HOSTS AND GUESTS

D0076761

HOSTS AND GUESTS

THE ANTHROPOLOGY OF TOURISM

SECOND EDITION

VALENE L. SMITH *Editor*

upp

UNIVERSITY OF PENNSYLVANIA PRESS *Philadelphia*

Copyright © 1989 by the University of Pennsylvania Press
All rights reserved
Printed in the United States of America

Library of Congress Cataloging-in-Publication Data

Hosts and guests.
  Bibliography: p.
  Includes index.
  1. Tourist trade.   I. Smith, Valene L.
G155.A1H67   1989   . 380.1'4591   88-27795
ISBN 0-8122-1280-0 (pbk.)

LIBRARY
ALMA COLLEGE
ALMA, MICHIGAN

CONTENTS

PART V
TOWARDS A THEORY OF TOURISM

PREFACE

VALENE L. SMITH

The first edition of *Hosts and Guests: The Anthropology of Tourism*, published in 1977, was a pioneering work that legitimatized the American academic study of tourism, and provided both a preliminary theoretical perspective and twelve case studies documenting the impacts of tourism. The book owed its genesis to the first national academic symposium on tourism, held in conjunction with the 1974 Mexico City meetings of the American Anthropological Association. Also in 1977, the World Tourism Organization (WTO) was created to replace the International Union of Official Travel Organizations, which had functioned since 1925 for the purpose of promoting and developing tourism in the interest of economic, social, and political progress of all nations. However, the authors of the first edition must admit to some myopic ethnocentrism in their 1974 "discovery" of the impacts of tourism. As we soon learned, there was a significant body of knowledge in Europe, dating to as early as 1899 (Cohen 1984), for that continent was the first to experience mass tourism.

The first edition of *Hosts and Guests* was well received and widely cited. This work and several others that appeared almost simultaneously—notably DeKadt (1977) and MacCannell (1976)—sparked research in several disciplines. The result has been far greater understanding of the nature of tourism and its effect on the structure of society. In 1978 it was suggested to each author that a second edition might be feasible in a decade (Smith 1978); that idea has been realized here.

This second edition of *Hosts and Guests* assesses some of the many changes that have occurred in tourism in the past decade. By retaining the salient elements of the original studies, and updating them through field-work and more recent theoretical perspective, this edition provides a historical framework for examining the nature of tourism in a series of global examples. To date, no other comparative tourism study exists, with time-depth documentation by the same author(s)—in fact, it is even rare within the discipline of anthropology as a whole.

Every case study, with one exception (Rayna Reiter, "The Politics of Tourism in a French Alpine Community"), has been recently reexamined and the concluding perspective updated. Unfortunately, Theron Nuñez, who is credited with the first published article (1963) in the American literature and who wrote the original final chapter in this work, was physically unable to complete its revision. However, his former student James Lett ably completed the conclusion, and Nuñez read it prior to his death. I am grateful to all the authors for their dedication to the tasks entailed in the preparation of this volume. Only chapters 1 and 2, by Graburn and Nash respectively, remain unchanged, a decision that reflects their discretion.

In the decade between the two editions, tourism has continued to burgeon. No one now doubts its importance or questions its future as one of the leading world industries, unless global terrorism directed at tourists persists and expands. Government agencies at every level from the international down to small towns have adopted a progressively more active role in the use of tourism as a developmental tool. Noteworthy are the activities of the WTO headquarters in Madrid, serving its 108 member nations on the international level as a consultative clearinghouse. The WTO library is an important research collection even though many of their in-house reports are necessarily confidential.

In the first edition most authors encountered a common and major problem: the difficulty of differentiating between the roles of modernization and tourism in the process of culture change. There were no prior guidelines. The most important contribution of this second edition is the opportunity to document for each of the case studies the changes that have occurred through time, and to assess the relative importance of tourism vis-à-vis modernization in acculturation. Although each site differs, as does each author in his interpretation, the research undertaken in the intervening decade indicates overall that tourism is *not* the major element of culture change in most societies. Given the pervasive indigenous demands for modernization, for the materialism and gadgetry that make human lives physically more comfortable and easier, the labor-intensive tourist industry has progressively served as an economically viable and socially permissible vehicle to provide wage employment. Tourism is especially favored where significant segments of the population have minimal education or technical skills, inasmuch as other industries may require extensive training.

Whereas in previous years tourism development was commonly a private enterprise, and tour operators chose their destinations and found venture capital to construct resorts and hotels (and were sometimes favored with tax and investment incentives), government agencies currently promote tourism as a panacea for underemployment in economically depressed areas. On the U.S. domestic level almost every state has funded a state tourist office which sponsors advertising, conferences and publications. California has the best manual to date for marketing rural tourism (Hetherington 1987), America's new-found business of attracting urban visitors to the countryside to craft fairs and festivals (Jordan 1980).

Almost greater than the growth of tourism itself has been the increase in research, both in anthropology and in the allied social and environmental sciences. Many national and regional meetings in several disciplines now include one or more research papers on tourism, even if special tourism sessions are not planned. Parallel to this growth are the quantity and quality of articles published by research-oriented journals, especially the *Annals of Tourism Research* with a circulation reaching more than seventy countries; and the fact that tourism journals are also regularly published in several Asian countries, including Korea, India, and the Philippines.

Even greater recognition should probably be given to the role of tourism in applied anthropology, and the growing interface between industry and academia. Esoteric studies on the nature of tourist motivations for travel have direct applications in marketing strategies. The use of mitigation techniques to resolve conflict between hosts/guests, non-national managers/native employees, and land-use planners/environmentalists augurs well for greater professionalism in tourism management. Many travel industry conferences regularly schedule one or two sessions on tourism research as part of their format, and anthropologists, geographers and psychologists thus find employment as industry consultants.

The result of the proliferation of tourism research, new journals, industry-generated studies, and even the extensive literature published by WTO is the difficulty of maintaining a complete bibliography. Already extensive in the first edition, the bibliography has been updated and expanded, but deliberate deletions are evident and inadvertent omissions regrettable.

INTRODUCTION

The Nature of Tourism: A Definition

Tourism is difficult to define because business travelers and convention-goers can combine conferences with tourist-type activities; but, in general, a tourist is a temporarily leisured person who voluntarily visits a place away from home for the purpose of experiencing a change. The motivations for individuals to travel are many and varied, but the foundation of tourism rests on three key elements (all must be operative) which form an equation:

Tourism = leisure + discretionary + positive local
               time   income   sanctions

In the Western world and especially in the U.S., the amount of leisure time available to an individual has, in general, increased since World War II. The workweek has decreased from sixty hours to forty-eight hours, then to forty hours per week, and for some occupations the workweek in 1988 already stands at only thirty to twenty-four hours. Personal preferences plus labor union demands have effectively lengthened paid vacations from two weeks to three, four, or more, especially for longterm employees. In addition, the dates of observance for several national holidays have been shifted to Mondays to provide for additional three-day weekends. Early retirement (at as young as age fifty-five) and increased longevity (American overseas travelers age eighty or older are not uncommon), of Americans with substantial pensions and investment income have created a significant generation of youthful senior citizens for whom tourism is an important and recurring activity.

Discretionary income is money not needed for personal essentials such as food, clothing, housing, health-care, transportation, and so forth. However, the inroads of inflation combined with vague uncertainties concerning the future (including the threat of nuclear war, political terrorism or the spread of epidemic diseases such as AIDS) have tended to discourage the habit of "saving." As Graburn notes (chapter 1), the Protestant work ethic was once pervasive in the U.S.: to work was right, moral, and satisfying. This work philosophy has largely disappeared among Americans born after World War II. The modern generation seeks instant happiness, and its work goal is to earn money with which to play. Translated into tourism, the extra money once saved for home, car, or a "rainy day" becomes the means to travel.

On a broader scale, American wives were not commonly employed outside the home until World War II, when women were needed for the manufacture of war materiel. Having become accustomed to wage income, and with public sanctioning of their dual role as employee and house-wife/mother, the numbers of working wives has grown consistently since the mid-1940s. Many American women feel that their "double workload" earns the family's discretionary income. Therefore, working wives are often the decision-makers in choice of family vacation destinations (Smith 1979). Further, if cash is not immediately available to prepay travel arrangements, credit cards permit taking the vacation and paying for it even months later, on the installment plan.

The sanctions for travel are closely linked to the motivation and therefore the kind of travel to be undertaken. These are multiple, varied and complex. For example, in the U.S. job mobility is often quite widespread and frequently linked to the breakdown of the family (and vice versa). Especially in metropolitan centers, there may be substantial numbers of lonely urban dwellers. Their motivations and travel destinations are highly varied, but a sampling may be instructive:

> To escape the pressures of city life, they can opt for a quick and quiet weekend in the country, away from the telephone. They may also have a second home (chapter 10) as a permanent hideaway, or pursue hobbies such as skiing and sailing; or, alternately, they may *enjoy* the city's attractions of museums, theater, and gourmet restaurants. Which one of these—or many other choices—is decided upon will depend on how much time and money is available, as well as peer group approval.
> To find fresh air and outdoor recreation, one could visit a local city

park (an acceptable, inexpensive activity); one could also go halfway around the world to walk in a similar garden. Whether one's peers and society approve the latter activity (given the fact that one is spending time, money, and energy) becomes a matter of sanctions.

Lonely city dwellers often use tourism as a means to meet and make new friends; cruises and "singles only" tours are travel industry promotions to help meet vacation preferences for this group.

Sanctions may regulate vacation style. In Europe it is considered appropriate for a university student to hitchhike from country to country across the Continent and stay in youth hostels because he is expanding his education; an American trying to do the same thing in the U.S. would be viewed with great suspicion. In the U.S., it is socially preferable to travel by plane; to ride a transcontinental bus carries a stigma of poverty. In Europe, trains and railroad stations are noted for their good food; in the U.S., most stations have no food service and trains provide only snack bars or precooked meals.

The tourism formula and accompanying examples are cited because I believe them to be prophetic for tourism in the future. To date, the world's most industrialized nations have generated the greatest percentage of tourists, and Germans, Americans, French, Japanese, Swiss and Swedes are frequent travelers. However, as underdeveloped countries develop modern economies, their citizens will similarly benefit from increased income and shortened hours of work. Already the stimulus for personal travel is evident. For example, India was once a Third World country. In 1987, thanks to the "Green Revolution" and modernization, India ranks as one of the world's ten leading industrial nations. Local newspapers now regularly carry many ads for domestic tourism ("Spend 5 days 4 nights in Simla/Darjeeling/Srinagar . . . price includes round-trip air, hotels, sightseeing"), with quoted prices to be paid in rupees. The positive cultural sanctions favoring tourism are already operative, and with increased leisure and greater discretionary income, more Indians *will* take vacations and travel within their own country. A guide in India expressed the hope that domestic tourism by Indians traveling within their own subcontinent will eventually help break down the language disputes and provincialism that continue to fracture government efforts toward national consolidation.

Similarly, I believe that eventually tourism in China, Taiwan, and Korea will greatly increase, first as a form of domestic tourism within their respective countries; then, in years to come, Chinese, Taiwanese and Koreans will become tourists to adjacent Pacific rim nations, and finally overseas visitors. Thus the predicted increase in world tourism will probably come in large measure from the Pacific rim countries whose populations total half of the world's, and whose economies are just beginning to generate the components for tourism of leisure time, discretionary income, and public sanctions for travel.

Indicative of other possible trends, the Japanese government in 1987 drew up a plan to double the number of Japanese tourists traveling abroad to ten million by 1991, estimating that they would spend almost us$11 billion in that year. This first known example of a government advocating foreign tourism is designed to "help narrow Japan's wide trade surplus and to increase its national ties with other nations. A total of 5,520,000 Japanese traveled overseas in 1986 but, although a record, it represented only 4 percent of Japan's population" (*Wall Street Journal*, 16 September 1987). And in the same year, the Canadian government announced the "First Global Conference, Tourism—A Vital Force for Peace" to be held in Vancouver in October 1988. Thus tourism, already the world's largest industry—with worldwide spending for domestic and international travel valued in 1986 at us $2 trillion, or about us $2.5 billion a day (Waters 1987)—seems destined to maintain that standing, and increase in importance in a variety of social and economic milieus.

Types of Tourism

Tourism as a form of leisured activity structures the personal life cycle to provide alternate periods of work and relaxation (Graburn, chapter 1). As work gives way to leisured mobility, individuals find re-creation in a variety of new contexts. Different forms of tourism can be defined in terms of the kinds of leisured mobility undertaken by the tourist, and may be identified as five types:

Ethnic tourism is marketed to the public in terms of the "quaint" customs of indigenous and often exotic peoples, exemplified by the case studies on the Eskimo, the San Blas Indians of Panama, and the Toraja in Indonesia. Destination activities that stimulate tourism include visits to native homes and villages, observation of dances and ceremonies, and shopping for primitive wares or curios, some of which may have considerable intrinsic value to the art historian. Frequently these tourist targets are far removed from the "beaten path" and attract only a limited number of visitors motivated by curiosity and elite peer approval. As long as the flow of visitors is sporadic and small, host-guest impact is minimal.

Cultural tourism includes the "picturesque" or "local color," a vestige of a vanishing life-style that lies within human memory with its "old style" houses, homespun fabrics, horse or ox-drawn carts and plows, and hand rather than machine-made crafts. Destination activities include meals in rustic inns, folklore performances, costumed wine festivals, or rodeos reminiscent of the Wild West. This is peasant culture, illustrated by the case studies on Bali and Spain. Host-guest stresses may be maximal because the rural peasant areas are often readily accessible from tourist resorts, and large numbers of visitors come for the very purpose of observing and photographing the lives of peasants who become objects of study *per se*.

Historical tourism is the Museum-Cathedral circuit that stresses the glories of the Past—i.e., Rome, Egypt, and the Inca. Favored destination activities include guided tours of monuments and ruins, and especially light and sound performances that encapsulate into a brief drama the life-style and key events that textbooks record. Historical tourism tends to attract many education-oriented visitors, and tourism is facilitated because the targets are either in or readily accessible to large cities. An institutionalized tourist industry, or "tourist culture," usually exists to cater to a stream of visitors, and host-guest contacts are often impersonal and detached, and primarily economic rather than social, as shown by the case study on the Iranian Jewish merchants.

Environmental tourism is often ancillary to ethnic tourism, attracting a tourist elite to remote areas such as Antarctica to experience a truly alien scene. Because environmental tourism is primarily geographic, many education-oriented travelers enjoy driving through mountains and countryside to observe man-land relationships. Popular destination activities include tours of local industries such as tea farms and processing plants in Japan or Ceylon, or salmon canneries in Alaska. One of the recognized bases for the popularity of the Polynesian Cultural Center is the tourist's ability to "visit the Pacific"—to see how material culture adapts to environment as well as to sample native foods and see a variety of dances—within an hour's drive of Waikiki. Host-guest contacts in this category vary widely and must be assesed locally.

Recreational tourism is often sand, sea, and sex—promoted by beautiful color pictures that make you want to be "there"—on the ski slopes, the palm-fringed beaches, the championship golf courses, or sunning in a deck chair, and attracts tourists who want to relax or commune with nature. Destination activities center upon participation in sports, curative spas, or sunbathing, as well as good food and convivial entertainment. Las Vegas epitomizes another type of recreational center: gambling, "name" shows, and the away-from-home freedom to indulge in the new morality. Again, host-guest relationships vary widely but may be influenced by the seasonality of some types of recreational tourism, which may require imported labor to handle massive influxes, or by radical changes in land values when favored sites are converted to a monetarily more profitable use, as in the case study of the three North Carolina coastal towns.

The Impacts of Tourism

Since the publication of the first edition of *Hosts and Guests*, a great deal of research has been directed toward a fuller understanding of the impacts of tourism. Because of the magnitude of the tourist industry, the great complexity of tourist motivations and expectations, and the diversity of cultural responses to tourist arrivals, it is impossible to provide a comprehensive overview in this short introduction. However, some generalizations reflect recent research and will provide background information appropriate to the individual case studies.

The major stimulus for the development of tourism is economic. Tourism is labor intensive, especially for a minimally skilled labor pool, and ranks high as a developmental tool, particularly for underdeveloped areas worldwide and even for rural districts in the United States. Supporters point to the value of the so-called new money brought by the tourists into the host area which, if it were a hard currency including the German mark, Japanese yen, Swiss franc or U.S. dollar, could be valuable foreign exchange with which to buy food, pharmaceuticals, farm machinery, and other items needed for development or survival. Further, all new funds recirculate through the local economy several times, in the "multiplier effect," and directly benefit local businesses that are not tourism related. Several case studies, such as those that focus on Bali, the Polynesian Cultural Center, and the San Blas Indians, illustrate the positive economic gains from the tourist trade.

Refinements in research methods have provided new insight into the economic role of tourism vis-à-vis other industries. Early economic studies suggested that profits earned by foreign investors were commonly siphoned back to the source of capital in a process known as economic leakage. However, as Pye and Lin (1983, p. xiv) show, when the tourism sector becomes increasingly integrated into the domestic economy, the degree of leakage is proportionately reduced. Similarly, the authors responded to the criticism that dollars invested in tourism might be better spent in other potential industries, by pointing out, in their Asian example, that the Korean foreign exchange leakage in the important electronics industry was 50 percent and in the machine industry it was 23 percent. The foreign exchange leakage in tourism to Korea was only 19.7 percent. Similar figures could be cited for other Asian countries.

Where wide economic disparities exist between hosts and guests, or where narcotics usage is widespread, tourists may be singled out for robbery or terrorism—not because they are tourists, but because they are easy targets. Even sophisticated travelers are often unaware of cultural differences in body language; their attention may be distracted by the novelty of a strange environment; or they may be intent on a personal interest. Many are simply careless. For the criminal, it is safer to prey upon the tourist—a temporary guest who, having been victimized, departs for home at the end of the vacation and seldom returns to prosecute the perpetrator even if one is apprehended.

Most of the case studies report tremendous growth in the number of visitors during the period between the first fieldwork and the present account. Accordingly, many of the initial contacts between hosts and guests have changed appreciably during the intervening years. The first visitors were novelties, studied by the hosts, and, because tourism was new, job opportunities for the indigenous population were limited. Most inhabitants had no usable job skills. However, by the late 1980s, tourism was no longer an oddity. Models of success where local employees obtained positions of considerable responsibility can be found in many tourist areas. Further, if qualified native workers are not immediately available at a new tourist site (such as a resort), individuals can be recruited from an already functioning facility elsewhere. Motivated employees who have perceived tourism to be an avenue for upward mobility have repeatedly proven this to be true. As a case in point, in Tana Toraja (chapter 7) during my 1986 visit, the fully bilingual local guide used his earnings to pay tuition for his schooling toward a degree in engineering. An elder brother had similarly served as a guide during his university undergraduate years, then decided on a career in tourism and was enrolled in a doctoral program at the Sorbonne. Ultimately, upon degree completion, he expects to join the Indonesian Ministry of Tourism and help develop tourism in the area.

Economic strains do exist, however, and some of the most sensitive factors relate to the seasonality of tourism, which may leave hotels empty, carriers and tour operators with idle wheels, and employees jobless. Unless a pervasive, sound economic base exists, individuals who are tied to tourism experience either "feast or famine." Tourism is also very sensitive to external variables over which the local industry has very little control, including fluctuations in currency values and the political climate. Tourists flock to centers where their purchasing power makes travel a "good buy," and avoid areas where political terrorism and military activities might threaten their lives. There may also be an ebb and flow in the popularity of any destination for economic reasons. Ski resort operators know this in relation to weather: skiing is popular and profitable during years of good snow but the losses are disastrous in times of drought. Plog (1974) has charted the rise and fall of destinations in relation to their popularity and the kinds of tourists they attract. However, skillful marketing—expensive, but effective—can overcome some of the problems associated with seasonality. The state of Alaska has made a major advertising commitment for 1988 to stimulate winter tourism, and make the Iditarod race (chapter 3) a world event, thus overcoming tourist aversion to the Arctic winter.

The advent of large-scale tourism often necessitates the transfer of local control to a central government which has the power to compete internationally for the tourist trade by offering concessions, in the form of favorable taxes or negotiated land values, to induce major hotel chains to construct facilities. And only governments can solicit and obtain tourism grants from United Nation funds or from other governments to be used for infrastructure improvements or hotel/resort construction. When the tourist industry is managed by outsiders, to whom the profits flow, tourism becomes a form of imperialism (Nash, chapter 2) and may develop into neocolonialism. However, the case studies indicate that the San Blas Kuna have retained local control, and that the Eskimo now have a major financial interest in the tourism to their area. Indeed, the world trend in tourism is towards privatization of the industry, either by direct local ownership or through franchising, even though marketing is most effective on a regional or group membership basis.

The economic effects of tourism upon the arts and crafts industries merit mention. The case studies on Bali, the Eskimo, and the San Blas Indians all show that tourism has served to regenerate traditional industries by providing an enlarged market for native products. Deitch (chapter 11) shows that tourism has been important in the renascence of Indian arts in the Southwest United States, and Loeb (chapter 12) discusses religious art. None of the authors discuss the "trinketization" of aesthetics created by the curio shop marketing of cheap goods of non-native manufacture. Again, the question must be asked: Who benefits, and in what proportion—the alien manufacturer, or local entrepreneurs who have the capital to buy, inventory, and sell this "airport art"?

Culture change, in the form of modernization, has made impressive inroads into the backward areas and the poverty pockets of the globe, and the process is both ongoing and accelerating. The generations born after World War II adhere far less to traditional values and mores; they seek active participation in the coming "new order" and want to share in its benefits. Cheap radios and cassettes have brought world news and rock singers into native huts and heightened local awareness of, and demand for, roads, clean water, better medicine, electricity, and entertainment. The façade of cultural homogenization appears on almost every village main street (including those of the Kuna, the Eskimo, Tana Toraja, and Bali): hamburger stands, coffeehouses, video stores, and repair shops for motorbikes, cars, and trucks. Thus the question that haunted most authors of the earlier edition of this book and other researchers in tourism a decade ago (namely, "Is tourism a major agent of culture change?") seems to have been largely resolved. The guide I met in Tana Toraja responded to that question with a straightforward, "Tourism is not important in our lives—we see the world on television every night"; significantly, too, Kotzebue Eskimo operate their own media stations.

The tourist trade does not have to be culturally damaging. Many tourists want to forsake the "tourist bubble" and seek opportunities to meet and become acquainted with local people. The Ecumenical Coalition on Third World Tourism (ECTWT), headquartered in Bangkok, has sought ways to curtail some of the negative effects of tourism. Prostitution, drug abuse, alcoholism, and juvenile homosexuality—though not necessarily caused by tourism *per se*—are increased due to the presence of many outsiders (as is also true of the areas surrounding army bases). In Sri Lanka ECTWT reports, for example, that children who "beg" at airports and attractions often earn more cash in one day than their farmer-fishermen parents can earn in a month; a factor that serves as a basis for family disruption. An interesting and potentially useful device to prevent the negative cultural impacts is the use of an educational film aboard the numerous charter aircraft that bring many of the visitors to Colombo for a week's vacation. The film portrays insensitive behavior by the tourists toward religious shrines, and toward juveniles, as well as nude bathing on beaches—the latter particularly offensive to the modest Singalese.

Tourism can be a bridge to an appreciation of cultural relativity and international understanding. However, catering to guests is a repetitive, monotonous business, and although questions posed by each visitor may be "new" to him, hosts can become bored as if a cassette has been turned on. If the economic goals of mass tourism are realized and the occasional visitor is replaced by a steady influx, individual guests' identities become obscured, and they are labeled "tourists" who, in turn, may be stereotyped into national character images (Pi-Sunyer, chapter 9). As guests become dehumanized objects that are tolerated for economic gain, tourists have little alternative other than to look upon their hosts only with curiosity, and, too, as objects. To overcome this impersonal attitude, some tour operators are developing "alternative tourism" formats that feature one-to-one interaction between hosts and guests, including overnight stays in private homes. In a form of cultural mitigation, some major hotel chains have instituted training programs to teach "service" and "friendliness" to employees, and provide tangible rewards for the "employee of the month" who has received the most compliments from guests.

Ethnic and cultural tourism promise the visitor the opportunity to see at least some portions of the indigenous culture. Apparently, some culture traits, such as public rituals, can be shared with outsiders without disruption, at least as long as the numbers of spectators remain small. Social stress becomes apparent, however, when tourism invades the privacy of daily lives, as among Kotzebue Eskimo, or when participants in a ritual are engulfed by grandstands full of paid audiences. Still, modernization is rapidly changing most of the tourist realm. As it does so, many problems previously associated with host-guest relationships are diminishing. Disparities between rich and poor are not as great if for no other reason than the cash flow generated by one or more decades of tourism has provided the means for employees to satisfy some of their material aspirations. Tourism is no longer an oddity, and although the people whose culture is the object of tourism may need to transfer what Nuñez (chapter 14) terms "front stage" in their lives to a private sector, a worldwide cultural homogenization is underway. As a consequence, model cultures become much more important.

The Role of Model Cultures

Model cultures have been successfully developed as reconstructions of a historic past in, for example, Williamsburg, Plymouthe Plantation, Old Sturbridge Village, and Mystic Seaport in the United States, as well as in the many folk museums of Europe. These turn time back a century or two, affording a scale against which visitors can measure progress, and be reminded of the hardships encountered by their forebears. Many are also "living museums" where schoolchildren may spend a day or two and learn history firsthand. In addition to Hawaii's Polynesian Cultural Center (chapter 13), other ethnographic models include Fiji's Orchid Island, Bangkok's Rose Garden—Thailand in Miniature, and Korea's Folk Village. Smaller versions operate in cities such as Jakarta, Manila, and Cairo. Popular and profitable, these models appear to meet the ethnic expectations of the tourist. Although only a reconstruction of the life-style they had hoped to observe, these models offer a more accurate ethnographic view than is reflected in the modern native culture, and allow the visitor the freedom to wander and photograph at will.

Model cultures also offer another distinct advantage, especially at tourist sites where the physical presence of humans may cause damage. The actual Paleolithic caves of Lascaux (France) with their world-renowned polychrome paintings, are now closed to the public to prevent exfoliation of the paint; however, the surrogate display is in some ways more graphic than the original. Similarly, the Viking settlement at L'Anse aux Meadows in northern Newfoundland would have been destroyed by visitors tramping through the archaeologic pits, but the now-reconstructed village provides a fine interpretive center that documents the Viking ventures into the New World, and fully merits its number one rank on the United Nation's World Patrimony list. Even the spread of popular fantasies, in the Disneylands of Tokyo and Paris, provides forms of model cultures for "children of all ages" for they too have internal "theme villages" and fairy-tale motifs.

Further construction of model cultures is to be expected and should be warmly received as long as the models remain reasonably accurate: model cultures have the great advantage of structuring tourist visits to a site away from the daily lives of ordinary people. I, at least, would prefer to visit a Tana Torajan model than an inhabited village, and to photograph paid performers in traditional costumes rather than have individuals demand money for each picture taken, as is the common practice among Panama's San Blas Indians.

Come One or All: The Effects of Numbers

To a host population, tourism is often a mixed blessing: the tourist industry creates jobs and increases cash flow but the tourists themselves can become a physical as well as a social burden, especially as their numbers increase. In addition to the types of tourism suggested earlier, it appears a touristic typology can be drawn, accounting for their numbers, their goals, and their adaptations to local norms (Table 1).

Explorers quest for discovery and new knowledge but in a shrinking

TABLE 1
FREQUENCY OF TYPES OF TOURISTS AND THEIR ADAPTATIONS TO
LOCAL NORMS

Type of Tourist	Numbers of Tourists	Adaptations to Local Norms
Explorer	Very limited	Accepts fully
Elite	Rarely seen	Adapts fully
Off-beat	Uncommon but seen	Adapts well
Unusual	Occasional	Adapts somewhat
Incipient Mass	Steady flow	Seeks Western amenities
Mass	Continuous influx	Expects Western amenities
Charter	Massive arrivals	Demands Western amenities

planet, their numbers are sharply restricted. By definition, they are not tourists and traditionally are almost akin to anthropologists living as active participant-observers among "their" people. They easily accommodate to local norms in housing, food, and life-style, bolstered by an amazing array of Western technology including "walkie-talkies," dehydrated foods, portable chemical toilets, oxygen tanks, and medicine.

Elite tourists are few in number and usually include individuals who have been "almost everywhere" and who now, for example, choose to spend US$1500 for a week, to travel by dugout canoe, with a guide, on the Darien River in Panama. They overnight in Kuna Indian homes, sleep in hammocks, get thoroughly bitten by chiggers, eat native food, and chance the tourist "trots." They differ from Explorers because they are "touring"— irrespective of whether they planned the trip in great detail in advance or not, they are using facilities that could be prearranged at home by any travel agent. However, they adapt easily with the attitude that "if they [the natives] can live that way all their lives, we can, for a week."

The Off-beat tourist includes those who currently visit Toraja Regency to see the funerals, "trek" in Nepal, or go alone to Point Hope as part of an Alaskan tour. They seek either to (1) get away from the tourist crowds, or (2) heighten the excitement of their vacation by doing something beyond the norm. In general, they adapt well and "put up with" the simple accommodations and services provided for the occasional tourist.

The Unusual tourist visits South America on an organized tour, and buys an optional one-day package tour to visit the Kuna Indians, as an alternate to a day of shopping in duty-free Panama. By chartered small plane, tour members fly to a coastal airstrip where an American guide provides a motorboat to tour two or three off-shore villages; shopping for *molas* (chapter 4) is encouraged and, for a fee, tourists may photograph the women and/or the interiors of their houses. The tourist tends to be "interested" in the "primitive" culture but is much happier with his "safe" box lunch and bottled soda rather than a native feast.

Incipient Mass tourism is a steady flow of people, and although the numbers are increasing, they usually travel as individuals or in small groups. The tourist industry is only one sector of the total economy, and hotels usually have a mix of guests including domestic travelers and businessmen as well as tour groups. This phase of tourist activity is exemplified by many "popular" destinations such as Guatemala, or the summer visitors to the Arctic, the latter secure in their guided tour, heated buses, and modern hotels. These tourists seek Western amenities, and, totally ignoring the fact that at great expense the hotel room in the Arctic has a private bath, many of these visitors would complain about the "ring around the bathtub."

Mass tourism is a continuous influx of visitors who inundate Hawaii most of the year, and other areas at least seasonally, including the European resorts (part III), and Northern Hemisphere "winter vacation" lands such as coastal Mexico and the Caribbean. Mass tourism is built upon middle-class income and values, and the impact of sheer numbers is high. Because of the diversity of individual tastes and budgets, in Europe, for example, the tourists are everywhere—hitchhiking at the roadside, riding trains with their Eurailpasses, or huddled around a guide who is attempting to be heard above the voices of other guides in some crowded museum. With a "you get what you pay for" attitude, they fill up hotels of every category, pensions, and hostels *but*, as a common denominator, they expect a trained, multi-lingual hotel and tourist staff to be alert and solicitous to their *wants* as well as to their needs. The "tourist bubble" of Western amenities is very much in evidence.

Charter tourists arrive en masse, as in Waikiki, and for every 747 planeload, there is a fleet of at least ten big buses waiting to transfer them from the airport to the designated hotel, in the lobby of which is a special Tour Desk to provide itineraries and other group services. Should an individual ask even a simple, "What time does the tour bus go?," the immediate answer is, "What *group* are you with?" The "you" in the reply is spoken as to a "living thing" and not as to a personality. Charter tourists wear name tags, are assigned to numbered buses, counted aboard, and continually reminded: "Be sure to get on the right bus." Given the requisite organization that makes Charter tourism a high-volume business, to avoid complaints tour operators and hotels have standardized the services to Western (or Japanese) tastes, and there are "ice machines and soft drinks on every floor." For Charter tourists, even destination may be of very little importance, especially if they won the trip as part of an incentive sales program, or it coincides with tax-free convention travel.

The frequency of tourist types seems to approximate a pyramid (Figure 1), in which the bold triangle is a scale of increasing numbers, from top to bottom. An inverse triangle suggests the role of the host culture penetrated by the increased flow of tourists. Explorers and Elite travelers, by virtue of their limited numbers, usually make little impact upon the indigenous culture, for hotels and other services are seldom required. Their presence may be unnoticed except by the few who meet and serve them. The Off-beat and Unusual tourist commonly stays at roadhouses or hotels that locals also use, and gets about by local transportation (including the use of the school bus, for the very occasional groups who visit). The money they spend is a welcome addition, their presence is seldom disruptive, and children may delight in "talking English" with someone other than their teacher.

However, as the number of tourists progressively increases, it appears different expectations emerge and more facilities are required to handle them. When Charter tourism appears, I suggest that nationality is no longer locally significant, for the only economic base able to generate Charter tourism is Western society, whose members are fast approaching cultural and economic homogeneity.

The stressful contacts between hosts and guests also appear to increase, proportionate to the larger numbers. I believe that the critical point in the development of a successful tourist industry occurs at or near the intersection of the two triangles, when members of Incipient Mass tourism "seek" Western amenities, with the result that these facilities begin to be economically or even visually important, as "tourist hotels" and privileged parking places for tour buses. The local culture is probably at the "Y" in the road, and should decide whether to (a) consciously control or even restrict tourism, to preserve their economic and cultural integrity; or (b) to encourage tourism as a desirable economic goal and restructure their culture to absorb it. The first choice has been made by the economically powerful but socially traditional oil states adjacent to and including Saudi Arabia who refuse tourist visas. Bhutan, the tiny land-locked mountain kingdom in the eastern Himalayas, developed a second alternative (Smith 1981). Given the negative model of adjacent Nepal whose tourism was dominated through the 1970s by the drug cult and "hippies," Bhutan opened its borders to tourism in

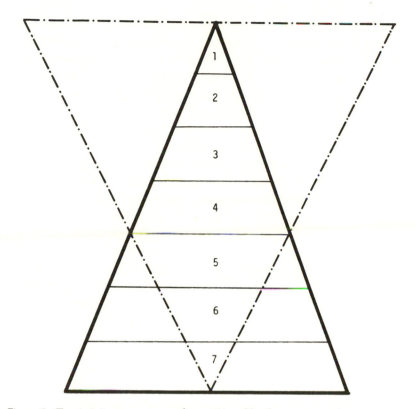

Figure 1.   Touristic impact upon a culture ($\triangle$) and local perceptions of visitors (∇), expressed in types of tourism: 1. Explorer; 2. Elite; 3. Off-beat; 4. Unusual; 5. Incipient Mass; 6. Mass; 7. Charter.

1974, permitting only one thousand visitors per year, each of whom paid a minimum of us$1000 for a week of group travel on a fixed itinerary. By restricting the number of visas issued annually, the Ministry of Tourism hoped to generate hard currency income and also to limit social interaction, so that little direct contact occurred between village Bhutanese and visitors. A 1986 WTO study praised the system and encouraged its perpetuation with little change. However for 1988 the government of Bhutan has closed some monasteries to foreign access because of the "growing materialism" among monks, which was generated by visitors who thoughtlessly made token gifts of money, candy, pencils, and so forth to young trainees.

Cultural impact studies can serve tourism well and indicate which elements of a specific culture are "public" and can be marketed as "local color" without serious disruption. As Greenwood reassesses the *Alarde* in Spain (chapter 8), the festival has survived economic exploitation. Although now changed in format, its existence has made Fuentarrabia a nationally known tourist destination, and helped preserve it as a community by providing local employment in shops, pensions, and in other services. For many people, small-town living is less expensive and pleasanter among family and friends than life in major urban centers: correspondingly, one of the significant trends in tourism currently, and projected to be of greater importance in decades ahead, is the effort to disperse tourism into the countryside and small towns, to better distribute its economic benefits. In this regard, however, it is imperative that cultural assessment be undertaken to identify potential tourist use, and to develop marketing plans that will maximize the benefits of tourism without negative sociocultural impact.

If a group can survive the transition from Incipient to full-blown Mass tourism, then it may ultimately achieve what Kemper (1976) has termed "tourist culture," or a process of full accommodation, so that large numbers of tourists are part of the "regional scenery," as in charter tourism to Hawaii.

Tana Toraja (chapter 7), a highland area in Sulawesi, Indonesia, dramatically illustrates the potentials of tourism *and* the need for fundamental planning. When Europeans first discovered its unique funeral ceremonies (ca. 1973), and government recognition that this cultural trait was a marketable commodity followed, Toraja moved from Elite to Charter tourism in only five years. Tourism became a viable economic means for widespread modernization; unfortunately, no one anticipated the demand for grave-marker souvenirs. Restrictions on public access to the sites should have been instituted immediately, for the effigies can be seen effectively from a viewing platform only a few yards distant.

However, tourism and the tourists themselves should not become scapegoats for the malaise of society as a whole. Throughout history and worldwide, the Fausts have sold their souls for a sou. In a world that many social scientists believe to be overpopulated (as does the government of the People's Republic of China), the desperately poor (or those who are simply greedy) will sell whatever they have to those who will buy—even their children, as well as their cultural patrimony. In fairness, one must consider that deep-seated economic problems which have little or nothing to do with tourism exist in many countries, including the U.S. The case study on Tonga (chapter 5) is instructive here. Urbanowicz points out that the islands are overpopulated, there is no additional land available, and that the importing of goods strains the economy, triggering inflation. However, if the strictures of careful scientific analysis were removed, it would be easy to conclude that food prices soared because of the fourteen thousand air visitors to Tonga in 1985. It is patently easier to blame a nameless, faceless foreigner who comes (and goes) than it is to address and solve fundamental problems.

As tourism expands and the numbers of visitors increase, so too will the problems. However, many more avenues now exist to mitigate stresses in the interaction between hosts and guests, as the following case studies show.

California State University, Chico

I

TOURISM AND LEISURE:
A THEORETICAL OVERVIEW

Tourism as a manifestation of leisure presupposes a socioeconomic milieu in which money and time-away-from-work can be accumulated to be spent at will. Tourism as a form of mobility suggests that culturally sanctioned reasons exist for leaving home to travel. In this theoretical introduction to the nature of tourism, Nelson Graburn in chapter 1 traces the history of tourism and discusses why tourism arose in the forms in which it exists today. In chapter 2, Dennison Nash considers the economic bases for tourism, and why tourism arose in the places where it is found today. Both authors treat tourism as an organized industry, catering to a clientele who have time and money and want to spend them, pleasurably, in leisured mobility or migration.

1

Tourism: The Sacred Journey

NELSON H. H. GRABURN

The human organism . . . is . . . motivated to keep the influx of novelty, complexity, and information within an optimal range and thus escape the extremes of confusion [This is Tuesday, so it must be Belgium] and boredom [We never go anywhere!].

D. Berlyne (1962, p. 166)

The anthropology of tourism, though novel in itself, rests upon sound anthropological foundations and has predecessors in previous research on rituals and ceremonials, human play, and cross-cultural aesthetics. Modern

This paper is derived from a series of revisions made of the remarks that I delivered as a discussant to the Symposium on Tourism, organized by Valene Smith at the American Anthropological Association meetings in Mexico City, November 1974. A draft of this chapter was presented as "The Anthropology of Tourism" in June 1975 and discussed at a meeting of the faculty of the Department of Anthropology at the University of California, Berkeley, to whom I direct my gratitude for many suggestions and criticisms. In addition I owe particular thanks to Sheldon Rothblatt and Ian Dengler of the Department of History at Berkeley, for suggestions concerning the development of tourism in European history, and to Valene Smith I owe special gratitude for her stimulating pursuit of this new branch of anthropology and for particular insightful comments on the nature of travel itself, which are incorporated in this chapter.

tourism exemplifies that part of the range of human behavior Berlyne calls
"human exploratory behavior," which includes much expressive culture
such as ceremonials, the arts, sports, and folklore; as diversions from the
ordinary, they make life worth living. Tourism as defined in the introduction does not universally exist but is functionally and symbolically equivalent to other institutions that humans use to embellish and add meaning to
their lives. In its special aspect—travel—it has antecedents and equivalents
in other seemingly more purposeful institutions such as medieval student
travel, the Crusades, and European and Asian pilgrimage circuits.

All Work and No Play Makes Jack a Dull Boy

A major characteristic of our conception of tourism is that it is *not* work, but
is part of the recent invention, *re*-creation, which is supposed to renew us
for the workaday world, a point emphasized by Nash (chapter 2). Tourism is
a special form of play involving travel, or getting away from "it all" (work
and home), affording relaxation from tensions, and for some, the opportunity to temporarily become a nonentity, removed from a ringing tele-
phone. Stemming from our peasant European (or East Asian) traditions,
there is a symbolic link between staying : working and traveling : playing,
which may be expressed as a model (Figure 1).

Norbeck (1971) points out that in Western society and Japan, and particularly in Northern European-derived cultures, the work ethic is so important that very strong moral feelings are attached to the concepts of work and
play, including an association of what is "proper" in time and place. From
the model, compulsory or serious activities such as making a living properly
take place in the workaday world and preferably "at home." Conversely,
"proper" travel is voluntary, does not involve routine work, and therefore is
"good for you." A majority of Americans and Europeans see life as properly
consisting of alternations of these two modes of existence: living at home
and working for longish periods followed by taking vacations away from
home for shorter periods. However, some sanctioned recreation is often an-

Figure 1. Working/traveling matrix.

	Stay	Travel
Voluntary	"Doing nothing" at home	Tourism and/or recreation
Compulsory/ Serious	Work (including schoolwork and housework)	Occupations requiring travel

other kind of "hard work," especially in the rites-of-passage or self-testing types of tourism such as those of youthful travelers (Teas 1976; Vogt 1978). Many tourists admittedly return home to "rest up" from their vacations.

The model also indicates that staying at home and *not* working is considered improper for normal people. Many would complain that to not go away during vacations is "doing nothing" as if the contrasting "something" must take place away from home or it is "no vacation at all." The very word vacation comes from the Latin *vacare*, "to leave (one's house) empty," and emphasizes the fact that we cannot properly vacation at home.[1] People who stay home for vacation are often looked down upon or pitied, or made to feel left behind and possibly provincial, except for the aged and infirm, small children, and the poor. Within the framework of tourism, normal adults travel and those who do not are disadvantaged.

By contrast, able-bodied adults who do not work when living at home are also in a taboo category among contemporary Western peoples. If they are younger or poorer they are labelled "hippies," "bums," or even "welfare chiselers"; otherwise they may be labeled the "idle rich." In both cases, most people consider them some kind of immoral parasites.

The other combination—work that involves compulsory travel—is equally problematic. Somehow, it is improper to travel when we work, as it is improper to work when we travel. The first category includes traveling salesmen, gypsies, anthropologists, convention goers, stewards, and sailors, and our folklore is full of obscene jokes about such people—for their very occupations are questionable, whatever their behavior! Alternately, people on vacation don't want to work, and justifiably complain about their "busman's holiday." Among them are housewives whose families, to save money, rent a villa rather than stay in a hotel; doctors who are constantly consulted by their co-travelers; and even anthropologists who are just trying to vacation in a foreign country.

To Tour or Not to Tour: That Is the Problem

Tourism in the modal sense emphasized here is but one of a range of choices, or styles, of vacation or recreation—those structurally-necessary, ritualized breaks in routine that define and relieve the ordinary. For the

---

1. Though the sense of "leaving one's house" now implies a holiday or tourism, it was originally intended to describe the itinerant work of people such as craftsmen, apprentices, and circuit judges. Such changes in meaning from holiday = to celebrate a holy day in the home community, and vacation = to go off to work, to the present usage reflects the post-Renaissance changes in ideology that account for the rise of modern tourism.

present discussion our focus is consciously on the more extreme examples of tourism such as long distance tours to well-known places or visiting exotic peoples, in the most enchanting environments. However, the most minimal kinds of tourism, such as a picnic in the garden, contain elements of the magic of tourism. The food and drink might be identical to that normally eaten indoors, but the magic comes from the movement and the nonordinary setting. Furthermore, it is not merely a matter of money that separates the stay-at-homes from the extensive travelers. Many very wealthy people never become tourists, and most "youthful" travelers are, by Western standards, quite poor.

The stay-at-home who participates in some creative activity such as remodeling the house, redoing the garden, or seriously undertaking painting, writing, or sports activities, shares some of the values of tourism in that recreation is involved that is nonordinary and represents a *voluntary* self-indulgent choice on the part of the practitioner. Still others who, through financial stringency or choice, do not go away during vacations but celebrate the released time period by making many short trips, take the nonworkaday aspects of the vacation and construct events for the satisfaction of their personal recreational urges. Even sending the children away to camp may count as a vacation for some parents. Though not tourism in the modal sense, camping, backpacking, renting a lake cottage, or visiting relatives who live far away function as kinds of tourism, although their level of complexity and novelty may not be as high.

The Sacred and the Profane, or, A Change is as Good as a Rest

Taking our cue from Berlyne, who suggests that all human life tries to maintain a preferred level of arousal and seeks "artificial sources of stimulation . . . to make up for shortcomings of their environment" (Berlyne 1968, p. 170), tourism can be examined against its complement: ordinary, workaday life. There is a long tradition in anthropology of the structural examination of events and institutions as markers of the passage of natural and social time and as definers of the nature of life itself. This stems partly from Durkheim's (1912) notions of the sacred—the nonordinary experience—and the profane. The alternation of these states and the importance of the transition between them was first used to advantage by Mauss (1898) in his analysis of the almost universal rituals of sacrifice, which emphasized the process of leaving the ordinary, i.e., sacralization that elevates participants to the nonordinary state wherein marvellous things happen, and the converse process of desacralization or return to ordinary life.

Leach (1961, pp. 132–36), in his essay on "Time and False Noses," suggests that the regular occurrence of sacred-profane alternations marks important periods of social life or even provides the measure of the passage of time itself. The passing of each year is usually marked by the annual vacation (or Christmas), and something would be wrong with a year if it didn't occur, as if one had been cheated of time. "The notion that time is a 'discontinuity of repeated contrasts' is probably the most elementary and primitive of all ways of regarding time. . . . The year's progress is marked by a succession of festivals. Each festival represents a temporary shift from the Normal-Profane order of existence into the Abnormal-Sacred order and back again." The total flow of time has a pattern, which may be represented as in Figure 2.

Vacations involving travel, i.e., tourism, since all "proper" vacations involve travel, are the modern equivalent for secular societies to the annual and lifelong sequences of festivals for more traditional God-fearing societies. Fundamental is the contrast between the ordinary/compulsory work state spent "at home" and the nonordinary/voluntary "away from home" sacred state. The stream of alternating contrasts provides the meaningful events that measure the passage of time. Leach applies the diagram to "people who do not possess calendars of the Nautical Almanac type," implying that those who have "scientific" calendars and other tacit reminders such as newspapers, radio, and TV rely on the numerical calendar. I believe the

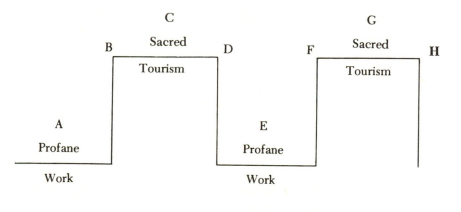

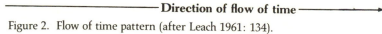

Figure 2. Flow of time pattern (after Leach 1961: 134).

"scientific, secular" Westerner gains greater meaning from the personal rather than the numerical in life. We are happier and better recall the loaded symbolic time markers: "That was the year we went to Rome!" rather than "that was 1957," for the former identifies the nonordinary, the festive, or ritual.

Each meaningful event marks the passage of time and thus life itself. Each secular or sacred period is a micro-life, with a bright beginning, a middle, and an end, and the beginnings and endings of these little "lives" are marked by rituals that thrust us irreversibly down life's path. Periods A and C in Figure 2 are both segments of our lives but of a different moral quality. The profane period, A, is the everyday life of the "That's life!" descriptive of the ordinary and inevitable. The period of marginality, C, is another life, which, though extraordinary, is perhaps more "real" than "real life." Vacation times and tourism are described as "I was really living, living it up . . . I've never felt so alive," in contrast to the daily humdrum often termed a "dog's life," since dogs are not thought to "vacation." Thus, holidays (holy, sacred days now celebrated by traveling away from home) are what makes "life worth living" as though ordinary life is not life or at least not the kind of life worth living.

Our two lives, the sacred/nonordinary/touristic and the profane/workaday/stay-at-home, customarily alternate for ordinary people and are marked by rituals or ceremonies, as should the beginning and end of lives. By definition, the beginning of one life marks the end of the other. Thus, at time B, we celebrate with TGIF (Thank God It's Friday) and going-away parties, to anticipate the future state and to give thanks for the end of the ordinary. Why else would people remain awake and drink all night on an outbound plane en route to Europe when they are going to arrive at 6:40 A.M. with a long day ahead of them? The re-entry ritual, time D, is often split between the ending-party—the last night in Europe or the last night at sea—and the welcome home or welcome back to work greetings and formalities, both of which are usually sadder than the going away.

In both cases the transition formalities are ambivalent and fraught with danger or at least tension. In spite of the supposedly happy nature of the occasion, personal observation and medical reports show that people are more accident prone when going away; are excited and nervous, even to the point of feeling sick; and Van Gennep (1914) suggests that the sacralization phase of symbolic death lies within our consciousness. It is implied in phrases such as "parting is such sweet sorrow" or even "to part is to die a little." Given media accounts of plane, train, and automobile accidents, literally as tourists we are not sure that we will return. Few have failed to think at least momentarily of plane crashes and car accidents or, for older people, dying while on vacation. Because we are departing ordinary life and may never return, we take out additional insurance, put our affairs in order, often make a new will, and leave "final" instructions concerning the watering, the pets, and the finances. We say goodbye as we depart and some even cry a little, as at a funeral, for we are dying symbolically. The most difficult role of a travel agent is to hand someone their tickets to travel to a funeral, for the happy aspect of the journey is entirely absent, leaving only a double sorrow.

The re-entry is also ambivalent. We hate to end vacation, and to leave new-found if temporary excitement; on the other hand, many are relieved to return home safely and even anticipate the end of the tense, emotion-charged period of being away. We step back into our former roles (time E), often with a sense of culture shock. We inherit our past selves like an heir to the estate of a deceased person who has to pick up the threads, for we are *not* ourselves. We are a new person who has gone through re-creation and, if we do not feel renewed, the whole point of tourism has been missed.

For most people the financial aspects of tourism parallel the symbolic. One accumulates enough money with which to vacation, much as one progressively acquires the worries and tedium of the workaday world. Going away lightens this mental load and also one's money. Running out of money at the end of the holiday is hopefully accompanied by running out of cares and worries—with the converse accumulation of new perspectives and general well-being. The latter counteracts the workaday worries with memories of the more carefree times. In turn, they stimulate the anticipation and planning for the next vacation, and F and G will be different from B and C because we have experienced times A through E.

While traveling, each day is a micro-model of the same motif. After the stable state of sleep, the tourist ventures forth to the heightened excitement of each new day. Nightfall is often a little sad for the weary tourist; the precious vacation day is spent. Perhaps the often frantic efforts at nightlife on the part of tourists who may never indulge at home are attempts to prolong the "high"—to remain in the sacred, altered state—and delay the "come down" as long as possible.

The Profane Spirit Quest: The Journey Motif in Tourism

Life is a succession of events marked by changes in state. It is both cyclical, in that the same time-marking events occur day after day, year after year, and it is progressive or linear in that we pass through life by a series of changes in status, each of which is marked by a different (though similarly structured) rite of passage. An almost universal motif for the explanation and description of life is the journey, for journeys are marked by beginnings and ends, and by a succession of events along the way.

The travel involved in tourism is more than geographical motion or a symbolically-altered state. For Westerners who value individualism, self-reliance, and the work ethic, tourism is the *best* kind of life for it is sacred in the sense of being exciting, renewing, and inherently self-fulfilling. The tourist journey is a segment of our lives over which we have maximum control, and it is no wonder that tourists are disappointed when their chosen, self-indulgent fantasies don't turn out as planned.

A journey is seldom without purpose, but culturally-specific values determine the goals of travel. In many American Indian societies, a young man left the camp alone to travel and suffer, and to meet the right spirit in order to advance to the next higher status on the journey through life. In India, in medieval Europe, and in the Islamic world, people made difficult pilgrimages to find spiritual enlightenment. Visitors to Las Vegas are also enlightened and often return home with a flat wallet, having sacrificed dearly for their pleasures.

Even if one regards tourism as voluntary, self-interested travel, the tourist journey must be morally justified by the home community. Because the touristic journey lies in the nonordinary sphere of existence, the goal is symbolically sacred and morally on a higher plane than the regards of the ordinary workaday world. Tourists spend substantial sums to achieve the altered state—money that could be invested for material gain or alternately used to buy a new car or redecorate their homes.

"Human exploratory behavior," says Berlyne (1968, p. 152), "is behavior whose principle function is to change the stimulus field and introduce stimulus elements that were not previously accessible." Thus, as art uplifts and makes meaningful the visual environment, so tourism provides an aesthetically appropriate counterpoint to ordinary life. Tourism has a stated, or unstated but culturally determined, goal that has changed through the ages. For traditional societies the rewards of pilgrimages were accumulated grace and moral leadership in the home community. The rewards of modern tourism are phrased in terms of values we now hold up for worship: mental and physical health, social status, and diverse, exotic experiences.

In medieval Europe, travel was usually for avowedly religious purposes, as were pilgrimages and crusades; for ordinary people travel was difficult and dangerous, and even for the ruling classes, who also traveled for reasons of state, travel required large protective entourages. Those who could afford it often retired to retreats or endowed religious institutions in their spiritual quest for the ultimate "truth." It was the Renaissance that changed the world-view by bringing forth the kind of consciousness that provides the cosmological foundation for modern tourism: the idea that truth lay outside the mind and spirit. In all fields this outward, materialist turning, this urge to explore and understand, showed up in such new forms as the new astronomy, the explorations, the new historical and scientific investigations of the fifteenth and sixteenth centuries. Means of land and sea transportation improved, and curiosities and exciting tales of discovery were brought back from all over the world.

By the seventeenth century the aristocracy and the wealthy were traveling to and in Europe to see the evidence of old historical truths and to converse with the discoverers of the new geographical and scientific ones. For eighteenth-century England the Grand Tour became a fully developed institution; the tourist motive for going abroad was not only cultural but highly educational and political. The post-medieval decline of the universities and the great public and grammar schools as institutions of liberal learning meant the rise of alternative means of instruction: the tutor and the tour were the two principal ones. Milord went abroad not only to see the classical sights, but to learn languages, manners and accomplishments, riding, dancing, and other social graces. The tour was deemed a very necessary part of the training of future political and administrative leaders, as well as patrons of the arts.

The Industrial Revolution took hold at the end of the eighteenth century and set in motion further changes affecting travel and tourism. It enhanced the need for scientific exchange and learning, for trade and raw materials, and for imperial expansion (see Nash, chapter 2). In addition it gave rise to the romanticism that glorified nature and the countryside, ideas stemming partly from the formerly neoclassical pastoral games of British and French aristocracy. As the Grand Tour in its elitist form declined in significance, new modes of transportation and new political arrangements made travel safer and cheaper for the bourgeoisie.

Thomas Cook, a Baptist minister and social reformer, taking advantage of the new railway system, in 1842 organized an all-inclusive tour to a temperance meeting. Other successful and morally uplifting tours followed; Cook combined his visions of democratic travel and the promotion of sobriety, with the chance to profit financially from the opportunities for taking townspeople to the countryside or abroad. His tours expanded from the Lake District, Wales, the Isle of Man, and Scotland, to reach France, Italy, and the glories of the Middle East by the 1870s. Promoting railway expansion everywhere, and the standardization of hotels and restaurants, Cook's coupons and later traveler's checks made travel easy for the masses, opening approved parts of the world to the inspection and edification of the educated middle classes. Imitators arose in Europe and America, and travel-made-easy followed closely on the heels of imperial and commercial expansion.

Displaced from their command of the historical and cultural centers of Europe and the Far East, the aristocracy pioneered another form of tourism, which was later to become a form of mass escape: the ruling families and the very wealthy began to leave their palaces and their homes for recreational and health reasons on a regular, yearly basis. Not since Roman times had this been done on such a massive scale. Prior to the eighteenth century the royal families regularly moved between their several castles, for the hunting and falconry seasons; and after the Renaissance a larger part of the ruling stratum began to take "cures" at spas within their own countries, such as at Bath or Baden-Baden. These were the forerunners of the strongly recreational theme in tourism. Starting in the eighteenth century and becoming the mode in the nineteenth century, luxurious rivieras were built along the Mediterranean and Adriatic shores to house the royalty and idle rich from the nations of Northern and Eastern Europe. Like the national health spas they displaced, these resorts were often only thinly disguised excuses for gambling and more lascivious pleasures. As the winter abodes for the Northerners were opened in the warmer South, this pleasure-seeking trend led to the establishment of Monte Carlo and other casino resorts. By the beginning of the twentieth century even rich Americans came to partake of the idle winter life-style, and great liners and trains made long-distance travel safe all over the world for those who could afford to pay.

The final cultural revolution that set the stage for the mass tourism of today was prompted by the First World War. Not only did this catastrophe pauperize the elite rivieras, but it did away with many of the ruling families and other European aristocrats whose fortunes had fueled the life-style. By the 1920s the newly wealthy Americans came to be the dominant taste-makers, not only in Paris but along the Côte d'Azur. The winter vacation retreats of the elitist "international set" became summer pleasure resorts. No longer was nature shunned and white skin universally admired. American experience in Florida and the Caribbean, along with an increasing realization of the healthy aspects of exposure to sunlight (pioneered by the discovery of Vitamin D and German experiments in World War I) made the suntan fashionable. An air of freedom from the old mores and the overthrow of the (superficially) stuffy old aristocracies brought out the excesses of the 1920s in every sphere of life. Features of the life-style of common people were studiedly imitated, folk music and jazz were heard, and a snobbish kind of "slumming" that equated dark skins with sexuality provided a spark for these changing attitudes, which are now well nigh universal. During this period aspects of "ethnic" tourism and anthropology itself became popular. Though the Depression put a lid on some of the excesses, the themes of nature, recreation, and ethnic interest were securely added to the previous cultural, historical, and educational motivations that underlie tourism today.

Nature Tourism and Cultural Tourism

Symbolically, Nature tourism has two different manifestations, both of which are strongly with us. The purest form is represented by Environmental tourism (McKean, chapter 6) where varied aspects of the land, sea, and sky perform their magical works of renewal—it's the "pure" air, the soothing waters, or the vast vistas that are curative. In its most extreme form the absence of humans is a factor: "There I was, the only person for miles . . . alone in the woods." If Nature is curative, performs magical re-creations and other miracles otherwise assigned to Lourdes, God, or *gurus*, the medicine is weakened by the presence of other humans. To share is to lose power. Recently, Environmental tourism has bifurcated into Ecological tourism (see Figure 3), wherein the tourist tries to leave as little effect from his visit as possible—concentrating perhaps on photographs and tape recordings—rather than the variant, Hunting and Gathering tourism. The latter includes environmental tourism and nature appreciating, including hunting, wherein little thought is given to impact, and at least some souvenirs are brought home.

To others, however, Nature in the "raw" is nice but somewhat boring because there is no dialogue; Nature is unresponsive even when threatened by capture on film or violation by campfire. Another way to get close to Nature's bosom is through her children, the people of Nature, once labeled Peasant and Primitive peoples and considered creatures of instinct. Interaction with them is possible and their naturalness and simplicity exemplify all that is good in Nature herself. What more exciting and uplifting experience could one imagine than to share a few words or, even better, a meal and a bed with such delightful people? Again, the magic is spoiled by the pres-

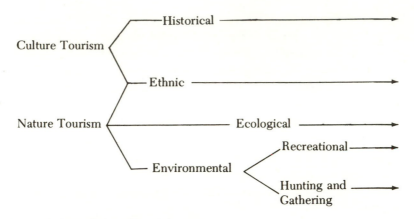

Figure 3. Interrelation of touristic types.

ence of too many other tourists. The approach to Nature through Her People is Ethnic tourism (Swain, chapter 4, Smith, chapter 3), whereas the use of Nature for her specified attributes of sun (tanning), wind (sailing), snow (skiing), surf (fishing), and sky (gliding) is Recreational Tourism.

The relation between the various forms of tourism is diagrammed in Figure 3.

Each touristic type has its own special scale of values and its hierarchy of prestigious places, i.e., those having more "magic." However, two or more kinds are frequently combined in one trip. For instance, one might visit the museums and cathedrals in Europe (Historical) and then go to Northern Scandinavia to see the Midnight Sun (Environmental) and the Lapps (Ethnic), or one might combine the Historical, Cultural, and Ethnic by touring India. Certain types of tourism are closer in fact and function than others; for instance, Ethnic tourism is a combination of Culture and Nature tourism. Others are conceptually further removed, such as Cultural tourism, with its emphases on the great traditions, in contrast to Hunting and Gathering tourism represented by African hunting safaris. Within these categories of tourism, there are an almost infinite variety of substyles including class, and ethnic and national variations. The rush of urban Germans to the southern and western coasts of Europe is different from the Scandinavians' junket to the Adriatic; the French take to their countryside quite differently from how the British take to theirs. The levels of preferred arousal and the nature of the touristic goals vary almost as much by age group and personality as by national origin and sex, and cannot all be described here.

The Holy Grail: Symbols and Souvenirs

Few tourists come home from a vacation without something to show for it, whether it is matchcovers, folk art, or rolls of exposed film. The type of vacation chosen and the proof that we really did it reflect what we consider "sacred." The Holy Grail is the myth sought on the journey, and the success of a holiday is proportionate to the degree that the myth is realized.

Souvenirs are tangible evidences of travel that are often shared with family and friends, but what one really brings back are memories of experiences. As Carpenter (1973, p. 17) puts it so well:

> The connection between symbol and things comes from the fact that the symbol—the word or picture (or artifact)—helps give the 'thing' its identity, clarity, definition. It helps convert given reality into experienced reality, and is therefore an indispensable part of all experience.

The chosen style of tourism has its counterpart in types of souvenirs. The Environmental tourist is usually content with pictures and postcards but the Hunter and Gatherer wants rocks and sea shells, or even pieces of an archaeologic ruin. Bolder members bring back heads or even whole animals to stuff, to testify to their vacation glory. The Ethnic tourist rarely has the opportunity to bring home the "whole Primitive" but is content with arts or crafts, particularly if they were made by the ethnic for his/her own (preferably sacred) use. Items made specifically for the tourist market have much less symbolic appeal, and this authenticity is often overstated (Graburn 1976).

The limitations of tourist travel, especially for jet-setters who cover so much ground so fast, diminish experienced reality and the momentos and souvenirs serve as cues by which to relive the experience at a slower pace. In photography, to get oneself in the picture is common to tourists of both Occidental and Oriental origins as evidence of identity and placement. If they are not afraid of soul-loss, native peoples often project themselves into tourists' pictures as a momentary escape from their environment and as a means of "getting into" the imagined happiness and affluence of the tourist's home situation. As one impoverished African in a remote ex-colonial country said to the anthropologist who was taking last-minute photos of all his informants, "And when you develop the photo, please make me come out white."

"Wish you were here"

Tourists almost ritualistically send postcards from faraway places to those whom they wish to impress as well as to those they love. Partly, it is to let the latter know they are well and enjoying themselves, and partly to be re-membered and awaited. Conversely, the sacred charisma rubs off; those left at home feel partly uplifted, though perhaps jealous, when they receive such cards and may even display them near their work desks or on bulletin boards. The next best thing to traveling is to know someone who did.

Yet if they did go along, had already been there, or were about to visit the same area, there would be heightened excitement in sharing, which par-allels Huizinga's (1950, p. 12) observations about play:

> The [co-traveling] community tends to become permanent even after it is over . . . the feeling of 'being apart' together in an exceptional situation, of sharing something important, or mutually withdraw-ing from the rest of the world and rejecting the usual norms, retains its magic beyond the duration . . . surrounds itself with an air of se-crecy . . . dressing up . . . disguised together as other beings.

Even aboard jets, we all know the "stranger on the train" phenomenon, or the "shipboard romance" that didn't last. The magic of sharing a touristic activity lasts only when (1) the event is really nonordinary; (2) participants initially share similar value systems; and most importantly, when (3) they already know each other or are in the same profession or institution. The popularity of conferences (held in vacation settings such as Hawaii or Disney-land), or touring groups of farmers or attorneys as well as "in-house" travel planned for factory workers, attest to the fact that the magic of tourism is enhanced by group identity and, later, reliving the experience with associ-ates. Analogous to the truism that "Distance is to love as wind to fire; it enflames the great and puts out the feeble," experiences shared at a distance strengthen relationships between the like-minded but may push others fur-ther apart.

Tourism is rife with snobbery, and within each of its basic forms hier-archies of rank and prestige exist that illustrate the continuum and the con-trast between the ordinary/nonordinary. Obviously, what is extraordinary for some—for a rural Britisher, a trip up to London to the theater—may be an almost daily affair for others (a London suburbanite). Thus one man's excitement may be another man's boredom and threshold from which the more urbane measures his sacred.

To measure the hierarchies of prestige, the journey motif suggests that the further removed from the ordinary, the better; the sacred/profane motif suggests that the more extraordinary, the better; while the time measuring aspect suggests that the longer the period or more frequent the trips, the better. Each theme can be translated into the one-upmanship of the genre of tourists. For the young, rebellious Ethnic and Environmental tourist (or non-tourist as they proudly claim), distant and exotic places such as Kathmandu or Goa are "in," and prestige is enhanced by the length of uninterrupted travel.

Others of a more rugged bent, the elite tourists, emphasize the struggle against Nature, and gain their prestige through solitude, and a high degree of self-reliance in the communion. Driving alone from Cairo to Capetown, or daring raft trips down wild rivers are pale imitations of what were once rugged individual efforts worthy of Explorer's Club membership.

A common theme in these contrasting examples of Ethnic and Environmental tourism is the emphasis on the "spirit quest" or the self-testing, often maturing, pioneer endurance that they both effect in their different ways. This spirit quest may be imagined, for Cohen (1973) suggests that modern drifter-tourism is as safe and commonplace as riding a New York subway. Nevertheless, these apparently dangerous and effortful styles of tourism seem to attract the young, as a kind of self-imposed rite of passage to prove to themselves and to their peers that they can make their own way in life—probably never to repeat it later on. Or, this high adventure attracts the affluent, often highly educated middle-aged for whom social constraints and a Depression denied their youthful wanderlust. Money is not the criterion of prestige. For the youthful traveler, Cohen (1973) notes that voluntary poverty is the sacred/nonordinary quality of tourism for the middle-class "Nomads from Affluence."

In sharp contrast is the tourism of the timid—often parents of the youthful travelers—who have money and don't mind spending it, as long as they can carry the home-grown "bubble" of their life-style around with them. They rely on the advice and blandishments of tourist brokers in order to live as comfortably as at home or even more luxuriously, for the holiday is nonordinary, and one should eat, drink, and spend beyond the rules of the ordinary. Though undoubtedly enchanted by the view of God's handiwork through the pane of the air-conditioned bus or the porthole, they worship "plumbing that works" and "safe" water and food. The connection with the unfamiliar is likely to be purely visual, and filtered through sunglasses and a camera viewfinder. These tourists are likely to have the greatest impact on the culture and environment of the host peoples both by virtue of their greater numbers and by their demands for extensions of their home environments for which they are willing to pay handsomely. Cohen (1973) points out that mass drifter-tourism stimulates the hosts to maintain specially designed receptive institutions, even if the travelers are unaware of the degree to which they are being catered.

Although the outward rationale for tourism has as many variations as there are tourists, the basic motivation seems to be the human need for recreation. Tourism is one manifestation of the fulfillment of this need—one that, because of the more affluent economic status of the developed world, is enabling many people to see "how the other half lives."

University of California, Berkeley

2

Tourism as a Form of Imperialism

DENNISON NASH

A concern with tourism by anthropologists would seem to be related to a general interest in culture contact and sociocultural change that has animated so much of our sociocultural inquiry in recent years. The tourist, like the trader, the employer, the conqueror, the governor, the educator, or the missionary, is seen as the agent of contact between cultures and, directly or indirectly, the cause of change particularly in the less developed regions of the world.

Recent analyses of culture contact have suggested that an understanding of the immediate contact situation may not be enough to fully comprehend it. Some reference to larger contexts may be required. Adams (1974, p. 240), for example, states, "Both social change and social continuity require interactive processes with the significant interactions in some respects confined to single communities, in others to multiple groups in time ordered settings, in others to whole regions, in still others to interregional contacts whose historical role was far out of proportion to their limited scale and frequency." And Magubane (1973) has pointed out the too-restricted scope of many studies of culture contact in Africa, and called for a consideration of

The author wishes to thank Robert Bee, Scott Cook, James Faris and Bernard Magubane for discussions that helped in the preparation of this chapter. Assistance also was provided by the University of Connecticut Research Foundation, the Camargo Foundation, and the Centre des Hautes Etudes Touristiques (Rene Baretje, director) in Aix-en-Provence.

the broader context of colonialism in which such contact occurs. He is one of a number of scholars who have brought theories of imperialism to bear on the kind of contact situation that has tended to preoccupy anthropologists. Though his and much other anthropological work on imperialism tends to be of Marxist persuasion and on the side of the underdogs in the Third World and elsewhere, one need not be a Marxist or a revolutionary to see the easy applicability of concepts of imperialism to such situations.

Imperialism

At the most general level, theories of imperialism refer to the expansion of a society's interests abroad. These interests—whether economic, political, military, religious, or some other—are imposed on or adopted by an alien society, and evolving intersocietal transactions, marked by the ebb and flow of power, are established. Such transactions will have various consequences for the societies involved. As I have indicated elsewhere (Nash 1970), a formulation of the imperialistic process at the present state of our knowledge does not require the acceptance of a particular interest (e.g., the economic) as crucial, nor does it require the notion of the unwanted imposition of some interest on an alien society. The possibility of voluntary acceptance by a native people and voluntary participation in transactions that further expatriate interests are an essential part of this conception of imperialism.

Changes in the relative power of the partners in an imperialistic transaction can transform or even lead to the breakdown of the relationship between them. Whatever happens between the partners will have greater or lesser consequences for their societies. The trading of such consequences in the less powerful partner society is, as this book demonstrates, grist for the anthropologist's mill. It is the nature of the sociohistorical processes which lead to these consequences which is less well understood.

Tourism as a Form of Imperialism

If the investigation of tourism is to be truly anthropological, it should not be confined to a narrow range of societies or contact situations but should endeavor to comprehend the phenomenon wherever it occurs. Perhaps it will not be possible to consider all tourism in a single theoretical scheme, but theoretical formulations of tourism should be as broadly applicable as possible. Since there appears to be no *a priori* reason why the principles governing internal tourism and external tourism should differ, the field of investigation ought, at least at the outset, to include both. An anthropologically useful theory of tourism would have the potential to embrace such varied events as skiing at St. Moritz, vacation activities on the Black Sea, New York's special relationship with the Catskill Mountains, the Victorian English winter community in Nice, ancient Romans in their country villas, thermalism in Ancient Greece, and possibly Muslim pilgrimages. In all such cases the focus of the inquiry ought to be on tourist-host relationships involving transactions between groups.

The association of tourism with industrial or modern society has been noted by a number of authors (Boyer 1972; Enzenberger 1962; Greenwood 1972; Nuñez 1963). However, if one takes tourism to imply leisured migration and all that is associated with it, as does Boyer, then it is difficult not to find it in preindustrial societies (Sigaux 1966, pp. 9–19). There is a problem in isolating leisure in hunting and gathering societies, but some aspects of their perpetual migrations (e.g., the visit to religious places by Australian aborigines) might be considered a sort of prototourism. In Ancient Athens, where citizens had much leisure time, Duchet (1949) states that people traveled for pleasure or education, sport, religious purposes (festivals or pilgrimages to sanctuaries), and reasons of health (spas). Ancient Romans vacationed in country villas. Medieval pilgrims, a possible variety of tourist, overcame obstacles to travel to visit religious centers. And some French monarchs in what was an essentially agricultural society were noted for their visits to and between country châteaux. It seems clear, therefore, that tourism is not totally confined to industrial or modern society; but it also is true that only in such a society does it become a pervasive social phenomenon.

The necessary cause of tourism, as it has been defined here, appears to be a level of productivity sufficient to sustain leisure. If productivity is the key to tourism, then any analysis of touristic development without reference to productive centers that generate tourist needs and tourists is bound to be incomplete. Such metropolitan centers have varying degrees of control over the nature of tourism and its development, but they exercise it—at least at the beginning of their relationship with tourist areas—in alien regions. It is this power over touristic and related developments abroad that makes a metropolitan center imperialistic and tourism a form of imperialism.

It may be useful to have an extreme, almost ideal-typical example in mind in beginning to explore the touristic process. The North American vacationer who insists on American fast-food hamburgers, coffee with his meals, hot running water in his bedroom and the use of the English language is a familiar image. Here is a person from a highly industrialized country expecting, even demanding, that his vacation life abroad meet expectations he has come to take for granted at home. Beyond this vacationer there often stands a metropolitan touristic infrastructure that, in effect, sees that his expectations are met. The tourist and his supporting infrastructure engage in transactions with a native people. Such transactions, which are marked by a disparity of power, may involve not only individuals of a given touristic phenomenon but will depend also on the relative significance of different social structures for understanding it.

The touristic process involves the generation of the touristic impulse in productive centers, the selection or creation of tourist areas to serve their needs, and the development of transactions between the productive centers and tourist areas. These transactions, centering on the host-guest relationship, have various consequences for the parties involved and develop according to laws we have yet to discover. This chapter makes some preliminary observations about different aspects of this touristic process and suggests some research questions that are likely to provide significant information about it.

The Generation of Tourism

As mentioned above, the origins of tourism are to be found in conditions of higher productivity, especially in industrial society. It is questionable if there is tourism among hunters and gatherers, and there is only a slight amount in agricultural societies. Higher productivity, associated with technological advances, has made possible the development of leisure classes as well as an improved material apparatus for travel. Tourism arises when people use the available means of travel for leisure-time pursuits. At the point in the industrial cycle where significant tourism appears, people are beginning to live in a society where productivity is great enough, the horizons broad enough, and the social mobility significant enough to nourish the touristic impulse. Though people could stay home in their spare time, they now have the desire and an increasing opportunity to tour. Who has the opportunity will, of course, depend on the distribution of leisure and resources in a society, but in an advanced industrial society widespread tourism is to be expected. Many people in such a society have come to expect a trip or a vacation away from home at some point in the year. Such expectations may be temporarily frustrated by economic conditions, political events, or military developments, but the aspirations have been normalized and are not likely to disappear so long as the industrial base remains.

What are the factors which generate the touristic impulse? It would seem advisable to divide this question into two parts: (1) What are the factors that tend to produce leisure? (2) What are the factors promoting migration during leisure time? Undoubtedly, productivity is associated with leisure, and attention to economic factors, as a somewhat ethnocentric Veblen (1899) has shown, is important in explaining it. One might posit a universal need for variation or "recreation" in humans, as does Graburn in this volume, but unless people are freed from the work routine by adequate productivity, there will be no possibility of satisfying that need. Also, such a need probably would be to some extent acquired and therefore would vary with social conditions. Here one is reminded of the characteristics of the so-called modern mentality that a number of authors (Inkeles 1969; Lerner 1958) have attempted to describe. A "modern" person has broader horizons and is prone to travel. If he lives in a modern city he may want to flee from its problems, a point emphasized by those authors (Boyer 1972; Duchet 1949) who implicate urbanism with tourism. Whether or not he migrates in his leisure time will depend on opportunities and facilities to travel abroad.

Without facilities for travel, of course, there would be no migration and hence no tourism. In the Middle Ages travelers had to move on poor roads, cross innumerable frontiers, pay many tolls, endure brigands, and put up with scarce and inadequate lodging. Indeed, as Gaulis and Creux (1975, p. 11) point out, *Pendant les siècles, le voyage n'était qu'une suite de contretemps* ("Throughout the centuries, travel was a series of difficulties"). Modern means of transport have changed all this and have opened up vast touristic possibilities. Boyer (1972, p. 134) has argued that the coming of a railroad usually produced a dramatic increase in visitors to a tourist area. Improved means of transport also would seem to be related to an increasing desire to travel.

In summary, the factors associated with the appearance and development of tourism are an increased productivity that creates leisure, psychological mobility associated with broadened horizons, and improved transport and communication facilities. Obviously, these factors are interrelated, but a greater weight probably should be assigned to productivity than to the others. Any so-called touristic "need" ought to be derivable from these factors. As indicated above, I believe that positing a universal need for variation of experience takes us only a short way in our attempt to explain tourism. Any such need probably varies with social conditions operating on the potential tourist in a negative way, as does a crowded, alienating urban existence, or positively, as with a modern, liberal education.

The Creation of Tourist Areas

Touristic expansion takes place according to the needs and resources of productive centers and their people. What tourist realms tend to be selected or created, and what purposes they will serve, vary with their accessibility as well as with the character of the centers involved. More southern regions, for example, often have become vacation meccas for the peoples of northern industrial nations; and the kind of services they are expected to perform or wishes they must fulfill often are given in the travel literature. The young Goethe (1962) thought that Italy offered a particular kind of fulfillment for romantic northern souls, and Thomas Mann (1930) saw Venice as a place where constricted northerners opened up and came apart. One cannot begin to account for the character of the Costa del Sol without reference to north-western Europe; turn-of-the-century Nice without reference to England and Csarist Russia; or Miami Beach and the Catskills without referring to New York City. Of course, tourist areas are not entirely the creation of met-ropolitan productive centers. Native peoples sometimes take the initiative and often actively collaborate in their establishment. Even then, however, they take as a significant point of reference the availability and needs of cer-tain metropolitan centers. To the extent that they take these into account, they are collaborating in the touristic expansion (and thus the imperialism) of such centers.

What are the factors causing certain alien regions to become tour-istically linked with specific metropolitan centers? Undoubtedly, cost must be considered. Forster (1964, p. 219) points out that adequate and cheap transport must be available and that the tourist area must have a slightly lower standard of living than the region from which it draws tourists. Though this generalization would seem to fail in a number of cases where tourists migrate to urban or more industrialized areas, it does point to the significance of cost in accounting for the selection or creation of tourist areas. Forster also suggests that such places must be different enough to sat-isfy the touristic impulse. Such differences, however, must be compatible with the touristic needs of specific metropolitan centers. Such compatibility sometimes is described as charm, beauty, or excitement, but it must always be assessed in terms of metropolitan expectations or needs. Not too many years ago, Puerto Vallarta was a relatively isolated, sleepy little fishing vil-lage, but it became the answer to some metropolitan touristic dreams in-volving sun, sea, and an unspoiled, picturesque landscape inhabited by a friendly, easy-going people. At the close of World War II the area that is now Vail, Colorado, was a mountain wilderness distinguished by, among other things, its deep and long-lasting snow cover. Its potential for satisfy-ing the needs of a nation experiencing the beginnings of a skiing boom was recognized by a group of entrepreneurial businessmen who mobilized the necessary resources to transform the area into a modern ski resort. Both Puerto Vallarta and Vail had features of potential touristic significance for certain metropolitan centers. They were chosen and, with the collaboration of their inhabitants, developed because of their compatibility with metropolitan dreams. Their fate thus became linked with exogenous forces over which they were to have less and less control.

We need to know more about the forces that generate specific touristic aspirations because they will tell us which places in the world are likely to come under what metropolitan touristic pressures. The boom in pleasure skiing is an example. How did it come about? What needs in a society and its people does skiing serve? If we know that people want to feel free and daring and that they can feel that way on skis, it is possible to chart the areas of the world where appropriate ski resorts might arise. Whether or not they would be developed would depend on a number of factors, among them transportation, skiing technology (including cable cars, snow making machines, ski equipment, etc.), the collaboration of native people, and certain economic resources. In considerations of this kind one might want to probe deeply into motivations and their sources. If, as Farber (1954) has suggested, travel is conceived to be a "magic helper," why is a certain kind of travel to a certain place thought to be more efficacious? Or if, as Enzenberger (1962) has argued, one function of tourism is to help people flee from distasteful work roles, why is flight in a certain direction thought to be more desirable? Here, methods of the market researcher, such as those being used in studies commissioned by the United States Travel Service (U.S. Department of Commerce 1972), can be of use in making predictions.

In any transactional view of imperialism one cannot forget the role played by native peoples. I have suggested above that some native peoples may be rather active partners in the creation of tourist resorts. What are the forces causing them to seek out or consent to touristic development? Where disparities of power are very great, as in the case of military conquest, such a question may be of little significance, but it is not possible to ignore the fact that the development of a tourist area usually depends on some local cooperation. This is especially apparent when a powerful country such as Soviet Russia chooses not to cooperate. In the post–World War II period when other countries eagerly pursued the tourist "dollar," the Russians resisted the intrusion of international tourism into their homeland; they began to cooperate only after a relaxation of the Cold War and their own development of what they considered to be adequate touristic controls and facilities.

A society may use its power not only to prevent or promote the establishment of touristic relationships, but also to select what for it seem to be
advantageous ones. Some kind of maximizing model such as that used by
Barth and his associates (1963; 1967) would be particularly helpful in analyzing early and later choices of indigenous peoples in the development of
tourism in their societies. With time, their power to shape the course of
touristic transactions with metropolitan centers would vary. This in turn
would affect the existence and nature of the tourism that depends for its
development on their cooperation.

Touristic Transactions

With the creation of a tourist realm, various social interactions are set up
between tourists, their hosts, and the organizations and societies they represent. These transactions, which can be long or short term, cyclical (e.g.,
seasonal) or noncyclical, and simple (as in a tourist-host relationship) or
complex (involving an elaborate touristic organization), come to be based
on understandings about how the parties involved will treat each other and
on the conditions that could bring about the termination of the relationships. If a native people are murderous, nasty, disease-ridden, or embroiled
in political conflict, the relationship could be threatened by metropolitan dissatisfactions. If, on the other hand, the brokers of tourism attempt to interfere in internal political affairs or desecrate local institutions, the hosts might
seek to end the touristic relationship. Guerrilla fighters sometimes deliber-
ately violate the implicit terms of a touristic contract in order to further
their political aims, and metropolitan centers may restrict or end the flow of
tourists to a given area if the terms of their contract are not honored. Similar to any other social relationship, the relationship between tourists and
their hosts includes certain understandings that must be agreed and acted
upon if it is to be maintained. What are these terms, and what are the conditions defining them?

Touristic transactions are defined, first, by the condition of strangerhood. The tourist is almost an ideal-typical example of what Simmel
(1950, pp. 402–7) had in mind when he formulated his conception of the
stranger. Simmel saw the stranger as a temporary sojourner who does not
share the essential qualities of host group life. As a result, interaction between him and the hosts tends to take place on a more general, impersonal
level. Simmel (p. 407) says, "Strangers are not really conceived as individuals, but as strangers of a particular type." The tendency to generalize or

categorize, which also characterizes strangers' conceptions of their hosts, suggests the type of relationship common in the modern world.

Not only do strangers and their hosts treat each other as types but also as objects. Where disparities of power are great, as in the early stages of colonialism, this can lead to prejudice and discrimination by the colonizers and a variety of familiar responses among the colonized (Fanon 1968). People who treat others as objects are less likely to be controlled by the constraints of personal involvement and will feel freer to act in terms of their own self-interest. This tendency often is tempered by the development of controls involving force or legal mechanisms and the intervention of external agencies such as governments or military bodies. This is one reason why transactions involving tourists usually cannot be successfully analyzed without reference to broader social structures with which they are connected.

Strangers are notable also for their tendency to clump together with their fellows (Nash 1970, pp. 108–22). Finding themselves uninvolved and often confused in a foreign situation, they may begin to build a familiar social network involving people from home. As a gap between this stranger group and the hosts solidifies, certain intergroup specialists such as the diplomat, the community relations expert, and the concierge, or organizations such as the World Association of Travel Agents, must be mobilized if successful stranger-host relationships are to continue. These mediators, who have been called "culture brokers" play an increasingly important role as social differentiation proceeds. Any analysis of the tourist-host relationships, therefore, probably will require a consideration of some group of stranger-tourists and the agents and organizations that mediate their relationships with the hosts.

The terms of tourist-host transactions are defined not only by the condition of strangerhood but by the nature of tourism itself. As a tourist, a person is at leisure, which means that he is not bent on shaping the world, only experiencing or toying with it. If the tourist is to pursue peculiarly touristic goals, others must perform more utilitarian functions. To put it more succinctly, others must serve while the tourist plays, rests, cures, or mentally enriches himself. Accordingly, he finds himself separated from those in the touristic infrastructure who serve him by the different, if complementary, nature of the activities specified in the touristic contract. The hosts can be a nation of hotel-keepers perfectly adapted to service, as in Switzerland, or Muscovite waitresses grudgingly performing it, but the work-leisure distinction continues to separate them from their guests. Even if they come from the same cultures and understand each other perfectly, the basic attitudes they bring to their relationship with each other are distinguished along lines specified by the differences between work and leisure. The difficulties attendant upon the development of liaisons between hotel guests and employees provide an illustration of the social barriers involved. Even in new club-style resorts, where the difference between host and guest is minimized, it cannot be eliminated.

In sum, tourists are separated from their hosts by the facts of strangerhood, the work-leisure distinction, and whatever cultural differences obtain in a particular situation. Any viable touristic contract must take into account these facts and make some provision for dealing with them. The tourist is not usually expected to make the adaptations necessary for involving himself in the essential life of the host society. This "privilege," which is resented by some tourists, may be one reason for the combination of envy and disdain shown by more acculturated expatriates for their tourist countrymen (Nash 1970, p. 129). But if the tourist is not expected to make the adaptations necessary for him to get along in a more or less foreign situation, who is? That burden tends to fall on the hosts, and it is one of the prices they pay for having tourists in their midsts. It is apparent that many of them willingly—even eagerly—pay this price. Here again, some kind of maximizing model derived from exchange theory would assist in understanding host calculations; but the fact that native people usually "choose" to take on the additional responsibilities of adjustment necessary for dealing with tourists suggests that the incentives or constraints in the direction of touristic development are very great and that the tourist benefits in his adaptations vis-à-vis hosts from the considerable economic, political, or military power of the metropolitan center he represents. Of course, calculations may go awry, and what may have appeared to be a very profitable venture may turn out in the end to be extremely costly. The decision to expand tourism may be seen by certain entrepreneurial hosts to require some compromises with tourists and their way of life, but the additional compromises demanded by developing tourism may not be foreseen. When the hosts find themselves dealing also with hotel-keepers, transportation people, travel and publicity agents, sanitary engineers, and the like, and making adjustments in the areas of life these represent, they may begin to have second thoughts about the wisdom of their initial calculations.

What kind of research endeavors would be appropriate for the analysis of touristic transactions? Microsocialogical analyses of tourist-host and tourist-tourist relationships using, perhaps, some variation of Goffman's (1959; 1967) approach to social relationships would give us some insight into the immediate social world of individual tourists and their hosts. In addition, institutional analyses of the nature of tourism would be essential for understanding why individual relationships take the form they do. Finally, some kind of exchange theory would help us understand why in a given situation certain forms of touristic transactions emerge. Such investigations would assume the generation of certain forms of tourism by particular metropolitan centers.

The Consequences of Tourism

Anthropologically viewed, the consequences of tourism may be seen to flow from the peculiar nature of the intergroup contact involved. Since that contact often (but not always) involves representatives of groups differing in degree of productivity and power (the tourist area usually being the less productive and powerful), investigations focusing on the modernization, urbanization, or development of a tourist area (Nuñez 1963) or the effects of exploitation by the dominant metropolitan center (Pérez 1973–74) ought to be of considerable scientific value. However, an alternative approach that focusses on touristic universals and their consequences for the individuals and societies involved also would seem to be indicated.

Since the touristic transaction is a two-way street involving interaction between metropolitan centers and tourist areas, there is no *a priori* reason to rule out a consideration of consequences to both ends of the relationship. Anthropologists' sympathies may lie with the underdog and the exotic, but they must recognize that one-sided transactional analysis is necessarily incomplete no matter how unequal the relationship being studied. Here, Hallowell's (1957) paper concerning the effects of the frontier is instructive.

In the tourist area the consequences of tourism derive from the introduction from outside of a new sociocultural reality. This reality, to which the native people and their social system must adapt, amounts to a transiently populated, externally based leisure class and its accompanying goals or expectations. The principal social adaptations that the hosts must work out in regard to this reality are between groups or societies and classes. The touristic arrangements created to deal with the foreign guests invariably include a serving class whose mission it is, first of all, to deal with strangers from other groups or societies. As Boyer (1972, p. 171) points out, the development of tourism is reflected in the local occupational structure by an expansion of the service center of the economy. Tourists must be transported, accommodated, and assisted with the many problems of getting along in a foreign place. Secondly, some provision for their leisure activities must be made. Such provisions may be extremely simple, as in providing access to a beach in the Canary Islands, or elaborate, as in the construction of Tivoli in Copenhagen. Investigations of the consequences of tourism in tourist areas ought to begin from an analysis of the individual and collective adaptations made by a host people in regard to these inevitable service functions. Such adaptations may be considered the primary consequences of tourism.

Though it probably is too early to begin to generalize confidently about touristic adaptations, one would expect them to be accompanied by at least some psychological and social conflict. In the tourist area, the necessity for at least some of the hosts to function as marginal men or culture brokers in order to deal with tourists and their metropolitan sponsors creates a pressure for acculturation in the direction of metropolitan cultures, learning how to carry on superficial, objective transactions, and providing for leisure needs. The acquisition or reinforcement of such qualities (including unfulfilled aspirations) could lead to social conflict among hosts, between hosts and guest, and also create intrapsychic conflict between incompatible personality dispositions. Additional social and psychological conflict could emerge as a result of competition over, or differential involvement in, the touristic enterprise. Examples of such conflicts have been provided by Lewis (1972), Nuñez (1963), and several chapters in this volume. The individual and social mechanisms that are developed to resolve these conflicts and thus facilitate the adjustment of the host society to touristic imperialism could be important factors in social change. Any investigation of the dynamics of the touristic process would have to consider them in some detail.

On the metropolitan side, the consequences of tourism derive from the creation and existence of a mobile leisure class and the infrastructure supporting it. As indicated above, tourism can serve a variety of social and psychological functions for a metropolitan center and its people. Does a vacation on the Baltic Sea, in Montecatini Terme, Acapulco, or the mountains of Hokkaido revive flagging energies, release threatening impulses, satisfy wanderlust, or assist or confirm vertical mobility? How do tours to distant places serve the economic, political, military, or religious needs of a people? Is it possible that the principal psychological consequence of tourism for the metropolitan side is an awakening or heightening of discontent (They'll never get me to go back to Indianapolis!)?

Where industrialization is far advanced and tourism widespread, a travel "industry" emerges, concerned with travel as an end in itself. It would be appropriate in such cases to speak about the institution of travel. Such an institution may be seen to serve certain social and psychological needs, but it also will develop needs of its own. What these self-serving needs are and how their fulfillment affects other institutions in the metropolitan society and with tourist areas would be an interesting subject for anthropological inquiry. In any study of the evolution of tourism, such an investigation would be essential, especially in accounting for its metropolitan-dictated development.

The Evolution of Tourism

So far, the implicit model underlying this analysis of tourism is not unlike that proposed by Malinowski (1945), who saw the world of contact and change in the colonial situation as consisting of three orders of sociocultural reality: the native or traditional, the modern or industrial, and the transitional. Such a model may be appropriate for treating early tourist contacts where tourism involves only some of the people on each side and the consequences of the interaction are not far reaching. But with continued contact, the transitional may engulf the traditional. In such circumstances the contact model proposed by Gluckman (1947) or Balandier (1951) for colonial situations would seem to be more appropriate. It would then be possible to speak of a transitional touristic social system emerging out of touristic contact. This system, which would center on the tourist-hosts relationship and the roles played in it, would be populated by transient tourists and all those hosts and metropolitans who participate in tourism. It would involve associative and dissociative social relationships by more or less committed maximizing people. There would be agreement and disagreement about the touristic goals of the system and the means used to attain them. The system's economic structure would be based on touristic service functions, and other social structures would reflect this. Finally, there would be power centers directing the system's development. Such a system, which could be a part of other systems (e.g., the colonial), might involve whole societies as in the U.S. Virgin Islands, and be multinational in scope as in the Pan American Airways empire.

Gordon Lewis, in his discussion of the U.S. Virgin Islands, provides an almost ideal-typical example of a touristic social system. For him (Lewis 1972, p. 129) the Virgin Islands "can be seen as a prime illustration of the general character of Caribbean parasitical tourism. They belong to the Caribbean subgroup of pure tourist economies, like Bermuda and the Bahamas, which are dependent almost entirely upon their ability to sell themselves to

North American affluent societies." Lewis describes in some detail the conflicts that have developed over tourism and the various interests involved, but points out (p. 130) that "all . . . differences yield to a united front when the total image of the economy is challenged."

Lewis (pp. 137–38) implies that all present-day tourist areas dependent on North American metropolitan centers are evolving along a path leading to the kind of "anti-civilization" found in San Juan or Las Vegas. It would be premature to suggest, however, a universal evolutionary scheme for analyzing the development of touristic systems. Forster (1964, p. 218) points out that there is no inevitability in the process of tourist development. A brief survey of specific cases would seem to bear him out. How can one make general statements that would include the development of the touristic systems of Cannes, Leningrad, Acapulco, Davos, Miami Beach, Paris, the Promised Land, Pennsylvania, Stratton Mountain, San Sebastien, Sochi, or Kiawah Island?

Any attempt to make broad or narrow generalizations about the evolution of touristic systems requires an identification of those parameters that are especially significant in sociocultural change. Among these are the needs of the metropolitan center(s), the distribution of power in the system, the economic base, and the social divisions relating to tourism. Some discussion of metropolitan touristic needs already has been given above. Here the role that these needs and their development play in the evolution of a touristic system must be added.

Because a tourist system, once established, must meet the touristic needs of one or more metropolitan centers, it will inevitably reflect in its evolution the development of such needs. Moreover, if we assume a competitive situation and maximizing human beings, there will be a pressure towards increasing responsiveness to metropolitan events. This means that the modernization or rationalization of a tourist area, which may have begun with a major effort to attain the minimal level necessary for interesting, accommodating, and serving tourists, will continue as a reflection of subsequent developments in this dimension in the metropolitan center. How exact a reflection it will be will depend on where the power lies in the touristic system. If considerable power is retained by those whose goals are at variance with metropolitan needs (as, for example, in Moscow, Paris, and New York), developments in the touristic system will reflect such needs with lesser fidelity. On the other hand, if power is entirely in the hands of metropolitan expatriates or their local agents, the touristic system will develop along a line that is increasingly dictated by metropolitan needs and their development.

As was suggested above, the economy of any tourist system will tend to become externally oriented and concerned with those service functions that provide for touristic needs. Cohen (1974, p. 250) points out that an expansion of a group's resource base outside its boundaries will alter the degree of dependence of occupational roles on outside resources. In the case of tourism the outside resource is the tourist. The adaptive response to his presence on the economic level is the development of the necessary service occupations to deal with him. The expansion of the service sector, in particular those jobs whose primary or secondary function is attending to transient expatriates and their sponsors, has implications for the economy as a whole and for the rest of the society. I will not attempt here to assess the practical desirability of such a development nor discuss the advisability of balanced economic development. Such important questions can be answered by the economist, more particularly, the economist in his role as advisor.

Insofar as other aspects of social organization are related to the economic structure, changes in that structure ought to be followed by other noneconomic changes. Not only would there be a strain towards consistency with the new economic arrangements, as in the Virgin Islands where even the churches tend to support the touristic "line" (Lewis 1972, pp. 128–29), but inconsistency or conflict between sectors of the touristic system, notably between the better and lesser served by the touristic economy, would arise as well. In some cases the introduction of tourism will exacerbate existing social cleavages; in others new cleavages will appear. Such conflict and associated psychological conflicts can generate additional changes in the touristic system as people work out ways of coping with them.

To sum up, the evolution of a touristic system is seen here to be subject to the actions of both exogenous and endogenous forces. Exogenous forces, which emanate from one or more metropolitan centers, involve the generation of touristic needs and tourists, the selection or creation of tourist areas, and the establishment of direct and indirect tourist-host transactions. The people of a tourist area may enter into a developing tourist system with varying degrees of enthusiasm. Their principal adaptation involves the development of a service economy and the necessary sociocultural changes to go with it. This service economy is externally oriented and focussed on providing for the needs of transient, leisured strangers. Such developments will tend to produce inter- and intrapersonal disjunctions constituting the principal endogenous sources of change in the touristic system.

It is not possible at this point in the anthropological study of tourism to make significant general statements about the evolution of touristic systems, but if investigations are confined to narrower classes of historical circumstances, as in the studies of Forster (1964) and Greenwood (1972), it may be possible to begin to build an empirically based theory of tourism within the conceptual framework of imperialism suggested here. The need for such a theory will grow as tourism grows, and since that growth is intimately related to industrialization, that need would seem to be very great indeed.

University of Connecticut, Storrs

II

NASCENT TOURISM IN NON-WESTERN SOCIETIES

The endeavor to record the customs of exotic societies before they vanish into the mainstream of a one-world culture has engaged a growing body of anthropologists for more than a hundred years. Popular accounts of "primitive peoples," rather than scholarly ethnographies, have penetrated school curriculums at every level, and laid the foundation for the tourist's quest to adventure. The powerful, modern taste-makers—the media with its travelogs, and especially the National Geographic Society with its magazine and documentaries—have created strong visual images that beckon the tourist. The culture brokers have converted the anthropologist's "hidden corner" of the world into a focal point for ethnic tourism. In each of the following case studies, tourism to the area is still nascent due to its limited numbers or seasonality.

Each author develops an individual theme: in chapter 3 I have chosen to examine tourism among the Eskimo in terms of locally-differentiated impact; Margaret Swain in chapter 4 analyzes tourism primarily in terms of sex roles; Charles Urbanowicz assesses the economic problems of Tonga in chapter 5, and Philip McKean in chapter 6 and Eric Crystal in chapter 7 provide interesting comparisons and contrasts in their two Indonesian case studies. Hindu Bali with its millenia-old ceremonial traditions seems better able to receive and cope with continuous visitors than the more isolated Toraja, for whom tourism is still new. Both authors, however, note that for diverse reasons tourism to Indonesia apparently strengthens local social bonds.

3

Eskimo Tourism: Micro-Models and Marginal Men

VALENE L. SMITH

Fascination with the Far North and especially with the Eskimos whose culture enabled them to survive despite the duress of Arctic cold, has lured many individuals to adventure there. In the Alaskan Arctic, the focus of this study, the first visitors were nineteenth-century explorers including Bering, Beechey, and Kotzebue (Oswalt 1979). Their journals, when printed on hand-set presses, stirred the imagination of many school boys. Financially unable to become a ship owner or captain, they signed on as sailors in the hundreds of whaling crews that penetrated the Bering Straits and western Arctic Ocean for a half-century, beginning as early as 1849. Letters and tales to their families, as well as the gifts of ivory scrimshaw, provided further stimulus to other travelers, including California naturalist John Muir and the educator-missionary Sheldon Jackson, both of whom were well-known writers. The Gold Rush of 1898 brought tens of thousands of miners to the north Alaskan coast, and their recollections added to the Alaskan lore.

Because of these historical accounts and the vast popular literature of this century, augmented by the many documentary films descriptive of their life, Eskimo culture is now an attraction—an ethnic commodity of commercial value—but one that no longer exists in its traditional form. Progressive modernization has transformed Eskimo villages into what I term "white man's towns where Eskimo also live." Tourists in the 1980s are surprised to

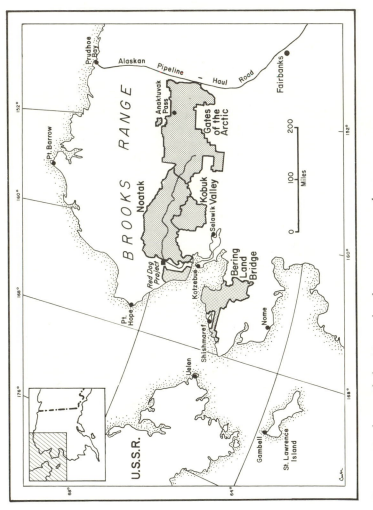

Figure 1. Northwest Alaska: National parks, monuments, and preserves.

find most Eskimo now live on a wage economy and in Western style. However, the stereotype of the Arctic climate and its snow-covered vastnesses is still an environmental asset. Tourists want to see the "Midnight Sun" and momentarily experience the geographic conditions in the "Last Frontier" of America. For most tourists, the Arctic is a once-in-a-lifetime visit and it is ironic that high season tourism occurs in summer when warm, sunny days, flowering tundra, and ice-free seas are nearly the antithesis of tourist expectations. Despite industry efforts to promote off-season tourism, few individuals participate because they fear the very conditions they wish to know.

The air-travel age has made the Alaskan Arctic readily accessible to increasing numbers of travelers. The recent U.S. national policy to set aside vast areas of northwest Alaska for preservation as wilderness but with provision for recreational use seems almost certain to change the type of tourism to the area, and to increase the flow of visitors in the decades to come (Figure 1). This case study examines the development and impacts of tourism in northwest Alaska in three phases: (1) Early Tourism, to 1971; (2) The post–Land Claims era, 1971 to 1987; and (3) the Future.

Early Arctic Tourism: Eskimo Contacts with Outsiders

The Eskimo of the Bering Straits are noted for their long tradition of involvement in aboriginal intercontinental trade with Siberians (Ray 1975), and their inter-ecologic trade with other Eskimo subgroups along the coast and in the hinterland. They became entrepreneurs par excellence, made long sledge journeys for the purpose of trade, and developed a minimally stratified society that accorded considerable status to shrewd traders (Smith 1966). To receive strangers (albeit from within the Arctic) and to turn a profit through barter are part of their heritage that may go back a thousand years.

In one of the few documented examples of aboriginal tourism, Northwest Coast Eskimo planned months in advance for their annual summer trip to the rendezvous on Kotzebue Sound that lasted for as long as six weeks and included sports contests and much intertribal dancing and singing. In anticipation, individuals made new clothes, prepared new songs, and looked forward to meeting old friends. Most significant of all, everyone who *could* go did so, even if they were not directly involved in the trading activities. It was a "summer vacation trip" based on leisure time, discretionary wealth, and was sanctioned by their peers.

When the hundreds of whaling schooners and White traders began to appear (augmented later by the presence of the miners) the Eskimo found a tremendous new trading opportunity. Traditional skills enabled the Eskimo to serve as buffers of survival for the outsiders, and Eskimo hunted, fished, trapped, and sewed as they had always done. This time, they received non-Arctic strangers and turned a cash profit. Few members of this alien horde gained much knowledge of Eskimo ethos, but they returned home imbued with respect for the native culture and disseminated the image of the Eskimo's unique ability to survive in the far north. These transient in-migrants of nearly a century ago laid the foundation for the present ethnic tourism.

Christian missions were founded in most Alaskan coastal villages in the 1890s. Once again, Eskimo in general welcomed these newcomers, and if there was no cash profit, the presence of missions was considered a positive influence. Christianity *per se* is not incongruous with many values inherent in the Eskimo world-view, and the church reinforced native sanctions against the widespread and disruptive use of alcohol. In many instances, missions provided much-sought medical help, started schools to equip Eskimo with the suddenly mandatory skills of English and arithmetic to cope with a new, patently irreversible world, and distributed welfare to the needy. Aged Eskimo informants from my fieldwork in 1950 who had personally known the missionaries accorded them great respect and affection.

The missions also had a negative effect upon Eskimo culture. The church hall, for instance, superceded the traditional men's house, the *karigi*, as a meeting place, and prayer meetings and Christmas parties replaced the aboriginal Messenger Feasts. Very important to Eskimo tourism is the role and attitude of the dominant sects toward native dancing. To name a pertinent few, the fundamentalist churches at Kotzebue and Nome effectively suppressed all native entertainment; the Episcopal mission at Point Hope and the Roman Catholic mission at King Island encouraged Eskimo aesthetics and constructed meeting halls to replace the *karigi* as a dance place; the Presbyterians at Gambell were passive, and dancing persisted. The "marginal men" of Eskimo tourism reflect this philosophical division.

Following sixty years of massive outside contact (1850–1910), the Arctic coast settled into a quiet rut, intercontinental trade ceased in 1926 by government fiat, and inter-ecologic trade sharply declined, then faded. Unlike the transient predecessors who had relied upon Eskimo products, the few new outsiders were salaried government employees who came to stay and work in the newly developing schools, hospitals, and allied services. Annual supply ships imported their needs of Stateside origin. The Eskimo entrepreneurs were still there, but the marketplace was empty.

In 1934, the Alaska Steamship Company offered an Arctic Cruise for tourists aboard their aging supply vessel, the S.S. *Victoria*. The service was so popularly received in Nome that the Chamber of Commerce sponsored a dance for the passengers and staged Eskimo dances, craft demonstrations and athletic events (Norris 1985). The ship made several voyages each summer until the eve of World War II, which permanently ended all passenger ocean travel to the Arctic until the 1980s.

The air-travel age opened the Alaskan Arctic to a new type of tourism in 1946 when a Wien Airlines bush pilot, Chuck West, conceived the idea of expanding their struggling business by selling short summer air tours to Nome and Kotzebue (West 1985). Kotzebue was a small, dominantly Eskimo village of less than five hundred inhabitants with one trading post, café, post office, movie house, and airstrip. Nome, founded as a White town during the 1898 Gold Rush, had seen a surge of military activity during World War II at its large air field but the permanent population of two thousand was quite stable. The Eskimo in Kotzebue thronged to the airport to greet the little planes carrying the occasional tourists whom they thought would restore the market for native handicrafts and services. Nome merchants similarly longed for newcomers to revive their faltering business. But, like the cruise ship visitors of two decades earlier, these air tourists came with cameras to snap a few pictures, purchased only a few small "souvenirs," and departed.

The tourism format created in the late 1940s has changed very little over the years. Visitors who purchase the two-day package tour are predominantly middle-aged and middle-class, and have campered their way up the Alaska Highway through Canada or cruised north through the Inside Passage. From a gateway city—Fairbanks or Anchorage—they extend their Alaskan vacations to include the visit to the Bering Straits. The cost for the tour is comparatively modest considering that the flight is more than six hundred miles each way, and includes sightseeing and hotel accommodations. Essentially proportionate to the consumer price index, the two-day air tour price in 1946 was us$75; in 1974, us$200; and in 1987, us$400. Participants fly to either Nome or Kotzebue for a local bus tour and overnight stay. In Kotzebue, there is an Eskimo dance performance, and in Nome, guests try gold-panning and see a dog-team demonstration (using a sled on wheels, driven by a White); then they fly to the alternate community for another bus tour, and return by air to their gateway. In each airport, they are outfitted with brightly colored parkas that serve to heighten their tourist identity.

Visitors to the Alaskan Arctic are seldom demanding or critical, and are satisfied with simple accommodations and plain fare. Most are pleased to sample Arctic char (a bland fish) or reindeer stew; a few will even taste more exotic native foods such as frozen black *muktuk*, or raw whale skin and blubber. Despite their commonly stated desire "to see how Eskimos really live," tourists are shepherded around the community in a motorcoach for a kaleidoscopic impression, with a white guide to explain native culture. The guide is usually a college student, hired for the season, with no prior Arctic experience. Few tourists have face-to-face interaction with Eskimos aside from the few natives hired to serve and entertain them, and then only in passing. Very brief periods of leisure are set aside for shopping in White-owned curio shops where tourists purchase postcards and token examples of Eskimo crafts, mostly scrimshaw and carved ivory. The comparative cost of the tour, the mass market, and its middle-class orientation generate few true "collectors" of the native art forms, which have considerable intrinsic value but are little known outside the Arctic.

Since its inception with the cruise ships, modern tourism in the Alaskan Arctic has been almost exclusively an external operation, financed and managed to benefit the carriers by providing a passenger load. Aside from more frequent air service and lower rates generated by the tourist trade and some minor infrastructure improvements, the host population whose culture and environment are the tourist attractions have profited only tangentially from the tourist trade. Increased revenues from passenger traffic help to reduce freight rates and thus lower the cost of living, since most fresh foods—meat, bread, vegetables, and dairy products—are all shipped by air freight from Anchorage or Seattle. Though summer tourists compete with the seasonal influx of business travelers, scientists, and engineering and construction crews for the use of limited facilities, a very small percentage of the host population derives any direct monetary benefit from tourism.

Tourism from 1946 to 1971 had a different impact on each of the two target communities of Kotzebue and Nome, because of variances in their local traditions and group involvement. Analysis of these disparities provides a clearer understanding of the historical process of tourism on the micro level. One cannot discuss "Eskimo tourism" in general but rather tourism in individual Eskimo centers as well as the incipient desire of the small outlying villages to participate for anticipated economic benefits.

Tourism in Kotzebue
Kotzebue lies just north of the Arctic Circle on the Bering Sea coast, and by virtue of location is the administrative and transportation center for north-

west Alaska. Archaeologic sites suggest a continuous occupancy from the fourteenth century (Van Stone 1955), and the local Eskimo, the *Kikitaruk-miut*, were very active in and probably controlled the extensive aboriginal trade that centered here. Their success as entrepreneurs provoked jealousies with contiguous groups, and it is germane to note that this is one of two reported Arctic sites where slat armor (indicative of warfare) is recovered. Legends particularly emphasize hostility as recently as one hundred fifty years ago with Eskimo from Point Hope, a different dialect group with a slightly variant, more truly maritime economy.

The historic town of Kotzebue, with an estimated 300 Eskimo population, was founded with the advent of the mission in 1897, and so great was its influence, within a few months all local Eskimo had joined the California Yearly Meeting of Friends and sworn abstention from alcohol, tobacco, *and* dancing. Gold Rush activity enticed other Eskimo to Kotzebue, but the residual aboriginal power then mandated to in-migrants a two-year probationary residence based on strict adherence to the established Christian tenets as a prerequisite to permanent settlement. Aboriginal dancing and music were effectively suppressed for all early Eskimo in Kotzebue.

Transformation of the aboriginal village into a modern metropolis seemingly parallels urban growth elsewhere. The indigenous Eskimo replaced sod igloos with frame houses on their traditional homesites, the most-favored for sea mammal hunting. The increasing in-migrants, attracted to the growing town for proximity to schools, hospital, and other desired services, of necessity built their homes on the periphery. The persistence of strong family ties and minor dialect differences in their native tongue created enclaves of "foreign," or ethnic, subgroup settlements at less favored beachline locations or on back roads, and formed the basis for community factionalism (Smith 1968).

When tourism commenced in 1946, few native Kotzebue Eskimo were available to serve as brokers for their culture because of religious sanctions. However, tour operators readily found their dancers among the small colony of Point Home Eskimo who, as Episcopalians, had maintained their aesthetics. Thus, a historically disliked, ethnic out-group of "marginal men" became the cultural entrepreneurs and entertained tourists for a profit. The same progressively aging individuals dominated local tourism throughout this period. Among them, a gregarious male Eskimo with a long record of White association and better-than-average bilingualism assumed the leadership role (Seveck 1973). In 1953 Wien Alaska Airline salaried Chester Seveck and his wife, Helen, on an annual basis and then sent them on winter promotion tours throughout the United States, Hawaii, Mexico and Europe to dance and generate tourism. Dressed in traditional furs and mukluks, they became veritable symbols of Eskimo culture, well known to the travel industry, and depicted in travel brochures worldwide. Chester's face is the 1980s logo painted on every Alaskan Airline jet.

As the numbers of visitors slowly increased, Kotzebuers became proportionately more disenchanted with tourism in general and with Point Hopers in particular. Considerable alienation seems centered on the brief, half-hour dance show. In the early years, the dance performances were sporadic, staged only when justified in terms of the numbers of tourists in town. Then quite a number of Kotzebue Eskimo trickled in to watch, for acculturation had lessened their ties with the church, and older members among them vicariously enjoyed reliving the days of their youth, although they were not made welcome to participate. As the town grew and daily mass tourism began, the numbers of Eskimo spectators at the now-nightly summer dances increased, straining facilities. At this point, nonperforming Eskimo were openly discouraged at the door, and finally a US$2.50 admission fee was levied. From the anthropological perspective, it is unfortunate that the tour operators were insensitive to a widening spectrum of involvement, but the employer/employee bonds were firmly established.

Handicrafts for tourist sales are another source of alienation. Aboriginal Kotzebue Eskimo became entrepreneurs because their resource base was limited, especially in ivory, and they were inferior carvers. However, tourist contacts readily indicated to the Point Hopers that an excellent market existed for "old things" easily obtained by raiding the archeologic site only three miles south of town. In violation of the National Antiquities Act, Point Hopers (and some white residents) almost systematically plundered Eskimo graves for salable "loot." Considering the half-forgotten tales of pitched battles between two aboriginal villages, this was a signal affront.

Spatial geography is another salient aspect of this micro-model. During the early years, tourists were housed in makeshift quarters above the airline's office, situated at the *south* end of town in a so-called central business district—a complex of buildings housing trading post, coffee shop, theater, and post office—that met tourist needs. The few overnight visitors seldom ventured much beyond this area, and their impact was minimal.

A decade later, Wien Airline constructed an enlarged Alaska-style roadhouse at the *northern* end of the traditional village and on a very slight curve in the beachline. To reach the essential services of the business center, tourists walked round-trip past traditional Kotzebue homes, with the ob-

Plate 1. A 1968 view southward from the Wein Airlines tourist hotel at Kotzebue, Alaska, with Eskimo hunting and fishing activities visible.

vious opportunity to "snap photos" of daily life. Further, from the hotel's second-story verandah, guests looked south over the entire length of the beachline with a commanding view directly onto the vestiges of Eskimo activity, including butchering (Plate 1).

One of the environmental aspects of Arctic tourism is to "stay up and see the Midnight Sun." After the dance performance finished at 9:00 P.M., the increased number of tourists strolled the beachline, at the very hour when hunters returned and butchering commenced. Tourist expectations were suddenly met—these were the things they came to see, and the pictures they wanted, of Eskimo doing "Eskimo things." By the mid-1960s, the tour packages were bringing to Kotzebue an average of twenty-five to thirty persons per day during the three summer months. Eskimo working on the beach at traditional subsistence tasks wearied of answering repetitive questions day after day and complained about tourists who took *muktuk* and fish from drying racks, smelled it, and threw it on the ground as if it were garbage. Above all, the many Eskimos flying as passengers aboard the airplanes that included tour parties reported overhearing the departing visitors brag about the "pictures I got," and interpreted the remarks as ridicule, which cuts deep into native ethos. In response, Eskimo women began to refuse

Plate 2. To screen their seal butchering from tourist eyes, Eskimo women in Kotzebue erected makeshift barricades. (Photo by Ira Latour, 1969)

would-be photographers, then erected barricades to shield their work from tourist eyes, and some finally resorted to hiring a taxi to haul seals and other game to the privacy of their homes for processing (Plates 2 and 3).

Tourism in Nome
The townsite of present-day Nome is on the windy, often storm-battered southern coast of the Seward Peninsula. Native subsistence resources appear to have been minimal, and no archaeologic settlement is known. Nome was founded as a White town during the Gold Rush era when thirty thousand miners created a flourishing frontier city. The Eskimo who now live there are in-migrants from a widespread region attracted to the wage economy of mining, barging, and other services. With one exception, no core group occurs. Several religious sects maintain churches, but most Eskimo appear to be drawn to the fundamentalist Covenant Mission, which discourages native aesthetics although it operates a radio station of region-wide importance because of partial programming in Eskimo.

Mass tourism began in the early 1960s with the construction of first one, then several, good hotels reflecting the dominantly White orientation

Plate 3. Butchering was traditionally a time of Eskimo socialization and cooperation. Under the impact of tourism some Eskimo women hired taxis to drag carcasses home, to be butchered in private. (Photo by Ira Latour, 1969)

of the town. Promotional materials stress the historic component of tourism and focus on the "days of '98," with the opportunity to pan for gold. However, since outside capital and management control the tourist industry, local white residents appear disinterested in tourism and have not even developed a "honky-tonk" bar to entertain seasonal visitors. It might prove fruitful to compare Nome with another Alaskan "ghost town," Skagway, where historic tourism appears to involve much of the White community with substantial monetary gain.

By a fortunate coincidence, ethnic tourism became possible in 1959 with the permanent resettlement of Eskimos from King Island, as a result of the closing of their BIA (Bureau of Indian Affairs) school. More traditional and subsistence-oriented than most groups, indicated by their continued use of *umiaks* (skin-covered boats), the King Islanders are a dialect and residential group. They clustered their houses around a government-built Council Hall that functioned as a surrogate *karigi* for male ivory carvers (an art form in which they excel) and as a dance place. The Catholic Mission, to which most belong, had long encouraged dancing, and King Islanders have a rich repertoire of elaborate masked dances as well as the commonplace social styles.

Tourism in the Nome micro-model was originally highly structured, but with positive differences because the village was a discrete unit situated about a mile east of Nome. Tourists were bused to the village at 7:00 P.M. for an anticipated hour's visit that included a craft demonstration, blanket toss, and dancing, and then were immediately returned to their hotel with little opportunity to wander among homes or to observe and photograph other facets of the native life-style. In essence, visitors made a short stay in a "model culture," were entertained, and went away. Since the arrival was anticipated, and since the King Islanders were in their own milieu, a discernible host-guest relationship existed. Most King Island Eskimo attended the dances regularly as a cohesive social activity, and juveniles and youths frequently joined the dances spontaneously as fully functioning members of their own culture. Tourists in general seemed more satisfied with the Nome exposure to Eskimo culture for, although there was still little face-to-face contact, the participation of a larger group of all ages lent credibility to the visit.

Comparable to Kotzebue, the Eskimo who participated as culture brokers in Nome were an "outgroup": marginal and the object of adverse comment (verbalized jealousy) by other, more urbanized, noncohesive Eskimo. Among King Islanders, touristic leadership was vested in an individual with marked bilingualism whose salary and participation in airlines-sponsored promotion tours were not completely compatible with persistent male norms.

Elite Tourism in the Outlying Villages

In the early 1960s, the airlines advertised "Off-Beat" tours to Point Hope and Gambell, remote small villages accessible by air from Kotzebue and Nome, respectively. A few elite tourists—rugged individuals with interest, time, and money who disdained minimal accommodations and services—pioneered tourism to these areas. However, the tours were discontinued after several unsuccessful seasons because there was little to attract these "pathfinders." Those who hoped to see a "real Eskimo village" were disappointed because habitations were the same weathered frame houses, and in summer most of the active hunting families had moved to camps located miles away. The villages were semi-deserted with minimal subsistence activity. Even if a dance performance could be arranged, the fee was fifty dollars. Further, adverse flying conditions frequently prevail in both areas, and to be "weathered" for several days is often disruptive to a travel itinerary.

Elite ethnic tourism was a failure for the visitor, but villagers did not comprehend the reasons. They only recognized that when people came, they spent money that, no matter how limited, added to the minimal cash flow. To encourage more tourism became village goals but differentially expressed, according to the local micro-model.

Twice in the course of my fieldwork, the Point Hope Village Council formally sought guidance to expand their latent tourist industry. They perceived three hallmarks of success. First, their relatives and friends living in Kotzebue were making a good living from tourism, and it would be lucrative to the entire village if transferred to Point Hope. Second, they had copies of the brochure prepared by the (white-dominated) Chamber of Commerce in Kotzebue and naively assumed that this was the advertising that brought thousands of tourists to Kotzebue each summer. Third, Point Hope villagers enjoy the five days each June when they host with great success the several hundred Eskimo who come by chartered plane to celebrate the traditional whaling festival. The practical considerations of capital to build a suitable hotel, the inordinate costs of food and other supplies, and the summer ground fogs and adverse flying weather all fell on unhearing ears. They did not recognize the touristic requirements vis-à-vis those of their Eskimo guests who "camped out" or crowded onto the floor of family homes and ate the abundant native foods. Nor could they anticipate the possible village disruption occasioned by mass tourism. Point Hopers perceive tourists as a seasonally constant source of income as well as an interesting influx of out-siders to redeem the monotony of their daily lives.

Gambell, on remote St. Lawrence Island in the Bering Straits, is diffi-cult to access because of foul weather—severe storms accompanied by high seas, strong winds, and persistent summer fog. Belonging to a different lin-guistic group (Yupik) from other north Alaskan Eskimo, Gambell Eskimo had ties that were strongest with Siberia, prior to the closing of that inter-national boundary in 1926. Although Eskimos from Gambell do travel to Nome, perhaps most frequently for medical treatment, they have remained one of the most traditional subsistence groups, hunting walrus and whale from *umiaks* even in 1987.

In 1966, even elite tourism had scarcely touched Gambell, and available housing was a mere canvas Quonset hut with a kerosene heater and a "honey bucket" in the corner to serve as toilet. However, like Point Hopers, they dreamed of tourist income because cash to buy even rifle shells was in very short supply. Suddenly in 1967, national travel trade journals an-nounced an Alaskan Centennial Year Pageant to be held in Gambell on three Saturdays, one each month, that summer. Tourists could join charter air-craft from Anchorage and Fairbanks and for a us$5.00 local fee, visit the village and the Museum (constructed for the occasion), have lunch, and see the dance pageant. The bold plan was inspired and directed by the capable resident White couple whose leadership role as teachers is well-stated by Hughes (1960, p. 314), "The school would therefore seem to have been one of the positive contributions of the White world to village solidarity."

Analysis of Early Arctic Tourism
Major cultural change was underway in Kotzebue and its hinterland during the decade of the 1960s. To provide more social services for Eskimos, the federal government encouraged in-migration to this Arctic air hub. Many Eskimo found steady summer employment in construction of the U.S. Pub-lic Health Service hospital, the high school, or working for the barge com-pany and airlines responsible for importing the required building materials. Subsistence hunting and fishing almost ceased, and the few who continued "in the old ways" were looked down upon. Now, almost entirely on a cash economy, Eskimo opened bank accounts, bought cars to drive on the three miles of roadway around Kotzebue, and enlarged their homes, adding in-door plumbing and running water and then insuring them against fire. The material aspects of Eskimo culture were virtually gone, and young Eskimo, in general, ridiculed their past.

Tourism nearly doubled both in volume and value for Alaska and the Arctic during the years 1964–1970 (Alaska Division of Tourism 1974). Given the widespread wage employment and the negative Eskimo image, only "marginal men" (the aged and the outgroup) were willing to be identified with tourism and to serve as culture brokers to meet the tourist expectations as best they could. Admittedly, the tourists *were* disappointed not to find igloos and dog teams, but surprisingly few regretted their visit. Most were caught up in the fascination of the long days (environmental tourism) and were greatly interested in the changes taking place in the Arctic. Themselves middle-aged, they identified with the past, and were enamored of Chester Seveck and his peers. Fortunately, these "marginal men" were reliable interpreters of a rapidly vanishing culture.

Tourism in the Post-Land Claims Era: 1971–1987

The seeds of change for Alaskan tourism date to the Native Land Claims Settlement Act (1971), which transferred control of most land in northwestern Alaska to either the native regional corporations (the shareholding entities created to administer accrued native funds) or to state and federal governments. For the first time in their history, Eskimo had a voice in their self-determination, and among their ranks were a number of well-educated, sophisticated leaders charged with the responsibility of wisely investing corporate funds to assure stable future income for Alaskan natives.

For Eskimo at least, the settlement act came as a shock: land claims had been awarded because of their aboriginal culture and their traditional use of the land, and these—the very things the tourists had come to see—the Eskimo had abandoned and lost. Each native corporation, therefore, created a cultural entity to collect, store, and use pertinent aspects of their traditional culture for new textbooks and a revival of their language and traditions.

Also in this period, mass tourism began in the Alaskan Arctic. Jet airplanes with larger payloads arrived twice daily in both Nome and Kotzebue, bringing up to one hundred tourists per day, and as many as 10,000 visitors in a summer season.

Kotzebue Tourism

Fortunately, the Eskimo leadership of the Northwest Alaska Native Association (NANA) regional corporation based in Kotzebue had traveled widely

observing tourism elsewhere and was able to use that experience to the organization's benefit.

Although the package tour program was still operated from Seattle in
conjunction with the airlines, NANA soon entered the tourist business, and
by 1975 had purchased the only hotel not airline-owned. A year later, tourists were accommodated (along with the stream of government visitors) in
the new NANA-owned, US$2.2 million complex, the *Nul-luk-vik* Hotel
(Eskimo for "the resting place"). This fifty-five-room facility offers superior
travel amenities including dial phones, color television, a dining room,
beauty salon, and small gift shop. Initially the hotel also maintained a cock-
tail lounge/bar but the presence of inebriated Eskimos created security and
social problems and it was closed.

John Schaeffer, then-president of NANA and a frequent visitor to Hawaii, is a great admirer of the principle of the cultural conservation stressed
at the Polynesian Cultural Center (see chapter 13). To create a similar kind
of historical model that would illustrate the ancient Eskimo life-style, NANA
constructed a traditional sod igloo five miles south of town in 1976 and appropriately furnished it to simulate aboriginal living. An Eskimo couple
who served as reindeer herders for NANA's recently reinstituted herd also
served as local guides. Tourists appreciated the opportunity to drive across
the tundra, see the wild flowers, pick a handful of blueberries, and enjoy this
bit of the ethnic tourism of which they had dreamed.

Also in 1976 the dancing performance was transferred from the airlines
building to Cudd Hall, the Episcopalian church center, and local Eskimo
were once again free to attend, though few participated aside from the aged,
paid Point Hope troupe led by Seveck. On several occasions five big tour
buses, each with their white driver-guide, shuttled visitors on their scheduled
round of activities but encountered some problems with roads "blocked" by
stalled cars. The buses suffered an inordinate number of minor mechanical
difficulties; a few native houses were splattered with whitewash, "Tourists,
Go Home." NANA wanted tourism for the economic benefits of jobs and
cash flow but it was evident that a small cadre of young dissidents had decided to use tourism as one of their several targets for disruption.

In 1976 NANA received as a gift from a now-defunct Anchorage taxi-
dermy store several hundred professionally mounted animals, which became the basis of a new tourist show. Housed in a large new building
constructed for the purpose, the animals are displayed in habitat groups, illuminated by a fast-paced multi-media script created by Walt Disney Productions. This half-hour show is followed by a professional slide show
highlighting Eskimo culture, and terminates with a fifteen-minute live

dance performance. Performed twice daily in 1987 in conjunction with tour schedules, the admission of us$25 per person is included in the package price, and no Eskimo attend. (NANA did hold several open-house performances for the community when it was new, and offers free performances to school classes to reinforce children's knowledge of Eskimo culture.)

In 1980, NANA carefully investigated the possible purchase of the Seattle-based company that promotes tours to their area. The motivation was primarily economic, to prevent "leakage" of the profits outside the area and place more control of tourism into Eskimo hands. However, NANA executives soon learned what industry insiders know well: the rate of return on venture capital invested in tourism enterprises averages only three percent (less than that earned in a bank savings account), and carries considerable risk. Their considered decision to shun direct participation in travel-industry marketing and sales should be carefully noted by policy-makers among other indigenous groups, for NANA has been conspicuously successful in their other commercial enterprises. For the financial benefit of their Eskimo shareholders NANA owns and operates, among other enterprises, an Anchorage-based Marriott food-service franchise, several hotels, construction companies, and the security agency that protects the Alaska oil pipeline.

NANA created *Maniilaq* as their cultural entity, whose activities have revitalized Inupiaq (Eskimo) values and traditional subsistence pursuits. In contrast to the earlier philosophy of hunters as "second-class citizens," living off the land is now a sanctioned alternative life-style which takes advantage of most modern gear: fiberglass boats, high-powered outboard motors, ski-doos and expensive rifles. In the present town of Kotzebue (population 3500), no dog team exists and very little that is picturesque remains to be photographed. Instead, the visitor sees the community college, senior citizen center, and several department stores where modern delicatessens package sandwiches to order, the bakery decorates birthday cakes, and brides may select from a variety of lace gowns.

In part because of the sustained tourist throng, but mostly because of the increasing vehicular noise and dust generated by the many trucks and cars in use on Kotzebue roads, a number of hunter families now have summer homes fifteen miles across the Sound on the sandspit of Sheshalik, an ancestral camping place. In the summer of 1987, virtually no seal, beluga or *ugruk* (bearded seal) were butchered on the Kotzebue beach within tourist view. Although a few salmon nets were still set along the shore near the hotel, very few fish were filleted to dry in the sun. Eskimo townsmen on a full-time wage-based economy now live in modern houses valued at as much as US$150,000, set on small urban homesites worth US$50,000. They can afford a second home or vacation camp to which they commute in a few minutes by power boat. Families consider this a normal summer vacation. The Eskimo are frequent tourists, and travel regularly to visit friends or relatives living in the "lower 48." Disneyland in Anaheim is the most popular vacation destination and prosperous young Eskimo families consider it a must-see for their children. Hawaii is also popular and frequently visited by direct airlink from Anchorage.

The "marginal men" of Kotzebue tourism whose knowledge of aboriginal culture provided their employment are virtually all deceased. Chester Seveck died in 1985; in 1987, his widow, Helen, dressed in a fancy fur parka and accompanied by a young woman apprentice, continued to greet arriving tourist groups. Despite the efforts of Maniilaq to create a new dance troupe comprised of younger members, the blue-jean clad, gum-chewing adolescents are patently embarrassed and lack basic skills and understanding of the meaning of the songs and dances. Mature adults *can* dance but have better jobs in the booming community and are disinterested in the daily touristic routine.

Forty years of Kotzebue tourism had provided seasonal income for a small participating population whose lack of formal education and senior age status would probably have precluded other cash wages. Although they were "marginal men" to a society in the midst of rapid modernization, and, indeed, often were ridiculed by their grandchildren, now that their lives are a memory their contribution is viewed with nostalgia. An era has ended, and fortunate are the thousands of tourists who shared, even briefly, the opportunity to hear Chester Seveck (and his peers) talk about their lives and perform the songs and dances they had learned as children. The future Eskimo Interpretive Center (described below), accurate as its displays will be, cannot substitute for the human element.

Nome Tourism

The demise of Eskimo tourism in Nome in the mid-1980s is even more dramatic than that of Kotzebue, in this case the product of a labor dispute, for the values of the core group, the King Islanders, appear to have remained essentially intact. Instead, the tour brokers have substituted (with great effectiveness) the Gold Rush theme, and thus provide each of the two communities featured on the two-day tour with a completely separate identity—an effective marketing tool.

A devastating storm in November 1974 completely destroyed King Island village (miraculously, without loss of life). Prefabricated materials were immediately flown in by the U.S. government, and houses were assembled in an aircraft hangar, then sledded to their site. Within months neat rows of new homes were aligned on streets contiguous to the eastern end of Nome's urban sprawl, and set back from the beachline for safety from future high waves. Regrettably, the damaged Council Hall was not rebuilt and the dance performances were shifted to the basement of a hotel, destroying the former host-guest relation and the group solidarity the performances had reinforced. Ethnic tourism in Nome disintegrated as only the aging outgroup of performers were willing to be bused to the hotel to "dance for money." As some of the old-timers passed away, their ranks were filled by more aggressive middle-aged individuals, and *they* brought along their youngsters and encouraged them to dance as well. At first, it seemed like a renewal of community solidarity, but when the tour company was asked to pay wages for these "volunteers" (even toddlers), they refused to do so for economic reasons and Eskimo participation stopped completely.

The King Islanders seem not to care; most prefer to hunt and fish, and during the summer of 1987 a large colony camped on the beach about ten miles east of Nome far removed from tourist access. They continue to carve in ivory, and sell their wares to white-owned shops in Nome that do a good business in the souvenir trade. But with other, more lucrative jobs available to Eskimo in shipping, construction, and gold-mining—at least part-time—tourism has lost its luster as a source of income. However, all King Islanders do dance at community-wide special events, and are greatly appreciated by the spectators.

The more than eighty years of white domination in Nome is particularly evident in its newest tourist attraction, the famed Iditarod Trail Dog Sled Race held annually in March. The longest and most difficult race of its kind in the world, it begins in Anchorage and terminates 1049 miles (and some 18 days) later under a wooden arch on Nome's Front Street. White "mushers" have borrowed from the Eskimo the breeds of dogs and the technology, and made it their (expensive) sport, while the native population watches and cheers.

Point Hope and Gambell Tourism

The discovery of oil and its development transformed the north coast of Alaska during the 1970s. Barrow, the northernmost community, grew into a 3500-citizen modern community, complete with underground utilities, large public buildings, and even public bus service scheduled every twenty minutes throughout the day. Aided by astute lawyers, Eskimos of Barrow incorporated as the North Slope Borough with the legal power to tax oil production companies. The village of Point Hope was invited to join the borough (in the hope that oil reserves might also be found in their area), and the two villages share a US$30,000,000 annual (1986) budget.

Among the many changes facilitated by this windfall oil tax was the relocation of the village of Point Hope inland, from its former exposed coastal site where high waves and ice were eroding the beach cliffs and endangering homes. Amidst the new multi-colored houses aligned along defined streets, a new high school was opened. Representative of the high living standards now enjoyed in the borough, this Point Hope school (like its counterpart in Barrow) even has a heated indoor swimming pool. Nightly bingo games are a popular entertainment as an alternative to color television, and here also a bus circulates through the village of 500 persons every ten to fifteen minutes. An eight-room roadhouse-style hotel provides accommodations and meals to visiting officials and maintenance crews at a (1987) daily cost of US$150. The café is staffed by Eskimo cooks and open to Eskimo; and home-made pastries as well as hamburgers and French fries are popular fare. Tourism is uncommon—except during the Whaling Festival held annually the first weekend in June—because of the village's well-known modernity.

In the 1980s, Gambell was once again advertised as a tourist target, this time as short-term host for small groups of amateur ornithologists or "birders" traveling aboard one of the adventure cruise ships. Using the ship as their hotel, passengers come ashore to buy ivory and baleen handicrafts—at which local craftsmen excel—and the souvenir income is welcome. In addition, some small groups of birders have come by air for a short stay, again whetting a local desire for the economic benefits of tourism. Several documentary films portraying traditional Eskimo life-style have been made at Gambell, and their exhibition on public television renews interest by elite travelers. In 1988, a small, roadhouse-type hotel was intermittently under construction, delayed due to disputes between the contractor and the local council over allocation of future receipts. Whatever the outcome, Gambell will probably continue to attract a few tourists, even amidst the Eskimo hostility to outsiders who attempt unpaid amateur photography of subsistence activities.

The Future of Arctic Tourism

Tourism to Alaska grew rapidly in the early 1970s under the impetus of oil exploration and development which, in turn, triggered public interest; in 1977 the value of Alaskan tourism amounted to US$90 million. In the suc-

ceeding decade, tourism increased by only 10 percent, confirming a prediction in the earlier edition that "once the pipelines are completed, an
expensive 'normalcy' may prevail in Alaska." However, because of the decrease in oil sales prices worldwide, the overall economy of Alaska slumped
markedly during the 1980s. Consequently the value of the tourist dollar to
the state's income became proportionately greater than any time in the last
thirty years. In 1987 the state of Alaska funded an aggressive tourist promotion program as a source of seasonal employment and tax revenues, and
every White community of any size has a visitor center which is well
stocked with brochures and a friendly, informed staff. (Thus, Nome has a
visitor center but Kotzebue does not.)

Ethnic tourism—as a real-life exposure to traditional Eskimo culture—
has obviously ended in Alaska. It is also almost equally extinguished in both
Canada and Greenland, where tourism has *not* been either as numerically
pervasive or chronologically persistent. This observation merits attention
because of the ongoing argument as to whether tourism is a major agent of
culture change. Certainly for the Arctic, government actions to provide
better housing, education and medical care for native populations have been
the key element in the rapid process of modernization and acculturation.
And the Eskimo themselves were quick to adopt and adapt, for picturesque
as their aboriginal lives may have seemed in description, in actuality the
darkness, the cold, and the fear of starvation, accident and illness were stark
realities to be faced regularly.

Cultural and historical tourism have been well developed in Alaska in
the 1980s, in splendid new museum exhibits. Historical renovation and reconstruction continue to expand. But the major change in Arctic tourism
lies ahead in many new and diverse recreational facilities just being made
available to the public. The Alaska Lands Act (1980) created or expanded
eight national parks and established two national monuments and ten national preserves. The Arctic portions of these new public lands (Figure 1),
carved from traditional Eskimo terrain, include:

> NOATAK NATIONAL PRESERVE, a 2.6-million hectare wilderness that
> includes the largest untouched river basin in the U.S. offers canoeing
> along its 685-kilometer course, all above the Arctic Circle;
> CAPE KRUSENSTERN NATIONAL MONUMENT protects 5000 years of
> Eskimo history within its 218,000 hectares along the Chukchi Sea;
> BERING LAND BRIDGE NATIONAL PRESERVE protects the remnants of
> the ancient Indian/Eskimo migration route in its one million hectares;
> KOBUK VALLEY NATIONAL PARK supports steppe tundra and the only
> active Arctic sand dunes within its 688,000 hectares, and is drained by
> rivers noted for fine canoeing; and

GATES OF THE ARCTIC NATIONAL PARK encloses 3.3 million hectares in the heart of the scenic Brooks Range.

Kotzebue and Nome will serve as the gateway cities for the first four named above, and at Kotzebue an interim US$2.2-million facility will be in service in 1988 as a United States National Park Service interpretive center, with emphasis on the archaeological significance of the Bering Straits as the migration route used by the early native Americans who populated the New World. White entrepreneurs are starting new guide and float plane services, and undoubtedly some Eskimo will also participate.

Already evident on the tour buses in the 1980s were the first of a new type of Alaskan tourist—younger, more interested in recreation, and often traveling with their children. With energy to hike and camp, and in many instances with double incomes or other personal assets to afford air taxi access to these wilderness areas, these tourists herald a new era. In addition, the U.S. National Park Service already holds the right-of-way for a 600-mile highway from Fairbanks west to Kotzebue and, although expensive, its construction seems only a matter of time, public demand, and funding.

Known mineral deposits (copper and jade) exist in the Kobuk drainage; others may be found, including oil in the Bering Straits or even Kotzebue Sound. In 1988 the haul road is completed from the Bering Coast to Red Dog, site of the world's largest zinc mine which opened in summer 1988 and, with its lead and silver byproducts, will have a mine life of some fifty years. The Red Dog Mine adds 400 permanent new jobs to the Kotzebue area, and is the first harbinger of many anticipated changes. In addition, the Park Service has been meticulous in requiring adequate impact studies to prevent environmental damage, and the scene of caribou peacefully grazing next to the oil wells at Prudhoe Bay should be reassuring.

For 1988, NANA has signed an agreement with a "lower 48" tour operator to develop a new motorcoach tour route from Fairbanks along the "haul road," past the Gates of the Arctic National Park, and overnight at the NANA Arctic Inn in Prudhoe Bay. Eskimo tourism in the future is therefore no longer to be restricted to a so-called home village; instead, Eskimo investment capital may expand into contiguous (or even remote) regions.

Anaktuvak Pass, one of the few inland Eskimo villages in Alaska, in the midst of the Gates of the Arctic National Park, may well become a supply center for the hikers and rafters who will visit this area in the years to come. Part of the affluent North Slope Borough, Anaktuvak already has an admirable small museum, and a tiny hostelry to provide food and housing. The town has gained a widespread reputation as the manufacturing center for decorative caribou skin masks (widely believed to be aboriginal but, in truth, a craft that dates back only twenty years).

Residents of Shishmaref, a small Eskimo village in the midst of the Bering Land Bridge National Preserve, hope to profit from their location by obtaining touristic employment as guides and selling some of the many bone carvings that glut the two local stores. In 1988, a new, longer airport runway permits better access, but no tourist facilities for food or lodging were yet available.

Micro-Models and Marginal Men

Ethnohistories of tourism are still rare. This case study recounts what few fieldworkers have shared: more than three decades of commitment to the study of tourism, both academically and within the travel industry, combined with the opportunity for regular, personal reassessment of tourism impacts in a single geographical area. The individual details of Arctic tourism are relatively unimportant, but the composite picture presents a story that needs to be told: a unique contribution to understanding the process of tourism development in relation to cultural change. Many of the implications derived from this study have counterparts in other touristic settings and thus are global in their extent.

In the Alaskan Arctic, tourism—even mass tourism that, in three months, introduces four times the total population of a community—has not been a significant agent of culture change. As documented throughout the text, it was the natural resources of the Arctic—originally furs and marine mammals—that brought the first Western contacts. The other major extractive industries, gold-mining and petroleum production, soon followed and continue to be important to the local economy. In addition, Alaska's strategic position between two political superpowers, the United States and the USSR, influences the military presence. Many Eskimo have been active members of the Alaska National Guard throughout their adult lives and are regularly sent out for training and maneuvers. These factors, together with a post–World War II government philosophy dedicated to providing Native Americans with maximal opportunities for comprehensive medical services, education, and employment, have been the prime agents of culture change. Tourists in the Arctic are no different than the other Americans whom Eskimo have seen in metropolitan Alaska, or who have continuously lived among them for nearly a century. Host-guest contacts are too minimal for most Eskimo to recognize or be interested in the presence of a European.

Economically, all Eskimo have directly benefitted from tourism through the resulting development of increased air services: pilot weather information, improved search and rescue operations for lost boats and missing hunters, cargo planes for exporting their salmon catch, and, for many years, the airlink that made it easy for young Eskimo to go "outside" (the Arctic) to boarding schools and universities. And a few individuals employed for seasonal tourism by hotels, restaurants, and the airlines have personally profited from this industry.

Indirectly, mass tourism (though not necessarily the presence of tourists themselves) and the land claims settlement have contributed to the renaissance of Eskimo culture as they have shown the Eskimo that their culture is of great interest to tourists who are prepared to pay substantial sums to visit the Arctic to see the Eskimo life-style. This reaffirms the sense of ethnic self-worth that had been eroded in the early years of this century by missionary, health, and school personnel in their efforts to relieve the then-pressing problems of disease, hunger (even starvation), and accidents that were integral elements of aboriginal Eskimo culture. The Maniilaq staff's activities that have revived Eskimo aesthetics have also been effectively reinforced through tourism as the increased numbers of outside visitors are an expanding market for souvenir crafts. Within the past five years, observation suggests that the number of artisans has doubled, the volume of ivory carvings and scrimshaw has at least tripled, and many items not formerly displayed in curio stores are now available for sale in some quantity. Many of the new carvers are young (since the craft is now taught in school) and the completed pieces are very small. This bodes well for the future of the industry. Tourists prefer small, inexpensive souvenirs which in turn require less raw materials—a desirable factor, too, in wildlife conservation. Further, the new cultural self-confidence and the quantity of native-made items have all but eliminated the plastic trinkets of former years and even the "fake art" carved from African vegetable ivory. Among the newer crafts are former utilitarian goods such as finely made bark baskets and skillfully stitched fur-clad dolls; there is a renewed emphasis on masks, as well as a few new graphic artists (the latter specializing in contemporary rather than traditional motifs).

NANA's multi-media show and dance exhibition at their Arctic Museum of the North in Kotzebue also officially reinstated Eskimo dance and music in the native ethos through the mechanism of tourism. In addition, NANA has helped to revive the concept of the annual Kotzebue summer gathering with the July Fourth festival of competitive sports, dances and *muktuk*-eating contests, followed by a craft fair advertised as a "Trading Rendezvous." Widely attended by residents from all outlying villages, the event promotes social cohesion, and is a form of domestic tourism. The presence of tourists also positively reinforces the sanctions for Alaskan Eskimos to join the tourist ranks and travel beyond the Arctic.

This ethnohistory of tourism also illustrates the role of micro-models, which differentiate the impact(s) of tourism even within a limited area of the same geographical resource region. The aboriginal origins of the Eskimo of Point Hope, Kotzebue, and the King Islanders (now of Nome) are presumably the same, and date back thousands of years; yet, in prehistoric times variations in dialect and habitat emerged to make them separate peoples in the native perceptions. Despite Westernization, those differences persist, like nationalistic enclaves within metropolitan areas, and may, in part, fashion the direction of tourism development. Counterparts to the Alaskan example can be easily established. Particularly representative are island domains such as the Caribbean, where behavior toward tourists is shaped by nationality: French, Dutch, and English shopkeepers, taxi drivers, and guides all have culturally specific ways of interacting with outsiders. Switzerland, among the highly industrialized countries, is a striking example of ethnic contrasts, with its trilingual base and the associated differences in architecture, land use, and even religion.

Inherent to each micro-model are various internal power and leadership structures (comparable to the North Carolina example, chapter 10). In this Eskimo study, early tourism was directed from outside the Arctic, and even when Kotzebue's NANA leadership had the opportunity to take control, they chose not to for economic reasons. However, as recreational tourism expands in the future and involves direct federal government administration of national lands, it is probable that NANA and similar native corporations (as in Nome, with jurisdiction over Gambell and Shishmaref; or the North Slope Borough with interests at Anaktuvak Pass, Prudhoe Bay, and Point Hope) will generate Eskimo leadership.

Lacking any other source, Chuck West sought and found his tourism personnel in 1946 among the marginal men whose counterparts exist today worldwide. The term *marginal men* is used here without a specific referent. It is devoid of prior definitions of ethnicity or minority role to allow freedom to examine various forms of marginality that exist among a host population. In both target communities, the Eskimo who danced and demonstrated crafts were members of a minimally defined minority who overtly retained their aesthetics and were in a position to capitalize upon their knowledge. Because younger Eskimo had more formal schooling and marketable job skills, they were better able to obtain wage employment and to realize Western aspirations for material possessions. They did not want to be identified with the stereotype of fur-clad hunters or skin-chewing women, and eschewed or ridiculed this touristic performance. Consequently, the older generation entered the marketplace to sell the one thing they knew—their ancestral life-style.

Elsewhere in the tourist realms, many examples parallel the Eskimo marginal men: Fijian "fire-walkers," Tahitian nightclub dance troupes, Indian snake charmers, and—almost everywhere in the Third World—unlicensed "local guides" who frequent tourist destinations, hoping to serve for a fee. As in Kotzebue and Nome, these culture brokers are an ethnically distinct outgroup. Chester Seveck was a good anthropological informant respected by his peers for his veracity and knowledge of traditional culture. However, Kotzebue Eskimo identified Chester as being from Point Hope and thus a "salt water man" (Point Hope Eskimo still practice whaling, which was never part of Kotzebue subsistence techniques), a near-shaman, and as a person who had worked for Whites for many years in the nontraditional role of reindeer herder. Even this partial listing of personal traits is sufficient to identify Chester as marginal to his own people, and very "marginal" to Kotzebue. Further, all aging Eskimo, despite their tolerant respect, envied Chester and Helen their income, their nice clothes, their overseas travel and the material benefits they were able to give to their children and grandchildren. Their money made them even more marginal. Average tourists, however, saw none of this disparity; they enjoyed Chester's theatrics and accepted his stories without question. For the sincere ethnic tourist, however, the question becomes, Is the interpretation about a native culture, when described by a culturally marginal guide, accurate? This concept seems particularly applicable to tours of archaeological ruins which may be interpreted by so-called guides who have never read the site reports.

Bilingualism is the hallmark of the "marginal man," but certain personality traits are apparently also necessary—charisma, charm, wit, gregariousness—and make jobs in tourism attractive to individuals who believe it to be a glamour industry. They may indeed gain considerable upward mobility through wages and the opportunity for travel and, if circumstances permit, through interaction with foreigners they may obtain hard currencies as tips, engage in black marketing of local currencies for additional profit (Lehmann 1980), or serve as intermediaries in a range of illicit activities as pimps, hustlers, and narcotics peddlers. These entrepreneurs may differ sharply from the norms of their subculture yet to be one of tourism's "marginal men."

Relationships between host and guest are a blend of value orientations. For the most part, historic Eskimo contacts with American whalers and gold-seekers were positive and financially profitable, which predisposed their initial welcome to American tourists. The early contacts between Russians and Bering Straits Eskimo are little-documented, but Russian penetration further south in Alaska and among the Aleuts is associated with the Russians' great cruelty. Accounts of Russian atrocities among Yupik Eskimo and Aleuts became legendary among the Inupiaqs; Nome and Kotzebue Eskimo are still hostile toward anyone Russian, although they have not seen any in several decades. Had the first modern tourists been Russian, the reception to tourists might have been less cordial. Many Micronesians, Guamanians, and Filipinos have a similar attitude toward the recent invasion of Japanese tourists: tolerance and moderation for the financial gain of the host cannot, in one short generation, erase the memory of loved ones subjected to brutality or killed in battle against the would-be World War II conqueror whose "armies" are now guest honeymooners and holiday-makers aboard tour buses.

Tourism, especially mass tourism, modifies the local scene in many ways, some of which may be quite subtle, as in the use of geographic space. For hundreds of years, aboriginal activity centered on the beach at Kotzebue; Eskimo igloos (and later homes) faced seaward to watch for returning hunters. Now that the food quest takes place in the supermarkets, a beach location is considered undesirable because of prevailing winds and accumulating ice. New homes, by preference, are on back streets. The site of the first hotel (see Plate 1) was once a source of host-guest friction, but today the needed new hotels should have beach frontage from which guests can look westward across the Sound to photograph a midnight setting sun reflected in the Arctic sea.

Highly structured bus package tourism—Graburn's "tourist bubble" (chapter 1)—described here for Nome and Kotzebue provided little opportunity for visitors to learn much about the lives of their co-nationals; their fellow Americans. Costs of construction, operation, and maintenance necessitate high prices for hotel rooms; even groceries for a summer picnic lunch seem expensive to nonresidents who are often shocked at store prices. Only elite or off-beat tourists venture to visit on their own; mass tourists, lacking entrée to the Eskimo community, almost never stay after the tour party departs. Visitors thus suffer from the myopic ethnocentrism often evident among individuals from industrialized countries visiting a so-called primitive people. Sadly, they do not know that Eskimo reindeer herders of the 1980s have studied Soviet techniques in Siberia as guests of the USSR; that members of NANA and other regional corporations in the Arctic are global travelers who attend many types of professional meetings such as anthropological congresses in Paris, and medical symposia in Switzerland; and that Eskimo have political networks and attend meetings with their Greenland and Canadian counterparts.

Package tourism to the Arctic undoubtedly will continue because it meets a need for the short-term tourist. However, beginning in 1988 in Kotzebue, the U.S. National Park Service interpretive center will focus on the archaeological significance of the Bering Land Bridge and the natural history of Northwest Alaska; with the anticipated increase in visitors who will raft the rivers and lakes and be involved in sports fishing and hunting, it is to be hoped that more positive interaction will occur between hosts and guests. Prediction is difficult, but more "marginal men" will probably appear—and will be needed—as guides, for the Arctic environment is still formidable, and the mastery of survival skills takes years, patience, and practice.

California State University, Chico

4

Gender Roles in Indigenous Tourism: Kuna Mola, Kuna Yala, and Cultural Survival

MARGARET BYRNE SWAIN

Travel accounts about the Kuna of Panama portray an isolated ethnic group accessible to tourists. "'Intruders,' Cuna Natives Mingle in San Blas" (*Denver Post*, February 1, 1981) headlines a United States newspaper's travel section. "Panama's Primitive San Blas Islands: Indians Manage to Hold onto Pre-Colombian Lifestyle Amid Cruise Ships" (*Hartford Courant*, November 13, 1983); "Crossroads In Panama" (accompanied by a photo of "Cuna woman pounding grain in the San Blas Islands," L. Sloane, *New York Times*, February 15, 1987) are captions for other Kuna tourism features. Just how extensive is this tourism and what role do the Kuna have in it? These questions are addressed by viewing *indigenous tourism*, controlled by the Kuna, as a type of self-sustaining development.

One measure of this development is the role opportunities tourism generates for women and men. Gender roles have shaped the Kuna response to tourism: Kuna women produce *mola* artwork of fabric appliqué and maintain a marketable image of ethnicity; Kuna men produce and maintain the political forum that shapes the group's interactions with outside interests, including tourism. Local tourism can offer roles different from those open in the national economy. Role choices generated by Kuna tourism are now available through self-employment, private business, and cooperative ventures, including a woman's sewing cooperative (Productores de Molas), hotel services employment, and the Kuna Yala Wildlands Investigation Project (PEMASKY). These roles have evolved to produce and manage *mola* business and to promote and manage tourism in Kuna *yala*, or territory. Gradually the Kuna may realign complementary and cooperative gender roles to maintain their own society (Swain 1978, pp. 324–5). Group stability is enhanced if indigenous tourism development provides balanced opportunities for women and men.

The San Blas Kuna

The "Kuna" are the "Cuna": both spellings are used but the Kuna themselves are standardizing on the *K*. A majority of the Kuna indigenous group, numbering about 30,000, live in a semi-autonomous reserve along Panama's Caribbean coast (Figure 1). This reserve, the Comarca de San Blas or "Kuna Yala," extends about 200 kilometers northeast to the Colombian

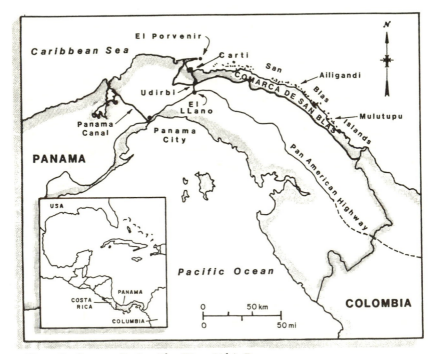

Figure 1. Comarca De San Blas (Kuna Yala), Panama.

border, and fifteen kilometers inland to the continental divide. Numerous coral islands provide living sites for the majority of some fifty Kuna communities. Preferred matrilocal residence is cited in the 1945 *comarca* constitution as "the foundation of the communal organization" of Kuna society. Each Kuna village is governed by a *congresso* comprised of all adult males, with leadership elected by consensus. All village *congressos* are organized within a pan-*comarca* government, the *Congresso General*. Only Kuna may own land in San Blas, and new foreign businesses must have permission from the Congresso General.

Subsistence activities, migrant wage labor, and the commercialization of fishing, coconut trading, and textile production (of *molas*) provide Kuna sustenance. The local cash economy, including tourism services, continues to develop. The Kuna are "unique among tropical forest dwellers in Central America for their unusually well organized and cohesive society . . . [which] enables the Kuna to retain their cultural identity while confronting outside influences" (Houseal et al. 1986, p. 10).

Kuna Indigenous Tourism

The newspaper headlines cited above create the impression that the Kuna are being invaded by tourists. In 1975 this was a reasonable prediction, if Panamanian government plans for massive tourism development in San Blas had been carried out (Swain 1977, p. 74). By 1987 tourism in San Blas was low-key and, most importantly, controlled by the Kuna themselves. In the intervening often turbulent years, the Kuna have evolved a strategy of tourism development using both "ethnic" and "ecological" emphases. It is "indigenous tourism": tourism based on the group's land and cultural identity and controlled from within by the group. The Kuna have chosen development assistance from the outside which complements local financial, political, and institutional factors and thus promotes the sustainability of new developments (Morss et al. 1985, p. 218).

Ethnic Tourism

"Ethnic" tourism, the marketing of tourist attractions based on an indigenous population's way of life, was a very minor part of the Kuna economy by the 1940s and slowly grew in importance. *Molas* became popular souvenirs from Panama and the Canal Zone in the following decades. Visitors began to fly out to San Blas to experience Kuna life firsthand. Photos of Kuna women and their *mola* art became a staple in advertisements for Panama's tourist trade. By the 1960s there were four tourist facilities in San Blas, one Kuna-owned, and the *mola* cooperative was being formed. This type of tourism "is a form of ethnic relations . . . where the very existence of the ethnic boundary creates the tourist attraction" (van den Bergh and Keyes 1984, p. 346).

MacCannell (1984, p. 388) has suggested that "when an ethnic group begins to sell itself . . . as an ethnic attraction, it ceases to evolve naturally. The group members begin to think of themselves . . . as living representatives of an authentic way of life. Suddenly any change in life-style is not a mere question of practical utility but a weighty question which has economic and political implications for the entire group." In Kuna villages, *congresso* gatherings are held almost every evening. Life-style issues are often discussed in these meetings, but it would be easy "to exaggerate the struggles between the generations and the sexes or take them too seriously" (Howe 1986, p. 232).

The nature of the ethnic tourism development, like ecological tourism, is concerned with boundaries. As Gamper (1985, p. 251) has commented on MacCannell's thesis, "While the overt culture traits may indeed become 'museumized' for commercial reasons, the different processes that seem to be involved in generating and maintaining ethnic groups continue to operate." In Kuna tourism these processes have evolved around issues of territory, *mola* art, and tourist facilities.

Ecological Tourism

For the Kuna, a definition of their "ethnic group" includes a concept of territory. Breslin and Chapin (1984, p. 31) have noted that, "so conscious and proud are the Kuna of their culture, so fluent in discussing it, they can sound like a convention of anthropologists. . . . [They] invariably stress the identification of their culture with a specific expanse of land—the Comarca of San Blas." They quote an eloquent speaker as saying, "If we were to lose this land, there would be no culture, no soul."

The beauty and location of Kuna Yala is another factor in tourism development. Besides excellent diving available off the islands, the inland mountainous rain forest has its own appeal. "Ecological" tourism is a celebration of the natural environment "wherein the tourist tries to leave as little effect of his visit as possible" (Graburn 1977, p. 27). This is the type of tourism the PEMASKY group is working to develop.

Protecting this territory of Kuna Yala is of utmost importance to all Kuna. Kuna political leaders often struggle over issues of sovereignty. In 1976 the clash between national tourism plans and Kuna interests reached crisis proportions creating a schism in Kuna leadership. By mid-1977 the political division had been resolved and the national tourism plans shelved (Moore 1980; Howe 1982). After several non-Kuna tourist resorts were violently terminated, only Kuna-controlled tourism business has been allowed in San Blas since 1982.

During the same period of time, a group of young Kuna men were moving to protect the inland boundaries of their reserve from encroachment along a road which would ultimately link Panama City with the San Blas coast (Breslin and Chapin 1984). This group, PEMASKY, has utilized international resources to develop a strategy of protection of their rain forest through "scientific tourism" (Caufield 1982; Houseal et al. 1986). Many issues of land and off-shore rights must be resolved between the Kuna and the national government before Kuna plans can be fully realized.

Indigenous Tourism
The fact that the Kuna have a territory to protect is significant. The Kuna are not typical of the "un-grounded" peoples frequently found in ethnic tourism development: "Touristified ethnic groups are often weakened by a history of exploitation, limited in resources and power, and they have no . . . natural wonders to deflect the tourists' attention away from the intimate details of their daily lives" (MacCannell 1984, p. 368). These peoples must often "reconstruct" or re-create their ethnicity, and, if possible, reclaim their land.

A unique culture and land base have kept the Kuna image attractive to tourists over the years. If either Kuna society or the tourist's expectations change, then the marketing of Kuna tourism must adapt in order to continue. The Kuna are in a position now to model ways in which indigenous tourism can be sustainable development. Kuna tourism development depends on *local* control. At the ethnic group level, the Kuna as a whole seek control over outside interests. At the individual level, every Kuna woman and man responds to local controls determining their roles within the group. Gender or shared roles may evolve in the group to maintain their unique way of life and territory, and to adapt to economic change. Indigenous tourism can be a buffer, providing an alternative to economic development under outside control and exploitation or to direct incorporation into the national society.

The Extent of Kuna Tourism: From a Tourist's Perspective

The three newspaper accounts cited above were all written since the Kuna took active control of tourism in San Blas. No mention is made of various issues shaping Kuna tourism, including an organized *mola* business; the road into Kuna territory from Panama City; and current political tensions over sovereignty. However, these stories give some indication as to why the Kuna are such intriguing tourist "attractions." Part of the attraction for some tourists and travel writers is that the Kuna seem to control their tourism so well.

The *Denver Post* story by Birnbaum (February 1, 1981) maintains that the flight from Panama City to San Blas is harrowing but worth it, for

> how often can you spend a mere 30 minutes and be transported to another world? Here live the Cuna Indians . . . who are known—if at all—for their short haired women who wear distinctive gold rings in their noses and for their molas . . . [which] are found almost all over the civilized world.
>
> Though the Cuna are famous for their commercial interests . . . toadying to tourists is not at all prevalent. Visitors who come to see this unusual escapist paradise should be prepared for rather primitive living conditions. . . . The lure is an atmosphere that allows a visitor to feel a part of the Cuna village rather than an intruder in an unspoiled culture. . . . The major enterprise is negotiating for molas. . . .
>
> The preservation of Cuna culture has not been without a price. An attempt by the Panamanian government to annex the San Blas territory . . . [in the] "War of 1925" was a complete Cuna victory. Though the modern world invades the San Blas Islands in the form of radios, schooling, and the many Cuna who work in Panama City and the Canal Zone, the Cuna culture today remains as zealously protected today as it was hundreds of years ago. . . . [These] sociological holdouts are extremely savvy when it comes to commerce, so they take the best of what the outside world can offer them and use it to sustain and nurture their otherwise unmodern lifestyle. . . . [Their chiefs] keep most of [their world] closed to outsiders. The exceptions . . . all occupy just one small corner of one end of the island chain.

Tourists also approach San Blas by sea, sailing in boats ranging from private yachts to cruise liners. Over the years, tours have made sporadic stops in the "tourist islands" open in the Carti area. Carti area women are renowned throughout San Blas for their fine *molas*, and the villages visited by tourists maintain an "unmodern" appearance. From 1984 to late 1985 thirty-two liners, carrying as many as 900 passengers each, were recorded visiting the Carti area (Tice 1986). Two Panama Canal cruises were making a port-of-call in San Blas during 1987 (Plate 1). The smaller line could carry ninety-two visitors a week for this six-month season, but cruises were infrequent. Both of these lines have worked with John Mann, an American who

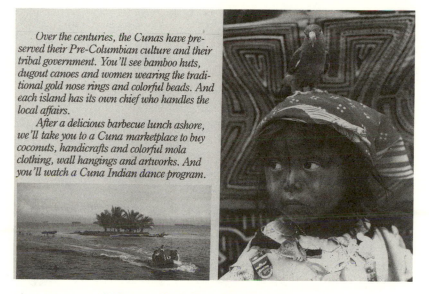

*Over the centuries, the Cunas have pre-
served their Pre-Columbian culture and their
tribal government. You'll see bamboo huts,
dugout canoes and women wearing the traditional gold nose rings and colorful beads. And
each island has its own chief who handles the
local affairs.*

*After a delicious barbecue lunch ashore,
we'll take you to a Cuna marketplace to buy
coconuts, handicrafts and colorful mola
clothing, wall hangings and artworks. And
you'll watch a Cuna Indian dance program.*

Plate 1. From a 1987 Panama Canal Cruises Brochure. Reprinted by permission, ©
1987 by Exploration Cruise Lines, Inc.

has been dealing with the Kuna for more than twenty years. Though Mann
once ran his own tours in the region, he now stays on the tour boat lecturing
the tourists on Kuna society, and does not disembark.

Mann is noted in *The Hartford Courant* (Kerins, November 13, 1983)
story on a one-day cruise stop in San Blas. He "told us what to expect and
how to act while on the islands. For example, taking photos of the Indians
is . . . encouraged, but the subject expects a quarter for her efforts." The
story's first mention of the Kuna is of women who, "all decked out in brilliantly hued blouses and skirts, and sporting an astonishing amount of
jewelry, including nose-rings, add even more color to the exotic scene"
(Plate 2). Photo subjects are "almost always women. . . . Unlike the children and males, who smile a great deal, the women appear rather somber.
Perhaps it is because they seem to be in charge of all money-making endeavors. It is they who make and sell the product for which the Cunas are best
known: . . . molas. . . . [L]earning to sew them is part of every young girl's
education. . . . Expect to pay between us$7 and us$15 a panel."

The writer also reports that most Kuna "live pretty much as their ancestors did hundreds of years ago. . . . [A]lthough the islands are part of the

Plate 2. Kuna women celebrating the fiftieth anniversary of the 1925 Kuna revolt against Panama. (Photo by Walt Swain, Ailigandi, 1975)

Republic of Panama, the Cunas really govern themselves. . . . [A chief] looks after local affairs. . . . A congress of chiefs meets whenever the need arises, which is not very often." In daily life, Kuna women sail to the mainland to wash, play, and obtain fresh water; Kuna men practice subsistence farming, cultivate coconuts, and fish. This article notes that "coconuts are their most valuable crop, an important part of the diet and the source of a lively business in trading."

This information is probably also from John Mann. Watching men tend coconuts is not a regular tourist activity, nor do many tourists see Kuna women selling their coconuts to traders. The coconut trade is solely with Colombia and, like tourism, reinforces their ethnic group. Kuna autonomy is aided by the cash income from coconuts and " [by not selling to Panama] . . . playing one outside power off against another" (Howe 1986, p. 14).

After a "brief and friendly encounter" with two men carving a canoe, and a final stop at the nicest island ("fewer tourists"), it is time for the travel writer to leave: "I remember John Mann saying that the Cuna welcome visitors, but there are things to do, meals to prepare, babies to feed—so as happy as they are to see you come, they're just as happy to see you go."

A one-day plane trip to the tourist islands was the recommended way to see San Blas in the *New York Times* travel story (L. Sloane 1987, pp. 23, 32). Sloane writes: "The residents, Cuna Indians, have long maintained a communal way of life, with the men tending coconut trees, and the women creating intricately layered, multicolored designs called molas for which visitors can bargain and buy for as little as $10." Lunch on this tour is catered by a local Kuna hotel.

In the 1987–88 edition of *South America on $30 a Day* the Kuna are portrayed as having lived in the San Blas for centuries with little change except for men adopting Western clothing from working on the mainland. Men are multilingual, while "females speak only Kuna. . . . As the result of a new interest in mola designs, Kuna women have achieved a certain fame in fashion circles. . . . [and] are their own best advertisements . . . fascinating and authentic, no tourist show here!" The authors note that it is possible to stay overnight in San Blas where it is "primitive, but fun."

Tourism is a two-way exchange. Tourists—people on the outside—must want to visit and buy goods; local people on the inside must be willing to produce goods and services for sale. The travel writers cited above help illustrate what is marketed as Kuna tourism. The Kuna help market themselves: what they sell will motivate indigenous tourism development in the future.

There is tourist appeal in viewing the Kuna as "sociological holdouts." These tourist accounts communicate an image of Kuna women that is strong, conservative, and attractive. The writers agreed that: the women are concerned about making and selling *molas* while the men are busy doing non-tourism work; their society is communal and removed from national control; most tourism activity happens in a selected few Kuna communities; and the Kuna depend on outside interests to bring tourists into San Blas, but once there tourists deal directly with Kuna. It is interesting to note that none of these writers called the Kuna a matriarchy as, frequently, tourist accounts in the 1960s and 1970s erroneously asserted.

Tourism in Kuna Society: Gender Roles and Change

Why were there stories of a Kuna matriarchy? The dynamic image of Kuna women and matrilocal residence were thought to mean that Kuna women "ruled" their society. Female presence in the domestic domain, however, is offset by male-dominated ritual and political roles in the public domain. Female debut rites, an appreciation of *mola* work, and a societal focus on the matriset all contribute to a complementarity of female and male status. The division of labor in Kuna society often reflects an interdependence of the sexes. Bilateral inheritance is reinforced by an individual's right to personal earnings.

Change is evident in contemporary Kuna society. Virtually every community now has a national system elementary school, and three islands have regional secondary schools. Adult San Blas Kuna literacy in Spanish rose from 33 percent in 1970 to 49 percent in 1980. This is particularly relevant for women whose literacy rate was 21 percent compared with 49 percent for men in 1970 (approximate, from the National Census of Panama). The Kuna are noted as being "the best educated tribe in Panama, and perhaps in Central America. Many Kuna students study at the National University and abroad, and the number of professionals has grown steadily during the past decade" (Breslin and Chapin 1984, p. 31).

Modernization and a mixed cash and subsistence economy in San Blas have a number of effects on occupational roles. Urban employment in more permanent skilled work is available for Kuna with education and training. Several very acculturated islands have a steady flow of male and female migrants to the mainland. For the majority of Kuna men, temporary labor migration is the usual source of cash. For the majority of Kuna women, female temporary, unskilled employment in the national sector is literally not worth their time (Swain 1982, p. 106). National census figures for San Blas illustrate the disproportion of the sexes in residence: eighty-six males to one hundred females in 1980. Most women travel away from home very infrequently. In San Blas villages, health clinics, schools, and various agencies of the national government and religious missions provide salaried jobs for a few professionally trained Kuna (women and men).

Other sources of cash in the San Blas are self- or household-employment in the sale of *molas* and coconuts and in small businesses. Voluntary, cooperative societies (*sociedades*) are an alternative form of employment. Everything from catering Kuna girls' "Inna" debuts (Sherzer 1983, p. 230) to running stores, coastal shipping, and cropping coconuts, have been organized as *sociedad* businesses. Some *sociedades* have both women and men members, others are only men. *Sociedades* are a preferred form of business in San Blas, which can accommodate individuals of varying skills, training, and ages while maintaining cooperative aspects of Kuna society.

Some physical changes in Kuna villages have had a particular impact on women's role activities. Households with both electricity and potable water have gone from 10 percent in 1970 to 30 percent in the 1980 national census. Howe (1986, p. 134) counted eleven villages with aqueducts installed or planned and thirteen with electricity in 1982. These changes have a direct effect on the women's available time for producing *molas* (Swain 1978, p. 220). Women in these villages no longer have to spend hours each day bringing fresh water from the mainland, and in the daytime hours they can see to sew better than in the night.

Kuna Molas *and Tourism*

Kuna tourism grew out of the *mola* trade, expanding from a subsistence activity/art form to a marketable art form for cash. *Mola* work developed as an appliqué technique for decorating women's tradecloth clothing. The two-panel *mola* blouse construction seen today was in use by the beginning of this century. During the Kuna's 1925 revolt against Panama, one issue was the forced change of the Kuna women's dress from *mola* to modern. *Mola* dress became highly symbolic of ethnic identity for the Kuna themselves (Plate 3). Especially talented women and men design and cut *mola* work.

Plate 3. Elizabeth Pacheco sewing together *mola* panels to make a blouse. She would be insulted by any inference that her *molas* are machine-sewn. (Photo by Walt Swain, Ailigandi, 1975)

Sewing *molas* is women's work but "woman-like" men also do the intricate handwork.

Kuna women sell used *molas* and new *"turista"* trade *molas* to visitors in San Blas. Ten dollars for one panel is a low price in the 1980s, and most *molas* range from US$20 to US$50 each, especially in the tourist islands. *Molas* are also locally used as barter. A service allowing patients to pay charges with *molas* at the only hospital in San Blas was managed by a Kuna woman buyer for several years until the business was reorganized by the hospital without a Kuna "middleman." In Panama, women sell to people on the streets, in Steven's Circle in the Canal Zone, and in small *"bohiós"* along the urban waterfront (Bertha Brown, personal communication).

Mola wholesaling to urban shops and dealers has been primarily a male activity, reflecting men's roles as collective bargainers with non-Kuna. The practice of women selling their *molas* to male middlemen is decreasing (Sherzer 1983, p. 7). A distinction should be made between the male wholesaler versus the male household head who sells his family's *molas*. The former often exploits women in nontourist villages by offering them very low prices, then reselling the *molas* in the Carti tourist area or the city; the latter is a case of complementary gender roles.

The activities of one Kuna family (Patera 1984; Anne Wenzel, personal communication) illustrate household *mola* marketing. The family lives outside of the Carti tourist area and therefore must depend on irregular local tourist trade or send their *molas* out for sale. The household head, "Joe," has developed his own fresh seafood and grocery businesses in San Blas. "Elena," his wife, sews *molas* constantly. Joe will help out by doing machine sewing on *molas* when necessary. Their household includes four children, one of Elena's sisters, and extends to another sister's family living close by.

Joe periodically collects *molas* from the household and takes them into the city for sale. *Mola* sales can be precipitated by a need for cash. When the family decided to put a seven-hundred dollar downpayment on an apartment in Panama City, Joe brought in seven-hundred dollars' worth of *molas* from the family's coffers to sell to a collector. Several years earlier, this same friend of Joe's bought some of Elena's fine *molas* sewn from designs in a textile museum book.

These *molas* had been made for their eldest daughter's trousseau but she had "gone modern" and did not want them. This daughter later attended high school in Panama City. She speaks English and has worked as an urban buyer for her father's store. Sewing *molas* is not something she plans to do; the early choices this young woman has made increase her future options.

Because of young Kuna like her, some *mola* collectors feel that this is probably the last generation of Kuna to make *molas*.

The Mola Cooperative

Concern over the future of *mola* sewing was one motivation for starting a women's *mola* cooperative, "Cooperativa de Productores de Molas de San Blas," in 1965 with Peace Corps aid. By 1968 this organization had grown from one sewing class to a pre-cooperative (differing from a *sociedad* because of national legal status and a paid manager) with 200 members on seven islands. Carti Sugtupu was and has remained the only co-op community from the "tourist islands." The initial success of the "*mola* co-op" was based on its appeal to all Kuna, from the conservative to the modern in the society. This organization was a first in Kuna society in two ways: the first all-women owned and operated business; and the first pan–San Blas cooperative of Kuna communities.

Different kinds of *mola* production businesses formed during the 1960s in response to market demand. Some were run by outsiders, who flew in to gather up commissioned work and leave off the next batch of piecework materials. Other retail *mola* businesses were run from Panama with Kuna middlemen. The *mola* co-op generally paid better for similar work on items ranging from traditional panels to toys and modern-style clothing decorated with a *mola* technique. The ultimate in *mola* production, a factory of sorts, was started in 1975 by the national artisan's program and the Panamanian Institute of Tourism (IPAT) in Panama City. Here the women received a monthly salary of us$55. Sentiment in the San Blas was particularly negative about this venture (Swain 1978, p. 180). Commissioned piecework has remained a preferred source of business for both the *mola* co-op and nonco-op sewers. In the city, a business called "My Name is Panama" had become a major source of *mola* piecework commissions in the late 1980s.

Since 1968, the Congresso General has gradually acknowledged the *mola* co-op by allowing, then inviting, members to be on their agenda. At first the co-op flourished with a retail store in Panama City then, after the Peace Corps left Panama in 1971, cut back to wholesale trade only. In 1973 Adela Lopez, a bilingual urban Kuna woman, became the *mola* co-op manager. The first few years of her work were spent consolidating the organization. In 1974 the *mola* co-op had grown to 390 members and was officially recognized by the Panamian government. By 1975 members were generating approximately us$1000 a month total income. Co-op expenses included materials and the manager's monthly salary of us$100 (Swain 1978, p. 177).

The co-op developed, but was hindered by a basic lack of funds. Despite their co-op status they could not acquire credit from Panamanian banks. In 1978 their situation improved when the *mola* co-op obtained an Inter-American Foundation (IAF) grant of us$30,000 for a capital base, education, and equipment. The capital was used for fabric purchase and a revolving reimbursement fund (Tice 1986). Co-op membership grew to 1000 by 1980 and to 1500 members from 17 communities by 1984. The co-op again had a store in Panama City and actively sought special orders. In 1985 the co-op held a juried bank-sponsored *mola* exhibition in Panama, which awarded us$750 for future marketing. Adela Lopez was an organizer, and forty women from eighteen communities participated.

Success and support were encouraging for Adela Lopez, but after thirteen years as manager she decided to leave the co-op in August 1986. The co-op manager's job entails finance and business arrangements, dealing with the co-op board of directors, and holding educational programs. It is difficult work and the salary has remained low. Co-op product quality control and pricing, compared to the current market, have been constant problems. The sentiment that women in the co-op never really get to see the money they earn continues to fuel member discontent, despite the increase in co-op funds.

Adela Lopez took about sixty members of the *mola* co-op from her home community with her and formed her own business using family connections in San Blas. The former members are now employees working for piecework pay. Sources of work include old contacts and IPAT contracts. The *mola* co-op did not collapse. Co-op management passed to the next most senior member who is from the same island as Adela Lopez and also lives in Panama City. Even the co-op on their home island remained functioning in 1987 despite a 70 percent reduction in membership. Total co-op membership was about 1400. Adela Lopez's *mola* business may be a logical progression in the development of *mola* marketing roles as women take greater control of their own production. The co-op was the first all-female Kuna business; now there is another, private one. Many changes are possible, including the co-op or other groups of women opening *mola* tourist stores in San Blas.

Mola co-op participation has also affected gradual realignment of political gender roles in some villages. Kuna ideally attribute ritual speaking and curing roles to men and women, but in practice men have overwhelmingly predominated in the recorded past. In the past twenty years the co-op has offered opportunities for the development of female leadership roles and served as a forum for discussion (Howe 1986, p. 117). These opportunities were outside of direct male control. On the island of Mulutuppu "women hold 'gatherings' with their own leaders and discuss such matters as their *mola* cooperative and women's tasks in the village. . . . They are strikingly parallel to the men's 'gatherings'" (Sherzer 1983, pp. 70–71). A few women have now become active junior officials in their village *congressos*.

The *mola* co-op bylaws have no requirements as to a member's sex, and there are a few male members. In the 1980s a Kuna woman was appointed *"intendente"* or governor of San Blas in the Panamanian government. These may be signs of changes to come. Certainly, the *mola* co-op as a response to tourism trade is also providing a base for women to address the politics of tourism as well.

Kuna Yala; Island Facilities for Ethnic Tourism
The first tourist facilities in San Blas were developed by foreigners. The earliest was started by "Jungle Jim" Price in the 1940s on the Panamanian government-controlled island of El Porvenir in the "tourist zone." His operation lasted into the 1970s. No hotel service was available there in the 1980s. For the Kuna, the main impact of his business had been to provide a place for *mola* shoppers to stay. Two other foreign-operated resorts were started in San Blas during the 1960s. In both cases the American entrepreneurs apparently failed to go through the Congresso General for legal permission to build, although they dealt with the three *caciques*, the regional elected leaders of the Kuna (Howe 1982). These resorts were not sanctioned by the Kuna group as a whole.

In 1965 W. D. Barton rented an island site on which he would build "Islandia." Located in the middle of the San Blas chain, this resort was removed from other facilities and cruise boats in the "tourist islands" to the west. Barton was successful in attracting tourists. He promised to train Kuna in the hotel business, but his relationship with the Kuna was poor. In 1969, following a dispute with the Kuna over back wages and rent, the resort was burned down. Barton rebuilt his operation on the same site but did not repair relations with the Kuna. His resort was burned down again in 1974. After this Barton did not return despite IPAT efforts to negotiate for him. Some local Kuna benefitted financially from the island rent, jobs, and tourist trade, but the Kuna's overall negative experience with this resort set the stage for future events.

In 1967 Tom Moody negotiated a lease for uninhabited Pidertupo Island to develop a resort near El Porvenir. From 1969 on the Congresso General regularly told the Moody family to leave because of their unsanctioned status. The problem was not resolved for more than a decade in part because the Moodys did try to work with the local Kuna community. The Pidertupo resort could accommodate fourteen guests. At a rate of US$100 a day they were booked well in advance. The resort brought in local tax revenues and tourist trade, but still the Moodys were not welcomed in Kuna Yala. The Moodys' lease of US$200 a year and their unwillingness to let Kuna fish nearby or come ashore (Howe 1982, p. 17) added to growing tension.

Resolution of the 1975–77 Kuna Congresso General leadership crisis over IPAT plans for massive tourism development in San Blas solidified Kuna opposition to outside tourism development. In the spring of 1981 the Congresso General issued a warning that the Moodys would not be safe after 20 June (Howe 1982). On the twenty-first the resort was attacked. Tom Moody was shot and beaten, requiring a two-month hospital stay. Local violence the next day between pro-Moody Kuna and Kuna National Guards sent to restore order resulted in the death of two guards. During the same time a group of Kuna went after John Mann, the tour guide, but he was safe on a cruise ship. Mann tried to keep his own tour business going, but closed down after a few months. This was the end of the foreign tourism business in San Blas.

While Islandia was burned twice, a Kuna-run hotel just across the lagoon at Ailigandi was struggling to pay off its debts. The Hotel Las Palmiras owes its existence, in part, to Islandia. One of the people Barton had hired to work for him quit, then worked out a plan with a local restaurant *sociedad* to build a Kuna tourist hotel. The 300-member *sociedad* was the largest private group of women and men in San Blas (Holloman 1969, p. 216). The hotel opened in 1965 with five rooms, a restaurant and a snack bar. Ten paid jobs are rotated monthly among qualified members. Several other jobs (chief cook and motor runner) are permanent. After more than twenty years of operation, the hotel is in need of repairs but has remained open. It has yet to become a major financial success.

Toward El Porvenir in the west there are two other Kuna-run hotels. Both are extended family ventures somewhat like a small, private *sociedad*. Luis Borgos's Hotel San Blas on Nalunega is the "primitive but fun" establishment with no running water or electricity noted in tourist accounts. In 1987 the cost was US$20 a day, with fishing trips and sightseeing to other islands available.

On Wichubwalla, Alberto Gonzales runs the Hotel Anai ("My Friend"). During the year 1977–78 Gonzales leased his hotel to a Panamanian, but local hostility led to the outsider being removed to Panama (Howe 1982).

Plate 4. Mulatupu Community Dance Troupe at Kuna celebration. (Photo by Walt Swain, 1975)

Since the 1970s Gonzales has expanded his hotel to a ten-room facility with baths, electricity, and a pool. Accommodations cost US$50 a day in 1987. Gonzales uses the new El Llano-Carti road, when passable, to bring in supplies. Both hotels are promoted by the Panamanian airlines which offer Kuna-catered day trips and one-night package tours.

Outside of the tourist area there are Kuna pensions on several of the larger islands. Individual tourist service ventures come and go. Many communities have daily plane service that tourists can use. Visitors to Ustupu, east of Ailigandi, can take advantage of the Kuna culture center and diving tours. A number of villages have secular ethnic dance troops for their own and tourist entertainment (Plate 4). Hotels and pensions provide some local employment, stimulate the *mola* trade and recreation businesses, and expand the local economic base. In the late 1980s these were all small-scale operations.

Kuna Yala: Ecological Tourism
Transportation to and from San Blas has been a longstanding problem. The twenty-five-mile El Llano-Carti road was started more than fifteen years

ago as a spur off the Pan-American Highway toward the Atlantic coast. By the early 1970s land was being cleared by new settlers on either side of the road. Popular sentiment to "conquer the Atlantic" was promoted by the national government in a search for arable land. To reach the Atlantic, however, the road must cut across Kuna Yala to the coastal community of Carti, in the primary tourism area.

The Kuna considered a road into their territory a mixed blessing. Easy access to Panama would be welcomed, but the threat of Panamanian settlers laying claim to Kuna land was a real concern. Furthermore, Kuna beliefs teach that the forest is a sacred home of spirits. Vast tracts of virgin forest have been maintained. In the littoral area near the villages on the coast among agricultural plots there are untouched "spirit reserves" where the spirits are appeased and curers can gather medicinal herbs (Breslin and Chapin 1984, p. 34).

While road construction forged ahead necessary environmental impact studies were not done, despite a national government contract with the United States Agency for International Development (USAID). As Kuna concern grew over the road's progress into Kuna territory, a small group of young men from the Kuna Youth Movement set up an experimental agricultural station in 1975. This station was at the point where the road entered the reserve, Udirbi, 2400 feet above sea level on the continental divide. Toward Panama the view is of land decimated by slash-and-burn agriculture and cattle grazing. Toward the San Blas Islands the view is of thick, undisturbed tropical forest.

The purpose of a station at Udirbi was to create a presence for control of non-Kuna immigration and to develop appropriate uses for the land. The Udirbi movement gained the support of the Kuna Workers Union in 1976 and the Congresso General, which provided some us$36,000 for the project (Caufield 1982). The Kuna youth, lead by Guillermo Archibold, tried to raise many different crops and domestic stock that had been successful along the coast; nothing worked. The deeply weathered tropical mountain soils were pronounced unfit for permanent agriculture or cattle by a national Ministry of Agriculture team called in by the Kuna in 1979 for technical support (Houseal et al. 1986, p. 17).

In 1980–81 the Udirbi group turned to CATIE, a regional agricultural research center in Costa Rica. CATIE confirmed that the land was best left undisturbed, and worked with the Kuna to develop the concept of a forest park for "scientific tourism." They also developed an international network for technical and financial support. USAID funds were used to train Archibold and others in park management at CATIE headquarters and for a feasibility study. Project funding sources over the years have also included IAF, the Smithsonian Tropical Research Institute (STRI), the World Wildlife Fund, and the MacArthur Foundation, which awarded a us$225,000 grant (McGeary 1986, p. 31). Cooperation has also been developed with various Panamanian agencies and the University of Panama despite on-going disputes with the national government over resource rights and boundaries.

The Kuna Yala Wildlands Investigation Project (PEMASKY) is now supported by a twenty-person Kuna staff. The proposed park or ecological reserve encompasses 60,000 hectares of wildlands, from coastal areas to tropical forest. Archibold is director of PEMASKY, serving as the park's technical director, and Aurelio Chiari is administrator. Nine staff are trained as rangers. Some of the forest rangers will be Kuna National Guards, others will be trained as guides. The border area of the reserve has been patrolled by fifteen to twenty volunteers who are sent out every other week by Kuna communities (Breslin and Chapin 1984, p. 34). A second pan–San Blas cooperative, after the *mola* co-op, has been formed by Kuna men "to manage the land and water resources of their nearly autonomous homeland" (McGeary 1986).

Objectives of the project include demarcating and protecting the reserve boundary; promoting scientific investigation of the ecosystem and inventorying rare flora and fauna; and developing ecological or "scientific" tourism. Toward all these aims a center called Nusigandi is being built at the original Udirbi site. Housing is planned for park staff and some fifty "scientific tourists." Tourists coming through on the new road to the islands will be oriented to Kuna ecology at an environmental education center. The learning center will also serve non-Kuna colonists adjacent to the reserve, teaching appropriate land use techniques, and serving as a resource for Kuna students. The park is intended to be a model of conservation and effective indigenous political action. The Kuna's many ideas for projects outside of the park area including productive forests, export crops, coconut intercropping, fish culture, and encouragement of scientific study and controlled tourism, make their future promising. Guillermo Archibold has noted that "the potential of the Kuna reserve lends hope to the preservation of renewable natural resources in the tropics" (in Huber 1986, p. 15).

Conclusions

Indigenous tourism development will be self-sustaining when the financial, political, economic, and institutional aspects mesh to support on-going tourism efforts. For the Kuna, their society's emphasis on communal work and the evolution of *sociedad* businesses set the stage. Cooperatives have become a primary form for development. Co-op accountability rectifies *sociedad* management and bookkeeping problems that have slowed growth of some Kuna projects like the Hotel Las Palmiras. Private ventures such as the hotels San Blas and Anai and the new women's *mola* business also have incentives to sustain and grow.

Two new pan–San Blas organizations have been formed in response to outside pressures and a potential tourist market. The women's *mola* cooperative and the men's wildlands project are institutionalized projects with ample local input. They both obtained funding and technical training from outside sources; encouraged group self-reliance and membership participation; have broad regional political support from the Congresso General and national standing; and have grown over time, seeking to refine and expand cooperation.

These organizations are similar but not equivalent. The Productores de Molas co-op has grown slowly through time, and in contrast to PEMASKY, they have had relatively little financial and technical support. An explanation for this seeming imbalance is found in the nature of Kuna indigenous tourism. One factor is gender roles. Certainly, Kuna women as a whole do not have the public organizational and political skills that men are raised with in their society. Second, there is the regional power of the Congresso, where one leader went so far to predict that "when there are women in the congresso, we will no longer be Kuna" (Swain 1978, p. 285).

As women in many nations discover, Kuna women working in Panama find that "women and men tend to be treated differently. They do not enter into the labor force in the same rhythms; they are channeled into different economic niches; their patterns of internal migration differ; their access to capital is unequal; their rates of employment are distinct" (Bossen 1984, p. 8). This is readily reflected in Kuna migration patterns and the *mola* co-op's low level of financing.

In general, local tourism development also differentially affects women and men. In many cases it is not possible for women or men of the same group to find work where they live, and outsiders are primary beneficiaries. When the Kuna have not been in charge of tourism development (*mola* and hotel ventures), previous gender roles and migration patterns have been reinforced. When Kuna are in charge, some role choices have evolved: women are moving from co-op leadership to community roles; PEMASKY is developing new local occupations that could reduce migration of men and women. Local employment in indigenous tourism could affect any evolution of Kuna gender roles. One day there may be Kuna women forest rangers; the Congresso may change to incorporate the voices of all women; Kuna men may stop temporary migration; and, *mola*-making may be considered Kuna work, not women's work.

As Graburn (1984, p. 415) has noted, *molas* are tourist art, the material symbols of "new formulations of identity . . . often defensively constructed to both meet the demand and modify the cultural content of group life. This dialectic is not always one that moves in the directions intended or understood . . . by the planners or social scientists." The interaction of tourist market demand and the Kuna's response is another factor shaping Kuna tourism. The travel writers promote a sense of "cultural preservation," yet no longer refer to the Kuna as a mythical matriarchy. A greater knowledge of their subjects is evident on both sides. The Kuna appreciate the symbolic and economic power *molas* have in Panama's tourist trade. As one Kuna noted, "in an event of a major crisis with the government, the Kuna could bring it to its knees by having all the women replace their *molas* with western dress" (Howe 1982, p. 15). Cultural pluralism as a tourist attraction is important to Panama's economy. It is basic to indigenous tourism.

To support this pluralism, the Kuna need an economic base. *Mola* sales in and of themselves can stimulate only limited income. The Kuna continue to have a mixed subsistence and cash economy with much promise for future development if they maintain Kuna Yala with its natural resources. Tourism gives Panama a stake in the survival of Kuna Yala as well. Ultimately the factors shaping Kuna tourism are issues of power and control. Power and control must be balanced between the Kuna and the nation of Panama (cultural pluralism); with multinational tourist interests (tourism market dynamics); and, within the ethnic group, between individuals (gender roles). As more Kuna become shareholders in tourist companies and are trained in tourism businesses, these factors will shape indigenous tourism development.

In many nations, the question of cultural pluralism or integration of minority cultures is a factor in national tourism plans (see Pi-Sunyer 1982, p. 10). Despite differences in national size and political systems, the Kuna can serve as a model for other groups on a course toward indigenous tourism. For example, in Yunnan Province, China, ethnic tourism highlighting twenty-four minority groups is of growing importance. Many of these groups live in semi-autonomous regions that are becoming accessible to travelers. Minority women make souvenirs based on their ethnic dress. The Sani Yi minority group has other similarities with the Kuna, including population size; a geographically attractive setting with established tourism; and circular migration to sell goods to tourists in the city. It will be interesting to see if the Sani Yi and other groups around the world will be able to evolve from ethnic to indigenous tourism. Only if the national benefits make it feasible will the group have control of its own tourism development.

More nations are beginning to recognize that "the ability of indigenous peoples to successfully manage their resources is important in sustaining national development" (Houseal et al. 1986, p. 10). The Kuna are at the forefront. They are using indigenous tourism as a means to an end: cultural survival.

University of California, Davis

5

Tourism in Tonga Revisited: Continued Troubled Times?

CHARLES F. URBANOWICZ

Prologue

The following is a revision of a chapter published in 1977. Fieldwork for the earlier chapter was conducted in the Polynesian Kingdom of Tonga in 1970 and 1971. Since then, I have not been back to Tonga but have followed Tongan matters through published works (including Tongan government documents) and contacts with individuals in Tonga or individuals who have been to Tonga. For archival research, I have turned to the excellent resources of the Library of the University of Hawaii and the university librarian, Renee Heyum.

Background

The Kingdom of Tonga lies in the heart of fabled Polynesia, approximately 550 miles southwest of Samoa and 450 miles southeast of Fiji. The tiny kingdom encompasses approximately 289 square miles and supports an estimated (1986) population of one hundred thousand, giving an average density of more than 346 persons per square mile. The actual usable land available for settlement, however, is only 190 square miles, giving a true density of 532 persons per square mile.

The population is not evenly distributed and the largest island of the group, Tongatapu (one hundred square miles, population of 57,411), is the economic center for the archipelago. The second largest population of Tongans (15,068) is located on the islands of Vava'u, 180 miles northeast of Tongatapu. Tongatapu has been the historic residence of Tongan royalty, and Nuku'alofa, the capital as well as the largest city and the main tourist attraction, is located there.

Formerly a British protectorate, Tonga achieved independence in 1970 and entered the British Commonwealth of Nations in that year. The constitutional monarchy dates to 1875 and the current monarch, His Majesty King Taufa'ahau Tupou IV acceded to the throne on his forty-ninth birthday on 4 July 1965. Tongan is the official language, but English is the second language and most Tongans are bilingual. The population is ethnically homogenous and 98 percent of the population is Tongan. Tongans are also stalwart Christians and in the 1976 census, which listed 90,085 inhabitants, only 233 respondents failed to declare a religious affiliation. The most recent census, conducted in November of 1986, reaffirms this Christian aspect of the kingdom.

Tourism in one form or another has existed in Tonga since the mid-1960s. One could argue that in 1966, when 14,581 passengers arrived on a cruise ship (up from 6398 in 1965) tourism had come to Tonga to stay. Tourism has grown considerably since I became involved with Tonga in the late 1960s: tourism (and the economic impact of tourism on Tongans) has been increasing due to extensive promotions that stress the beauty of unspoiled Polynesia, where English is spoken and where there is a king and queen.

Although Tonga is the last Polynesian kingdom, it is far from being the storybook land of culture brokers. Tonga is an overpopulated and underdeveloped tiny nation, struggling to maintain its cultural integrity in the face of twentieth-century changes. There are serious internal economic problems in Tonga for which, I believe, tourism is not the total solution. This case study examines the impact of tourism on the Tongan economy and the problems associated with the advent of mass tourism. It also provides information for the reader on one individual's perspective on tourism in Tonga for the past eighteen years: and that perspective is not a very positive one.

The Economic Problem

Tonga continues to be a nation of small landholders. Despite government efforts to modernize and increase food production, the natural resources of the islands are inadequate to feed the local population and the increasing number of tourists. For greater cash flow, however, Tonga has also become an exporter of agricultural commodities to meet consumer demands for Western products. It is interesting to note that while various amounts of frozen fish, live animals, and fruits and vegetables are *exported* to generate hard cash, meat and chicken account for a large portion of Tonga's annual *imported* foodstuffs.

In addition to foodstuffs and a variety of other items (including Tongan handicrafts) exported to raise funds, one of the major "exports" from Tonga that result in cash returning back to the kingdom are Tongans themselves: Tongans abroad send back millions of dollars in what have been called "invisible earnings" (categorized as remittances or gifts) from relatives overseas in Hawaii, New Zealand, or California. In 1974, for example, overseas funds to Tonga resulted in T$3,582,000 injected into the economy and in 1980, for comparison, Tongans overseas sent T$10,728,000. It is important to note here that because of changing exchange rates over the time period discussed in this chapter, (nearly two decades), all dollar amounts are given in Tongan currency relative to the times discussed: exchange rates for Tonga dollars have ranged from US$.92 to US$.86, and in 1987 one Tongan dollar was exchanged for US$.70.

Inflation has eroded Tongan purchasing power over the past eighteen years, as indicated by the Consumer Price Index (CPI). Established in 1969 with a base of 100.0, the CPI is based on the purchasing power of a "typical" Tongan family. Biased toward food items (64 percent of all items on the index), the CPI has risen steadily (Figure 1) ever since tourism began in the kingdom.

Another critical problem for Tonga is unemployment, and in an island world where land is important, many adult Tongans are landless. Although every Tongan male, upon reaching the age of sixteen (and becoming a taxpayer) is entitled to land for crops and for a home, there simply is not enough to go around. In 1966, 57 percent of all men over sixteen years of age who were entitled to tax allotments were landless, and by 1976 this number had increased to 64 percent. There are not many opportunities for jobs in the tourism sector of the Tongan economy, and since 1971 thousands of Tongans have gone overseas to work.

This "export" item has benefitted the Tongan economy but has also created problems: family life for wage earners who go overseas is disrupted and it has also created problems with the "host" countries that receive these (and other) islanders. On 1 December 1986, for example, the New Zealand Government lifted certain restrictions on visitors to New Zealand from Tonga, Fiji, and Western Samoa. In a mere eleven weeks, some 11,500 islanders had arrived in New Zealand, "many under the impression fostered

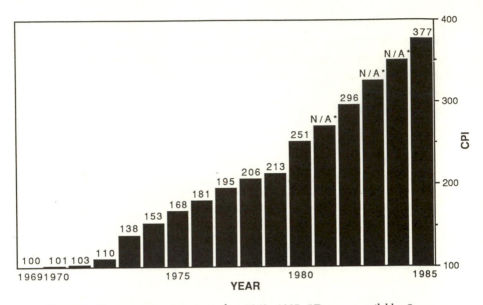

Figure 1. Tongan consumer price index, 1969–1985. *Data not available. Source: Various Tongan government publications.

by travel agents that they could settle in the country permanently" (Barber 1987, p. 30). The New Zealand government terminated the program on 18 February 1987, but not until some 5000 Tongans had traveled to New Zealand on fifty special flights. It was reported that the kingdom ran out of passport forms and that this rush to leave Tonga left Tonga with a "shortage of nurses and teachers" (ibid.).

Tonga, like many of the island nations of the Pacific, continues to undergo massive acculturation. It is not surprising that in their 1970–75 development plan, Tongans viewed tourism as having the greatest economic potential for the kingdom, both as an employer of labor and also as a source of foreign exchange. In the five-year period of 1982–1986, tourism earnings brought some T$37,878,997 into the kingdom: an impressive figure when one considers that the budget for the entire kingdom for 1986–1987 was T$57,300,000.

The Economic Role of Tourism

Tourists arrive in Tonga by private yacht, by cruise ships making a one- or two-day stop as part of a longer Pacific itinerary, or by air from Samoa, Fiji,

New Zealand, or Hawaii. In 1958 guests to Tonga were an elite group, when only three cruise vessels landed passengers at Tongatapu, and some special flights brought a total of sixty-four air passengers from Australia. Tourism, however, has grown steadily and rapidly, and more growth is anticipated, including tourism to areas other than Nuku'alofa. In 1973, cruise ships began scheduled visits to Vava'u, 180 miles north of Tongatapu, and twenty-four ships brought 9463 tourists to that island. In 1975, 17,500 tourists visited Vava'u and in 1985 there were 23,043 visitors to that island.

Foreign exchange receipts make tourism one of the top two income generators for Tongans (along with agriculture and livestock products). Table 1 clearly points out the monetary impact of tourism in Tonga from 1975,

TABLE 1.
SELECTED TOURISTS TO TONGA BY CRUISE SHIP AND PLANE: 1958–1986

Year	Number of Passengers	Number of Ships	Number of In-Passengers	Number of Flights	Tourism Earnings
1958	1715	3	64	N/A	N/A
1959	2600	5	45	8	N/A
1960	N/A	7	189	23	N/A
1961	2866	4	308	35	N/A
1962	3677	6	524	66	N/A
1963	4355	6	668	75	N/A
1964	5626	10	992	117	N/A
1965	6398	8	1174	144	N/A
1966	14,581	20	1460	146	N/A
1967	14,240	14	2883	231	N/A
1968	11,111	12	3465	182	N/A
1969	18,111	19	4326	230	N/A
1970	21,025	24	4001	324	N/A
1971	23,500	32	4000	314	N/A
1972	27,259	29	4599	358	N/A
1973	31,502	48	6356	403	N/A
1974	36,308	44	6403	397	N/A
1975	44,968	45	6770	N/A	T$1,700,000
1976	43,074	N/A	9312	N/A	T$2,224,150
1977	44,683	54	11,023	N/A	T$3,358,623
1978	52,275	49	12,090	N/A	T$3,980,884
1979	36,171	42	12,189	N/A	T$3,919,226
1980	39,521	37	12,505	N/A	T$6,584,823
1981	45,229	46	12,611	N/A	T$6,006,133
1982	43,869	36	12,443	N/A	T$4,406,306
1983	49,586	38	14,482	N/A	T$6,222,564
1984	43,911	46	13,713	N/A	T$6,170,581
1985	41,748	46	14,216	821	T$10,079,346
1986	N/A	N/A	~15,211	N/A	~T$11,000,000

N/A = Not available

Source: Various Tongan government publications

when tourism "earnings" were singled out as a category at T$1,700,000, to approximately T$11,000,000 for 1986! Tourism is definitely increasing in Tonga, and the length of the stay of the "typical" tourist is increasing: while cruise-ship passengers visit for an eight-hour day, in 1985 the average tourist stayed 8.7 nights in the kingdom, spending an average of T$402 per person.

The government of Tonga is interested in developing tourism for apparent economic benefits. The Tonga Visitor's Bureau (TVB) was created in 1971 to work toward that goal and it is the TVB's function to disseminate information to promote tourism. A typical mailing from the TVB will include promotional literature on the kingdom and will state that "we hope that this book on Tonga will assist you in encouraging and promoting visitors to the Kingdom of Tonga." Such a cover letter was included with a copy of a 1978 book entitled *Tonga* (by James Siers) wherein the author wrote:

> The jet lands at Tongatapu and the visitor disembarks to go through immigration and customs formalities in a friendly atmosphere which sets the tone for the visit. Next comes an unhurried drive into town to a choice of accommodation. The Dateline Hotel offers first class tourist accommodations but there are a number of motels and guest houses which are typically Tongan: ultra friendly and concerned for the guest's welfare. As the majority of these are located in Nuku'alofa, it is possible to visit places of interest on foot. There is the Palace and a Chapel on the waterfront; the Royal tombs nearby; the markets where the stall-holders proudly display the abundant produce of Tonga's rich soil—tomato, cucumber, cabbage, lettuce, peppers, melons, citrus fruits in season, papaya and mango and the taro and yam for which Tonga is famous. There are many other things besides, including souvenirs. The people are justly famous for their handicrafts, especially tapa cloth made from the bark of a tree and beautiful basketware. (p. 7)

From this the reader gets a fairly good idea of the "image" that the TVB (and the travel agent) is trying to sell to the potential guest. A survey of tourist "likes" and "dissatisfactions" taken by the TVB indicated that many visitors felt that most Tongans did not know enough of their own culture and history (or at least the aspects of touristic interest), so the TVB published a pamphlet for local distribution to remedy this particular complaint.

Tongans have built airstrips to encourage tourist travel to outlying islands and the government continues to allocate substantial sums of money for hotel expansion and construction. With the help of overseas backing (from Australia, Japan, and West Germany), new hotels have been constructed on Tongatapu and Vava'u. Japanese companies have also expressed an interest in joint investment with the Tongan government for facilities that would serve the public and especially entice the now rare Japanese traveler to Tonga.

In September 1986 the Japanese government confirmed a grant to Tonga of T$4,850,000 to construct a "handicrafts and cultural resources centre" in the capital of Nuku'alofa on the island of Tongatapu. King Taufa'ahau Tupou IV has traveled to Japan, exchange clubs have been established, and Tongans have been encouraged to visit Japan. In 1976 the Japan/Tonga Friendship Fellowship opened a resort clubhouse in Tonga in an effort to develop growing contacts and increase guests to Tonga.

Tourism, however, increases the economic problems in the kingdom, especially the need for additional imported foodstuffs. Air passengers have to be fed, and although many enjoy the local fruits and bread (made from the imported flour), few would be content for long on the relatively bland Tongan diet of yams, taro, and fruit. Tongans are, indeed, competing with the tourists for the imported foods. The ever-increasing quantities of food that must be imported to feed the increasing number of tourists contributed to the steadily rising CPI. A similar situation prevails in Fiji, as Ward (1971, p. 171) noted more than a decade ago:

> Some (Fiji) hotels, in the interest of greater economy and convenience, only provide a strictly limited choice of meals and the sort of meals which tourists expect to receive in their home countries, e.g. of the steak-hamburger-mixed grill variety. Many hotels argue that this is all the tourist wants although the best hotels do provide more extensive menus. The majority (of hotels, however) do provide the food which is produced and consumed by the local inhabitants and this compounds the problem of buying requirements from domestic producers.

Ward also states that despite the availability of many local foodstuffs tourists might consume, hotels in Fiji prefer to purchase their requirements overseas because, it has been argued, "they can only then be assured of continuity in supplies and of a consistent high standard of quality."

Tourism has grown rapidly in Tonga, but it could evaporate just as quickly. Tongans occasionally have experienced situations when the anticipated tourists have failed to arrive. In 1972, at least forty tour groups cancelled their planned air visits to Tongatapu because the tour operators could not be assured of making airline connections from the kingdom to other points on the itinerary; one can see in Table 1 that cruise-ship visitors appear to have peaked in 1978. The TVB attributes the steady increase in air visitors to consolidated and improved marketing of Tonga, with a media

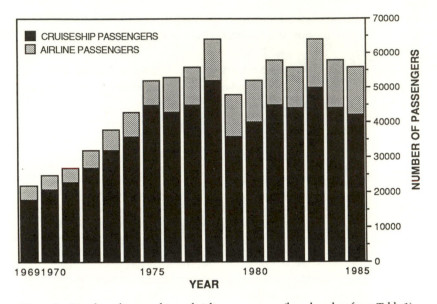

Figure 2.   Number of cruise-ship and airline passengers (based on data from Table 1).

campaign in Australia and New Zealand, and some joint promotions of Hawaiian Air with the West Coast of the United States.

It is interesting to construct a bar chart which indicates, in gross numbers, the combined number of cruise-ship passengers *and* air visitors to this tiny Polynesian kingdom and to compare this chart with the steady increase in inflation over the same time period (Figure 2). There is, I believe, a direct relationship between increased tourism and increased inflation in the kingdom of Tonga.

Because of fuel and labor costs, long-haul cruises such as those that stop at Tonga are not as profitable as the short-haul, fast turnaround cruises that operate weekly or biweekly in the Caribbean (Waters and Patterson 1976). Future cruises to Tonga might continue to decrease, seriously affecting businessmen in Tonga. Awareness of the potential loss of revenue from tourism should serve to reinforce the Tongans' awareness of the potential for disaster if their economy is tied too closely to tourism. While short-term cruise passengers consume little of the imported foodstuffs, airline guests (whose stays range from five to eleven days) must be fed for the duration of their visit. The host-guest competition for food and natural resources will further contribute to inflation.

What Price Tourism?

Tongans have become the victims of their own tourism. Exceedingly happy when ships dock with a thousand passengers (and several hundred crew members) who inject thousands of dollars into the economy in an eight-hour period, Tongans are even happier when the ships depart at dusk. The physical impact of a thousand tourists on one town on a tiny island is tremendous, especially when most tourists are bused to see *all* the sights of the island.

The tourist literature has brought the visitors here "to observe the traditional Tongan way of life in the *natives' own habitat*" and the shore excursions promise that you will "see the daily work routine of men and women—gardening, weaving baskets, cooking, washing and their many other activities. This village walking tour offers you an excellent opportunity to photograph the Tongan people as they really are" (Itinerary for the International Institute, 2 June 1974). Tongans cannot tolerate being regarded as members of a "cultural zoo" and Kirch has recently written of *Tourism as Conflict in Polynesia: Status Degradation Among Tongan Handicraft Sellers* (1984). Under these circumstances, there are few opportunities for a true host-guest relationship to develop.

Ordinarily, tourists have heard something about Tonga long before they arrive, and they anticipate "seeing" Tonga, but, all too often, cruise passengers get only a look at a "phony-folk-culture" in action or a Disneyland of the Pacific. Air guests, fewer in number than cruise guests (but staying longer), may have a somewhat different experience. They have the opportunity to enjoy the recreational facilities of a tropical island and they also have the opportunity to see more of the island at a gradual pace, to meet some of the truly hospitable Tongans, and to share a cross-cultural educational experience. The actual experiences, of the tourist, however, can fall short of this ideal.

The increasing number of visitors entering the last Polynesian kingdom can be impressive when compared to the indigenous Tongans who are year-round inhabitants. Rajotte, in a 1977 work entitled "Evaluating the Cultural and Environmental Impact of Pacific Tourism," stated that any attempt to ascertain the impact of tourism on a Pacific community should "begin by relating the tourism flow to the size of the island community into which it is injected" (1977, p. 44). With 60,000 Tongans in 1958 and 1769 tourists for the entire year, the Tongan-to-tourist ratio was 33 : 1. With 100,000 Tongans in 1985 and 55,964 ship and air passengers, the Tongan-to-tourist ratio was barely 2 : 1.

TABLE 2.
TOTAL OF VISITORS AND EXCURSIONISTS ARRIVING IN TONGA: 1981–1985

Category	1981	1982	1983	1984	1985
Air Visitors	12,611	12,443	14,482	13,713	14,216
Cargo-ship Passengers	33	38	81	116	173
Yacht Visitors	875	648	1252	1290	1687
Naval Vessel Crew Members	627	2707	1180	2032	1462
Cruise-ship Passengers	45,229	43,869	49,586	43,911	41,748
Cruise-ship Crew Members	21,641	20,926	24,166	20,947	19,320
Foreign Vessel Crew Members	N/A	1369	1747	2760	2593
Total Visitors and Excursionists	81,016	82,000	92,494	84,769	81,199

"The Tonga Visitors Bureau uses the following criteria to define visitors/tourists and cruise passengers (excursionists). Visitors/Tourists: Any person visiting Tonga other than those usually resident within the Kingdom for any reason other than following an occupation renumerated from within Tonga. Visitors include persons travelling for pleasure (recreation, holiday, health, study, sport, religion), and for business, family reasons, missions, or meetings. The stay must be a minimum of 24 hours (over night) and accommodations must be in a hotel, guest house, or in a private home. Persons classified as yacht visitor arrivals may depart by air, ship, or yacht. From this definition, the Tonga Visitors Bureau reports its visitor statistics by three modes of travel: Visitors by Air, Visitors by Ship [and], Visitors by Yacht. Cruise passengers (Excursionists): as defined above visiting ports [in] the Kingdom by cruise ship but not utilising any land accommodations within the Kingdom. . . . the statistics presented are not based upon a sample but are an analysis of *all Immigration Cards for the year* [emphasis added]."

Source: Taumoepeau, Semisi P., *Visitors Statistics 1985.* Research and Statistical Section, Tonga Visitors Bureau, Nuku'alofa, Tonga 1986, pp. 6, 8.

The Tonga Visitor's Bureau has developed a sophisticated tracking system in an attempt to assess the impact of *all* visitors to the kingdom. In February of 1986, the Fifteenth Annual Statistics Report was published with data from a standardized format adopted in 1985 to "reflect the current requirements of those persons involved in the South Pacific travel industry, especially in the areas of planning, development and marketing" (Taumoepeau 1986, p. 5). Utilizing their data for 1985 (Table 2), including all individuals who entered Tonga, the 1985 total for all "Visitors and Excursionists" was 81,199 or a ratio of 1.23 visitors and excursionists to each Tongan!

The fact is granted that *not* every single one of these 81,199 individuals touched Tongan soil or interacted with Tongans (and many of these, especially cruise-ship crew members, were probably counted more than once in the tally), but the impact of these "guests" on the "hosts" is increasing: what happens when tourists outnumber the Tongans for any given year? Forster (1964, pp. 217–22) pointed out that one of the fascinating aspects of the tourist process in the Pacific is the deliberate creation of a "phony-folk-culture," which the indigenous inhabitants develop to provide "authentic native culture" to the tourists. For example, a popular tourist "attraction" is a disply of dances in Tonga: the program may contain almost a dozen Fijian, Tahitian, Hawaiian, or New Zealand dances performed by the Tongan dancers, but show only one or two Tongan dances. The fact is granted that a Tahitian *tamure* has a tremendous amount of visual impact, and a Fijian fire dance is dramatic, but Tongan dances have a beauty and symmetry of their own that should be performed for visitors to Tonga.

It is this alteration of their basic culture that has prompted Tongans to consider legislating the tourist industry. They seek to ensure the active preservation of the traditional Tongan way of life and culture by integrating traditional patterns into mass tourism and not making traditional culture a contemporary "phony-folk-culture."

The substantial amount of quickly generated cash derived from cruise-ship passengers (in return for an "authentic" Polynesian feast, shore excursions around the island, and the purchase of handicrafts), when placed into circulation in the port towns, can be the occasion for a party. Drinking may commence even before the ship has weighed anchor. Tongans still enjoy their traditional *kava* drink, but as stated elsewhere, when individuals begin to consume more alcohol than *kava*, in violation of their Christian ethic, it is an indication that the basic fabric of their culture and society has shifted (Urbanowicz 1977).

Conclusions

Deep-seated economic problems induced by a growing indigenous and tourist population have almost engulfed the tiny islands of Tonga. The glitter of tourist money seemingly promises a substantial portion of much-needed economic help, but will it bring more "troubled times"? The current substantial cruise business might be considered relatively benign in that visitors are short-term, and they arrive and depart at a scheduled hour. Comparatively little capital or space is required to cater to their needs, aside from docking areas and taxis or buses. Further, the money that the cruise passengers spend is largely for local services (transportation, amusement, and for handicrafts as souvenirs) and directly benefits individuals.

A threatened demise of the cruise industry, to be replaced with an increasing number of air travelers, may be potentially more disruptive to the economy and to the culture. To accommodate air visitors, hotels and resort facilities must be financed and built, but they must occupy land, already in short supply in Tonga. Given the small size of the capital of Nuku'alofa as well as the Island of Tongatapu itself, one must imagine the impact if one thousand guests were continually present, day *and* night, demanding that their needs be met, including Sunday, the traditional Tongan Sabbath and a day of rest. Although air travel is steadily developing, the advent of mass travel could "Waikiki" the beaches, and inundate local culture, as has already happened in certain parts of the Fiftieth State.

Tonga will certainly never approach the tourist volume of Hawaii (estimated to be 5,600,000 visitors in 1986), but Tongans could certainly take some hints from the tourist industry in Tahiti. For example, in all of 1967, Tahiti had a mere 16,200 tourists and it wasn't until 1979 that the 100,000-visitor mark was passed; in 1986, Tahiti's visitor count was a phenomenal 161,238 and with increased air carrier service in effect, officials are predicting 220,000 tourists a year by 1990. To anyone who has traveled to Tahiti it is clear that the number one complaint in Tahiti is the cost of food and beverages. Tahiti has been described by some individuals in three simple words: "beautiful but expensive," and the same might well be said for Tonga within the next decade.

The prime minister of Tonga (His Majesty's brother) has repeatedly stressed that Tongan culture can withstand the impact of modern tourism development. I, too, am certain that Tongans will survive; however, will they still be Tongans? Or will they become yet another example of a people who have been forced to abandon their traditions (or at least move them "back stage" away from prying eyes) to prevent their becoming the "quaint" customs of ethnic tourism?

The anthropological analysis of tourism differs from the statistical methods employed by economic planners in that the former assesses tourism's impact upon culture and the social milieu rather than being restricted to analyzing the balance-of-trade or the CPI. There is an important ethnohistoric component to cultural change, from past to present, just as there is a strong cross-cultural component that must be studied. Tongans must become aware of the changes that have occurred as a result of non-Tongan influences; they must also study the effects of tourism elsewhere in the Pacific islands. From these two sources, they should design for the future. Tourism *must be* properly controlled if it is to make a positive contribution to the economy, to the Tongan hosts, and to the non-Tongan guests.

Epilogue

It should be clear from this reading that I am not overwhelmingly ecstatic about tourism in Tonga or impressed with the impact of tourism as a world-wide phenomenon. Tourism has been with us as long as people have had excess time to travel and, too, excess funds to expend on traveling to locations distant from home.

Tourism will not go away because being a tourist allows the traveler to leave behind his own local "poverty" and see or experience a new localized (and often) Third World poverty that is not his own. As affluent tourists we leave behind the hardships of home and "visit ourselves" upon the hardships of others. As tourists (or travelers) we effectively leave behind the death and dying of our peer group: while we may see death and dying around us as we travel (just as we may see poverty and beggars as we travel), the people that we see are not "our own" people.

Travel or tourism is thus a bit of an escape from our local problems: an escape from the daily routine of paying mortgages, bills, and watching the stress level go up around us. As a tourist (or traveler) we are safely in the hands of the pilot or steward or cruise captain who will take us to our destination without our worrying about getting there. Traveling is an escape to the carefree times of childhood when someone else had to do the worrying for us, and traveling is here to stay!

California State University, Chico

6

Towards a Theoretical Analysis of Tourism: Economic Dualism and Cultural Involution in Bali

PHILIP FRICK MCKEAN

Tourism in Bali

Prior to World War II, Dutch ships brought passengers to Bali for a five-day tour of the island made famous in Europe when orchestras from Bali performed at the Paris Colonial Exposition in 1932. Artists, ethnographers, and other visitors spread the image of the exquisite aesthetic attainments of the Balinese. Following the Indonesian Revolution in 1945, President Sukarno used Bali as a retreat, and often entertained foreign dignitaries at his palatial home there. However, poor roads, small airfields, shallow harbors, and a permeating instability of both economic and political institutions in Indonesia inhibited tourism until 1969, when a more liberal government supported construction of a modern jet airport. Since then, visitors have increased from forty thousand to over one hundred thousand annually. Hotel facilities have been built along the coast at Sanur and Kuta, tour agencies and art shops have opened roads, electric systems, and other major investments in the infrastructure have been made, and a Master Plan for land use and development was commissioned by the World Bank. Mass tourism is now a social reality affecting the island in multiple ways.

The Theoretical Problem

A common theme in the anthropological study of tourism is the considerable cultural change wrought by the coming of tourists. Normal assumptions include that (1) changes are brought about by the intrusion of an external, usually superordinate sociocultural system, into a weaker, receiving culture; (2) changes are generally destructive to the indigenous tradition; (3) the changes will lead to a homogeneous culture as ethnic or local identity is subsumed under the aegis of a technologically-advanced industrial system, a national and multinational bureaucracy, a consumer-oriented economy, and jet-age life-style. Few analyses exist of alternative mechanisms available to indigenous populations to resist change, or to retain and even revitalize their social fabric and customs within the changed conditions wrought by the tourist industry. If this approach has not been considered by anthropologists, other writers have completely overlooked the possibility and typically turned up their noses in disdain at tourists and their effect on the host area. Concern that obnoxious, insensitive tourists will despoil Bali is widespread, especially among foreign intelligentsia, as the following passage indicates (Hanna 1972, pp. 2, 5, 6):

> Tourism, whether or not of a purely cultural variety, is now the boom industry in Bali; but jumbo-jet flights of joy seekers may blight the very enchantments that even the less cultured economy-class package-tour patrons are led by their hard-sell agents to breathlessly anticipate. . . . During the Sukarno years the island had unhappy experiences from tampering with the artistic traditions. Today's distortions, which are just as deliberate, are as artistically if not as politically sinister. This, then, is the 'Waikiki-anization' of Bali. . . . Even the less sensitive tourists are starting to deplore it, and the more thoughtful Balinese are bracing themselves to withstand the worst.

This pessimistic hand-wringing for the return of the "good old days" is founded on the assumption that the Balinese will be willy-nilly, passive receptors of a total package of "modernization." Further, these critics have ignored the varied surrogates that enable groups to respond to both internal and external stimuli. Presuming that monolithic and uniform results will occur, these observers fail to appreciate the differential, selective changes that may occur within a cultural tradition. Although socioeconomic change is taking place in Bali, I argue that it goes hand-in-hand with the conservation of the traditional culture. My field data supports the hypothesis that tourism may in fact strengthen the process of conserving, reforming, and recreating certain traditions. The effects of tourism are examined in terms of two contrasting theoretical constructs—economic dualism and cultural involution—to assess the validity of the hypothesis.

Economic Dualism

In the simplest theoretical analysis, I posit two extremes: (1) a "tourist world" in which total sociocultural change occurs in the area affected by tourism and the host area becomes modeled after the patterns of the visiting groups; *or* (2) a "native world" in which no change occurs, and life-as-usual-prior-to-contact goes on. These are extremes on a continuum, and each should be viewed as an "ideal type."

If separation between the two "worlds" is emphasized, the apparent continuity or persistence of each must be explained in terms of a system that enables transactions to take place, but which binds them so that they are essentially autonomous and noninterfering. The Dutch economist J. H. Boeke noticed a separation between two sectors of the Indonesian economy—the capitalist and the peasant—and reasoned that there must be profound causes for the "dualism." Boeke felt that the peasant was not particularly "rational" in his economic behavior, and that he was less interested in saving and investing than in traditional goals such as gaining status, performing rituals, and building solidarity with neighbors. Capitalists, on the other hand, strive to exploit scarce resources and make profits, thereby responding "rationally" to the economic forces of supply and demand.

Boeke's theories of economics are based on a series of evolutionary phases, with capitalism at its climax in both its "Eastern" as well as "Western" guises. A unilineal and monolithic quality pervades his analysis (1953, p. 14):

> In each phase (pre-capitalistic through late capitalistic) society may be said to be uniform, homogeneous; it evolves as a whole, in all its expressions, whether spiritual or material, cultural or economic; there is harmony and coherence between the different social phenomena; one spiritual conception pervades all.

Modern Balinese, however, have *not* become exclusively "capitalist" persons, in antithesis to the "pre-capitalistic" persons posited by Boeke (1953, pp. 12 ff.). Nor have they, as Boeke asserts for the Southern Asian Chinese or Indian minorities, "been absorbed by, and become independent on, the fully developed western capitalism" (1953, p. 15). Through a selective process, the Balinese have found ways to increase their cash flow without becoming "capitalists" nor following totally the socioeconomic trends that Boeke predicts. Boeke also develops several corollaries to describe the advent of capitalism, including these essentials: "a sharp distinction between business and household, and the continuous harrowing of the latter; the commodity-character of all products; a steadily growing division of labor, with its counterparts: organization and planning, in contracts and in corporations" (1953, p. 13). In contrast, Balinese organizations that promote and arrange tourism primarily function through family and neighborhood ties.

Boeke uses several specific traits to characterize "Eastern forms of industry," which are listed below, and examined in terms of my data for their appropriateness to characterize tourism on Bali:

> 1. Aversion to capital; i.e. conscious dislike of investing capital and of the risks attending this. (1953, pp. 101–5)

Many hamlet cooperatives have worked strenuously to acquire the necessary capital to upgrade their orchestras, to obtain costumes, and rebuild the meeting halls used as performance centers—based on the risky expectation that they would be able to attract paying tourists on a regular basis. They have, in effect, invested in their cultural traditions, and planned for repayment, with accrued interest that could be both monetarily and culturally.

> 2. Only slight interest in finish and accuracy. (1953, pp. 101–5)

One who has viewed a *legong* dance in Peliatan (Plate 1), a mask carved by Ida Bagus Gelodog, or a statue carved by Ida Bagus Tilem, or examined the construction of decorations at a Balinese cremation, is likely to disagree with the preceding statement. The evidence in Bali, at least with reference to the best workmanship, does not support Boeke's assertion. However, the "tourist junk art" assuredly does lack "finish and accuracy."

> 3. Lack of business qualities. No attempt is made to compute the profitableness of a business or to find the most economical system of utilizing labor. (1953, pp. 101–5)

This generalized statement is not difficult to counter. For example, a royal family who owns the Pemetjutan Palace in Den Pasar maintains careful record of profit and loss. This family operates a variety of income producing schemes: promotion of paintings, a gift shop, a weekly dramatic performance catering to the tourist market.

> 4. Failure to come up to even the minimum requirements of standard and sample. (1953, pp. 101–5)

Plate 1. *Legong* dancers shown at a temple gate. Although adapted from indigenous religious celebrations, even tourist performances require extensive training and fine costumes. (Batubulan, Bali)

While some handicrafts may fall under this judgment (weaving and carving, which are produced in large numbers by poorly trained workers), it is inaccurate as a whole, for the detail in architecture, temple ornamentation, costuming, and dance are evaluated critically. Balinese carefully distinguish between high and low standards in their traditional culture. Even in the products available to tourists, it is not true that there is a lack of "quality control." Sanctions may be imposed by an island-wide consultative body of artists and government officials (LISTIBIYA) and by a Conservatory for the Arts (KOBAR). Informal sanctions from villagers (laughter, for example) prevail on those who carve or dance poorly and have also served to maintain high quality among many of the artists and craftsmen in Bali. There are, of course, "sweat shop" production centers catering to the assumed lower standards of the mass tourist market.

Boeke asserts a unilateral development of economics, and further projects it into the life-styles, laws, and beliefs pervasive in a society. He views the "pre-capitalistic" societies of the East, especially Indonesia, as losing out to Western-oriented "late capitalism." The dialectic is a false one

Plate 2. A local leader of the *gamelon* orchestra who also carves and farms, shown with some of his children. (Sesetan, Bali)

in Bali, for adaptive alternatives exist to link the local economy to the international one without destruction of the former. Nor does the economic development accompanying tourism necessarily lead to "late capitalism" in Bali. No mutually exclusive choice is enforced between the multiple roles available to Balinese. The traditional roles have not been entirely replaced or substituted with those found in the capitalistic West. In significant ways, the advent of the tourist industry has meant an *addition* of roles: the coming of tourists to Bali has strengthened the "folk," "ethnic," or "local" survival of Balinese, rather than leading them into the homogeneity of the industrialized world. Their traditional roles as dancers, musicians, artists, or carvers are now alternative and additional sources of livelihood for individuals and whole communities (Plate 2). By no means has the traditional ethos perished, and a complex selective process is operative. Some social units have gained greater cohesion while simultaneously profiting from the tourist industry (a group performing dances, for example). Other social units (such as residential groups) have been necessarily modified. The nuclear family has become more important, especially in the residence compounds for employees provided by the Hotel Bali Beach and other tourist establishments. For this segment, the extended family is still supported, visited, and remembered, but at a distance. Only a few mobile, career-oriented young persons forsake it entirely.

Economic dualism as posited by Boeke is a theory with limited explanatory validity. The many economic interactions between Balinese and tourists bind the two groups in a common field.

Cultural Involution

A continuous syncretic process has occurred in Bali through which elements of the traditions are mixed so that it is practically impossible to distinguish them, yet it is possible to see adumbrations of each in the current blend. More of the ancient *Bali aga* traditions persist in the rural, mountain villages, and more of the modern occur in Denpasar's urban sprawl, but in both contexts it is not unusual to see a blend that is at first blush almost ludicrous. A young woman, for example, appropriately costumed for the festival in which she is to dance, may arrive at the village temple perched on the back of a Japanese 250cc. motorbike, driven by a male friend dressed in jeans and denim jacket. Later, he may appear in the festival acting the part of Prime Minister Gadja Mada in a legendary opera about the Madjapahit Empire. Both of them will participate in the rituals, which include the sacrifice of a live chick or duckling, the possibility of entering a trance, and offerings of rice, fruit, and flowers to the divine powers. Before dawn, as the celebration comes to an end, they will return home on the motorbike to sleep a little before attending classes in medicine or economics at the University. This example illustrates the gamut of historical influences that have created "Balinese culture." The process of synthesis is not unique to Bali, as Redfield has written (1955, p. 25):

> We have studied changes as processes; we see something happening to a native society or culture and we hope to discover significant generalizations. So long as things keep happening it is still a native society or cultural system that we see undergoing change. But when the effects of the outside influences become stabilized we begin to see a new and expanded total system in which part is of native origin and part is of Euroamerican origin.

That an "expanded total system" is coming into being in Bali is obvious. Knowing more of its configurations reward future researchers, and the present study attempts to describe and analyze only that portion of the system touching on tourism. Yet, mass tourism is a crucial aspect of the "expanded total system," for reasons of economics, social order, and aesthetics.

An ironic theme permeates this analysis: modernization in Bali is occurring; tourism introduces new ideas and is a major source of funds. Yet, the tourists expect the perpetuation of ancient traditions, especially in the performing and plastic arts, and would not visit in such numbers if Bali were to become a thoroughly modern island. Both conservatism and economic necessity encourage the Balinese to maintain their skills as carvers, musicians, and dancers in order to have the funds for modernization.

This process is "cultural involution," following the language of Geertz who introduced the notion of "agricultural involution" (1963a). Like Boeke, Geertz emphasizes the traditionalism of the Indonesian peasantry on the "inner islands" of Java and Bali; however, he attributes it not to ancient, indeed static sociocultural patterns, but to the impact of colonialism. Under that aegis, the productivity of the land was increased to absorb a rapidly growing population, and the resultant ornate, intricate social and subsistence systems are explained as "the overdriving of an established form in such a way that it becomes rigid through an inward overelaboration of detail." (1963a, p. 82). Geertz (1963b, pp. 106–20) studied in the town of Tabanan to the west of Denpasar. He found a variety of voluntary organizations (*sekahas*) all organized by the princely families; members were recapping tires, manufacturing ice and soft drinks, trading in coffee and pigs, running new bus routes and stores. He suggested that the noble *Ksatria* families were attempting to retain their power through economic activity since their political prestige had waned:

> Drawing upon the "duck-like" collectivism of the Balinese village and upon their own oligarchic traditions, some of Tabanan's more dynamic aristocrats have initiated a fundamental reorganization of the town's whole economic system. But now that the . . . groups have emerged into the strangely landscaped and ill-defined zone where neither the forms of ancient custom nor those of the modern West offer reliable guides to action, they are gradually coming to discover that these readjusted older patterns are insufficient to complete the task for which they set themselves: . . . Tabanan's [firms] fail to rationalize. (Geertz 1963b, p. 140)

Geertz believes that the princely mentality will not serve the thrust toward development and that the professional manager must come to the fore if there is to be complete modernization. Earlier he noted that the dangers in the Tabanan system were already evident: too many persons were employed for the work to be done, inefficiency was compounded by multiple claims on profits, so there was little capital reinvested by the princes, giving the businesses the quality of a "relief project" (1963b, p. 123). Yet, these criticisms of the development potential in Tabanan may be viewed more positively. If the enterprises do not fail completely, but manage to provide a living for the multitude of employees, then the princes have accomplished at least a part of what they set out to do, that is, maintain power.

More centrally, the liabilities accompanying these changes may become assets if the assumption that Bali needs to go down the path towards an "industrial society" is challenged (Geertz 1963b, p. 140).

If, in the absence of local resources, future "modern society" in Bali could not be supported by the production of petrochemicals or machine tools, then it appears that economic prosperity might be based on cultural production—the establishment of a truly "post-industrial" service industry, which is at least in part what tourism fosters. The entertainment, education, and care of international visitors would then pay the Balinese to do what they have learned to do so well for their own satisfaction—perform their arts and religion, their crafts and ceremonials.

The economic "rationalization" would favor retention of the existent social ties, which connect villagers in overlapping planes (Geertz 1959). The fact is that Balinese are traditionally tied or bound (*kaiket* in Balinese, or *terikat* in Indonesian) to a wide variety of groups—irrigation societies (*subak*), residential hamlet organizations (*bandjar*), temple groupings (*pura*), voluntary associations such as musical and dramatic clubs (*sekaha*), and patrilineal clans (*dadia*) (Lansing 1973). Adaptation with minimal dislocation to the Balinese would then be possible were these traditional social bonds retained to some extent, and in a process of involution not unfamiliar to the Balinese, reaffirmed and gradually rearranged to include their aspirations for more education, better health care, and a share of the technological wealth that accompanies hopes of development in Bali as well as throughout Indonesia. It is these linkages, or more precisely what these ties enable the Balinese to make with them, that will attract, educate, and entertain the tourists.

Hypothetically, a transition to "post-industrial society" in Bali would involve the more ancient social organization; however, another dimension emerges, which has implications for social order and cultural creativity beyond Bali. In contrast to the anomic and uprooted quality of modern urban life, which so many analysts have held to be endemic, in these Balinese efforts may lie a clue to future development of human bonds and loyalties, group responsibilities, and productivity, which might make all human life more humane. However, will temple ceremonies, religious observances, their attendant music, dances, and offerings become a kind of "floor show" for the guests as well as the Balinese? Could they ultimately become a hypocritical "fake culture," created by the secularizing tendencies of tourism, converting *homo religiosus* into *homo economicus?* If the Balinese (and we could extend this supposition to any group) can thus be "bought," so that economic gain is the sole value, then an argument encouraging tourism in Bali will be false prophecy, bad social science, and a plague for the Balinese. I do not foresee this happening as long as Balinese are bound to other Balinese by ties of religious ritual, cosmic orientation, and ancestral loyalty (cf. Boon 1974, p. 24). An analysis of the production of art illustrates Balinese involution. The maintenance of self-respect through "presentation of culture" may be one of the primary factors in continued Balinese existence as a unique cultural entity. In earlier times, "presentation of culture" was demonstrated to other Balinese, to the spirit realm, and to alien neighbors in Java who posed a political as well as a religious threat to the Balinese.

Graburn has described other societies in which the production of art for outsiders has heightened self-identity and self-value, and has encouraged appreciation of indigenous craft and creativity. Analyzing the carving of Canadian and Alaskan Eskimos, the Maori, and the Kamba of Kenya, Graburn (1969, p. 467) has suggested that a "special economic relationship" may develop wherein a small-scale society uses its special skills to its advantage, surpassing the efforts of the larger society: "The Eskimos know that the white man cannot or will not carve soapstone as well as they can. The same might be said of Navajo jewelry and Maori woodcarving."

He has proposed a typology of the "portable arts" for cross-cultural analysis (1) *functional fine arts*, which have great contemporary cultural and social significance to the people themselves, comparable to Balinese offerings and temple carvings; (2) *commercial fine arts*, made for sale to a specialized audience of patrons or connoisseurs, analogous to tapestries hung in Balinese palaces or ornamental carvings decorating the homes of the wealthy; (3) *souvenir arts*, made for sale to a wider audience, which in Bali include inexpensive carvings, paintings, masks, cloths, and jewelry; and (4) *assimilated fine arts*, including those attempts to copy or use the traditional arts of the outsiders by whom they are being influenced. The abstract paintings by the young painters of Ubud—who use "Western" colors and canvases, as well as styles to paint Balinese landscapes, fighting cocks, and portraits—or weavers who make tablecloths with Balinese designs on imported looms reflect this category. Graburn acknowledges that the typology poses some problems of classification, as with the Canadian Eskimo soapstone carvings, which range from "commercial fine art" costing thousands of dollars to the inexpensive, mediocre, hurriedly-done works of less careful craftsmen, which is "souvenir art." A comparable range also occurs in Bali. Graburn (1969, pp. 465–66) discusses the phenomenon of "airport art":

> One fairly obvious feature of the many cases discussed is the recurrent tendency toward simplification, increase in volume, standardization and eventually mass production on an assembly line basis. Such trends almost inevitably preclude the maintenance of functional fine arts, and lead through commercial arts to souvenir art. The volume may rise and the economic support afforded may increase temporarily; however, in such cases the produce must respond to the market and the whole venture becomes subject to the fast changing whims and taste of a mass culture. However, if the majority of the producers are really responsive to the market they will probably adapt and find other products which sell, as long as their own aesthetic impulses are held in abeyance.

In Bali the rush toward standardization and simplification of the souvenir arts exists without the total loss of either functional fine arts or commercial fine arts, because indigenous institutions continue to demand high quality craftsmanship as appropriate offerings for the "divine world." Balinese could ignore this mandate only at personal and corporate peril. In Balinese ethos, to offer inferior gifts to the divine powers, and incur their displeasure, would be silly and shortsighted. It is one thing to sell inferior goods to tourists who do not know or care about artistic expertise, but to shortchange the infinitely superior taste of the spirit realm would be foolhardy indeed. Thus, Balinese craftsmen remain responsive to the marketplace in their willingness to alter the themes of their carvings from *wayang* (shadow puppet) figures to animal figures—and even to busts of Sophia Loren and Raquel Welch—and also responsive to the "market" of the "divine world" whose tastes and expectations are believed to remain infinitely more exquisite. Graburn (1969, pp. 459–66) reported that in other non-Balinese cases, craftsmanship has suffered a loss in quality, because the quality of the spiritual realm evidently suffered from degradation, and the spiritual "audience" was no longer significantly viable. This is not true in Bali, at least not yet.

While the sacred realm authenticates and legitimates Balinese craft, dance, and drama, these aesthetic creations simultaneously receive economic encouragement from tourists. This involution illuminates the peculiar characteristics of classic tradition and modernity which combine to strengthen the Balinese cultural productivity and self-identity.

Field data suggests that Balinese cultural traditions may be preserved by involution. This contrasts with the assertion by both anthropologists and tourists that culture is a static entity, self-contained and isolated, that will wither like a fragile flower when exposed to chilling exterior influences. Graburn's thesis that artistic production may integrate and express the special identity of a minority group is applicable to the Balinese situation. Anthropologists need to develop hypotheses about the conservation of culture in the midst of economic and social changes wrought by the international tourist industry, as well as consider the theoretical significance of anthropological studies of tourism in general.

Conclusion: Bali and Tourism

The reciprocal effect of tourists on contemporary Balinese is profound, and certain to develop in unexpected ways in the future, no matter how visionary analysts may try to be. Nevertheless, I will conclude with some observations about what may be expected in the coming years, based on research experience.

The trend in Bali towards increasing economic dependence on tourism reflects the growing worldwide interconnection between nations. Bali is no longer an insulated, self-sufficient, socioeconomic unit, but is dependent on the world economic cycles, especially those of the developed industrial nations that permit citizens to travel at will. Bali may boom for a period of time, but if economic cycles follow historic precedents, there will be times of world economy slumps, which would distinctly affect contemporary Bali. The "luxury" of tourism may be an early casualty in a general economic depression. Those Balinese dependent on tourism would suffer a loss of income, and need alternate sources of income or "welfare" or "relief." The persistent and ancient ties of kin, neighborhood, and temple obligations might provide sanctuary for the unemployed or underemployed. Reactivated or enlarged traditional social groups could care for members in need, but only if individual family members now supported by tourism maintained their traditional obligations and roles during their halcyon days. If these ties were still extant, Balinese might then weather the economic storms (Lansing 1973). Insofar as the Balinese understand that tourism may

Plate 3. Tourists attending a performance of the Balinese *Barong*. (Batubalan, Bali)

not be a totally dependable source of income, this very uncertainty and fluidity of the industry is likely to encourage the conservation of the social bonds, if for no other reason than a kind of familial social insurance.

Bali is a prime example of ethnic tourism, or as it is termed on the island "cultural tourism." The tourists have become patrons for particular cultural or ethnic expressions, such as the confrontation of the witch (*rangda*) and the dragon (*barong*) (Plate 3), the so-called monkey dance (*ketjak*), and a wide range of wood carvings (cf. McKean 1977). Certain of these activities have become far more widespread in the past decade, and a kind of revitalization of folk arts is found in many villages. For example, school children are taught the *ketjak* dance and music in the elementary grades, and carving has also become a part of the curriculum. The identity of young Balinese is formed, in part, by the recognition that their skills are of value to visitors as well as to local audiences. If they carve or dance or perform in a drama sufficiently well, their abilities may become a source of profit to them and their families, and no small source of personal pride and satisfaction. I talked with several young dancers who recited "famous people and places" who had witnessed their performances, from Robert Kennedy to the Beatles. Memories of tours to Europe, Australia, or North America will be savored and shared.

So the younger Balinese find their identity as Balinese to be sharply framed by the mirror that tourism holds up to them, and has led many of them to celebrate their own traditions with continued vitality.

Certainly there are dangers for the Balinese in embracing tourism, and as in Toraja, the misuse of scarce resources, increased stratification with the "rich getting richer," or environmental and ritual erosion may be so damaging to the indigenous way of life that tourism could eventually be evaluated by both social scientists and local villager as a profound and disastrous blight. The results will depend to considerable degree on actions within the political structures.

The government will necessarily have a great deal to say about the benefits and liabilities that tourism brings to Bali or Toraja. The national government incorporated the growth of tourist facilities as part of the First Five Year Development Plan, and sustains it into the Second Five Year Plan (1974–79). Officials are naturally concerned with increasing the flow of foreign currency into Indonesia, and view tourism as a new and important source of funds. But the provincial and local political structures in Bali have attempted to counter the national pressures on them. They have sought to zone certain areas as "off-limits" to tourist development; they have insisted that the new hotels be erected no higher than the palm trees; they have organized artists and master teachers to review the quality of tourist performances and prevent ill-trained troups from performing; and they have prohibited the sale of tickets to certain cultural activities, such as cremations. They have sought to enforce the national prohibition against alienating land, so that hotels may purchase leases for extended periods, but not the unlimited rights to it. Balinese efforts to have the Hindu religion legitimated under the national Ministry of Religion have met with considerable success, and there is now a national organization, the Parisada Hindu Dharma, with headquarters in Bali.

Safeguards need to be initiated if thoughtless or exploitative tourism, from multinational corporations to Jakarta-based speculators, is not to dominate in Bali. The provincial authorities will need to be vigilant in enforcing existent laws and proposing new legislation on behalf of villagers. Hamlet-level leaders should be better trained and held responsible to both local and regional authorities for the actions of hosts in their treatment of guests. Inspection teams could be appointed by the government to make regular and thorough reports on the processes of cultural change and the impact of tourism; such teams might be composed of prominent international and national scholars, artists, journalists, and professional and working persons who would speak on behalf of the powerless, indicating new problems due to tourism. Such "internal policing" of tourism would be in the self-interest of both the Balinese and the Indonesian government; otherwise the extraordinary cultural riches of Bali might become so debased that they would no longer be of interest to travelers or valued by villagers themselves.

Underlying tourism is a quest or an odyssey to see, and perhaps to understand, the whole inhabited earth, the *oikumene*. Tourism can be viewed as not an entirely banal pleasure-seeking or escapism (MacCannell 1976), but as a profound, widely shared human desire to know "others," with the reciprocal possibility that we may come to know ourselves. As social scientists we need to acknowledge the phenomena inherent in contemporary tourism, and closely study locales with different histories, ecologies, indigenous traditions, and socioeconomic structures to assess the range of tourist-native interactions in a variety of situations. We need to test the theoretical analysis suggested here, that tourism may selectively strengthen local traditions and societies, and then re-examine conditions in Bali, with particular attention to social bonds and cultural performances, cultural involution, and aesthetic-economic interactions. Anthropologists may thus contribute to the expanding appreciation of the tourists and the toured, not only in Bali but throughout the world.

Epilogue

The novelist and journalist Robert Elegant started his visits to Bali in 1955 and has noted some of the cultural changes evident in the subsequent three decades at Kuta Beach: ". . . not long ago one of the loveliest villages of the coast—and now two miles of close packed bars, pubs, restaurants, money changers, supermarkets, boutiques and rooming houses largely populated by young Australians." He asks several penetrating questions central to our anthropological analysis, and to the future of the Balinese themselves: "The old Bali, then, is finished? Has the tidal wave of tourism sweeping over the East Indies washed away the idyllic culture that enchanted earlier visitors? With its hamburger joints, discotheques and Kentucky Fried Chicken outlets, has Bali succumbed to the gritty homogenization of the modern world?"

Elegant replies to these queries: "The short—and definitive answer is: By no means! Beset by invaders for millenniums the Balinese are responding to the latest incursion as they have past incursions, by becoming even more like themselves.

"The fabric of Balinese society is too strong and too flexible to be rent by easy money." (*New York Times* Travel Section, 8 March 1987, pp. 9, 26).

The observations of Elegant summarize that of many others who have visited and studied Bali in recent years.

Surely tourism has expanded enormously since I completed my field-work in 1971, on which the original contribution to this volume was based. And, just as surely, the on-going conservation of Balinese culture is a real-ity, as I have argued; indeed, "tourism may selectively strengthen local traditions and societies." I will turn to each of these topics with more con-temporary data.

The Expansion of Tourism

In 1985, three-quarters of a million tourists entered Indonesia, with 202,421 coming directly to Bali. This was an increase of 6.9 percent over 1984. For the first quarter of 1986, there was an increase of 12.4 percent for all of Indonesia, and 25.7 percent for Bali. Since the average stay was 10.9 nights, we may infer that a high percentage of the tourists who entered Indonesia also visited Bali, although I do not have exact figures: probably more than one-half million visitors touring an island with an indigenous population of 2,672,000 in 1985. Who were these tourists? Australians headed the list, followed by Japanese, other Asians (primarily from Singapore, Malaysia, and Hong Kong), then Europeans and North Americans. There were twice as many male as female tourists, broken into the following age groups: 20 to 29, 24 percent; 30 to 39, 26.9 percent; 40 to 49, 19.6 percent; other, 29.5 percent (data supplied by Office of Information, Consul General, Re-public of Indonesia, New York, from *Travel Indonesia*, July 1986).

The hotel accommodations for these increased numbers of tourists have also expanded with the opening of a new complex at Nusa Dua during the early 1980s. This hotel center was an important part of the Indonesian Five Year Development Plans (REPELITA II and III). The following numbers rep-resent hotel accommodations in Bali (beds): in 1979, 8155; in 1980, 8558; in 1981, 9176; in 1982, 16,460; and in 1983, 16,804 (*Statistical Pocketbook of Indonesia: 1983*, Biro Pusat Statistic, Jakarta, 1984, p. 240).

Two more large hotels, including Bali's first five-star operation, opened during 1984–85, with 680 additional beds. And Club Med started programs in Bali in 1986.

The economic effect of these increased tourists were evident not only along the strip developments bordering Kuta, Sanur, and other tourist-oriented roads from Denpasar to Ubud, but also in the national economic figures. Between 1979 and 1983 foreign exchange earnings from tourism increased from US$188 to US$358 million. These revenues were increasingly important to the Indonesian government as falling oil prices caused severe budgetary crises in Jakarta. To make it as easy as possible for tourists to visit Indonesia, the bureaucratic barriers for visa applications were lowered, so that no visa was required for stays of less than two months.

In the current Five Year Plan (REPELITA IV, 1984–1989) tourism is anticipated to grow 14 percent annually, reaching one million visitors (p. 76). Out of a total development budget of 5379 billion rupiah, the tourism sector is apportioned 216.2 billion rupiah (p. 22).

The presence of hundreds of thousands of tourists annually in Bali is therefore a fact of contemporary history and ethnography, and is not likely to diminish under normal expectations for world travel. The interests of the Indonesian government, the airlines, hotels, and travel agencies, along with the public and private sectors dependent on them are so committed to tourism that Bali will be promoted vigorously throughout the tourist-generating countries. Bali will continue to vie with the Caribbean cruises, European spas, and excursions to Sri Lanka, Nepal, China, and the South Pacific for "market share." Social scientists seeking to understand contemporary Bali will need to take this new phenomenon into account, for it will have an enduring effect on the Balinese and their culture.

Balinese Identity, National Culture, and Tourism

How do the Balinese cope with tourist-driven change in ways which allow them to retain their own identity? I have written that a process of "cultural involution" is at work, as economic necessity and social conservatism "encourage the Balinese to maintain their skills as carvers, musicians, and dancers." But there are other suggestions for the remarkable response of the Balinese, which seem to run counter to the prevailing cultural devastation wrought by tourism. Robert Elegant invokes a string of possible explanations for Balinese cultural stability; the centrality of religious ceremonies and religious bonds; hereditary social structures; the natural abundance of productive resources in a benevolent climate, leading to a harmony which is a "minor miracle." He concludes, "But Bali's stock in trade is miracles."

This Balinese "miracle" is, of course, rooted in the historic values and current behaviors of the Balinese as they interact with each other, with the provincial and Indonesian government, and with the international visitors. From the point of view of the tourist, seeking an idyllic experience, the attempts at interaction with Balinese are not always satisfactory. To be sure, viewing a staged performance or driving between the fields of terraced rice fields and admiring the ingenuity of the workmanship is usually extremely pleasing to visitors, but when they are approached by zealous merchants, pushing wares in a most aggressive fashion, the tourists respond to the crowds of peddlars pressing carvings, weavings, batiks, personal services or other offerings with distaste and even fear or revulsion. The vendors, many of them youngsters, encircle the tourist vans, surround beach strollers, and are not discouraged in their quest for business by cultural codes, governmental restrictions, or exhortations by tour leaders. The result can be disappointing to tourists and the Balinese alike, yet no solution is in sight.

In other areas of management, the local decisions of Balinese villagers have successfully kept tourists in the arena where the Balinese want them, that is, where the visitors do not interfere with their activities. At a provincial and national level, governmental authorities have sought to retain

Plate 4. A masked Bali dancer fitting his costume. (Photo by Karen Goodman)

Balinese culture as an example of the national motto, "Unity in diversity," and there have been strong incentives to value cultural continuity.

The current Five Year Plan puts much emphasis on development that will be in accord with "values of the national character based on Pancasila [Five Basic Principles]" (REPELITA IV, p. 117). The Plan also affirms the role of art and culture in development: "Regional arts will be upgraded to enrich the diverse national arts. The development of the arts will be carried out through quality improvement of traditional arts, upgrading of skills and creativity among the artists, provision of guidance to figures in traditional arts, stimulation of the younger generation's attention to traditional arts, improvement of the living standards of artists and cooperation among institutions and nations, particularly ASEAN countries" (p. 118).

An example of governmental management of the arts was evident at the Indonesian Pavilion of EXPO '86 in Vancouver, British Columbia, where

Plate 5. Balinese *legong* dancers preparing for a performance. (Photo by Karen Goodman)

musicians and dancers performed several times daily for thousands of fair-goers. While a variety of dances was presented, from Java and Sumatra as well as the outer islands, Balinese figured prominently in each show (Plate 4). During August 1986, in conjunction with the fair, the Indonesian government sponsored a *gamelan* festival, with musical ensembles from across North America, Indonesia, and, of course, Bali in attendance.

Not only is the Indonesian government promoting the regional arts as part of their emphasis on the development of a diverse but unified national culture, but there is also support in the Five Year Plan for research into the "reciprocal actions of the development process and the environment . . . influencing the conditions of the national economy in the future," and a call for "research on tourism development, including . . . the impact of tourism" (REPELITA IV, pp. 122, 123).

To further research on Balinese cultural phenomena, an institute of Balinese studies has been established, led by a group of indigenous anthropologists, historians, and linguists (Plate 5). The recognition of the importance of Bali in Indonesia has been strengthened by the growth of tourism.

In a province which has long been in the shade of Javanese political power, this growing recognition of a fundamental interaction between central and regional government is vital to all Balinese. As the Balinese manage the new economic and symbolic power brought by tourism, another dimension becomes apparent in the process of "cultural involution." The ever-adapting Balinese have used the power derived from tourism to gain status within the nation; they have turned to examine and preserve their own culture using the techniques of Western academic institutions, and have reached out to the rest of the world with their cultural performances on the international stage. Such a record requires continued admiration as well as expanded study by anthropologists.

University of Massachusetts, Amherst

7

Tourism in Toraja (Sulawesi, Indonesia)

ERIC CRYSTAL

Indonesia is the largest of the Southeast Asian states, but prior to World War II, tourism was largely confined to Dutch colonials and to occasional elite travelers who principally visited the island of Bali, noted for its ceremonial pageantry. The regime of the late President Sukarno (1945–66), with its anti-Western, often xenophobic policies, effectively discouraged tourism. Under the aegis of the "new Order" that came to power in 1966, tourism accelerated more rapidly in Indonesia than in any neighboring Pacific area country. Annual visits increased from a total of 20,000 in 1966 to 86,000 in 1968, and to 129,000 in 1970, primarily because of the changed political climate. Indicative of the new thrust towards development planning, the Director General of Tourism proclaimed the government's intent to move the "invisible export" [tourism] from its then eighth to third position as an earner of foreign exchange. The first Five Year Plan, implemented in April 1969 stressed tourist development in relatively accessible Java, north Sumatra, and the prime tourist target, Bali. Both foreign investment and tourism were encouraged consonant with the view that much-needed national development could be achieved only with massive infusions of Western capital. A Second Five Year Plan (1974) sought to actively promote tourism and to expand promotional activities to outer island areas including Sulawesi.

Sulawesi (formerly Celebes) is a spider-shaped island, lying east of

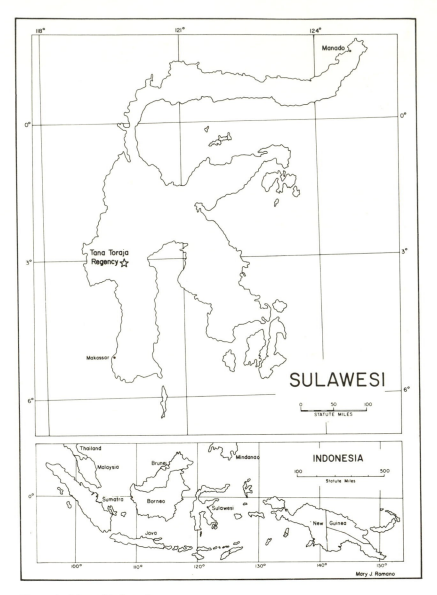

Figure 1. Map of Indonesia.

Borneo (Figure 1). The island population of nine million is unevenly distributed, with some six million inhabitants residing in the southwestern peninsular province of Sulawesi Selatan. This province is further divided into twenty-three Regencies, roughly equivalent to U.S. counties, of which all but one contain predominantly Muslim populations of Bugis/Makassar farmers and coastal traders. The inland Tana Toraja Regency lies at the northern extremity of the province, the population of 320,000 is minimally Muslim (5 percent), about 35 percent Christian, with the balance of the inhabitants adhering to their ancestral faith.

Aluk To Dolo (ceremonies of the ancestors), the traditional religion, includes elaborate rituals that routinely draw hundreds and often thousands of adherents together. Economic planners, seeking ways to attract the tourists to more remote areas, envisaged that these ceremonies would be of touristic interest comparable to the religious rituals of Hindu Bali, and would generate increased visitors and more cash flow. Towards that goal, in March 1973, the Toraja Regency government hosted a local conference on tourist development that was attended by entrepreneurs, civil servants, and religious functionaries of traditionalist, Christian, and Muslim faiths. Government agencies aired plans to make of Tana Toraja an important national tourist center, and solicited the cooperation of local leadership.

The air/sea gateway for travelers to Sulawesi is the capital, Ujung Pandang (formerly Makassar). However, in 1974 the average of six hundred tourists per month who visited the city strained the available accommodations designated as "international caliber." Tourist travel to highland Tana Toraja was once inhibited by a twelve-hour jeep trip, but recent road improvements reduced the drive to six hours by chartered car or bus. However, the elapsed travel time necessitates an average stay of two nights, and hotel accommodations suitable for overseas visitors are very limited in number. Reservations of existent facilities as much as six months in advance has forced the refusal of many impromptu booking requests in recent years. August is the peak month for tourism, with more than twice as many visitors arriving than at any other time.

Despite the long drive and minimal facilities, in 1971 (the first year in which tourist statistics were compiled), 58 overseas tourists visited the Toraja region (Table 1). I analyzed data for the first eight months of 1974, and found that 1376 tourists registered at hotels and pensions in the principal Toraja towns, Makale and Rantepao. Continental Europeans predominated, including 484 French, 144 Swiss, and 124 West Germans compared to only 135 Americans and 56 Japanese. Given then existent travel trends, the

TABLE 1
OVERSEAS VISITORS TO INDONESIA, 1971–1975

Year	Visitors to Indonesia	Visitors to South Sulawesi	Percentage of Sulawesi Visitors to National Total
1971	178,781	58	.03
1972	221,195	427	.19
1973	270,303	422	.15
1974	313,452	1908	.60
1975	366,000	6008	1.64

Source: Idacipta, P. T. *Master Plan for South Sulawesi Tourist Development* 2 (1976): 63.

numbers of Americans and Japanese are expected to increase as Toraja becomes better known. Regional, provincial, and local Regency funds have already been allocated for road and site access improvement and for the promotion of the Toraja region in government and private publications.

This case study assesses the impact of nascent tourism upon a small and fragile society, the Toraja, using a basic data base of 1974 with a brief postscript to highlight the changes from 1974 to 1976. In particular, it focuses on those aspects of traditional culture which draw visitors to a semi-isolated locale, the economic/political climate that encourages the advent of tourism, and the real and potential consequences of organized tourism upon ceremonial and secular aspects of Toraja life.

Toraja Culture

The approximate 192,000 Toraja who practice the traditional faith are bound together by a common language, an extensive network of family and kin, shared customs, and a mutual involvement in an elaborate ritual system founded upon the tenets of their ancient beliefs (Crystal 1976). Ceremonies of death periodically draw hundreds and often thousands together from scattered mountain homesteads. The most frequent Toraja rituals are funerals of one to seven nights duration that follow rigidly prescribed scenarios consonant with the status and economic resources of the family of the deceased. The largest death rituals involve the construction of substantial ceremonial grounds, include the sacrifice of scores of pigs and water buffalo, and present a full panoply of song, dance, and procession that center much of Toraja social life. The funerary traditions of these people are so deeply rooted, and so inextricably bound to indigenous conceptions of status, that even Christian converts adhere closely to the form if not the symbolic content of the great death rituals. Toraja funerals require a great deal of the energy and resources of the village community each year. Failure to reciprocate a debt of meat incurred during the ritual slaughtering of pigs and bovines is a cause for extreme embarrassment and loss of standing in local society. No effort is spared, including the pawning of irrigated rice land, to make good on obligations to neighbors and relatives.

The advent of the Dutch colonial administration in 1906 established health and educational institutions, transport links, and government administration. Far from being pristine, primitive isolates remotely secure in highland eyries, the people of Tana Toraja today are bound to external markets through their production of *arabica* coffee, participate in the national political process, and enjoy a mission-sponsored educational system unequalled elsewhere in the hinterlands of Sulawesi. Rather than attenuating indigenous ritual, access to external markets and to salaried positions for the relatively large number of educated Toraja has actually enhanced the scale of local funerary practice. Combined with spectacular population growth over the past seventy years (allegedly a six-fold increase) the modernization process has in fact occasioned larger and ever more sumptuous death ceremonies. Competition for social status is the rationale underlying the ongoing investment of time and resources in such ceremonies—a stimulus that has been accentuated by the rise of an indigenous, Christian-oriented middle rank group nurtured by local mission stations as a counter-elite to the traditionalist and mainly conservative nobility. Each Toraja death ceremony is ethnically cohesive, yet it expresses the competition for position and standing among individuals and family groups, and masks a demanding ethic of reciprocity.

Social life in Tana Toraja is marked by a constant round of funerary comings and goings. Death and funeral are temporally separated. Large funerals commence months, often years, after the passing of the deceased. The body is washed, wrapped in layers of homespun shroud, and reserved in the house until such time as economic resources can be marshalled to stage the seven-night ceremony (Plate 1). When the funeral finally occurs, grief has been largely assuaged by the passage of time. The mourning taboos regulating food and clothing are confined to select kinsmen or their surrogates. For most participants in the death ritual, and a lavish funeral renews reciprocal relationships through animal sacrifice and meat exchange (Plate 2), and allows for the expression of remorse at the passing of a promi-

Plate 1. Toraja funeral ground. In the forefront is a Lakkian catafalque housing the body.

Plate 2. Bearing sacrificial pigs to a funeral ceremony.

Plate 3. Traditional circle dances transpire at most Toraja rituals. Here, villagers dance the *Ondo* at Ma'bugi' ritual.

nent person. The honor shown the deceased is directly proportionate to the attendance, vigor, and splendor of his funeral.

Although less frequent rituals, such as those of agricultural renewal and trance, perhaps more cogently reflect the fundamentals of indigenous religious belief, the inevitability of death and the manner of its celebration in Tana Toraja render funeral rites a more or less regular feature of Toraja social life (Plate 3). Since rice is harvested once annually and the cultivation of alternate garden crops is not particularly intensive, much time and energy remain for the elaboration of ritual and status concerns. Save for four or five months of intensive irrigated rice cultivation (January–May), the balance of the year may at any time witness large death rituals—often easily accessible to foreign travelers and always appreciated with great interest by visitors to the region.

Political Environment

Until recently, however, commitment to death ritual was somewhat diminished in modernizing, elite circles, tempered by a consciousness of tension between customary village law and modern Indonesian values. Reflective of a generalized tentativeness and embarrassment toward village culture, this attitude mirrored the stance of foreign missionaries and indigenous evangelists who regarded traditional Toraja culture as fundamentally contradictory to the spirit of the modern (interpreted as monotheistic Western) world. Despite almost universal participation in reciprocal exchange in the funerary context, increasing numbers of local inhabitants subject to external influence shared the view that ritual activity must be constricted; consequently, the process of modernization inevitably presaged the disappearance of indigenous religious ceremony.

The most influential Christian organization in the Toraja region is the Gereja Toraja (Toraja Church), closely linked to the Gereformeerden Zendingsbond in The Netherlands. In the view of foreign and indigenous evangelists, the persistence of the autochthonous Aluk To Dolo religion presents a continuing challenge to the efficacy of local missionary activity. To the north, in other upland locales much more isolated than Tana Toraja, groups of highlanders have for decades universally embraced the Christian faith, abandoning *en masse* traditional religion. Yet, in Tana Toraja the best efforts of an expatriate Christian missionary force—numbering in 1971 eight Protestant ministers and fifteen Catholic priests—had yet to tip the balance in favor of a Christian plurality. Resistance remained strong in many quarters. Identification with the new faith brought with it access to education (almost all primary and most secondary schools in Tana Toraja are church affiliated) and entrée to modern Indonesian culture. A direct correlation exists between the image of modernity and conversion to Christianity (or Islam).

For most of the thirty-year history of the Republic of Indonesia, participation in the political process in Tana Toraja was predicated on both adherence to a monotheistic faith and affiliation with the dominant political party. Despite the constellation of Christian modernist and Aluk traditionalist factions, contradictions within the Christian ethos have persisted to the present. The strength of the Toraja Church may be measured in relation to its willingness to compromise with indigenous ceremonial tradition. Sects such as the Seventh Day Adventists—marked in Toraja eyes by their vegetarian ethic and absolute prohibition on consuming the meat of ritually slaughtered animals—have in their wide divergence from traditional practice succeeded in gaining very few converts (and these mostly from the lowest strata of society desiring to opt out entirely from the burdens of reciprocal exchange). The Toraja Church, with nearly 100,000 members, has validated participation in native ritual by its members as long as they abjure any role in Aluk sacrificial process as opposed to the reciprocal exchange of goods. Furthermore, Toraja Church funerals often parallel Aluk rites, with New Testament readings and sermons transpiring in an environment of bamboo ceremonial structures, tethered water buffalo, and slung pigs awaiting dispatch at specific times during the week-long ritual. Urban Toraja as well as rural rice farmers remain locked securely within the system of ritualized reciprocity, and often abandon their urban office desks to attend rural rituals where their own livestock are scheduled to be slaughtered.

A significant change in elite views concerning indigenous ritual has been effected in Tana Toraja in recent years. To some extent this change is merely a reflection of altered political postures at the national level. Parkindo, the party of Indonesian Protestants, had for two decades dominated the local legislature, controlling some 75 percent of the seats. Since 1969 the rapid efflorescence of the new and pervasive tourist ethic had dramatically influenced Toraja self-image as well as development planning. Following the Indonesian national elections of July 1971, the strength of established political parties has steadily diminished under pressure from Golkar (the alliance of "functional groups" that now dominates Indonesian political life as the state party). Just as parties such as the Islamic Partai Mulimin Indonesia and the Soekarnoist Partai Nasionalis Indonesia have in recent years been eclipsed in regions formerly secured under their control, so also has Parkindo now lost its former preeminence in Tana Toraja, reflecting but a shadow of its former power in the regional Toraja legislative council. Displacing Parkindo with its sectarian modernism was the local Golkar faction. Consciously secular in orientation, the government party has enlisted support from Christian, Muslim, and Aluk To Dolo communities; in fact, Aluk adherents currently outnumber Parkindo representatives in the local Dewan Perwakilan Rakyat II (Regional People's Representative Council). The official Toraja government view regarding indigenous tradition has radically changed in the years since Golkar swept to unprecedented victories throughout Indonesia. Where once fundamentalist rigidity banned gambling as sinful, now lotteries and cockfights are held under government auspices with tax monies accruing to development funds. Similarly, the Aluk To Dolo religion has been granted legitimacy by the Ministry of Religion. Aluk officials have been asked to participate as equals with Catholic priests, Protestant ministers, and Muslim notables at the formal celebration of national holidays and during the administration of oaths to court witnesses and newly elected government representatives.

The Tourist Ethic

Inclusion of traditionalist adherents of the Toraja religion in the governmental sphere constitutes a significant departure from previous Toraja political practice. Coupled with the reversion to a traditional market system and linked to the validation of the indigenous faith by the central government, the changes that commenced with the 1971 election signalled a profound attitudinal shift by the local elite towards their own cultural heritage. Closely associated with the above political developments was the rise to prominence of a tourist ethic, the realization that development prospects for Tana Toraja were unusually promising in the tourist field. The promotion and maintenance of the unique ritual system that attracted the attention of early foreign visitors to Tana Toraja became a goal of traditionalist villagers and urban modernizers alike. Thus a congruence of political, economic, and cultural factors tangibly reoriented attitudes toward traditional culture. Where once local leaders had sought to mask their involvement in indigenous ritual, had minimized the number of Aluk practitioners, had constructed new homes in nontraditional style, and, at least in the urban milieu, had manifested negative views concerning the foundations of Toraja culture, these perspectives began to change in light of the newly perceived relationship between tourism and development. Death ceremonies especially came to be reassessed in light of regional economic planning potential and national priorities. For the first time in many years the previously ignored Toraja region began to be featured in provincial capital newspapers, with favorable comments about indigenous ritual practice.

From an anthropological perspective, the short-term consequences of nascent tourism in Tana Toraja must be evaluated positively. Aluk To Dolo religious practice has received official recognition from government, and its adherents now participate in the legislative process. A formerly negative embarrassment concerning local culture has been transformed into positive encouragement of ritual practice by members of the modern elite. Significant changes in the political sphere over the last several years have been reflected in a dramatic alteration of self-image in the Toraja region. One important short-term result of the above is that Christian evangelical threats to the continued existence of the ancestral faith have been checked, as the power of the church and its political allies have abruptly diminished. In part, the effects of tourism in Toraja parallel those in Bali (McKean, chapter 6).

The long-term consequences of tourist influx present a somewhat less sanguine image of the future. Tana Toraja is semi-isolated, relatively over-populated, and presents limited opportunity for the expansion of land under cultivation. Theoretically, the growth of tourist income will provide funds that may trickle down to the village level and enhance living standards generally, but practical results of accelerated tourism may be far different. It appears that those most likely to benefit from the tourist trade are the outside entrepreneurs who send tour groups to Tana Toraja, and the few local merchants and hoteliers who accommodate tourists in the Toraja region. What benefits accrue to traditionalist Aluk villagers who are the mainstay of the ceremonial system? For instance, in 1969/70 some eleven million rupiah (US$27,500) were expended on the construction of a hotel facility by the government. Ostensibly this building was to function as a military hostel for high level delegations inspecting the hinterlands. In fact, the structure represented the first government-sponsored tourist accommodation in the region. Tastefully designed according to indigenous motifs and situated in a rural area overlooking the Sa'dan river, this large hotel cost money that, from the perspective of local requisites, might better have been used to eradicate endemic malaria, improve grain and vegetable seeds, or purchase fertilizers.

In 1971, the provincial press announced several major death ceremonies. One article proclaimed that facilities were being arranged for two hundred tourists; another suggested that food would be provided for overseas guests. Subsequently, an international English-language publication carried an Indonesian government-sponsored advertisement enticing tourists to Tana Toraja, now newly dubbed the "land of the heavenly kings." Such stories, aside from ethnographic inaccuracy, tend to create unreal expectations on the part of future visitors and provide a basis for exploitation of Toraja villagers in their new role of international "hosts." Dating to the era of Dutch colonial administration, occasional foreign visitors to Toraja funerals have been offered, free of charge, sleeping space and sumptuous meals prepared from the sacrificial animals. Of little consequence in the years past, this practice in an era of organized tourism now threatens to deprive village participants of their principal source of meat. Every gram of animal protein offered to tourists reduces the supply available to villagers, whose consumption of high grade protein is already limited to ritual contexts. Similarly, at large funeral feasts, both shelter and potable water are normally in short supply. To provide these essentials free of charge to an increasing number of tourist "guests," because the government seeks to stimulate tourism, becomes an economic burden upon simple peasants. In one known instance, a member of the deceased's family attempted to sell tickets of entry to the ceremonial grounds. Outraged kinsmen quickly thwarted the effort because tradition demands that all who wish to join in the rites of mourning must be welcomed without qualification. In another case, organizers of a major ceremony altered the normal course of the ritual to create for the several score foreign tourists a more dramatic and shorter spectacle. Conflict between traditionalist and modernist factions halted the ceremony until government officials stepped in and supported the innovators.

In an area of nascent tourism, problems in the host-guest relationship seem certain to occur. Government officials recently embarked on a misdirected tourist development scheme at Lemo, which is a prime attraction because of a large burial cave complex. The road to the site was greatly improved, and in accord with the local notion that good lavatory facilities are a constant preoccupation of Westerners, toilets were constructed although Lemo is less than twenty minutes from the customary tourist hotel. Great care was taken to whitewash the plaster walls with the brightest paint, to roof the new structure with gleaming galvanized iron, and to incise the lavatory doors with traditional patterns. Unfortunately this building was incongruously situated precisely in the line of sight from the parking area, and destroyed the once pristine vista of burial caves and funeral statues directly visible from the road. Of more consequence is the desecration of the striking ancient burial locale at Londa. Here a pristine assemblage of ancient carved burial vessels has been marred by the drawing of initials on wooden sarcophagi and painting of names on limestone-faced walls. Perpetrated in the 1960s by Indonesian visitors attending a national Christian youth group conference, this locale stands today as an ugly reminder of the malevolent potential of unregulated tourism.

Conclusions

The culture of Tana Toraja is a living example of autochthonous Southeast Asian architectural, craft, and religious tradition. Integrated politically into modern Indonesia, this rather isolated locale figured minimally in the national development planning until a new government began to promote international tourism by tapping the cultural resources of the population. As of the data base of November 1974, the relatively small scale growth of commercial tours to the Toraja Regency have had little negative impact and may even, in some cases, have supported a renewed interest in local ritual and artistic tradition, as McKean (chapter 6) has suggested is also true in Bali.

However, the possible long-term effects of a steady, if not massive, tourist influx must be considered. Almost as if he were writing specifically about Toraja, Nuñez (1963, p. 352) advises, "In the newly developing countries of today's world, when the larger society (particularly the formal apparatus of the state) takes special interest in previously overlooked rural communities, for whatever reason—tourism, nativist or nationalist—the anthropologist should be alert to the consequences." Predictions concerning the possible future effects of tourism must be tentative. Already, the tourist ethic in Sulawesi has drawn Tana Toraja into a position of unaccustomed prominence in provincial and national planning, compromising the highlanders' ancestral prerogative of ritual self-determination. Increasing tourism may necessarily lead to the commercialization of religious rites. If so, then Toraja ritual will become commoditized, and if one aspect of the ritual—the gift of food—is changed, can all other aspects of the complex customs associated with funerals remain untouched? As an alternative, the ritual process may be reorganized, turned into a "show" for the tourists with the potential of stripping the ceremonies of their integral meaning, as with the *Alarde* festival of Spain (Greenwood, chapter 8). To date the promotion and operation of tourism is external, and it appears that the primary benefits are also external.

There is every indication that tourism will become a constant and growing feature of Toraja life. Intelligent planning will be required if the deleterious effects of tourism such as the desecration of sites, sacrilege of ritual, and the victimization of traditionalist peasants are to be forestalled. Can the small Toraja region with its marked social, religious, and political factions maintain the delicate composite of cultural integrity, educational opportunity, and economic development that presently hold considerable promise? Will the tourist impact ultimately serve as a positive incentive for economic development, or become a negative stimulus to the dissolution of a fragile highland culture? No longer proud masters of their destiny and possibly soon doomed to become exhibitors of "quaint customs" for tourist eyes, the future of Toraja will depend to a great extent upon the foresight and capabilities of national, provincial, and regency officials.

Postscript

During 1976 I returned to Tana Toraja for brief visits in May and June, and for a six-week sojourn in August and September as consultant to BBC Documentary Films. The rapid development of tourism was startling, with a three-fold growth between my data base of 1974 and 1976 (Table 1). When I initiated the fieldwork in 1971, tourists were a curiosity (Plate 4),

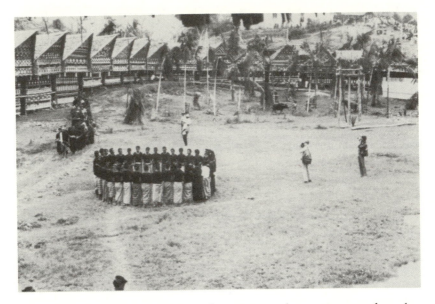

Plate 4. Tourist photographers: an early (1971) French tour group at a large funeral at Tondon village, Tana Toraja. The structures are temporary residences for the mourners.

but by 1976 tourists from Europe and North America had become a firmly fixed feature of the Toraja social landscape. *Asia Travel Trade* (February 1977, p. 23) estimates that 10,000 foreign tourists visited Sulawesi in 1975 and that the numbers increased to 12,000 in 1976. The official statistics cited in Table 1 are derived from reports submitted by local hotels. However, my informal queries of many 1976 visitors revealed they had not been asked to complete any registration forms and thus their presence was unrecorded. During August and September, I observed that hotels in Tana Toraja were filled to capacity with mainly European tourists. Some evenings the 150 seats in the two prime Chinese restaurants in Rantepao were occupied entirely by foreign visitors. Therefore, I believe the official statistics are too conservative, and that the *Asia Travel Trade* estimates are more realistic.

One unforeseen development in 1976 was the degree to which French enterprise had entered and now dominates the Toraja tourist market. Travelers originating in Paris, on Singapore-bound charter flights, made two-week trips around Indonesia including visits to Jakarta, central Java, Bali and Tana Toraja (total price about US$1000). Chartered buses met them at the

Province airfield as they arrived from Bali by plane, and drove them directly to Tana Toraja over 285 kilometers of newly improved, all-weather road. Five French nationals, stationed in Tana Toraja during the months of July through September, escorted the visitors and arranged local transportation. Duties of the expatriate guides also included arranging walking tours through the Toraja countryside and scheduling overnight sojourns in "picturesque" mountain villages where they could enjoy "local color."

The influx of tourists to Tana Toraja (at least 90 percent of all tourism in South Sulawesi Province flows to this area) has created new economic opportunities but also increased cultural and administrative dilemmas that have not been squarely confronted. Tana Toraja has experienced a boom in hotel construction, an inflation of land values in potential construction sites, and a rush to improve access roads to prime physical attractions. Accommodations available to visitors range from small US$1.50 per night guest houses to the international caliber Toraja Cottages (daily rate, US$30.00, double occupancy) opened early in 1976. Most of the nineteen hotels are owned and operated by native Torajas, and most facilities retain Torajan motifs in architectural style and decor. The magnitude and rapidity of the shift from nascent to charter tourism was totally unexpected, and administrative officials were ill-prepared to cope. Local governmental policy has quietly restricted hotel development to the environs of the Makale-Rantepao axis road, and also to date has dissuaded capital from beyond the borders of Tana Toraja to invest in the tourist infrastructure within the region. In view of the national policy to encourage tourism, and the "ripple" effect that tourism generates, the prospect that the industry will remain under tenuous local control is dim.

Tana Toraja may be unique, and worthy of on-going careful study, because of the dramatic change within two years. The area has passed directly from the obscurity of elite, ethnic tourism to become a target for cultural, charter tourism without passing through any of the intermediary stages (see Introduction). It is too soon to fully assess the touristic impact, but some trends are evident. The local Torajas are bewildered, and uncertain as to the choices open to them, or their outcome: (1) If they open their villages, and their ceremonies, to tourism for the sake of economic gain, they are victimized by the compromise of cultural integrity; (2) If they exclude the tourists, they are victimized by the inflation accompanying the influx, and enterprising neighbors reap the profits. Cultural conservatism does not "pay." During the tourist season of 1976 it was evident that rituals were being commercialized as "spectacles" for the foreigners, including being rescheduled at the request of foreign guides. Further, the disappearance of antiquities into the souvenir market indicated another potential cultural loss. My cautious optimism based on the 1974 data is strained, and further field research is needed. If, as anthropologists, we have the capacity to guide, our skills should be applied here and now lest this fragile mountain community, which has only its cultural traditions to attract tourism, loses both its heritage *and* the tourists.

Epilogue

This essay reflects upon the decade of tourist development which has passed between the writing of the original essay on tourism in Toraja for *Hosts and Guests* and 1987. The author has been fortunate to have been able to revisit the Toraja area in 1976, about a year after submitting the chapter for the first edition of *Hosts and Guests;* in 1983; and twice in 1985. During each of these visits attention was directed to the formal development of tourist enterprise and, more important in my view, to the perceptions of the tourist phenomenon as garnered from reactions of community leaders, urban entrepreneurs and rural village farmers in Tana Toraja. When the original discussion of global tourist issues commenced at the 1974 Mexico City American Anthropological Society meetings, tourism was a fresh and relatively unknown phenomenon in this area. Even the term *turis* was new to the lexicon of South Sulawesi Province. Was a *turis* a specific nationality, an important government guest, or an affluent visitor from afar just looking around?

In the intervening years the tourist industry in Toraja has developed with a rapidity that has startled government planners, surprised local inhabitants, and delighted those few Indonesian and foreign entrepreneurs with the capital sufficient to invest in what now is a well-established international business enterprise (Plate 5). Certain epiphenomena of the tourist influx have also shocked and saddened Toraja villagers, who look back wistfully to times when their major life crisis rites and precious heirloom artifacts were of no interest to outsiders. Unknown to foreign travel agents and, indeed, the world at large fifteen years ago, Tana Toraja is now an established international tourist destination. As of January 1986 Tana Toraja was designated the second most important tourist development region (after Bali) in all of Indonesia.

In order to assess the impact of tourism and the emergence of the formerly isolated Toraja culture area as a major focal point of international travel to Southeast Asia in the 1980s it will be helpful to recall briefly the

Plate 5. German tourists ponder a guidebook to Indonesia. (Bali 1987)

extent to which Tana Toraja was shielded from the outside world as late as 1969. Completing fifteen months of anthropological fieldwork in the area in May 1969, I had carefully noted that not one article concerning the Toraja region had ever appeared in the local South Sulawesi press. Indeed, more than veiled hostility toward the Toraja region was often expressed by Muslim lowlanders in the national capital. Twice (in 1953 and 1958) armed conflict between the largely Christian and animist Toraja had erupted in the Toraja homeland as irredentist Torajas reacted strongly to interference from the lowlands. During the years 1951–65 a widespread Darul Islam anti-government Muslim rebellion engulfed almost all of rural South Sulawesi in internecine conflict. From the end of World War II until 1965 Tana Toraja was essentially closed to the outside world. Foreign missionaries did reside in the area (sometimes escorted by armed convoy from the provincial capital of Makassar). Educational, church, and national political institutions evolved much more slowly here than in other areas of Indonesia. Contact with coastal cities, with the national capital at Jakarta, and with the outside world remained highly restricted in the quarter century between the displacement of the Dutch by the Japanese and the end of the Darul Islam rebellion in February 1965. Travel to the provincial capital was a difficult and oftentimes dangerous journey in those times of armed rebellion. As late as 1963 the *Bupati* or local government administrator of the Toraja area was assassinated when his jeep was attacked by Muslim rebels just a few kilometers south of the Tana Toraja border. Even in 1968–69, scheduled bus service to Makassar (renamed Ujung Pandang in 1971) was erratic. Only one scheduled departure left for the capital each day. No air link existed. The cost of goods ordered from Makassar was oftentimes 50 percent higher in Toraja shops due to transportation surcharges. In sum, Tana Toraja during the 1960s remained semi-isolated from much of the rest of the world. The dirt road leading to Tana Toraja from the coastal town of Pare Pare in 1968 was frequently impassable due to mud slides. The 180-mile journey to the province capital required either a large truck or four-wheel drive vehicle during much of the year. Bus trips sometimes took twenty-four hours as vehicles became mired in mud, broke down, or were hampered by rock slides.

The physical and political isolation of Tana Toraja persisted during the post-World War II years when most of Southeast Asia came to be influenced by foreign ideological, economic, and political forces. Political developments in South Sulawesi province thus tended to buttress the fundamental cultural conservatism of the Toraja. A living artifact of late neolithic Southeast Asian culture, Toraja architecture, ceremonial life, agricultural subsistence systems, and folk arts recall the most elemental traditions of Southeast Asia (Plates 6 and 7). Isolated and on the defensive, the Toraja region in the years 1942–65 remained relatively unaffected by the outside world. A handful of tourists and adventurers, travel buffs, and international church leaders did visit the region between 1963 and 1970. Tourist visits to the area began to make an impact as early as 1971. And yet at that early date the Toraja area was relatively unknown in Indonesia as a whole and had just begun to be reported on in international travel sections of newspapers. The watershed date for tourist development in the region was the 1974 Jakarta meeting of the Pacific Area Travel Association, where travel agents from around the world were given tours of Tana Toraja.

When my original article on tourism in Toraja was written in 1975, approximately 2500 tourists were recorded as visitors to Tana Toraja by local government authorities. Most certainly the total was underrecorded at that time due to lack of systematized data-gathering procedures. By 1983 South Sulawesi provincial tourist arrivals had risen to 30,000 yearly visitors; some 40,000 tourists (almost all of whom were destined for Tana Toraja) were recorded in 1985. In a decade the isolation of the Toraja area was irrevocably shattered. If in 1968 scheduled buses departed but once daily for the provin-

Plate 6. *Tongkonan*, traditional Toraja houses, present fascinating examples of traditional Toraja architecture. (1987)

Plate 7. Toraja traditional artists, such as this *makatia* funeral dancer, generate much tourist interest. (1985)

cial capital, now twenty buses roar down the all-weather highway from Tana Toraja toward the coast. The trip by scheduled ground transport that once frequently took twenty-four hours is now reduced to ten. A small airport was opened in 1984 in Tana Toraja, with thrice weekly flights linking the area to Ujung Pandang. Once veritably unknown even to most Indonesians, the Toraja region is now often discussed in the national as well as in the local South Sulawesi press. In response to international tourist interest in Tana Toraja, domestic tourists have begun to follow in the wake of European, Japanese, and American visitors. Prior to 1973 very few Muslim community leaders, academics, or entrepreneurs had ever visited the Toraja area. Indeed, most such individuals expressed no interest in the region, seeing little merit in visiting an area beyond the pale of Muslim civilization, inhabited by "dog-eating primitives," and adhering to strange cultural traditions centering upon gargantuan ceremonies of death. Now, in the wake of foreign interest, few South Sulawesi opinion-makers would wish to admit that they had never visited the nearby, world-famous Toraja area.

Major national companies such as Pacto tours escort tourists from their arrival in Jakarta through central Java, to Bali, and then on to Tana Toraja. Such domestic firms have worked out handling arrangements with foreign travel agencies that are not allowed to directly operate within Indonesia. Most Toraja believe that the great profit from Toraja tourism is remanded to domestic, non-Toraja tour companies headquartered in Jakarta with agents and facilities (buses and so forth) in Ujung Pandang. Toraja entrepreneurs (hoteliers, a few restaurateurs) of course have also profited from the tourist trade. Jobs have been provided for some tour guides (Plate 8), drivers, and, certainly, service personnel at the tourist facilities. No study has ever been undertaken to assess the amount of money flowing into the area from tourists. Clearly tourism has had little impact on most of the 75 percent of Torajas who subsist as village farmers. Only those villagers engaged in the fabrication of craft products for sale at major Toraja urban centers have been affected by the explosion of tourist arrivals in the area in recent years.

As visitors exit the Mandai airport just north of Ujung Pandang they are confronted with a new welcoming monument as they drive on to the main highway. "Welcome to Sulawesi" is incised in a large concrete monolith upon which is painted a large tourist map of South Sulawesi province. Three tourist destinations are noted on the map: Ujung Pandang City, Bantimurung Park, and Tana Toraja. Since the first discussion of tourist policy initiatives in South Sulawesi in the early 1970s, considerable confusion has reigned over prospective objects of tourist interest. Early tourist brochures

Plate 8. Toraja tour guide poses with "tourist shirt." (1985)

issued in Ujung Pandang identified the Ujung Pandang central mosque and central marketplace as objects of potential tourist interest (they have never attracted any attention whatsoever). Tourism to Toraja itself developed initially in spite of the provincial officials' skewed perceptions of Western tastes. Such perceptions (in some part based upon coastal bias toward the culture of the highlands) were never shared by Javanese officials in Jakarta, who early on appreciated the tourist potential of the area. Indeed, it was a Javanese general who, as commander of South Sulawesi regional forces in 1971, erected the ceremonial gateway welcoming visitors to the area at the southern border of Tana Toraja. Prior to this initiative no government official in South Sulawesi had ever made an attempt to identify the Toraja region as an area of special interest. Bantimurung waterfall and natural area is of passing interest to tourists. Ujung Pandang city, with its large Chinatown, historic Confucian temples, picturesque harbor region, and interesting curio shops does provide interesting diversions for tourists ultimately bound for Tana Toraja. But, in fact, the singular tourist attraction in the area is Tana Toraja itself. Thousands of tourists annually land at the Mandai airport north of Ujung Pandang and proceed directly to Tana Toraja without stopping either in the city or at Bantimurung Park on the road north. With the recent opening in 1984 of the Makassar Golden Hotel and the somewhat less impressive Hotel Marannu, first-class urban accommodations have become available in Ujung Pandang. The Makassar Golden is particularly noteworthy because it employs Toraja architectural motifs, dominating much of the prime waterfront area of the city. Replete with French restaurant, the hotel has a swimming pool, and ocean-view rooms listed at us$100.00 a night.

Tourism to Tana Toraja has clearly become a phenomenon of international significance. In South Sulawesi itself the tourist business has generated hundreds if not thousands of jobs and has indirectly accounted for major improvements in the local infrastructure ranging from the extension of runaways to handle Garuda DC-10 jumbo jets to the paving of the highway from Ujung Pandang through to Tana Toraja. Well-established tourist routes currently funnel visitors from Germany, France, Switzerland, the Netherlands, Japan, and, to a much lesser extent, the U.S. to Ujung Pandang and then through to Tana Toraja. Torajan culture, once spoken of in derogatory terms, is now featured nationally in Indonesia as a major and important component of multicultural Indonesia. The fact that the Toraja house was chosen as the design for the Indonesian 5000 rupiah bill (equivalent to us$5 when first printed) further underscores the degree to which the formerly isolated and sequestered Toraja culture has been promoted and nationally embraced. Calendars with neo-Toraja designs and motifs (models garbed in what non-Torajas imagine is traditional Toraja dress) are found in most hotel rooms in Ujung Pandang.

In the Toraja culture region itself tourist influence is apparent immediately. Driving across the southern border of Tana Toraja one passes through the now somewhat weatherworn cement ceremonial gate that welcomes visitors to the area. About 22 kilometers to the north in the center of Makale town are arrayed a number of traditional Toraja rice granaries, the only such structures in the area that serve no function other than to bemuse the locals and (theoretically) intrigue the visiting tourist. Small guest lodges are found on the outskirts of Makale town and several major hotels are situated along the road as it makes its way northward 18 kilometers to Rantepao, the larger of the two Toraja towns. At the central intersection here is a concrete monument in the form of a large Toraja ritual dish atop which sits a frayed wooden Toraja model house. Once again, these objects were constructed early in the 1970s in the first rush of enthusiasm for tourism. They are of no interest to either locals or foreign visitors but stand as mute testimony to the indigenous officials' misperceptions of foreigners' interests.

Many more hotels, small and large, thrive in Rantepao. Once every six days a large market assembles in Rantepao that does constitute a legitimate tourist attraction. One of the newer village trades is the fabrication of tourist art, much of it for the domestic market, some for export. Tourism has reinvigorated formerly moribund Toraja crafts such as weaving, ikat dyeing, and beadwork (albeit with gaudy new imported beads). Probably as many finely woven Toraja sun hats are sold to tourists these days as to local village women. Village artisans flock to the phalanx of curio stores that surround the principal Rantepao marketplace on market day to sell their wares to the proprietors. Model Toraja homes, sample incised house panels, food-serving trays, textiles, and basketry comprise contemporary Toraja folk and tourist arts. The traditional water buffalo market still takes place a half kilometer down the road. The sales of *tuak* rice wine, carp cooked with the jet black condiment *pamerasan,* and a wide array of fruits, vegetables and staples remain brisk as villagers throng to Rantepao on market day. Tourists come and observe and sometimes buy; however, tourists do not displace or dislocate the traditional economy.

Inside the curio shops that stand before the Rantepao market are sometimes found valuable artifacts: objects that have never been displayed in the Jakarta Central Museum. Toraja arts have become the object of intense bidding by international art dealers. Some of these objects are displayed on demand. Others must be viewed outside of Tana Toraja, where they are spirited away by thieves under cover of nightfall to far off trade entrepôts. Sacred painted or batik decorated cloths, termed *sarita* or *mawa*, are found for sale at prices ranging in the many hundreds of dollars. The sacred textiles of the Toraja in traditional times might never be sold or traded once utilized in a family religious context; nowadays rapid economic and social change (of which tourism is but one element) has rendered such valuable heirlooms as useful commodities in the eyes of some for financing a year of higher education, a trip to Jakarta, or a new motorcycle.

One of the sadder consequences of change in Toraja has been the accelerated loss of these precious heirlooms and cultural artifacts. There is no doubt that tourism has played a significant role in this process. In 1969 beautiful strands of ancient beads were sold in each Toraja market by itinerant vendors. By 1976 villagers in the marketplace and the vendors themselves reported that such old beads were becoming increasingly scarce due to demand by visiting French tourists. By 1983 such beads were "effectively" gone in the sense that they were out of the price range of the average village consumer. Tourists and itinerant international art dealers have demonstrated an insatiable appetite for old pieces of Toraja folk art. Newly crafted house panels, baskets, textiles, or carvings do not satisfy these most particular appetites; only the oldest, most weathered and most exotic-looking pieces will do.

Most devastating to the people of Toraja is the rape of ancestral statuary that continues unabated at this writing. The carving of ancestral images is common in a number of relatively isolated culture regions of Indonesia and, indeed, was highly developed in many parts of the ancient world. *Tau tau*, or funerary statues, in Tana Toraja are carved of extremely durable jackfruit wood. Only the largest death ceremonies are embellished with a near life-sized wooden image of the deceased. After interment of the deceased in a limestone cave vault, the statue is placed in a gallery near the burial site. In 1969, two years before the first depredations were recorded, Tana Toraja preserved literally thousands of such statues in burial sites spread over much of its 3000 square kilometers of territory. When my first article was written in 1975 I did not realize that the first highly selective raids on Toraja statuary were already taking place. By 1985 Toraja *tau tau* were bringing us$6000 sale prices in Los Angeles. During the past years agents with 300mm telephoto lenses have been dispatched from Western Europe to compose albums of "available" statuary from which potential customers could select their desired piece. Working in league with local Toraja thieves, foreign agents spirited the statues from Tana Toraja, and transshipped them by air and sea from Den Pasar, Bali, to overseas destinations. So sacred are these statues within Tana Toraja that no one would dare to openly sell such artifacts within the region itself.

In 1985 I was able to look into this phenomenon somewhat more closely. In two of eighty-one Toraja formal village sites, over half of the extant *tau tau* had either been stolen or destroyed within the past five years. The two prime tourist destinations in Tana Toraja are the impressive limestone burial sites at Londa and Rantelemo. The national Directorate-General of Tourism improved Londa by building elaborate concrete steps that descend to the mouth of a deep cave where archaic wooden sarcophagi and scattered bones of long deceased ancestors may be viewed. A gallery of *tau tau* figures rested for centuries above the cave, surrounded by the carved wooden doors of the many burial vaults that have been chiseled into the surrounding limestone cliff face. Over the past five years several statues had been stolen from this site. By July 1987 all statues had disappeared from the Londa site. At Rantelemo—which has, perhaps, the most impressive array of *tau tau* wooden statues anywhere in Tana Toraja—tourist development funds once again financed an excellent access road. Here at least two score statues have been stolen from the lower levels of the site. Where once seventy imposing traditional wooden figures were arrayed against a great limestone cliff wall, today only a scattered handful remain.

The loss of statues from the two principal tourists sites in Tana Toraja indicates the freedom with which thieves operate, the inability of local and national governments to confront the problem of thievery, and the futility of improving the infrastructure when elemental cultural preservation precautions are not taken. During two visits in 1985 I spoke extensively with Toraja villagers and community leaders. All interviewed were distressed at the theft of cultural artifacts. Whether Christian or Aluk To Dolo in religious orientation, all felt that the statues were an elemental part of their family heritage: highly valued representations of prominent ancestors whose memories have been revered for decades and generations. For each statue stolen intact probably two are destroyed in situ. During visits to several little-known burial sites, villagers led me to ancient sacred grottoes where beautiful statues lay dismembered and chopped into pieces. Often only the heads of the *tau tau* (which are oftentimes detachable) are taken. On occasion, three or four statues are destroyed in the process of extracting a particularly fine piece intact. Interviews with village chiefs in affected areas indicated that at least half of the statues in their villages have been stolen within the last four years. Some thieves have been caught; but the most severe sentence ever meted out was three months in jail.

As indicated earlier, accelerated social change in Tana Toraja should not be singularly attributed to tourism. Tana Toraja possesses the finest educational system in all of rural South Sulawesi. Developed over half a century by missionaries, Toraja Protestant and Catholic schools have produced high caliber high school and technical school graduates whose skills have been readily utilized in government service, the armed forces, and private industry. Very few employment opportunities are available within Tana Toraja itself. Out-migration of Torajas to the timber operations of Kalimantan, nickel mines elsewhere in Sulawesi, and civil service positions throughout Indonesia has accelerated contact with greater Indonesian culture, enhanced the local economy through significant monthly remissions, and created something of a residential building boom within Tana Toraja itself. Conversions to Christianity have continued apace as well, such that at present only 17 percent of the Toraja population is said to adhere to the traditional religion, Aluk To Dolo, with the balance embracing Christianity. National television is relayed to receivers from a station in the vicinity of Rantepao. Government schools are now accessible to all Toraja villages and, indeed, elementary education is compulsory. Toraja economy and culture have been much more closely integrated with national economy and culture than ever before due to increased communications, the extension of educational opportunities and facilities, and the placement of graduates in important and well-paying positions.

Despite the process of social change, Toraja adherence to traditional ritual form and ceremonial display remains strong. The single significant factor attracting tourists to Tana Toraja is the vital ceremonial system of the region that centers on ceremonies of death. Toraja is not a place to come and relax or to be entertained. It is a place to learn, study, and wonder at the complexity of Southeast Asian ritual, art, and natural beauty. All tourists to Tana Toraja hope to witness a traditional Toraja funeral (again and again visitors to Toraja rituals have commented, "This is the most interesting event I have ever witnessed"). Once rare curiosities at Toraja ceremonial events, tourists from afar now frequently attend the funerals of five days' duration in Tana Toraja during the months from May to September. The impact of tourists at these events varies greatly. Some tour companies are quite sensitive to the needs of local villagers—sometimes supplying a pig to festival organizers and packing in their own food and drink. Others have imposed greatly on the hospitality of the Toraja which traditionally commands that foreign guests be feted with food and drink as befits high-status notables entering a ceremonial site. In such cases, the coffee, cakes, and food shared with visitors are taken from the limited stocks available to ritual participants. Due to population expansion, Torajas frequently note that the portions of meat distributed at rituals have been declining in quantity in recent years. Some tour operators have been unconcerned about the consequences of imposing upon the hospitality of local villagers, most of whom eat meat only at rare ritual events. At this point in time tourist attendance at major funerals has become quite regular in Tana Toraja. Some villagers may ask for money if visitors wish to photograph them. Children very frequently beg for candy—and again and again tour operators and foreign visitors oblige.

Generally speaking, in regard to the accuracy of the information about Toraja culture imparted to tourists, there has been little effort to orient, communicate with, or educate visitors about traditional Toraja culture. In 1985 at least half of the guides leading foreign visitors around the area were of non-Toraja origin. Many of the Toraja guides, skilled in foreign languages, are third-generation Christians born in urban areas with little or no familiarity with their native culture. No visitor orientation center exists to meet the demonstrated visitor demand for accurate information. Despite the fact that all foreign tourists to Tana Toraja are cultural tourists, drawn to the area because of its impressive ceremonial system and vital traditional arts, to date no effective effort at communication concerning Torajan culture has been undertaken.

A great paradox is apparent in the Tana Toraja of today. Just at the time when much world interest is focused on this area (at least eight anthropologists currently engaged in Toraja studies; 40,000 visitors a year; major if illicit attention from international art dealers), the isolation of Toraja traditionalists remains almost complete. Despite the depredations of art thieves, the impositions of tourists at ritual events, and the economic and social forces of cultural change impelled by enchanced contact with the outside world, Toraja religious, artistic, and ceremonial traditions remain vital. Toraja rituals are genuine, not tourist shows. Yet no benefits of tourism accrue to those traditional leaders who vouchsafe much of the cultural heritage of Tana Toraja that draws so many tourists from afar.

Foreign tourists mightily desire to learn about the rituals that they are often fortunate enough to witness, are intrigued with the primal religious vigor of Toraja ceremonies, and are captivated as well by the traditional arts of the area that are laden with symbolic meaning. On the other hand, Toraja traditionalist leaders today find themselves very much on the defensive. Their traditional religion is under severe pressure from Christian evangelists who preach that to be modern one has to abandon the old Toraja ways. The tourist shop in the three-star Makassar Golden Hotel may indeed sell T-shirts emblazoned with the legend, "Tana Toraja—land of Aluk To Dolo," but few if any visitors will understand what that legend means. No ritual specialists in the Toraja hills will benefit from the sale of such clothing. Traditional Toraja ceremonies are the area's prime attraction for foreign tourists. Yet the guarantors of Toraja traditions, traditionalist villagers and religious specialists, benefit the least from the tourist influx. Those Toraja who have become cultural interlocutors for visitors from afar, the guides, are often estranged from their own traditional culture. Immersed in the study of foreign languages and the development of their own enterprise, they have little interest in approaching traditional religious specialists for information. Indeed, one of the most unfortunate characteristics of contemporary Toraja society is the widening conceptual chasm between those who wish to maintain a traditional world-view and agents, interlocutors, and institutions of change. Thus, the Toraja government school system has never sought to involve experts in Toraja folklore, oral history, performing arts, or ceremonial tradition in the classroom—ironic, indeed, in an area with a traditional culture so vital that it has attracted major international attention from around the world.

Within the past decade tourism in Tana Toraja has changed from a peripheral phenomenon intriguing to locals and bemusing to provincial officials into a major and probably permanent fact of local economic, social, and cultural life. It is probably fair to say that international tourist arrivals in the area up to the present have come about in spite of, rather than due to, government efforts to promote tourism in Tana Toraja. Serious central government concern for tourist development in Toraja followed long after European tour operators from France, Switzerland, and Germany independently discovered the attractions of the region, established working relationships with national tour companies, and stimulated, at least indirectly, the building of adequate hotel facilities in the region. Now, with the recent designation of Tana Toraja as the second most important tourist destination in Indonesia, only active government intervention in concert with local Toraja community leaders can preserve cultural artifacts, orient visitors, and regulate the imposition of external demands upon local village generosity. If significant efforts are not made to control the rape of sacred Toraja cultural artifacts, the approach to ritual events, and the communication of information to cultural tourists, the future consequences of the forthcoming mass tourism in Tana Toraja will be much more destructive than has already been the case. Unlike the resilient four million person strong civilization of Bali to the south, the relatively small (population 320,000), religiously heterodox, and intensely fragmented Toraja culture region is singularly unprepared to cope with a major tourist influx. Serious efforts to improve communication with tourists through the founding of a living museum/cultural orientation center, effective training of guides, and control of international traders in illicitly obtained cultural artifacts will be necessary if tourism is to be of some benefit to the people of Tana Toraja.

"It was," my village friend in the west of Tana Toraja sadly noted as we made our way down a steep mountain path, "when the tourists first came that our family statues began to disappear." Our journey took us down a narrow cliff-side path to a hidden grotto. Here were assembled some seventy *tau tau* statues, secreted from public view in a hiding place known only to a few village leaders. "Better to hide these forever than to see the images of our ancestors stolen to be sold in a foreign land," he remarked. Elsewhere, many such statues have been inserted into limestone burial vaults that had been opened on the occasion of a funeral. Statues inserted in burial vaults in this way will never again be placed on public view. In many villages, villagers—once proud to display their burial sites to visitors—fear for the safety of their heirloom ancestral images. Once semi-isolated and essentially closed to external influence, Tana Toraja today is open, vulnerable, and tentative about the ultimate impact of tourism. Tourism to date has neither strengthened the indigenous belief system nor induced much in the way of enhanced cultural understanding. Whether the next decade of tourism development in Tana Toraja positively contributes to the visitors' understanding of local culture, and renewed interest in Toraja traditions by local youth, or instead accelerates the commoditization of Toraja ceremony and artifacts will depend ultimately on the wisdom, commitment and intelligence of government planners, private entrepreneurs, and Toraja community leaders.

Center for South and Southeast Asia Studies
University of California, Berkeley

III

TOURISM IN EUROPEAN RESORTS

Europe—the continent that produced Greece, Rome, the Renaissance and the Industrial Revolution—has historically been host to more tourism than any other area. Even today most tourists in Europe are Europeans, vacationing away from home in some other country. In addition, Europe is an important historical-cultural destination for overseas visitors and especially for individuals whose forebears departed Europe a generation or more ago to colonize elsewhere, and who now still feel a sense of bond or identity with an ancestral homeland.

Mass tourism is pervasive throughout most of the continent, and the industry is well-organized and economically very important to many countries. However, the attraction of tourists to any given center is highly competitive, and governments have been active and influential in stimulating tourism. Despite good intentions to generate outside income, the promotional techniques have not always been beneficial as Davydd Greenwood shows in chapter 8 that government efforts, using "local color" as a "come-on," proved disruptive to the target community. In chapter 9, Oriol Pi-Sunyer provides an insightful analysis of the effects of mass tourism in changing interpersonal relations between European hosts and guests.

8

Culture by the Pound: An Anthropological Perspective on Tourism as Cultural Commoditization

DAVYDD J. GREENWOOD

Tourism is now more than the travelers' game. A few years ago, we could lament the lack of serious research on tourism, but now, like the tourists themselves, social researchers are flocking to tourist centers. This is necessary since tourism is the largest scale movement of goods, services, and people that humanity has perhaps ever seen (Greenwood 1972). Economists and planners have been tracing the outlines of this industry and its peculiarities, and many anthropologists and sociologists have begun to chart the social effects of tourism on communities.

The literature generally points out that tourism provides a considerable stimulus to the local and national economy, but it also results in an increasingly unequal distribution of wealth. Tourism thus seems to exacerbate existing cleavages within the community. It is not, therefore, the development panacea that a few hasty planners proclaimed. This nascent critical literature is useful because it places tourism-related development in the analytical perspective from which a variety of different development strategies

I am indebted to Pilar Fernandez-Cañadas de Greenwood for helpful substantive and editorial criticisms.

are being reviewed. The conclusion that tourism-related development tends to produce inequalities takes on added significance because it seems to parallel the inequalities produced by other development strategies, like enclave factories, capital formation schemes, and the "Green Revolution." This serves as a needed corrective to overly exuberant dreams of an El Dorado paved with tourism receipts.

Tourism is not a monolith. It is an exceedingly large-scale and diverse industry, operating in a variety of ways under differing circumstances. Necessarily this means that we must differentiate between types of tourism and the range of impacts tourism can have on local communities.

This case study concentrates on the promotion of "local color" as a part of tourism merchandising and its impact on one community.[1] For clarity and to avoid any possible misunderstanding on this point, my analysis is not a general indictment of the tourist industry, but considers only the use of "local color" in tourism. The pros and cons of other aspects of tourism are weighed elsewhere in this volume and in the literature generally.

Social researchers and moralists often speak cynically of the uses and abuses of "local color" by the tourism industry. Spokesmen for local cultures decry the vilification of their traditions by tourism. Planners, too, feel vaguely uncomfortable about this but are quick to point out how little we understand the potential impact of these practices. Lacking well-documented research into the implications of the use of local color in tourism, it is not surprising that neither planners nor local people can decide just how to approach the problem. This study attempts, in brief compass, to analyze the commoditization of local culture in the case of Fuenterrabia, Guipúzcoa, in the Spanish Basque country.

Can Culture Be Considered a Commodity?

Logically, anything that is for sale must have been produced by combining the factors of production (land, labor, or capital). This offers no problem when the subject is razor blades, transistor radios, or hotel accommodations. It is not so clear when buyers are attracted to a place by some feature of local culture, such as the running of the bulls in Pamplona, an appearance of the Virgin Mary, or an exotic festival.

---

1. By "local color" I mean the promotion of a commoditized version of local culture as part of the "come-on," a widespread practice with little-understood consequences.

Economists and planners dealing with tourism have papered over this difficulty either by considering local culture a "natural resource" (that is, as part of the land factor) or simply by viewing local culture as part of the "come-on" and focusing their attention entirely on the number of hotel beds and the flow of liquor, gasoline, and souvenir purchases. Such a perspective is not very helpful because in ethnic tourism settings, local culture itself is being treated as a commodity *sui generis.*

A fundamental characteristic of the capitalist system is that anything that can be priced can be bought and sold. It can be treated as a commodity. This offers no analytical problem when local people are paid to perform for tourists. Like the symphony orchestra of economics textbook fame, they are being reimbursed for performing a service consumed on the spot. It is not so clear when activities of the host culture are treated as part of the "come-on" without their consent and are invaded by tourists who do not reimburse them for their "service." In this case, their activities are taken advantage of for profit, but they do not profit, culturally. The onlookers often alter the meaning of the activities being carried on by local people. Under these circumstances, local culture is in effect being expropriated, and local people are being exploited.

We already know from worldwide experience that local culture—be it New Guinea aboriginal art and rituals, Eskimo sculpture (Carpenter 1972, 1973), Balinese dancing, bullfights, voodoo ceremonies, gypsy dancing, or peasant markets—is altered and often destroyed by the treatment of it as a tourist attraction. It is made meaningless to the people who once believed in it by means of a process that can be understood anthropologically. I think we have the social science tools to understand the fragility of local culture and the humanist's responsibility to put these tools to use.

Anthropological Definitions of Culture and Public Ritual

To develop this view of local culture as a commodity, working definitions of culture and public ritual are needed. I will follow Clifford Geertz's views here. For Geertz, *culture* is an integrated system of meanings by means of which the nature of reality is established and maintained. His concept of culture emphasizes the authenticity and the moral tone it imparts to life experiences, as he calls attention to the fundamental importance of systems of meaning in human life. By implication, anything that falsifies, disorganizes, or challenges the participants' belief in the authenticity of their culture threatens it with collapse. *Public rituals* can be viewed as dramatic enactments, commentaries on, and summations of the meanings basic to a particular culture. They serve to reaffirm, further develop, and elaborate those aspects of reality that hold a particular group of people together in a common culture (Geertz 1957, 1966, 1972).

As can be seen, the anthropological view of culture is far different from the economists' and planners' views of culture as a "come-on," a "natural resource," or as a "service." The anthropological perspective enables us to understand why the commoditization of local culture in the tourism industry is so fundamentally destructive and why the sale of "culture by the pound," as it were, needs to be examined by everyone involved in tourism.

The Alarde *of Fuenterrabia*

To analyze the process of cultural commoditization, I will use the specific case of a major public ritual in Fuenterrabia: the *Alarde*. Fuenterrabia's *Alarde* is a public ritual *par excellence*. It involves almost all the men, women, and children in the town during the preparations for it and includes a staggering number of them in the actual enactment.

The *Alarde* is essentially a ritual recreation of Fuenterrabia's victory over the French in the siege of A.D. 1638. This town was important from the fifteenth to the nineteenth centuries as a walled citadel standing almost on the border between Spain and France, where the Spanish and French crowns contested the rights to control the territory in the northeast corner of Spain. As a result, Fuenterrabia was besieged an immense number of times. Most famous was the siege of 1638, which lasted sixty-nine days and which the town successfully withstood, leading to the rout of the French army. Following this victory the town was accorded a number of privileges by the Spanish crown and was given an important honorific title to add to its official name.

But the *Alarde* does much more than simply commemorate a battle. Fuenterrabia is made up of the citadel, a fishermen's ward, and five local wards, each with a corporate identity and responsibilities. The walled city and the six wards of the town each send a contingent of children who play Basque flutes and drums, and march, dressed in the white shirt and pants, red sandals, sash, and beret symbolizing the Basques. They also send a contingent of men armed with shotguns. From among their young women, each ward elects a *cantinera* (water carrier) who is supposed to be the best flower of young womanhood in the ward. She dresses in a military style uniform and carries a canteen. Various nonlocalized occupational groups are also represented. There is a contingent of *hacheros* (woodchoppers) dressed in sheepskin cloaks, with huge black beards and tall black fur hats. The mayor and the town council dress in military uniform and ride on horseback, leading the procession.

After an early Mass, the groups form in the square outside the citadel gates. Each contingent of children marches through the gates and up the two-block street to the plaza where the somber fortress of Charles the Fifth is located, to the cheers and smiles of hundreds of relatives who crowd the streets and the overhanging balconies. The martial music is played with great fervor. The continual passing of each group, all playing a different tune, and the endless drumming have a profound effect on the bystanders.

Then come the mayor and town councilmen on horseback, symbols of leadership, valor, and nobility. They pass amidst general cheers and then dismount and move to the balcony of the town hall, which overlooks the main street about halfway up to the plaza, to review the parade. Lead by its *cantinera*, each ward's group of armed men then marches up the street and stops under the town hall balcony. After saluting, they fire a unison shotgun salvo with deafening effect. The trick is to fire as if only one huge gun has gone off, and the audience continually comments on how well or badly each ward does this. The men then march on to the plaza and form up there.

At the end of the parade, the mayor and town council rejoin the people, all now in the plaza. Together they fire a unison salvo that very nearly deafens all present. Everyone reloads and fires until he has run out of shells. With that the people begin to disperse. After rejoining their families, they walk down to the fishermen's ward for food and drink.

There are far too many elements in this ritual to permit a full commentary here. And, *Alardes* are not restricted to Fuenterrabia but are performed in many Basque and non-Basque towns. In each case, the details differ greatly (Caro Baroja, 1968).

A few basic points about Fuenterrabia *Alarde* should be made. The siege of Fuenterrabia was one in which wealthy and poor—men, women, and children, farmers, fishermen and merchants—withstood a ferocious attack together. The *Alarde* reproduces this solidarity by involving all occupational groups, men, women, and children, in the activity. The guns, by ward and then together, speak with one unified voice of the solidarity between the inhabitants that allowed them to survive. It is a statement of collective valor and of the quality of all the people of Fuenterrabia. It is an affirmation of their existence and identity at a time when most of the people earn money outside Fuenterrabia. It is a closing of wounds of gossip and bad faith opened up during the year of town life. The mayor and town councilmen, often thought of as dishonest manipulators rather than as good men, are momentarily transformed into the embodiment of civic virtue and valor to the death. The fishermen and farmers, in much of their daily lives trying to free themselves of the rustic and working-class identity their trades give them, are for a moment the embodiment of the poor but free and noble Basques with whom they affirm an historical identity. Together these people, who most of the time are divided, vulnerable, and confused, are a single spirit capable of withstanding the onslaughts of the outside world as they once withstood the siege of 1638.

There is much more to it, but this suffices to provide the flavor of the event. What is most important is for whom the *Alarde* is performed. It is clearly not performed for outsiders; it is a ritual whose importance and meaning lies in the entire town's participation and in the intimacy with which its major symbols are understood by all the participants and onlookers (the latter often having spent months sewing costumes, directing marching practice, and teaching music to the children). *It is a performance for the participants*, not a show. It is an enactment of the "sacred history" of Fuenterrabia, a history by its very nature inaccessible to outsiders, even when equipped with a two-paragraph explanation courtesy of the Ministry of Information and Tourism. A few unrelated outsiders have always been present, especially members of the Spanish elite who have been summering in Fuenterrabia since the time of the monarchy (Greenwood 1972). They are welcome, for they share some durable tie with the community. The presence of people who have no enduring relation to the community is much less welcome.

The *Alarde* is more than merely an interesting symbol of unity. As I am endeavoring to show in historical research on the Basques, the unique concept of Basque "collective nobility" is deeply involved here. By tradition, all people born in Guipúzcoa of Guipuzcoano parents were declared by that fact alone to have *limpieza de sangre* (no Moorish or Jewish blood), something that happened nowhere outside the Basque country. It gave rise to a unique situation: the Basques could assert that a cobbler, a farmer, a fisherman, a mayor, and a count were all equally noble. Though they recognized the differences in wealth and power, they asserted a common human equality by virtue of *limpieza de sangre* (Greenwood 1977).

Although the importance of *limpieza* is now gone, the equalitarian values arising from the idea live on in a Spain of stark class differences. To my mind, part of the importance of the *Alarde* is that it is the only occasion in which these ideas of equality and common destiny are given general expression. In this respect, the performance of the *Alarde* is a statement of their historical identity as Basques as well as an enactment of a particular moment in their history. The ritual is thus very important.

But the *Alarde* has the misfortune of taking place during the tourist season. The local population of Fuenterrabia is swollen fourfold; innumerable tourists drive in and out of town during the day to visit the beach, to watch boat races, to eat, swim, and take pictures of farms, old houses, and the city walls. The *Alarde* is listed by the Spanish tourism ministry in a national festival calendar that is given wide circulation. Tourism developers, a group including local politicians and contractors plus large national companies that specialize in tourism-related construction, have added the *Alarde* to their list of advertisable features about Fuenterrabia. Posters and other publicity for the *Alarde* are circulated, as is anything else that makes the town attractive to the tourism consumer.

I do not wish to give the impression that the *Alarde* is singled out for this treatment. In fact, in the "come-on," the *Alarde* is relatively unimportant. It lasts only one day, and by comparison with tourist interest in the fortifications, the frequent boat races, and the other attractions of the town, the ritual is of only passing interest. The *Alarde* is simply part of the list of "local color" to attract tourist receipts; it is an offhand addition to the basic tourism package.

The Turning Point: The Alarde Goes Public

This offhanded treatment of the *Alarde* is not reflected in the effect its incorporation into the tourism package has had on the people of Fuenterrabia. Though the *Alarde* is still a going concern, it is in trouble. It has suddenly become difficult to get the people to show and participate in it.

The turning point occurred while I worked in Fuenterrabia during the summer of 1969. The town streets are narrow and all the balconies along the street belong to private houses. The plaza must be cleared of people to make room for the military formations. Thus, there is very little room for onlookers in the narrow streets of the old citadel.

In 1969, the Spanish Ministry of Tourism and Public Information finished remodeling the old fortress of Charles the Fifth in the plaza and opened it as a part of their well-known chain of tourist *paradores* (hotel, restaurant, bar combination). It was personally inaugurated by Generalísimo Franco, an event commemorated on national television. Even a facsimile copy of Padre Moret's eyewitness account of the siege was published to add a note of "culture" to the occasion (Moret 1763). With the boost of national publicity, the municipal government felt obligated to resolve the problem of the onlookers. Not only should the people in the *parador* see the *Alarde*, but so should everyone else who wanted to. They declared that the *Alarde* should be given twice in the same day to allow everyone to see it.

In spite of the fact that the *Alarde* has not, to my knowledge, been given twice, the effect of the council's action was stunning. In service of simple pecuniary motives, it defined the *Alarde* as a *public show to be performed for outsiders* who, because of their economic importance in the town, had the *right* to see it.

The Aftermath: The Collapse of Cultural Meanings

There was a great consternation among the people of Fuenterrabia and a vaulting sense of discomfort. Soon this became the mask of cynicism that prefaces their attitudes toward the motives behind all business ventures in Fuenterrabia. Little was said publicly about it. But two summers later, I found that the town was having a great deal of difficulty in getting the participants to appear for the *Alarde*. No one actively or ideologically resisted, but in an event that depends entirely on voluntary compliance, the general lack of interest created serious organizational problems. In the space of two years, what was a vital and exciting ritual had become an obligation to be avoided. Recently the municipal government was considering payments to people for their participation in the *Alarde*. I do not doubt that they ultimately will have to pay them, just as the gypsies are paid to dance and sing and the symphony orchestra is paid to make music. The ritual has become a performance for money. The meaning is gone.

Conclusions: Culture by the Pound

This is undoubtedly a small event in a small place that few people will ever hear of, but its implications seem to be significant. The "local color" used to attract tourists to Fuenterrabia came to include a major ritual that the people had performed for themselves. Its meaning depended on their understanding of the whole system of beliefs reaffirmed by it through dramatic reenactment and commentary. It was not a performance for pay, but an affirmation of their belief in their own culture. It was Fuenterrabia commenting on itself for its own purposes.

By ordaining that the *Alarde* be a public event to attract outsiders into the town to spend money, the municipal government made it one more of Fuenterrabia's assets in the competitive tourism market. But this decision directly violated the *meaning* of the ritual, definitively destroying its authenticity and its power for the people. They reacted with consternation and then with indifference. They can still perform the outward forms of the ritual for money, but they cannot subscribe to the meanings it once held because it is no longer being performed by them for themselves.

I do not think this is a rare case by any means. Worldwide, we are seeing the transformation of cultures into "local color," making peoples' cultures extensions of the modern mass media (Carpenter 1972, 1973). Culture is being packaged, priced, and sold like building lots, rights-of-way, fast food, and room service, as the tourism industry inexorably extends its grasp. For the monied tourist, the tourism industry promises that the world is his/hers to use. All the "natural resources," including cultural traditions, have their price, and if you have the money in hand, it is your right to see whatever you wish.

As an analytical perspective has finally begun to develop with regard to the socioeconomic effects of mass tourism, it has become obvious that the increasing maldistribution of wealth and resultant social stratification are widespread results of touristic development. Various remedies are proposed as an attempt to counteract these problems. While these problems are serious and must be remedied, I am terribly concerned that the question of cultural commoditization involved in ethnic tourism has been blithely ignored, except for anecdotal accounts. The massive alterations in the distribution of wealth and power that are brought about by tourism are paralleled by equally massive and perhaps equally destructive alterations in local culture.

The culture brokers have appropriated facets of a life-style into the tourism package to help sales in the competitive market. This sets in motion a process of its own for which no one, not even planners, seems to feel in the least responsible. Treating culture as a natural resource or a commodity over which tourists have rights is not simply perverse, it is a violation of the peoples' cultural rights. While some aspects of culture have wider ramifications than others, what must be remembered is that culture in its very essence is something that people believe in *implicitly*. By making it part of the tourism package, it is turned into an explicit and paid performance and no longer can be believed in the way it was before. Thus, commoditization of culture in effect robs people of the very meanings by which they organize their lives.

And because such a system of belief is implicit, the holders of it are hard pressed to understand what is happening to them. The people of Fuenterrabia only express confusion and concern about their *Alarde;* they know something is wrong and do not know exactly what it is or what to do about it. The *Alarde* is dying for them, and they are powerless to reverse the process. Making their culture a public performance took the municipal government a few minutes; with that act, a 350-year-old ritual died.

That is the final perversity. The commoditization of culture does not require the consent of the participants; it can be done by anyone. Once set in motion, the process seems irreversible and its very subtlety prevents the affected people from taking any clear-cut action to stop it. In the end, many of the venerated aspects of Basque culture are becoming commodities, like toothpaste, beer, and boat rides.

Perhaps this is the final logic of the capitalist development of which tourism is an ideal example. The commoditization process does not stop with land, labor, and capital but ultimately includes the history, ethnic identity, and culture of the peoples of the world. Tourism simply packages the cultural realities of a people for sale along with their other resources. We know that no people anywhere can live without the meanings culture provides; thus tourism is forcing unprecedented cultural change on people already reeling from the blows of industrialization, urbanization, and inflation. The loss of meaning through cultural commoditization is a problem at least as serious as the unequal distribution of wealth that results from tourist development.

Postscript (1977)

As this essay was going to press, I received word of the tragic consequences of the *Alarde* of 1976. The now "public" ritual became a major political event. In the context of the acute political tensions in the Basque country, the *Alarde* seemingly provides a means of political expression. Apparently the *Alarde* was celebrated this year amidst an atmosphere of considerable tension. Late in the evening in the fishermen's ward, a boisterous crowd confronted the police and a young worker from the nearby town of Irún was killed. The sense of shock and anger was intense and will probably play a role in the political future of Fuenterrabia. Perhaps the debasement of the *Alarde* set the scene for this event, and perhaps not. However, it is certain that, given the magnitude of the potential consequences, we cannot afford to merely guess at the political implications of cultural commoditization.

Epilogue

"Culture by the Pound" was written as an expression of both anger and concern. In the years since, I have returned to Fuenterrabia only for a few days at a time and have not again witnessed the *Alarde*. I understand that it has become much more a public event and is imbued now with contemporary political significance as part of the contest over regional political rights in Spain.

Further reflection on what I wrote suggested to me the need to place the process described in the chapter within a broader context. After all, local cultures have been transformed by tourism, but so have they been by industrialization, urbanization, pollution, poverty, civil war, migration, and a host of other factors. Does tourism have unique effects? Are its cultural manifestations always negative? The anthropological literature on tourism does not yet provide very clear answers.

Within the study of tourism, there have been two basic approaches. The first concentrates on the political economy, making the case that tourism can have a substantial and disruptive impact on the local community. It is certain that the deleterious local effects of tourism continue to merit attention for their own sake and for their significant policy implications. Nevertheless, the seeming spontaneity of the anthropological focus on the disruption of the local community by tourism was not entirely accidental. It fit well with the notion of the pristine relatively static, traditional community plunged into the modern capitalist arena.

With that concept went the relative inattention to the communities' alternative patterns of economic development and a rather lapidary view of government policy and the international tourist economy. The anthropological reaction to these developments was dominantly negative and fit generically with the anthropological critique of modernization already well developed in literature on the folk culture and urbanization. "Culture by the Pound" and my earlier article, "Tourism as an Agent of Change: A Spanish Basque Case" (Greenwood 1972) are examples.

Another part of the anthropological response to tourism focused on its cultural dimensions, or, specifically, on tourism as cultural exploitation. Here anthropological voices blended with those of journalists and cultural preservationists to a degree, though I tend to believe that anthropology had more challenging things to say. In this vein, many anthropologists, including myself wrote of the cultural expropriation and demolition that tourism could wreak on local cultures. This critique is still valid and there are enough examples to confirm both the analyses and predictions. However, this perspective provides only a partial view of the process.

The historical and ideological basis for this critique deserves analysis in its own right. Every generation produces moralists claiming that theirs is the epoch when culture has collapsed, when traditions have been destroyed and values lost. Though the anthropological critiques confidently announced this theme, it is troublingly difficult to separate this moral discourse, traceable in an unbroken genealogy back to Plato (Caro Baroja 1963), from other forms of intellectual and political conservatism, even though the rhetorical tone of the critique of tourism is politically left of center.

Lévi-Strauss put this worry quite eloquently in *Tristes Tropiques* when he wrote:

> The alternative is inescapable: either I am a traveller in ancient times, and faced with a prodigious spectacle which would be almost entirely unintelligible to me and might, indeed, provoke me to mockery or disgust; or I am a traveller of our own day, hastening in search of a vanished reality. In either case I am the loser—and more heavily than one might suppose; for today, as I go groping among the shadows, I miss, inevitably, the spectacle that is now taking shape. My eyes, or perhaps my degree of humanity, do not equip me to witness that spectacle; and in the centuries to come, when another traveller revisits this same place, he too may groan aloud at the disappearance of much that I should have set down, but cannot. I am the victim of a double infirmity: what I see is an affliction to me; and what I do not see, a reproach. (1970, p. 45)

Are we correct that all local cultural values are being destroyed? Or are they changing once again, under the press of circumstance and from their own internal dynamics, while we, the anthropologists, disapprove of the changes or at the very least do not comprehend them?

To argue globally against cultural change is a startling position; to accept all change as good is mindless and cruel. The challenge, as yet unmet, is to conceptualize communities as a complex process of stability and change, and then to factor in the changes tourism brings.

To this end, the evaluation of tourism cannot be accomplished by measuring the impact of tourism against a static background. Some of what we see as destruction is construction; some is the result of a lack of any other viable options; and some the result of choices that could be made differently. Which is which is by no means an easy matter to decide, but it is clear that anthropologists have not met these problems head on.

Moral anguish was easier to express. But this had negative effects on tourism as anthropological subject because it did not suggest the ways that tourism offered opportunities for theoretical growth in the core areas of anthropology. Tourism was seen as a subroutine of a shopworn view of local communities and as externally imposed social change. There was nothing new in it; it was just one more example of our perverse age of modernization. But the objectification of local culture via tourism does not always destroy it; on occasion it transforms and even stimulates its further proliferation (Mathieu 1982; Greenwood 1982).

Tourism as a Set of Anthropological Challenges

Authenticity: Suggestions that tourism challenges anthropology on the theoretical center of its turf and demands the best efforts of anthropology's leading theoreticians and methodologists have rarely been made, and when made (e.g., MacCannell 1976), they have been ignored, at least until recently. On the surface, determining the authenticity of cultural elements and performances seems such a simple thing. It would appear that the anthropologist can simply observe what is presented to the tourist, compare it with the traditional models, and offer a judgment. But such a rendering is based on anthropological views of culture that should have long ago passed away.

To speak unproblematically of "traditional" culture is not permissible. All cultures continually change. What is traditional in a culture is largely a matter of internal polemic as groups within a society struggle for hegemony, and a matter of external judgment when the anthropologist constitutes a particular image of a culture as its "true" form.

Within any culture, there is a great deal of diversity. We have known for generations that people do not share many elements of their own culture, or at least, they understand them differently. Culture as "webs of significance" does not have a simple structure, summed up in a statistical mean called tradition.

What then does authenticity mean and why do tourists seek it? The concept of cultural authenticity is part of a much broader polemic about the meaning of history, long important in the Western world. We vacillate between allocating political rights on the basis of authentic racial and ethnic claims, and trying to convert all members of the population to political equals.

In many cases, being culturally authentic provides access to important political resources. In countries currently developing home rule statutes for internal regions, the ability to make political claims always follows in the train of comprehensive arguments about the authentic historical and cultural foundations that underlie those claims. At the same time, democratic constitutions often make arguments and allocate rights on the assumption that all human beings have certain qualities and rights in common.

Both of these views have led to excesses and received justifiable criticism. The allocation of rights on cultural grounds often leads to systematic invention of cultural traditions for the purpose of acquiring rights. At the same time, the allocation of rights through attempts to make the population homogeneous can lead contemporary society to the dilution of all that is local and idiosyncratic—the massification of global culture. Tourism necessarily operates within this conflictive arena.

Middle-class Tourists: Some of the prime beneficiaries of cultural homogenization are the tourists themselves, largely middle class, successful products of the great melting pot. Their thirst for cultural authenticity seems at once a recognition of the supposed cultural impoverishment that has accompanied economic success and world domination and a reinforcement of the sense of social superiority. While a voodoo dance is fun to watch, it is important that the process be tightly controlled and that nothing stands in the way of a return to suburbia some days later.

Thus tourist cultural performances provide an opportunity for a limited self-criticism of middle-class culture, a kind of pseudo-tragedy in which the affluence that makes touring possible is the very cause of the loss of cultural authenticity. At the same time, the ability to command cultural performances shows that one may be able to have it all without renouncing a comfortable middle-class life-style for the other fifty weeks of the year.

Tourism and Political Mobilization: From another vantage point, those groups seeking to establish or expand political rights by the reinforcement of their cultural traditions and ethnic identity see tourism as a double-edged sword. The ability to attract tourists to their locations is itself a ratification of cultural claims about uniqueness. The aesthetic dimensions of tourism that emphasize native architecture, art, and performances offer opportunities for cultural advertisements and consolidation. Yet the very process of packaging and merchandising ethnicity for tourism alters local culture in important ways, creating internal divisions that may be politically destructive or diluting local culture in ways that make it unconvincing to the natives.

Creative Responses to Tourism: Occasionally tourism engenders creative responses in local cultures and positively affects the trajectory of cultural development. The interest that tourists demonstrate in local culture, history, and artifacts can—under some conditions (and this is the key)—engender a positive local response. Interest in local culture, pride in local traditions, and an improved sense of cultural worth may develop. What has not been formulated with any precision is an analysis of the conditions that are conducive to this positive result and those that are not (E. Smith 1982; V. Smith 1982).

Certainly, anthropologists know that being observed itself can engender processes of reflection that lead to cultural elaboration, a subject that deserves much more detailed study in the context of tourism. We can also assume that this positive process involves important cultural change. Local culture, reformulated and revalued in the context of external interests, is itself transformed.

The Research Challenge of Tourism

No simple approach exists. To prohibit cultural change is nonsensical. To ratify all change is immoral. To occupy the turf in between requires that anthropologists link the study of tourism to the broadest theoretical issues in the discipline: culture as representation, cultural diversity, culture's dynamic properties, the importance of mythic authenticity, the character of intercultural interactions, and the links between political economy and systems of meaning. Cultural relativism, the identifying icon of anthropology, must be complicated and updated to deal with these realities. In this sense, the study of tourism reflects most current unresolved anthropological dilemmas and offers important opportunities for the theoretical and methodological development of our field.

Cornell University, Ithaca

9

Changing Perceptions of Tourism and Tourists in a Catalan Resort Town

ORIOL PI-SUNYER

Introduction

The majority of anthropological studies on tourism examine some aspect of the impact—social, cultural, or economic—that tourists or the tourist industry have on host communities and regions. This approach is rooted in the traditions of the discipline and can be paraphrased as community (or culture) reacting to external influences: the focus is on the community and community members and on how they cope, or fail to cope, with agencies and forces over which they exercise little control, but which may be tolerated inasmuch as they yield some measure of economic benefit.

The theoretical models that are brought to bear on the subject of tourism owe a great deal to modernization theory as it has been applied to rural transformation. Thus, in much the same way as the industrialization of the countryside is often taken as a "given" little affected by local desires and opinions, so, too, is tourism approached as an influence beyond local control,

This study is based on more than a dozen seasons of field research between the mid-1960s and 1987. Native knowledge, however, goes back considerably further: Cap Lloc is my ancestral village and I have some memory of it before the Spanish Civil War. I am grateful for all the help given to me by neighbors and officials; the interpretations are strictly my responsibility.

especially when the tourism in question is of the modern mass variety. Local feelings, it is generally assumed, are of secondary importance in the evolution of tourist industries since the customers are outsiders and the capital and management are seldom local. If physical resources are present, tourists will be catered to whether or not the natives feel inclined to assume service roles (Aspelin 1978; Lee 1978).

These assumptions and observations fit well the initial phases of mass tourism in developing and Third World societies; my own earlier work on foreign tourism in Catalonia makes use of such an impact model, and I see no reason to change the approach or the interpretation for the phenomenon as it manifested itself at the time.

However, what such a perspective may fail to pick up is the matter of process, since tourism, even in the same location, hardly remains a constant. In the mid-1960s, when I first began to look at tourism on the Costa Brava, the majority of tourists still formed part of the generation that had experienced World War II and its aftermath. They were interested in the affordable holiday, the Mediterranean sun and beaches, and the very novelty of foreign travel. Today, the tourists are the children and grandchildren of that postwar generation, and while sun and sea are still major attractions, they have grown up with travel and vacations as a normal part of life. They have also come to expect much the same degree of infrastructural support whether they visit Spain or some other European country. In a more subtle way, the passage of time has brought about an important structural change: the European tourist who feels comfortable and at home in a given location is increasingly likely to purchase property there and, in due course, to make it his retirement home. For Spain as a whole, we already have to think in terms of more than a million foreign property owners currently purchasing homes at the rate of 50,000 a year (Cullell 1987, pp. 1–3). Whatever else it may imply—and the matter is not unproblematic—a movement of this scale raises questions respecting the sharp distinctions between the categories of host and guest.

If a change is taking place in the composition of foreign tourism on the Costa Brava (and local officials and other informants tend to support such a view), even more important changes have taken place in the context within which tourism policies are developed. Most critical of all has been the transformation of Spain from a dictatorship to a democracy. Psychologically and culturally, this has done a great deal to end decades of peripheralization; politically, democracy has meant not only elected central and autonomous governments, but an important measure of administrative decentralization.

Without question, these political changes have functioned to make tourism and related issues, such as environmental protection and urban planning, questions about which local people not only have opinions, but the means to make these points of view known and considered as well.

In the meantime, tourism has not only grown to be the leading Spanish industry, but one so successful that it is responsible for two-thirds (twelve thousand million dollars) of the country's positive balance of payments (Vidal-Folch 1987, p. 16). Indeed, tourism is one of the few bright spots in an economy beset by high unemployment (some 20 percent of the national workforce) and the problems of industrial reconversion. Also, much in the same way as there has been something of a change in the composition of tourist traffic, the more than two decades of profitable seasons has had its influence on the inhabitants of the Costa Brava, most obviously in terms of economic security. Altogether, it should not surprise us that tourism is enjoying a considerably more positive image today than was the case a decade or more ago—an attitude not limited to those who make their living from this sector.

If some of the models that have been used to analyze the phenomenon of tourism fail to adequately take into consideration time and its changes as an element in social and intercultural relations, it is also true that they seldom draw attention to the impact of tourism at the interpersonal level: the social processes at work in tourist-host encounters. Some anthropologists have looked at this dimension (Brewer 1978; Pi-Sunyer 1977), but the matter has received substantially more attention from social psychologists (Pearce 1982, pp. 68–96). Obviously, it is in large measure through face-to-face encounters that the worlds of the visitor and the resident touch. But the ideas that one group harbors about another are more than the consequences of direct experience.

I will argue that the attitudes that residents hold respecting tourists are in part founded on direct experience, but are also strongly mediated by images and stereotypes concerning different types of visitors. These categories are not immutable; rather they are influenced by changes in tourism and by major societal transformations. In short, any examination of locally held ideas respecting tourism and tourists must be sensitive to important contextual changes within which lived experience actually takes place.

My approach considers the phenomenon of tourism as processual and embedded in overreaching institutions and structures. This study examines native perceptions concerning tourists in the Catalan Costa Brava, particularly in and around the town of Cap Lloc (a pseudonym). This is where I have witnessed the impact of tourism "on the ground" and the transformation of small fishing villages into major resorts. I have learned how my neighbors conceptualize tourism; how they achieve the balance between the good and the bad in the livelihood that now dominates the town; and how increasingly they have come to view the industry as something they can significantly influence as townspeople and citizens.

Natives and Outsiders: A Historical Perspective

Since the late nineteenth century, village communities in northeastern Spain have hosted a limited number of tourists including Catalans of urban background (often with ancestral roots in a given location), non-Catalan Spaniards, and foreigners. This section of Catalonia is part of the "Spanish marches," a region that for centuries felt the consequences of war and political conflict between France and Spain. The French frontier is nearby, and until the early nineteenth century, Cap Lloc was the site of a major Spanish military and naval base guarding the coast and protecting the hinterland from French incursions. Then, during the Napoleonic Wars, Cap Lloc and other adjacent villages came under French military and administrative control. Though not on the main artery across the eastern Pyrenees, the road to France was close enough to bring to Cap Lloc a quota of foreigners long before the boom in international tourism. In summary, the villagers' exposure to outsiders on the Costa Brava has been continuous for several centuries; these patterns of contact and interaction are at least in part linked to the integration of small communities into the sociopolitical fabric of modern state systems and are thus not unique in Cap Lloc and environs.

During this time, the people of Cap Lloc subtly categorized distinctions between native, stranger, and foreigner, as a guide to interpersonal relations and as a means of specifying how one should deal with whom and when. These folk categories, though, did not operate in a vacuum, but were tempered by cultural values that place substantial emphasis on the concept that each individual is a person, to be evaluated in terms of his or her merits. Bonhomie is not a dominant trait in the Catalan character; indeed, many observers consider the Catalan as somewhat dour and pragmatic. However, Catalans do have a sensitivity to good manners and a developed sense of fairness. These traits manifest themselves in a way that is particulary pertinent to our concerns: a consciousness of the duties inherent in the role of host and an expectation that the guest fulfill his reciprocal obligations.

This situation remained essentially unchanged until well after World War II. Writing of the Costa Brava as it was in the summer of 1947, Rose

Macaulay (1949, p. 36) describes a string of unspoiled fishing villages preserved from the "cosmopolitan smartness" that she felt vulgarized the French coast. Motoring from the French border to Barcelona, she encountered only three cars with "GB" (Great Britain) plates; had she returned twenty years later, she would have found tens of thousands of cars with foreign license plates and would soon have lost count of automobiles of British registry. Mass tourism began to reach the coast in the early 1960s, and the rapidity of its subsequent development coupled with its gross size tended to heighten the social impact. Although most villagers derived economic benefits from the influx, local people felt that they had very little control over the changes. Seldom verbalized as such (one did hear a lot about the "loss of tranquility"), tourism was conceptualized as a sort of mixed blessing, an attitude that the literature suggests was not unique to this part of the world.

The Phenomenon of Mass Tourism

Mass tourism is more than a mere quantitative jump in the incidence of travelers. It is essentially a post–World War II development, although its antecedents go back considerably earlier. Tourism on the present scale is clearly a reflection of the socioeconomic transformations experienced by the more developed Western societies since 1950; in short, it is a manifestation of mass consumption. In Europe, the expansion of the tourist market has transformed less-developed regions and countries into the summer playgrounds of the working classes and the lower middle classes of the more affluent nations.

Modern tourism, especially in southern Europe, differs also from earlier forms of leisure travel in that it is overwhelmingly a phenomenon of the coasts. For Spain in particular, the islands and the coasts account for some 90 percent of tourist destinations (Cals 1974, pp. 49–50; Cullell 1987, p. 3), leaving the interior a "paradise which has not yet been able to be sold to the tourist" (Cullell 1987, p. 3).

This geographic distribution can have important social and cultural consequences. In the past, foreigners and strangers were more likely to be found in cities than in rural locations, and it was the cities and towns that tended to contain ethnic and foreign minorities—all blending somewhat more easily in the overall anonymity of metropolitan settings. Furthermore, even without reference to such groups, the range of social and cultural variation in cities tends to be considerably greater than that encountered in smaller towns and villages. Moving to more recent times, the presence of tourists in cities simply does not make the same sort of visual and social impact as it does in the countryside and in newly developed resort communities.

In a small town such as Cap Lloc (some 6000 inhabitants in the mid 1960s; closer to 15,000 today), it is difficult to escape the tourists. They are present in their numbers day and night, walking the streets; frequenting the stores, the post office, and bars; driving in and out of town; and, of course, lying on the beaches. Virtually every tourist has great visibility and proclaims his alienness through dress, speech, and manners.

Although tourism may be regarded as just another "industry," it differs from other transformations of the countryside in one very important respect: tourism is a service-oriented operation that generally entails a great deal of face-to-face contact between visitors and residents. Mass tourism indirectly affects everyone in a small community, including other tourists who seek to get away from the beaten path and those who make a conscious effort to learn local ways.

In the past, those adventurous foreign travelers who visited such out-of-the-way communities as Cap Lloc seemingly assumed that it was they who had to adjust to the given sociocultural milieus; local people were scarcely expected to meet the standards of the visitors. If their stay was to be prolonged, then they largely entered the native system of accommodation and transportation, and lived as marginal natives. But the tens of thousands of tourists who made their way to Cap Lloc in the 1960s and 1970s were, for the most part, representatives of social strata with little prior experience of foreign travel. Also, they expected their wants and needs to be met according to some as yet poorly defined "international" standard. These attitudes often took the concrete form of quite vociferous objections to Iberian foodways and forms of structuring time—prejudices that are still echoed in the complaints of some tourists (*New York Times*, "Letters on Travel," 30 August 1987).

Needless to say, prejudice was not the monopoly of foreign visitors. Through local eyes—especially in the 1960s—tourists appeared to be well-off and privileged, except perhaps the "hippie" types that posed problems of categorization. We should also keep in mind that the generation of villagers I am discussing were living under a repressive dictatorship (for many years the mayor of Cap Lloc was an army major assigned to administrative duties) and that reasonably well-paying employment and sufficient food were still novelties.

While most residents were aware that the average tourist was not a person of great wealth, it was still difficult to translate socioeconomic concepts across cultural boundaries, especially in the case of summer visitors. What was obvious is that the tourist enjoyed leisure at the very time when the local inhabitant had to work hardest. Furthermore, as in the case of northern Europeans visiting the Mediterranean, somatic differences can be striking, which may bring into play the old myth that, in some subtle way, blond hair, blue eyes, and a light complexion spell money. Finally, most tourists are city people, again a very different world, particularly in the years under discussion.

In summary, the discontinuities created by mass tourism were in the main the consequence of a sudden change from a historic, steady interaction with a limited number of outsiders to the massive influx of short-term tourists. But we should also bear in mind that these villagers were, in common with other Spaniards, victims of one of the longest enduring modern dictatorships; repression generates all manner of responses, but it hardly fosters a sense of empowerment.

Natives and Tourists: The Cognitive Frame

All cultures engage in taxonomic exercises. The universe of experience is categorized, organized, and then related to in terms of culturally defined measures of equivalence and difference. No two models of reality are identical, even between subcultures. Cognitive structures of this type function as a template applied to all that is known or knowable, not the least in human relations. They allow individuals to relate to others in terms of perceived cultural and social distance; they help define, in any given or hypothetical situation, who belongs and who does not. Translated into ethnic relations, these guidelines demarcate boundaries of greater and lesser permeability and the bridges that are recognized to exist across such boundaries.

What happened at Cap Lloc is that with the advent of mass tourism a system of categorization that had functioned as a way of initially differentiating native, stranger, and different sorts of foreigner, became the primary mechanism informing social relations between residents and tourists. Today, as in the past, villagers readily produce fairly concrete descriptions of personality profiles distinctive to a variety of nationalities and ethnic groups. When the subjects are nationals of major European countries or of countries geographically close to Spain, the responses are fairly uniform. Disregarding Spanish ethnic groups, the sharpest delineations include the French, English, Germans, Italians, Portuguese, and Dutch. Most villagers also voice concrete opinions about Americans and Russians, although I suspect that the American image owes much to Hollywood and the ever-popular television series, while the Russian image may be attributed to the role of the Soviet Union as a world power combined with some memories of Russian participation in the Spanish Civil War.

In general, these images combine negative and positive evaluations of behavioral patterns or personal qualities. For example, the English are perceived to have the good qualities of nice manners, honesty, and general integrity. One cannot escape the impression that a degree of culture lag is involved in some common evaluative statements such as "The English always pay"; "Their children are very obedient"; and "You can depend on an Englishman's word." Some of the negative elements in this characterization also have a certain quaintness. English people are described as cold and aloof, haughty, and very demanding. In complaining about an English customer who made a fuss over the quality of the tea served in a restaurant, a middle-aged waitress quipped in Catalan to the local customers, "They are never satisfied, perhaps they think they are in India." True, this was some years ago; more recently I have been asked to shed light on such phenomena as British soccer hooliganism and the tribal markers of inner-city English youth.

English character, as it is still generally perceived, thus combines good points (steadiness, integrity, etc.) with elements that are viewed less favorably (social distance, stiffness, etc.). The stereotype exists as a generalized evaluation applicable to mass tourism. However, given a reasonable length of contact between an individual foreigner and local people, such stereotypes have always been amenable to adjustment. Thus, in the case of an Englishman who, back in the late 1960s, lived for some months in the village—a retired army officer who dressed in what locals regarded as very "English" attire and carried himself with dignity—the general consensus was that English national character as manifested in this individual made for an extremely agreeable combination. In the words of a local shopkeeper,

Sr. ——— is a real English gentleman. He has the English character, very correct. You can tell that he has a sense of discipline and order. No doubt this is the result of many years in the British army and before that having attended one of those expensive boarding schools they have in England. But he is not haughty and will always stop to say a word or two. He tries very hard to speak Spanish and has even picked up some Catalan. Yes, you could never mistake him for anything else but an Englishman, but he does not behave like a *lor* [a "lord," i.e., an aristocrat]. In the past, most of the English who visited the village came from the same educated classes, although not all were as understanding. Today, we generally get a much more rowdy group, drinking at all hours and keeping people awake with their noisy singing.

The man in question never failed to doff his hat to the women of the neighborhood, smile at the children, and greet the men with a cheerful "Good day." The comment of the storekeeper reflects a certain deprecation of contemporary tourists as being less educated and less well-mannered than those typical of an earlier generation. Over the years, I have heard this theme repeated many times, and to listen to some villagers, one is almost led to believe that visitors in the past were all upper-class people. This was hardly the case, but it is an example of how cultural categories are elaborated through a process of selecting some traits and ignoring others. More than this, though, it contrasts a problematic present with a past that is remembered as more predictable, more manageable.

Tourism and the Loss of Individuality

The Englishman described above did not fit the category of the typical tourist and it is just for this reason—for the purposes of contrast—that the case has been looked at in some detail. He lived in the village long enough for his qualities as an individual to emerge above the flood of thousands of other foreigners who overnight or stay one week or two. Many comparable examples could be cited of other outsiders, of different nationalities, who have similarly established their right to be considered as individuals and not just as stereotypes. In a culture where individual qualities are deemed so important, the loss of individuality represents the loss of an important human attribute.

The danger, of course, is that with the growth of mass tourism traditional stereotypes may become applied to all foreigners without the corrective factors that were normally applicable when guests were relatively few. This is more likely to occur when the average length of residence is short and the number of visitors high. Under these conditions, there is a temptation to apply traditional stereotypes virtually automatically, and with increasing emphasis on those attributes of ethnic group identification deemed most negative by the villagers. Thus samples of local conversation can at times suggest that *all* French people are pushy and bad-mannered, *all* Germans are stingy, and *all* Italians are untrustworthy. In the extreme, these stereotypes suggest that tourists as a group are unworthy of friendly consideration. Clearly, such a structure of belief facilitates—even legitimates—modes of interaction designed to capitalize on the ignorance of the average tourist; the traditional rules of social intercourse are simply waived or bent.

When I considered this problem ten years ago, I feared not only that the progressive application of stereotypes facilitated the exploitation of tourists ("Anything is good enough for tourists"), but that it was bound to have very negative consequences for the psychological well-being of the local inhabitants, as is generally the case when one group denies to the other essential human qualities. I attributed this process of the dulling of sensitivities to the pressures and the sheer magnitude of mass tourism (some 100,000 seasonal visitors by the mid-1970s) and to the sense of loss of control that such an influx implied. Tourists, I suggested, were increasingly being categorized as a resource: if culture and environment could be commoditized for purposes of mass tourism, it should not really surprise us that many locals perceived tourists in a comparable manner. How has this analysis stood the test of time?

Protecting "Our" Tourists

To begin to answer this question I will discuss some recent events and explain their significance in more general terms. For the second year in succession, the summer of 1987 was a particularly bountiful one for the anchovy fishery in the Gulf of Lyon. One consequence of this tremendous concentration of valuable fish in neighboring waters was the almost overnight transformation of Costa Brava towns into overcrowded fishing ports. In the process, Cap Lloc found itself the unenthusiastic host to a fleet of around one hundred large fishing vessels from every part of the Spanish coast, each with a crew of eight or nine men.

This "invasion" posed very real problems, most obviously hygienic and environmental. While the Cap Lloc port is quite extensive and well-protected, it simply lacks the facilities to meet the needs of this number of boats and the eight hundred or so crewmen that man them. By the middle of June, the harbor waters were filthy and it did not take very long for the local beaches to begin to suffer. The town doubled its clean-up efforts, but the problem could not be tackled at the source since the municipal government lacked jurisdiction over the harbor.

In the eyes of local people, the negative consequences of this massive incursion went far beyond the cleanliness of the harbor or the state of the beaches: it appeared to pose a genuine danger to livelihood, well-being, and the state of good relations with tourists. Very soon, "Save Cap Lloc" hand-bills, published by the "Cap Lloc Civic Movement," were being distributed in local stores. One that was given to my wife at the bakery refers to Cap Lloc as "our happy and prosperous tourist town" and goes on to describe the effects of last year's visitation as: "a homicide, attempted rapes, robberies, insults, quarrels, all of which led to undesirable publicity." The problems, we are told, continue and could have "international repercussions," presumably by endangering foreign tourists; indeed, something of the sort soon happened in a town across the bay when a young Dutch visitor was knifed by a fisherman.

I am not in a position to assess fully these dangers and problems (the fishermen in question may view matters differently), but I don't for a moment doubt that local opinion believes them to be real enough. What I have found particularly revealing in this series of events is the light they shed on the internal discourse respecting tourists and tourism. The handbills, written in Catalan and Castilian, were obviously for local consumption; in the aftermath of the stabbing, local and Barcelona papers carried angry letters describing the injured Dutch tourist as a friend and neighbor. Very similar judgments stressing the virtues of touristic harmony and warning of the dangers emanating from the anchovy fleet were voiced throughout the town in the summer of 1987.

Do such opinions indicate that tourism and tourists are now perceived in a significantly different manner than was the case in the late 1960s or even the early 1970s? I believe that this is, in fact, the case and that considerable evidence can be marshalled to support such a hypothesis. As noted earlier, one cannot discuss tourism on the Costa Brava without reference to political change. We should understand that modern tourism throughout Spain was the consequence of official development policies that stressed numbers above quality and were remarkably blind to negative effects, such as the deterioration of the human and physical environments and the extreme seasonality of a summer-oriented industry. I agree with Cals (1982, p. 255) that the Generalitat (the autonomous government) and the municipalities cannot undo many of the mistakes of the past, particularly those associated with speculative and haphazard development. Contemporary policies, he believes, should be based on the recognition that the Costa Brava is no longer a new touristic zone and that Catalonia is hardly a Third World country. These considerations should help frame realistic and democratic projects stressing "leisure, the second home, interior tourism and, in general, the quality of life" (Cals 1982, p. 260).

There would appear to be a shift in this direction, at least in the areas I know best. Environmental concerns are clearly much higher than they were even ten years ago, one result being a successful campaign to preserve an important stretch of coastal wetlands, another the recent election of an independent ecological candidate to the town council. If there is more awareness of environmental and ecological issues, part of the reason may be the very different world-view, the very different set of life experiences, that shape the perceptions of the average resident. Cap Lloc is far from a poor town, and while there is some concentration of wealth, small- and medium-sized businesses are the norm—over two-hundred different enterprises according to the town rolls. This distribution of wealth has aided tremendously in widening horizons. For example, many residents, particularly the younger ones, travel in off-season. Going to France hardly merits mention; trips to England and Scandinavia are not uncommon; and I have met several people who have crossed the Atlantic.

Nor is travel and off-season leisure the only significant change. Equally important, in my opinion, is the rise in general levels of education. It is true that historically there had always been a small core of resident professionals—the village doctor, the priest, the pharmacist, several teachers— but what we find today is a combination of more extensive career choices in the professions, a greater number of professional people, and a population with much higher educational qualifications. University training is no longer a rarity (as it still was twenty years ago), and many young people are moving into new fields and professions. No doubt some, such as my neighbor who is finishing her studies in archaeology, will be forced to look for work elsewhere, but contrary to the situation in the past when Cap Lloc was an impoverished village, the regional economy is likely to provide good prospects for all manner of trained people.

To sum up, Cap Lloc is undergoing very profound changes, some local, others more general, that help explain a shift in attitudes respecting tourism and tourists. The distance between hosts and guests has narrowed, tourism is no longer a new phenomenon, and citizens feel that they not only have the right, but the knowledge and experience, to help shape the future of the town and its major industry.

We should be aware, though, that tourism continues to raise some very important questions. The very fact that it is the major national industry can lead to various distortions. A tourism based on fewer people and higher value is a hope rather than a present reality; in the interval, the number of tourists entering Spain keeps increasing, and almost nine million of them stream across the nearby border point of La Jonquera every year (Anuario El País 1987, p. 362). Cap Lloc itself receives almost 400,000 visitors a year (La Temporada Turística 1985 a Catalunya 1986, p. 68) and the pressure of these numbers is well recognized by local officials (*Empordà Federal*, July 1987). Also, as other economic sectors falter, displaced workers are increasingly turning to tourism-related service jobs, most of which are poorly paid. Obviously, these people—and they are to be found at Cap Lloc as elsewhere on the coast—are hardly likely to form part of the changing cultural universe I have sketched in the above paragraphs.

No doubt tourism on this scale will always pose problems and there will always be a need for vigilance. But whatever difficulties lie ahead, they have a better chance of being addressed and resolved in a social and cultural environment that values common humanity over stereotype and caricature.

University of Massachusetts, Amherst

IV

TOURISM IN COMPLEX SOCIETIES

Humans everywhere seek status symbols to reaffirm their identity, and some Western tourists count countries as evidence of their widened experience. For others, the ownership of boats and second homes as forms of recreation are important. John Peck and Alice Lepie in chapter 10 examine the impact of dominantly American tourism upon three American communities and suggest a typology of power, payoff, and tradeoff to assess the differential effects of recreational tourism.

Souvenirs, derived from the Latin *subvenire*, "to come to mind," are an important symbolic adjunct to the tourist industry, providing the tourist with something tangible to take home while simultaneously providing local employment in an arts and crafts industry. The dramatic renascence and increased production of Southwest Indian crafts (Deitch, chapter 11) have been accompanied by an equal upturn in both quality and style, in sharp contrast to the "trinkets" that fill many curio stands elsewhere. However, as Laurence Loeb describes in chapter 12, the available supply of genuine antiques cannot meet the demands of expanded tourism, and in Iran a new industry has emerged specializing in the production of quality "fake art."

The Polynesian Cultural Center (Stanton, chapter 13) is an innovative tourist attraction that has attained great financial success in its thirteen years of operation, but for those who might seek to emulate it elsewhere there is a clear warning: the model culture has succeeded in Hawaii because of the large available audience engendered by mass and charter tourism but might not be a success were it to be undertaken as the primary attraction to an area.

10

Tourism and Development in Three North Carolina Coastal Towns

JOHN GREGORY PECK AND ALICE SHEAR LEPIE

As part of a regional planning project, in 1973 we undertook a study of the impact of recreational tourism on three coastal communities of North Carolina. A preliminary reconnaissance trip indicated the need to develop a framework or model around which we could quickly organize the data, given the complexities of the topic and the stipulated time-lines. As the model (Table 1) emerged, we recognized that it was a potential methodology that could be used to establish a topology of touristic development. Our hypothesis was that both the rate (magnitude and speed) of development and the amount of community involvement and control (power) over the change would affect the amount and distribution of payoffs and tradeoffs associated with increased tourism. We further suspected that of the two, power would be the more crucial factor.

Tourism is subdivided in terms of three criteria of central importance to the indigenous people: (1) power, (2) payoffs and (3) tradeoffs. "Power" in-

The research on which this case study is based was partially sponsored by NOAA Office of Sea Grant, under Grant No. 04-3-158-40, and the State of North Carolina, Department of Administration. The U.S. Government is authorized to reproduce and distribute reprints for governmental purposes notwithstanding any copyright that may appear hereon.

TABLE 1
TYPOLOGY OF TOURISTIC DEVELOPMENT

Rate of Change	*Power Basis*	*Payoffs and Tradeoffs— Effects on Life-Style of Community*
Rapid Growth	"Bedroom" communities Summer residents Specialized commerce (outside financing)	Rapid change of local norms New power structure and economy
Slow Growth	Individual developments Local ownership Expanding local commerce (local financing)	Slow change of norms Stable power structure Expanding local economy
Transient Development	Pass-throughs Weekenders Seasonal entrepreneurs (local financing)	Stable norms Individual mobility within power structure and economy Little overall change in local economy

cludes the ownership of the land that is developed, the source of the financing, the input from local people, and the relation of local traditions to the development projects. "Payoffs" includes benefits to the host culture from tourism, and potential changes in social mobility within the existing social order. "Tradeoffs" primarily involves the social impact, which changes the nature of the communities, such as the consequences of a shift from agriculture and fishing to commerce; a change from three-generation extended families to two-generation nuclear families; and the impact of a wider range of norms and mores on the existing methods of social control. These criteria suggested that dynamic tourism is divisible into three parts: *Rapid Growth, Slow Growth* and *Transient Development.*

Rapid growth occurs when corporations purchase and develop large tracts of raw land to the subdivision lot stage. The lots are then sold to a nonlocal urban market either as an investment or as a site for vacation or retirement homes. Within this context most of the profit realized from sale of the land flows out of the community; much of the labor utilized in the developmental building process comes from outside the local area; and many of the services developed to meet the needs of the new community are provided by outsiders as part of the developer's package.

Slow growth is primarily controlled by local landowners, and involves a substantially smaller number of newcomers and new homes. Development is locally incremental, proportionate to the stability or status quo of the population, and is comparatively unplanned. The occasional newcomers who buy into established businesses or open new enterprises become integrated into the traditional power structures of the communities.

Transient development refers to primarily a weekend and "special event" tourist trade that supplies seasonal income for local native entrepreneurs but requires relatively little cash investment to provide facilities or accommodations for the tourists.

To test the hypothesis we chose three coastal communities (Figure 1), each representing a different style of development yet sharing a number of features with the other two. Each community was small and geographically discrete, and populations ranged from 350 to 1600 people. None of the communities had full-time municipal employees, and local leadership was largely a combination of voluntary service groups and elected part-time officials. Each community was situated on an inland waterway (oceanfront property now is either almost completely developed or held by state or federal agencies) and had a mixed economic base of either local commerce and fishing or local commerce and farming. All three communities shared the process of change and nascent development.

The three target communities were expected to roughly approximate the three styles of tourism development in the topology. Oriental would reflect the rapid growth pattern because of several moderate to large-size real estate developments on its outskirts; Bath would resemble the slow growth aspect of the model because of the relatively stable land ownership patterns and the absence of large tourist developments; Harkers Island would represent the transient state of tourist development based on its position as a potential gateway port to the Cape Lookout National Seashore.

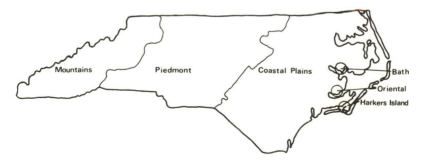

Figure 1. North Carolina.

Field Methods

As "outsiders," the customary role of participant-observer proved useful. Residence in local households validated the field worker's presence in the communities and afforded an intimate view of family life. In the routine daily cycle, daytime hours were normally spent in the community with a spectrum of townspeople of varied occupations and ages. Late afternoons were devoted to the household and socialization during the evening meal. Evenings were spent at church or other civic or voluntary association meetings.

One of the more useful, productive field techniques was an "essay contest" in the schools on Harkers Island. With administrative cooperation, the contest was conducted among fifth and sixth grade children for the best essay on "How tourists affect my community and my Island." Although prizes were awarded to the three best literary essays in each school, our anthropological interest was in the content of *all* essays. Other field methods included extensive interviews and review of historical data. From the wealth of material, three distinct community types emerged, each sharing many aspects with their counterparts yet maintaining their own individuality.

The Region

North Carolina is divisible into three general topographic areas. The Blue Ridge Mountains in the west contain some of the highest peaks in the eastern United States, and western North Carolina has relatively little industrial development, many small towns and hamlets, and a predominately rural, white population. The dominantly agricultural Piedmont section of North Carolina is an area of gently rolling hills containing most of the state's population and industry and most of the north-south arterial highways. East of the Piedmont lies the Coastal Plains of North Carolina: a 100- to 200-mile strip of flat, sandy soil stretching to the Atlantic Ocean.

Coastal North Carolina has a rich history. For over three thousand years, American Indians maintained maritime settlements and hunted, fished, and feasted upon the abundant shellfish taken from the estuaries and coastal shoals. During the early period of Colonial development, pirates sought the protection of the Outer Banks and the many estuarine and river systems served as safe harbors between their forays, and even today local folklore is rich with stories of Black Beard's buried treasure. Later, with the advent of three-masted clipper ships and the whaling industry, whaling stations and fishing villages were established along the Outer Banks. Their only means of communication with the rest of the world was by water. Fishing, ship-building, lumbering, and to a lesser extent plantation agriculture became the coastal zone's primary sources of revenue, but the communications and commercial channels remained by water.

An abundance of navigable waterways has been both a boon and a bane for North Carolina's Coastal Plains. The area is bisected from north to south by the Inland Waterway (a series of shallow estuaries connected by canals), protected from the fury of the Atlantic Ocean by North Carolina's Outer Banks. On an east-west axis, the area is intersected by a number of great river systems, including the Neuse and the Pamlico. These rivers, often several miles wide as they approach the sea, provide the necessary nutrients for bountiful harvests of fish and shellfish. A series of human habitations similar to isolated peninsulas grew up where ground communication and transportation between settlements are often many times the straight-line distance between points. Bridges across the major rivers are relatively few, and the interior areas of the peninsulas were, until recent times, almost impenetrable swamps.

Major changes in the Coastal Plains have occurred in the twentieth century. Despite relatively little in-migration since the Civil War, a series of major storms along the Outer Banks forced the abandonment of many fishing villages and their subsequent relocation within the protected waters of the estuarine and river systems. Massive corporate tree farming has replaced the harvesting of the virgin timber. Within the last decade, giant corporate farms began to assert a dominant position in the agriculture of eastern North Carolina, as well as open-pit mining of phosphate ores and large-scale draining and clearing of former swamp areas.

The coastal area had experienced significant changes since World War II: a rising population, increased affluence, the extension of improved highways to the coastal area, and a large market for "second" homes and recreation areas associated with the tourist industry. Coastal communities that over the last century had had relatively little contact with the outside world began to expand—first with new summer residents and tourists, later with retirees and "newcomers" who came to service the needs of the expanding communities.

North Carolina is rich in natural resources, and her coastal area is unrivaled for sheer beauty anywhere on this continent. Her greatest wealth, however, lies in the peoples of North Carolina. Inherent in this study is an analysis of the life-style, the "gut feelings" of North Carolinians and Down Easterners. Ahead lie choices involving values important to their life-style, between various kinds of tourist development, industrialization, and agri-business.

The Community of Oriental

Oriental is a river town situated near the mouth of the Neuse River where it empties into Pamlico Sound. Oriental is not an old town by coastal North Carolina standards. Prior to the Civil War, the Pamlico Bay area was divided into large plantations, and eighteenth-century homes can still be found around the town.

According to local legend Uncle Lou Midyette (pronounced mid-jet) sought a safe harbor from a storm around 1870, when he "clem a tree" and was enchanted with the area. He envisioned a bustling town and encouraged others to settle there by selling his land cheaply. This booster attitude continues today.

Many businesses in Oriental are composite two-generation, family-owned, and family-run. Typical are a construction firm owned by a county commissioner, his two sons, and their head carpenter; a gasoline station and a hardware-grocery owned by a local father and son; and a combination grill and beauty shop, housed in an old filling station. The grill is operated by the parents of the girl who runs the beauty shop.

The Oriental Marina, Restaurant, and Motel is run by a local widow, and her large bay-view restaurant has a regional reputation for its seafood. The local Rotary Club holds its dinner meetings here. On busy summer weekends the area around the motel stirs with activity as summer camps open and Oriental holds its annual sailing regatta.

Nearby is North Carolina's most modern crab processing plant. To its left is an oak-lined residential street, with large homes once built for lumber company executives or as hotels. Ten years ago they were in disrepair, but now many of them have been restored by summer residents. Beyond these riverfront mansions is the town's public park and fishing pier, a popular place for black residents and white tourists to spend a congenial evening, each commenting on the other's catch.

The established political and economic order in Oriental has traditionally been maintained by white male and female permanent residents forty years of age and older, who own and operate the majority of local essential businesses as well as the most profitable tourist establishments. Despite the decline in lumbering and tourism in the 1940s and '50s, these people have long-term cultural and economic commitments to the town.

In the face of a declining adult population, this core group filled multiple roles in various religious, political, and social organizations to provide continuity in the essential functioning of the community. They are now leaders who can "get things done" at local and county levels, and from whom newcomers, rich and poor alike, must seek informal sanctions and official validations that are necessary to live and work in Oriental.

This host group views Oriental's growth as a revitalization of a once dying town, and works actively and well with newcomers through the Rotary Club, and volunteer fire department, and other local institutions. They deem the influx of population as furnishing much-needed helping hands, rather than as a new group of outsiders competing for power and prestige. In their eyes, the solidarity of the town and its traditions is enhanced rather than threatened by the developing tourism.

Within the last ten years, Oriental has become an "in" place for a growing group of sailboat enthusiasts from Raleigh, the capital of North Carolina, who are enamored with what they perceived to be an "old New England Fishing Village" atmosphere and quality of life. These summer sailors are mostly professionals—doctors, lawyers, professors, and legislators—who, from early March to late October, drive with their families the two hundred miles from Raleigh on weekends to work and live on their boats or to fix up their "summer cottages," often renovated and repainted old homes left over from Oriental's prosperous lumbering past. They are usually affluent, in their forties, and they actively encourage others like themselves to buy summer homes as they become available. However, they are not involved in the rapid expansion of the retiree community and the "second home" real estate developments.

In addition to summer residents, many retirees and a growing group of college-educated, young entrepreneurs have settled in Oriental. Each group claims a strong sense of loyalty and love for the town and for its quality of life and has been integrated into the local scene through participation in service businesses and service organizations.

Completion of a Planned Unit Development resort project will attract more retirees as Oriental is within commuting distance of Cherry Point Marine Air Station, whose medical and post exchange facilities are of major value to retired military personnel. Most of these new residents are widely traveled, with administrative experience. They are accustomed to being busy, and see themselves as important and tend to integrate easily into service organizations such as the Rotary Club, where they predominate.

The retirees in Oriental typify a phenomenon found in all three of the communities studied. Many of the retiree couples consist of native-born eastern North Carolina women who went away to a university, then married and lived elsewhere, only to return later to their native area. Their in-migration tends to import husbands with a higher level of skills than the community norm. Occasional local resentment is aroused however, when these people wish to change the town "too much" or are insensitive to traditional lines of authority.

The college-educated young entrepreneurs are a relatively new phenomenon in eastern North Carolina and in Oriental. For several decades the area exported its college-educated youth as farming became increasingly mechanized and a shrinking population base offered progressively fewer job opportunities. Adventurous and aggressive youths found few rewards here and sought their futures in the North and in the bigger cities of the South.

This traditional pattern appears to be modifying, as a result of changing life goals and value systems among the young. Many of the young couples now settling in Oriental come from the eastern part of the state, but few have direct kinship ties in Oriental. They have been attracted by the quiet, small-town way of life and the newfound opportunity to make a good living in the new businesses generated by the summer sailors and the new retirees. These young people primarily integrate into the community through service clubs and churches, and in time can be expected to play their role in the local political arena.

The increased population and infusion of tourist dollars have improved the economy but heightened an awareness of differential income. Individuals on fixed or limited income, seldom directly affected by tourism but caught in an inflationary squeeze, sense a relatively great deprivation as the income and status of newcomers increase. Some residents are distressed by Oriental's growth and tend to view their declining purchasing power as a disruption caused by progress. They do not want more money; they only want to keep what they have.

Those on a limited or low income also say that they are being victimized by local merchants who have raised their prices to a level accommodating the more well-to-do newcomers. They feel that a progressive town is regressive by taxing them disproportionately for services that will not benefit them. They see no need for city water when they already have a well and pump and are resentful when tax revenues are used to provide Sea Vista—the new retirement community—with city services rather than repairing their own roads.

In addition, they see their neighborhood being invaded by weekend sailors with differing behavioral norms. The weekender's consumption of alcohol is felt by many to be immoral. They experience stress in their family when they must cope with the difference in child-rearing practices between themselves and the weekenders. Frequently they complain that vacationing children are allowed to run wild throughout town and that teenaged "hippies" hang out around town and "make love in the park."

Socioeconomic change in Oriental is subject to other counter trends. Many lots in the new development may be bought by outsiders for investment purposes and not built on. Other purchasers, in an era of tight money, may not be able to complete their payment schedule or to build. These empty lots and sections could remain mosquito-infested marshes, and, except for pockets of retirees and second home owners, it might become a neighborhood without people.

Oriental's growth, paralleling that of the national economy, seems to be slowing. Perhaps this will afford the community a period in which to integrate the differing goals of people who have settled and prevent it from being solely a Rapid Growth community, primarily benefitting outside investors. Newcomers are entering into Oriental's political process, and this seems the most promising road to community integration.

The Community of Bath

Bath, the oldest incorporated town in North Carolina, is a hamlet of only 350 people located on the north bank of the Pamlico River near its entrance into Pamlico Sound. The surrounding land is flat and empty, with stands of tall loblolly pine alternating with fields of corn, tobacco, and soybeans and areas of uncleared swamp land. The community has minimal stores and services. Most shopping is done in Belhaven or Washington, a fifteen-mile distance to the east or west, respectively.

Bath is a National Historical Landmark, with an air-conditioned visitor center offering the tourist a free movie on Bath's history, and where tickets may be purchased to tour the two renovated homes and other landmarks.

Tourists are hardly visible to the town residents. The restored homes are at opposite ends of a long, two-block street and sightseers are encouraged to *drive* the distance between the two houses. Even though the number of tourists is relatively small, the driving tends to reduce the interaction between the residents and the tourists.

Tourism in Bath serves local residents more than outside visitors. The visitor center and the renovated historical landmarks, built with locally-

raised funds, are properly to be admired by outsiders but are fully appreciated only by local residents. The antique shops advertise items for sale to
outsiders, but sell more to local county residents. Local history is primarily
for local rather than outside consumption and is a main focus of Bath's Colonial Book Club, the Historical Society, and daily conversation. By local assessment, tourists seldom stay more than two or three hours, but town-folk
will endure.

Life in Bath is kinship-based. The small resident population includes
families and kin who own much of the farmland around the town. Hence,
there is a sense of belonging to a kin group, to the land and its richness, to
the river, to the traditions and ways that have been a part of this eastern
North Carolina area since well before the Civil War.

Although a great deal of the timberland surrounding Bath is owned either by the phosphate mining companies or by a large wood-pulp and timber company, the traditional wealth is based in agriculture. The crops are
tobacco and corn, and in recent years, soybeans. The younger people, the
sons and daughters, live on the rural family farms, while the older people
have moved into town. There they live a quiet, comfortable, generally affluent life filled with childhood friends and a routine of never-too-busy to visit.
One of the comments frequently made about those who now work for the
phosphate mines is that "they never seem to have time to neighbor."

While making money is a goal for the retail and service businesses in
Bath, retaining an unhurried atmosphere is more important. The gift shops
and the visitor center are places where locals—friends and relatives—can
pass the time of day, relay a message, or stay to have a soda. The women
who work in the stores feel free to bring their younger children to play
while they work, or to supervise them from the shop. A gas station osten-
sively run for "through trade" gets very little of it; the two adjacent garages
are used for the storage of old and miscellaneous junked automobile parts.
The man who pumps gas is on a pension and takes little if any salary. His
reward is to be useful, and to be able to sit and talk with the other retired
men who gather in front of the station.

Outsiders whose destination is Bath are usually professionals from
Greenville or Kinston who either have a vacation sailboat at the marina or a
summer cottage in a section out from town, along the Pamlico River. They
purchase little in Bath except groceries or occasional bits of hardware and
gasoline. Store prices sometimes vary depending on whether or not one is a
local or an outsider. Rarely do the outsiders (sailing enthusiasts) and residents, who prefer motorboats if they can afford them, interact.

Bath, which has changed little in the last half century, will probably expand dramatically in the near future. Adjacent are some of the richest phosphate deposits in the United States. A worldwide fertilizer shortage has prompted companies with extensive mineral options in the area to begin or expand their strip-mining operations, which will create hundreds of new jobs. In the absence of an adequate local labor supply, the new employees will have to be imported.

Bath offers many attractions to the new residents. The school system is deemed better than average in the country; the town is installing a deep-well, central water supply system and plans a municipal sewer system. In addition, large tracts of open land adjacent to the city are potentially available for large scale housing subdivisions.

The future development of Bath will, in large measure, depend upon the continued expansion of phosphate mining in the area and upon the method of bridging the Pamlico River. The existent mines are located across the river, with limited access provided by a ferry service operated by the State of North Carolina on an hourly basis. The alternative to the four-mile ferry trip requires approximately fifty miles of driving west to Washington then east to Aurora, North Carolina. If access to the phosphate strip mines can be significantly improved, then Bath will grow and consequently will shift from the present Slow Growth phase to that of Rapid Growth.

Harkers Island

Harkers Island lies off the Carolina Coast about twenty miles east of Morehead City, and is linked to the mainland by a mile-long bridge and causeway. Until the 1930s, access was limited to private boats or the mail ferry.

Isolation once permeated the island, and old-timers remember when one could walk the entire length of this island freely, with the bay at one side and a dense buffer of forest on the other. In that era hunting and fishing were at will, anytime and anywhere on the island. Since construction of the two-lane, four-mile long highway three decades ago, most of the former rabbit, coon, and deer-hunting areas have been cleared for vacation home sites, and fishing sites are regulated.

Local entrepreneurs along the island road solicit some of the tourist trade by combining a seasonal business such as a restaurant, sports, or gift shop, or seafood stand with an essential, year-round island service such as a grocery, gasoline station, or repair shop. Shops are frequently run by one parent with the assistance of the children once they are out of school.

Local retailers prefer "pass-through" customers because they pay with cash, whereas islanders expect credit. While there is a seasonal rise in business tourist dollars do not continue to circulate in the community. With the exception of seafood caught by the islanders, all supplies must be brought from the mainland by middlemen.

Harkers Island has a stable, exclusively white population of 1600. Residents trace their origin to Diamond City, an eighteenth-century whaling town on Shackleford Banks, on the edge of the Atlantic Ocean, that was finally abandoned in the 1900s after a series of disastrous hurricanes. The present settlement was subsequently relocated landward on Harkers Island. Elements of the former whaling tradition persist in the construction of "flaired bow" boats for which the island is famous. Craftsmanship is still revered; the keel of the fine wooden boats is customarily hand-carved by the owner of the shipyard. Orders even come from Europe because Harkers Island is one of the few remaining sources of custom-made, wooden motor yachts.

Islanders still look fondly across the bay to their "banks" and love to hear the old people's stories about life there. A favorite trip for island families is to boat across the bay to the family's primitive squatter cabin, to spend a weekend swimming and gathering food from the sea. It is a peaceful time, away from modern conveniences and pressures, and they return home wistfully wishing there was a way they could bring back the old way of life.

The islander's concept of land ownership conflicts with that of the vacation home owners. The island is loved as a whole by the natives, and access to all its parts—beaches and open land alike—is considered an islander's birthright. Although land may be sold to outsiders, islanders still expect to be able to pull up their boats anywhere along the bay, and children are supposed to be able to walk and play everywhere. But outsider's bulkheads and "No Trespassing" signs block that inherent right. Frustrated outsiders, imbued with their legal rights, have taken islanders to court and even threatened to shoot at children who step across their lot line.

An indication of the hostility between islanders and outsiders is the vandalism of "outsiders'" vacation homes by local teenagers. By contrast, island fishermen also may have things stolen from their boats, but they usually find out who stole the items and then are able to put out the word that they would like the articles returned.

The concept of ownership also extends to the area between the banks and the island. Local fishermen resent the vacationing outsiders who aggressively stake out the best fishing spots. In addition, island fishermen see their work made harder by the sports fisherman who follows the commercial boats, steals from their nets, or unthinkingly tears their nets by running his motorboat over them. Commercial fishermen feel it unjust that sports fishermen are allowed to cut into the limited supply of fish upon which the commercial fisherman depends for his livelihood.

Natives see their island as a finite area that is gradually being taken over by outsiders through inflating land prices. Traditionally, three-generation extended families owned the land, but because of higher land prices many people now doubt that their children or grandchildren will be able to afford to stay on the island. In selling their land, they have also sold the joy of watching their grandchildren grow up.

Outsiders are almost never integrated into the community. An inward-focused world-view persists where "foreigners" are defined as any nonkin person living outside the island. To be truly accepted requires a church membership and the capacity to trace kin back to the fifteen or so families that came over from the Banks. Few summer people learn to understand the seemingly Elizabethan dialect the islanders speak. Even if they do become accustomed to the speech, the largely urban, middle-class tourist runs up against a rigidly fundamentalist closed society that coolly protects itself against the patronizing "quaint" or "backwards" label it gets from outsiders. Consequently, vacation lots are bought by outsiders who rarely stay for more than a week because they begin to feel isolated. To entertain themselves they encourage groups of friends either to come down and party with them or to buy adjoining lots.

A strong sense of loss and resentment permeates when islanders talk about the tourists. Islanders believe they are economically caught in a losing battle. Stories are told of people who sold bay property lots for more money than they had ever seen, only to discover that their land had been sold for less than its replacement value. They feel that the outside encroachment lessens the quality of life on the island.

Religion is very important to the islanders. Touring revivalists are still able to draw the biggest crowds of any event on the island. God's Will involves every aspect of the individual's life, and the intimate and comforting closeness they feel to Jesus reveals, for them, the direction their lives should take. For the more fundamentalist churchgoer, it is a joyous, liberating kind of religion that involves the whole body in its worship. For all island church members, religion is an involving association that encompasses their family, kin, and closest friends.

For the great majority, the Sabbath is a restful day devoted to church attendance, a big noon meal, and to visiting family. But weekend outsiders do not conform to this expected behavior, and resentment is deep towards streets congested with a steady stream of big cars pulling large fiberglass motorboats, or when spirited gospel singing is drowned out by the week-ender's power lawnmower or a boisterous party.

In the face of the tourist invasion, islanders are resigned to the attitude that there is little that can be done to modify the almost apocalyptic process they envision. Passivity in the face of God's Will is an interpretation that Fundamentalist religion encourages. Attention to the soul and that of the family is the most constructive course to ease dissatisfaction.

In addition to the religious introversion, Harkers Island has no truly functioning local political or governmental mechanisms. As a result, the community is poorly equipped to cope with the outside world, and with the internal problems of integrating rapid changes, when concerted group action or "political clout" is needed. Few members in the community are experienced in dealing with outside political entities. The future is problematic for Harkers Island. While today's tourism is still "transient," it has already been able to change the land use of the island, if not yet its social norms. More significantly, due to the lack of political strength and cohesiveness, the future development of tourism may be decided by people, conditions, and forces well outside the kinship, religious, and social networks of the islander community. Thus Harkers Island reflects the Transient Development stage in its early phases.

Conclusions

The three-fold model of tourism proved a useful device to distinguish between the three communities and the level of tourism associated with them. The nature of tourism in any given community is the product of complex, interrelated economic and political factors, as well as particular geographic and recreational features that attract "outsiders." The model also suggests that the *rate* of culture change induced by tourism affects the integration of the community, as well as the *magnitude* of the change. The nature of change associated with tourism must also be correlated with the *source of regulatory power*—that is, whether the host culture or an external force is the prime element. Power, both economic and political, emerged as the central differentiating factor in the impact of tourism. A strong local power base tended to direct the development toward compatibility with the local community and tended to foster integration of newcomers into the established network. Tourism may be assessed as an acculturation process with cyclical tendencies. In those situations where the acculturating groups have roughly equal power, a minimum of community disruption and disintegration will occur.

Epilogue, by John Gregory Peck

It has been almost fifteen years since the initial study of Bath, Oriental, and Harkers Island was completed. We have had three new presidents, two new governors, several economic upturns and downturns, and still the communities have persisted in their patterns of development and tourism. A brief "re-study" was made in the summer of 1987 to see what changes had occurred.

Harkers Island

To the tourist's eye, little seems to have changed on Harkers Island in the last decade and a half. Houses along the main road look a little older, perhaps, and traffic a little heavier, but there is very little that seems "new." The "Island" column in the city newspaper still recounts who is visiting whom, local births and weddings and deaths, and shopping trips made to Greenville or Morehead City. The ladies of the Mormon Church are once again assembling a Harkers Island cook book Thursday evening at the church and welcome all newcomers to help. The same families run the same stores, only the children are of a different generation.

Change is more apparent on the far side of the island, back where the boatworks are located. The "backroad" has been paved, and the area developed into half-acre lots. It strikes a city person as a strange development—a mixture of us$70,000- to us$120,000-houses interspersed with house trailers and campers. There are almost no vacant lots, and almost none for sale.

A few of the locals live here, but mostly this is an area of retirees—both permanent residents and summer people. Some are locals who moved away a long time ago, and have come home to the island to retire. This seems to be a community of older people; there are very few basketball hoops in the yards, few tricycles in the driveways, and no children playing.

The population of the island generally seems to be aging. The principal of the primary school talks of his declining enrollment—they've lost almost 25 percent of their student population in the last ten years, and a couple of teaching positions too. The names of his students are changing. It used to be that a handful of surnames would account for upwards of 60 percent of his students; nowadays, the old names are still there, but mostly there are new names and new families.

The language of Harkers Island is being lost as well. There are fewer of the old-timers left who still talk the "hoi toiders" (high tiders) away. Children quickly lose it when they go off-island, to secondary school, where they are teased by the mainlanders for "being different." It is only among the young who drop out of school and go to work "in the water" (i.e., fishing), that the distinctive language of Harkers Island remains, and this is a declining group, as commercial fishing continues to decline on the island.

Even the distinctive boat-building craft unique to Harkers Island has changed. One still sees the occasional boat under construction in a back yard or boat shed, its graceful gull-winged bow sweeping high, but most boat hulls are now made in the new factory on the far side of the island, and are made of fiberglass rather than wood.

The island people's roots on the Shackleford Banks are gone, too—bulldozed by the government to make way for a national park. A few still go there to show their children where Diamond City was, or where they had their squatter cabin, but there is little left now to have much significance.

More and more, the young people are leaving Harkers Island. There is no more land for them to settle and too few jobs. A few find homes in the trailer court developments that have sprung up on the mainland near the bridge to the island, but these are sad substitutes for island living—treeless and hot, without the breeze and the sound of the ocean. Others have gone off into the world; they may keep in touch as best they can, and they will visit and write, perhaps someday returning to their island.

Oriental

Things are humming in Oriental. From as far away as fifteen miles, the smart, attractive road signs of Sail Loft Realty, Oriental Reality, and Mariner Realty tell you of the many opportunities to participate in the casual affluence of this community, a resurrected pirate's retreat, designed for the '80s. One can live in Buccaneer Bay West, or Teach's Cove (Blackbeard's family name), Mainsail Point, or one of perhaps a dozen other small, new real estate developments scattered along the Neuse or Pamlico Sound. Participation is possible—that is, if one can afford the price of the lot (from us$20,000 to us$60,000 and up) and the home to be built on it.

There are three construction firms, in this town of 600 registered voters, that will see to the building of your house; five restaurants that will feed you well and appropriately; three full-service grocery stores to keep your larder full; a number of small shops and boutiques, like "Blackbeard's Treasure Chest," to indulge your every whim; and even a local florist shop. The latest addition to the town's list of amenities is "The Village Club," a "year-around social and physical fitness center," complete with indoor pool, cafe and lounge, and baby-sitting services.

The shopping area along the main street, near the river, is bright and crisp, with plenty of trees. The old houses have been converted into attractive shops and offices, and everything seems freshly painted and revitalized. One imagines that this must be what Cape Cod looked like, a generation or more ago, before it was "discovered."

With its active chamber of commerce and its forward-looking mayor and town council, Oriental appears to have embraced the benefits from its growing developments. It has both a municipal water system and a sewer system, and is an effective political force in the county. Oriental residents welcome the newcomers, most of whom live outside the political boundary of the town and are thus good for business but do not disturb the status quo.

The newcomers are often defined as "retirees," although many of them have not yet retired. Often they are the well-off and successful, in their mid-forties to mid-fifties. Their investment in a home near Oriental is an investment in their eventual retirement. They now come from all parts of the East Coast of the country, finding Oriental by word-of-mouth to be a viable (and less expensive) alternative location to summer homes and retirement homes in the more crowded sections of New England. They are the vanguard of the youth of the 1950s and 1960s, who have "made it" in the big cities and the corporate world, and are now planning and preparing for the ambience and affluence of their active middle years of retirement. They come because of the sailing afforded by the river and the sound; because of the climate; because of the charm of the town and its environs; and because of the reasonable cost of living they perceive Oriental provides them.

There are other newcomers, too: people who have come to work for the real estate firms, the banks and stores, the construction firms—the many service and retail jobs that are necessary to supply and support the growing population of the well-to-do. Often these newcomers will live in one of the nearby towns, or in the countryside, away from the water, where the cost of housing is less, and they earn a good living. They feel positive about their lives and their future, and development has been good for them.

Development has been good for many of the town's residents of fifteen years ago as well. Land has appreciated; the building that has gone on has been done by local landowners; and the projects have been small. Accustomed to the influx of tourists in the summer, the residents seem to have adjusted easily to their growth. The growth, however, has not benefitted everyone equally. The crab processing plants continue to be the main employer for the blacks of the area. Some of the old-time residents, particularly widows who retired to Oriental in the 1950s and 60s, find the new life-styles and new residents difficult to cope with, the cost of living high, and the increase in population confusing. For them, Oriental's promise of the future is bleak indeed.

Bath

Not much seems to have changed in Bath. The gas station garage at the edge of town has been torn down, and it has been said that a restaurant will be built there. However, if a visitor wants to stay at the motel across the street he still must find the man (now retired) who used to run the state liquor store (currently run by his wife) at the other end of town to get the key. A new fellow is operating the tire center and auto repair shop (us$3.00 to fix a flat), and of course, there's a new factory further down the road that manufactures high-tech charcoal filters, reportedly for the space agency. Yet, it does not *seem* as if much has changed in Bath.

An "outdoor drama" has come and gone since our initial study of Bath. Residing in Bath for ten summers, it brought in between 4000 and 7000 visitors each year. The visitor's center is doing well, too: almost 30,000 people visited last year to see the movie, pick up a brochure, or simply to ask questions. Still, not many of these visitors stay for long—most of them are on their way elsewhere, and are just passing through.

The town of Bath has had a land-use plan for a number of years, and has stuck to its policy of very limited development with surprising tenacity. While it has recently annexed Springdale Village, a community of nineteen houses, it has resisted attempts to develop marinas along the Pamlico. It has even gone to court over the matter, and the town has prevailed.

There are still only about 180 homes in the town, although there has been some change in who occupies the homes. As the old residents have died or moved away, their places have been taken by retired farmers moving in from the countryside. The charcoal filter factory employs mostly local people, so there's been no need to find housing for them. If there is a need for outsiders to spend time there, and they cannot find room with friends or kin, they can stay at the Bath Guest House bed-and-breakfast.

There have been changes, of course; perhaps the biggest change being that Bath is losing its school to consolidation, and there is much speculation as to what will happen to the old school building and playground on Main Street near the middle of town. Already some of the windows have been broken as happens when a building remains vacant. Another major change is the new municipal sewer system that just went into operation. Not everyone is happy with this change—many sewer and water bills went up almost 500 percent!

Over the years, a number of tourist developments have been established up and down the Pamlico, outside of Bath including Katnip Point, Sawmill Landing, Blackbeard's View, and Mixon Creek, which was developed by Weyerhaeuser, a major timber company. These developments seem to have had little impact on Bath itself. Because there is no big grocery store in town people generally shop elsewhere, though perhaps the tea room gets some business, as well as the liquor store and the gas station.

Phosphate mining at Texasgulf is about as it was fifteen years ago, and the ferry service across the Pamlico still runs once an hour, leaving Bath still much as it was half a century ago, poised on the edge of change.

Further Thoughts

In our original model, we indicated that both *rate of change* and *magnitude of change* would directly affect community integration. We also indicated that the *source of regulatory power,* that is, whether or not the host community had access to that power, would be the differentiating factor in determining the positive or negative impact of tourism on the host community. This view seems to have been supported by our further study.

Harkers Island, still only an unincorporated community and covered by county regulatory authority, has been the community most negatively affected by the in-migration of tourists. While the local churches—the area's primary source of community integration—still seem strong and viable, its school system is in decline. Because the younger generation of Harkers Islanders and their children are leaving, it will only be a matter of time until the church population ages and ultimately declines. The unique linguistic character of the island is also declining, as is its unique craft, the Harkers Island boat. The community's ties to its past, to the Banks, are gone. Its future seems to rest in "God's Will."

Oriental, with its strong and active local government, and commercial infrastructure, has fared well in the face of the increasingly rapid development of its tourist industry. The school system is thriving; most land that is being developed is owned by local people; and the newcomers are mostly affluent and value the town's appearance and traditions. There seems to be enough for everyone, and there is no "image of limited good," but rather an image of unlimited expansion. While some of the old-timers and locals may eventually get the designation "quaint," they will probably chuckle about it "all the way to the bank."

Bath has successfully resisted change by maintaining a strong town government, planning effective land-use, and by resorting to the court system to enforce its goals where necessary. It has maintained and improved its quality of life—and the quality of the River—most notably by completing its new municipal sewer system. This innovation may, however, become its Achilles' heel: with only 180 houses to pay for it, the cost of the system may become prohibitive. The need to expand its service base will inevitably present the town with choices, the most expedient of which may be the development of tourist housing linked to the marinas and access to the river.

Professor emeritus
North Carolina State University, Raleigh

11

The Impact of Tourism on the Arts and Crafts of the Indians of the Southwestern United States

LEWIS I. DEITCH

The role of tourism in altering segments of a traditional culture has not fully been examined. This study examines the impact of tourism upon the arts and crafts of the Indians of the American Southwest. Diffusion has been one of the major mechanisms of cultural change, but in assessing the role of diffusion the anthropologist has most often looked at the impact of trade, migration, war, and missionary contact. The tourist has been ignored as a potential source of new ideas that could alter or disrupt segments of a traditional culture.

The peoples of the Southwest have been exposed to European culture since the Spanish settled the Rio Grande Valley of New Mexico in the early 1600s. Their arts have experienced periodic infusions of new ideas, materials, and techniques. Art forms have flourished and waned. However, in the twentieth century (particularly since World War II) tourism generated many changes. Never before has there been such an abundance of Indian rugs, pottery, jewelry, *kachinas*, and baskets, nor have prices been so high.

Other art forms, such as paintings, are also rapidly developing. Throughout the nation, people are aware of the native arts of the Southwest, and many are eager to possess something Indian. For the first time since white contact, the Indian has a commodity that is sought by members of Western society.

This study examines the phenomenal growth of the Indian arts and crafts market brought about by their exposure to the rest of the nation through tourism and other factors, such as the national awakening to the importance of preserving those roots of the total American heritage that were a decade ago in danger of vanishing, and the Indian's self-awareness resulting from the Civil Rights movement, which has further engendered a pride in his traditions.

A Brief Historic Sketch

The concept of aesthetics exists in most societies, and such activities express an artistic sense of value and provide a measure of self-satisfaction. Among the Indians of the southwestern United States, arts and crafts have been integral to their culture for centuries. The present forms reflect an evolutionary process that has been heightened in the twentieth century by the creation of a commercial market of significant importance.

The sedentary cultures of the Pueblos trace their origins to pre-Columbian farmers who left a rich heritage in crop domestication, house construction, tool-making, and ceremony. At the time of Spanish contact, the Pueblo people were already well versed in the arts of pottery, baskets, cotton cloth, shell jewelry, and *kachina* figures. Other sedentary peoples also had developed the arts of pottery and basketry. Among the Papago, Walapai, and Ute, basket-making had reached a fine level of craftsmanship. The seminomadic ancestors of the contemporary Navajo and Apache (the Athapascans) were newcomers to the Southwest at the time of Spanish contact, and appear to have lacked the artistic sophistication of the Pueblo dwellers.

The Navajo were quick to learn new concepts. By the start of the eighteenth century they were weaving garments—a trait learned from contact with the Pueblos. During this same period, the Spanish introduction of sheep into the Rio Grande Valley led the Navajo and Pueblo to incorporate livestock into their economies and to the art of weaving in wool. The Navajo, however, more readily took to the domestication of sheep and goats as a major livelihood, and thus the weaving of wool garments and rugs became a more integral part of their aesthetic expression than it did among the

Pueblo peoples. The Navajo weavers experimented with designs and color, and began to use new commercial woolens such as bayeta and Saxony. By the mid-nineteenth century, Navajo skill in weaving reached a level of excellence as seen by surviving museum specimens. Among the Pueblo people, weaving was a male-dominated activity associated with religious ceremonies. In Navajo society the women became the weavers as ownership of livestock was vested in the matrilineal family.

During the mid-nineteenth century, another art form, silverwork, diffused into the Southwest from the Mexicans of the Rio Grande Valley. The Navajo first derived silver jewelry in trade for horses, but by 1860 they were manufacturing their own silver ornaments. From the Navajo, the trait spread among the Zuni and Hopi. The Rio Grande pueblos also developed silverwork from direct contact with the Spanish. The earliest Indian jewelry consisted of only silver. The use of turquoise, coral, and shell developed toward the end of the nineteenth century, and turquoise became the most valued stone. Turquoise has been used in the Southwest for centuries, primarily strung into necklaces. It has in many cases strong significance in ritual and ceremonial life, especially among the Pueblo peoples.

At first the Indians imitated Spanish styles, but as with weaving, new designs appeared including the so-called squash blossom, which many tourists consider "typically Indian." The design is a Navajo interpretation of the popular Spanish pomegranate worn as ornamentation during the mid-nineteenth century. Silversmithing has remained a male-dominated art form, as was also true among Spanish craftsmen.

The art of pottery-making nearly died out when the white man introduced metal pots. Likewise, basketry nearly vanished. Since these art forms served primarily a utilitarian purpose, only a few ceremonial pieces remained. However, the twentieth century brought about a dramatic revival of the arts of pottery and basket-making that rivals the ancient skills.

Early Twentieth-Century Impact

For most Indians in the United States, the coming of the white man spelled certain doom for traditional ways. The railroad, for example, heightened the pressure upon the Plains Indians and was a major contributor to the end of their way of life. So, too, in the Southwest, the Indian was threatened. However, since significant settlement did not occur until the 1880s, and the major influx commenced after the turn of this century, these Indians were spared much of the cultural devastation that disrupted other groups. Furthermore, in the 1920s the government began to reverse earlier policies aimed at assimilation.

The Southwest has long held a degree of fascination for Americans; its majestic canyons, vast and colorful vistas, and unique desert flora appealed to the frontier spirit of the American personality (Turner 1920). The blend of Hispano and Indian cultures further exemplified this romance. Most of the early twentieth-century visitors or settlers were drawn here because of medical advice from the Public Health Office and private physicians that the arid climate offered amenities for respiratory illness. White businessmen found that catering to these newcomers was profitable, and the first stage in the development of a resort industry commenced. Fortunately, the historic flavor of the Southwest manifested itself in an architectural revival of Spanish and Indian styles, and by 1930 these designs were widespread in use for private homes, public buildings, and hotels. Sante Fe, New Mexico enacted legislation prohibiting all but Hispanic-Indian construction and generated an awareness of and an interest in the people from whom the architecture was borrowed. The growing white communities needed recreation, and rodeos and fiestas were expanded and Indian ceremonies took on new meaning as rituals for outside enjoyment. The colorful pageantry of the "Wild West," the Spanish, and the Indians all stimulated tourists to come to the Southwest.

The Fred Harvey Company and the Sante Fe Railroad pioneered tourism and were very instrumental in fostering the Southwestern image. Begun as a curio business in 1899, the Fred Harvey Company later erected a chain of hotels along the Sante Fe route to facilitate stopovers and at adjacent scenic locations easily accessible from the railroad. With the exception of the rustic Grand Canyon lodges, all their hotels promoted the rich Spanish and Indian flavor, and included shops stocked with Mexican and Indian arts and crafts, staffed by native peoples. To the visitor this was the epitome of the Southwest, and nearly everyone bought something to take home. The trend continued and local residents also adorned their homes with handicrafts representative of the traditional cultures upon whose history the new image was being based. The Santa Fe Railroad constructed most of their stations in Spanish style and permitted Indians to sell their wares on the platform, thus further stimulating a market for such goods. Until the decline of passenger service in the 1960s, the stop of a train at Albuquerque was a colorful occasion as dozens of Indians lined the platform selling beads, jewelry, small pottery pieces, and other tourist-oriented curios. Often this was a traveler's first introduction to the romanticism of the region. It was fortuitous that the early twentieth-century settlers and health-seekers became interested in the indigenous cultures and historic traditions of the Southwest, and that the prime entrepreneur recognized their marketability as a tourist attraction. Otherwise, the decline of Indian arts and crafts would have paralleled other elements of their culture, as was true in other parts of the United States where white settlers paid little or no attention to the existing culture or to their aesthetics.

To best understand the early twentieth-century impact, each major art form is examined separately:

1. *Navajo Rugs.* During the nineteenth century, the trading post introduced aniline dyes, and Navajo weaving reached a dynamic level of brilliant color and design. The advent of the railroad brought an availability of colored, commercial yarns (Germantowns) that were used from the 1880s until the early 1900s. Many of these rugs represented excellent craftsmanship, both in design and in the quality of the weaving. But with increasing tourist interest, many traders encouraged rapid production, and as a result many rugs of the early twentieth century were inferior. Also during this period, many Navajo weavers turned away from the aniline dyes and began to use natural wool including dark browns and blacks.

Fred Harvey encouraged weavers to produce fine quality rugs and wall hangings that would appeal to tourists, with designs reflective of the nineteenth-century Navajo traditions, and to experiment with new designs. Thanks to his mercantile outlets, he could afford to pay higher prices and also absorb expanded production. Thus he prevented many of the earlier Navajo weaving traditions from being lost. Another entrepreneur, Don Lorenzo Hubbell urged weavers to produce rugs based upon predrawn designs he provided. Hubbell must be credited with helping to produce many fine rugs in the classic tradition as well as introducing the Navajo of the Ganado area to a deep red dye that has since become known as Ganado red (today a valued rug style). The quality of craftsmanship and design in Navajo rug weaving points to a latent sense of aesthetics added by weaving to the culture of a people who had previously been nomadic and had not possessed the technology through which their artistic values could be expressed. The Navajo simultaneously developed a new mythology to accompany rug weaving, and believe the art was handed down by Spider Woman. In honor of her, any rug with a border to the design must possess a slight flaw in the border (a spirit line), lest the weaver's soul be bound up in the rug. On the practical side, the Navajo woman gained new status and earned substantial income to keep pace in a world of ever-increasing economic desires.

Throughout the Navajo area, trading posts competed with each other to capture the rug market and thereby fostered local weaving. By the 1930s, it was possible to recognize regional patterns, and a rug was known by the name of the trading post near which it was woven. Many new styles emerged, of which the major ones are grouped as follows:

a. Yei rugs: Rugs portraying *yei-bichai* or ceremonial dancers, using a combination of natural wools and aniline dyes.

b. Vegetable dyes: Rugs that combine old geometric designs with the use of wools that have been dyed naturally.

c. Storm patterns: Woven mainly in the southwestern portion of the reservation, these rugs are characterized by sharp black and white contrasts with jagged lines that resemble lightning.

d. Two Gray Hills: Rugs of very fine quality (over one hundred weft threads to the inch) woven of carded natural colors into intricate geometric designs. By the 1930s these were the most sought-after rugs by those who wanted quality weaving.

Until the 1960s, prices were comparatively low, and the weaver received only a few cents per hour for her labor. Although traders often marked up prices to allow for considerable profit, most rugs could be purchased for less than US$25. Even considering the value of the dollar prior to World War II, Navajo weaving was not expensive, and local whites used the rugs as floor coverings. Although no accurate counts were ever made, the number of rugs produced per year was considerably less than today, and because of other modernizing influences many young Navajo girls were not interested in learning the arts of the loom. Thus the future of weaving among the Navajo showed definite signs of eventual decline. The postwar years, however, were to change that prospect.

2. *Jewelry.* The buying tastes of American tourists suggest that they often want "trinkets" as souvenirs, especially something that, unlike rugs or pottery, is a personal adornment. Its visibility says "I've been there," and Indian jewelry fits that category. Much of the jewelry was originally made for the Indian market, used as a display of wealth among Navajo people and as a medium of pawn among the Navajo and Pueblo people when spare cash was needed.

The tourist trade motivated the production of a wider range of jewelry styles including necklaces, rings, bracelets, concho belts, and bola ties. Silversmithing became a full-time profitable occupation for many men. During the early twentieth-century period, distinctive regional jewelry styles emerged as a result of individual creativity and the urging or suggestion of various traders. The main styles were:

a. Hammered silver: The original Indian jewelry made from silver dollars or Mexican pesos later gave way to designs hammered from sheet silver.

b. Sandcasting: This form of silver working is the most difficult to master and has not been widely adopted. A sandcast piece is formed in a mold usually of finely ground volcanic pumice.

c. Overlay: a design is cut out of one piece of silver, which is then joined to a second piece by means of sweating (heating). By oxidation, the cut out area is discolored to produce a tarnished appearance. Overlay is best associated with Hopi silver and was encouraged in 1938 by the Museum of Northern Arizona as a means of duplicating in silver the geometric patterns of Hopi pottery.

d. Silver and turquoise: Turquoise was set into sandcast pieces and on occasion into overlay. However, the best uses of turquoise were achieved by setting the stones into prepared casements (referred to as channel work) or by careful mosaic inlay. The Zuni became the experts of such finely delicate turquoise, shell, and coral work, although other groups used the same materials.

3. *Pottery.* The cultural flourish of classical pottery occurred among the Pueblo peoples prior to A.D.1300, and also among the Hohokam of the lower deserts. Exposure to the Spanish and later to the Americans led to a decline in pottery making among the Pueblos, Pima, and Maricopa as trade goods replaced the traditional storage and cooking pots. The increase in tourism during the early twentieth century created demand for small pottery pieces, but many of the older designs had been forgotten. Among numerous tribes, such as the Hopi, archaeologists and museums helped reintroduce traditional designs that were thought lost. A classic example of the revival of lost designs occurred during the 1920s, when noted archaeologist J. W. Fewkes was excavating near the Hopi First Mesa. One of the Hopi workers encouraged his wife to copy the designs. Fanny Nampeyo became one of the revivalists, and her pottery is today classic and exceptionally valuable (Sikorski 1968). Tourism thus restored a craft that had nearly disappeared, the one major difference being the decrease in the size of the pieces from those of former utilitarian value to those of saleable value.

4. *Basketry.* Basketry is one of the oldest art forms of the Southwest, and its manufacture has continued for ceremonial use while other art forms decline. Tourism during the early twentieth century appears to have had no effect upon basket manufacturing.

5. *Bead Making.* Like basketry, bead making is an ancient craft that has persisted among some tribes. Shell and coral beads were easily sold to early tourists and thus the art continued.

6. *Kachinas.* Among the Pueblo people, small *kachinas* carved as a symbolic likeness of the spirits that play an important role in their worldview served as a medium of instruction for the young. For the tourist, the *kachina* figures had great appeal. It is lightweight (carved of cottonwood root), and the variety of "grotesque" figures seemed to imply a connotation of "savage" and of "Indian" in the minds of the tourists. Since *kachinas* are sacred, touristic demands for the figures necessitated a change in their style, one that lacked the full symbolism and was more brilliantly painted using inexpensive tempera. Genuine *kachinas* were and still are available, but since the 1940s even they have been painted in poster colors. *Kachinas* are and always have been produced by men as they represent the sacred spirits with whom only initiated males have intimate association.

The New Awakening

During the depression years of the 1930s, tourism to the Southwest decreased, but the number of migrants traveling highway U.S. 66 to California rapidly increased. Military bases and aircraft plants built during the war years brought a new influx. Traffic through the area by rail and auto increased, and although people were concerned about the war, the market for Indian goods grew during the 1940s.

In the postwar decades of 1950 through 1970, with greater national affluence and increasing expenditures on highway construction, Americans took to the road. The national parks and resort areas became major foci of attention, and the Southwest became one of the favored locales. Advertising and publicity of the desert climate, the scenic attractions, and the romance of the Indian and Hispanic past paid off. The resident population rapidly grew with the expansion of the aircraft and electronics industries and the continued importance of military bases.

In 1960, most Indian handcrafts were priced well within the reach of the average American tourist or collector, most of whom did not consider them true art or valuable. They were curios of the Southwest, and even to most local residents they were decor elements that represented the flavor and romanticism that the Southwest had created as its image to the nation.

A combination of factors and events has changed the picture. Today Southwestern Indian arts and crafts are valuable. With prices spiraling, most quality objects are beyond the reach of the average tourist or collector. Production, price, and quality have all simultaneously increased. Although some old-time residents lament about the "good old days" of fine rugs and jewelry, the fact clearly remains that the classical rugs of the nineteenth century, and the old sandcast or inlaid jewelry, or the earlier pottery pieces, are artistically no match for the precision and quality of today's crafts. At the same time, the market is being flooded with much poorly-made art: imitation turquoise, silver plate, and commercial yarn rugs. Some of the merchandise is of foreign manufacture or made by Indians in assembly-line fashion by shops selling their products as "genuine" Indian-made. For example, rugs of Navajo design woven on shuttle looms in Mexico can be found in the Southwest. Normally they are sold as copies, but less reputable dealers may not be so honest and sell them as genuine Navajo rugs.

The Indian attitude toward handicrafts has changed rapidly. Until the "boom" in the Indian art market, these crafts were both a means of expressing the artistic values of each Indian culture as well as a way of providing extra revenue.

The Indian has always resented the exploitation of the crafts market, which tended to put him "in the blanket" as he once stood on a railway platform proffering his wares to the tourist who often cared little about its symbolism but bargained for something "Indian," bought from a *real* Indian. That subservient role has totally disappeared. Although some Indian entrepreneurs still set up sidewalk stalls around the plaza in "Old Town" in Albuquerque or on the Santa Fe Plaza, today they firmly hold to their price and little or no bargaining occurs.

The factors responsible for the rapid rise in the 1970s in the popularity of Indian crafts, in the accompanying price increases, and in the change in the Indians' attitude include:

1. *The Civil Rights Movement.* The success of the civil rights movement, especially among blacks, stimulated many of the tribal leaders in the Southwest to appraise the social and economic position of their people. In light of rising wages nationally, one obvious area of exploitation was in the sale or trade of rugs, jewelry, pottery, and other art objects. Tribal guilds were established as a means of assuring the direct sale of crafts and a better price for the artist; however, not all handicrafts are sold to tribal guilds. Much still enters the open market, and today most Indian craftsmen know the value of their work and demand higher prices for their labor. A pride in being Indian, and a desire to preserve and foster Indian traditions during the 1960s, have profoundly influenced the Indian artist who is now more concerned with tradition and fine craftsmanship than at anytime in the past.

Traditional sex roles still persist with few exceptions. Pottery making, basketry, and rug weaving are traditionally women's crafts while painting, jewelry, and *kachina* making are men's activities, with Pueblo men weaving cotton sashes and garments. Much of the work takes place in the home, but some of the more noted artisans perform at exhibitions and have furthered their own careers by such appearances. A strong sense of competition has entered into the production of fine pieces for exhibition at tribal, county, and state fairs as well as at museum shows, and the prize ribbons are greatly valued by more aggressive individuals. However, the majority of the craftsmen are only part-time artists, people who engage in handicrafts as a supplemental activity. Thus the majority of the Indian artists are unknown to the buyer.

2. *The Increase in the Southwestern Population.* By the 1960s, the Southwest contained over three million residents, a gain of several hundred percent over the 1900 figure and a gain of over 150 percent above 1940. This was mainly an urban gain fostered by economic opportunity and retirement. Consequently, the home market for Indian art was enlarged and the wearing of at least a piece of Indian silver became almost a Southwestern tradition.

By the mid-1980s, the Southwest population increased by an additional thirty-five percent and tourism is a multi-billion dollar annual industry. Greater emphasis is placed on the romanticism of the Southwest than was evident some twenty years earlier. Indian arts are featured in shops all across the region, often concentrating in specific downtown areas such as around the Santa Fe Plaza, in Old Town Scottsdale, at Tlaquepaque in

Sedona or along the old highway route U.S. 66 through Flagstaff and Gallup.

3. *The Increase in Tourism.* By the 1960s, most of the Southwest was accessible by road, and increasing numbers of retirees, winter vacationers, and "snowbirds" (temporarily leisured farmers from the wheat states of the U.S. and Canada) flocked to the Southwest for recreational tourism. The open spaces of the Southwest, the many parks and monuments, and the appeal of the Western frontier image—including an ethnic interest concerning Indian culture and life—have involved the area in mass tourism. A significant trend of the 1970s is the increased number of international visitors, notably Europeans and Japanese for whom the Grand Canyon and the Indians are a specific, preplanned target. Individual tourists also discovered the diversity and quality of Indian culture and art. Sales increased, stimulating production increases, and stimulating further Indian awareness among the tribes. As the merchandise diffused around the country and the world, interest was generated even among those who had not been to the Southwest.

4. *The "Americana" Trend.* During the late 1960s, partly as a result of foreign entanglements, pollution, and governmental mistrust, many young Americans began to look back to early Americana. Natural foods, communal living, and collecting of antiques, artifacts, and other bits of Americana became widespread. Indian crafts, especially jewelry, fell into this category, thus further increasing demand and helping to raise prices. This trend has continued into the 1980s, and has been heightened by a nationwide awareness of the richness and diversity of the American way of life.

5. *Investment.* Economic uncertainties prompted many investors to seriously consider solid objects such as fine paintings, ivory, and Indian art as sources for capital gain. Financial journals encouraged such collecting as sound investment, which motivated smaller collectors to invest, and this in turn further raised prices.

In addition to their increased value, changes in the art forms have also occurred:

1. *Navajo Rugs.* Today the emphasis is on fine-quality rugs using natural wool and vegetable dyes. Two Gray Hills, Tec Noc Pos, Chinle, Crystal, and Wide Ruins rugs are in greatest demand. Small saddle blankets and coarse weave rugs are less commonly seen. The average size of most rugs today is four feet by six feet. Yei rugs are more popular and their quality in weave and color has greatly improved. Few good quality rugs can be purchased for under US$100, and bargains are rare. Navajo weavers recognize the value of their skill, and tribal guild shops as well as traders pay well for fine-quality work. Large, well-woven rugs such as Two Gray Hills sell for prices as high as US$10,000.

2. *Jewelry.* Silversmithing is diversified, and in addition to the traditional items now includes silver platters, hollow ware, flatware, and decorative cigarette boxes. Designs have been expanded to include animal and

bird motifs such as the popular roadrunner. Navajo craftsmen imitate Zuni, Zuni copy Hopi, and even a sophisticated buyer is less certain of tribal origins. Turquoise quality has deteriorated because of the cost of high-grade stones, and the higher cost of silver results in small rings, thin bracelets, and lighter-weight necklaces. Mass distribution through chain stores means that many silversmiths work under contract with specific outlets in mind. Prices range from under US$20 for small rings to over US$8000 for fine squash blossom necklaces using premium quality spider web or Bisbee turquoise.

A recent innovation is the use of gold by several Indian jewelry makers. The workmanship and designs are of the highest quality, conforming to traditional patterns, but with a greater degree of style. High-grade turquoise adds to the overall Indian motif but the jewelry has a sophistication which competes with the most elegant European and American creations.

3. *Pottery*. Pottery continues to be made by the traditional methods of coiling, then firing in earth kilns; styles also remain traditional. The Hopi mesas—Acoma, San Ildefonso, and Santa Clara—are the major pueblo potters. The Maricopa and Pima also produce pottery. Most recently there has been a resurgence of undecorated Navajo pottery. As with the other major art forms, prices depend upon quality. A small Hopi pot may cost as little as US$50 whereas the Acoma pottery (usually larger in size) starts at US$200. The black San Ildefonso pottery may range up to US$10,000 or more for choice pieces, especially if signed by "Maria," the most noted of Pueblo potters.

4. *Basketry*. The traditional pattern of baskets remains unchanged. The Hopi and Papago literally dominate the market, but because of the tedious hours of labor they now turn out a greater number of small baskets. Apache water baskets have been scarce for years, but with the demand for genuine crafts regardless of their aesthetic appeal, even Apache baskets bring up to US$500. Good quality Hopi wedding plaques may sell for as much as US$5000.

5. *Bead Making*. Turquoise, shell, and coral beads are still found, but they are overshadowed by the silver jewelry.

6. *Kachinas*. Today the Hopi are almost the exclusive makers of *kachinas*, and are still willing to manufacture fine-quality genuine *kachinas*. The most popular *kachinas* depict a degree of motion, in contrast to the more traditional fixed stances. *Kachinas* are expensive with quality work priced from US$100 for a small doll (under ten inches) up to US$2000 for an eighteen-inch doll.

7. *Graphic Arts and Sculpture*. In the postwar years, two new crafts have developed: painting and sand painting. Stemming from the use of watercolor and tempera paints at school, many adult Indians have developed a distinctive style. Most of the paintings have a formal but graceful quality reminiscent of Chinese or Japanese art. Animals and birds are common themes; one Navajo artist is famous for depicting a large wild mustang or "spirit horse." Sand paintings are the most recent art form and are similar in style to the true sand paintings created as part of the Navajo curative cere-

monies. A true sand painting must be destroyed before dark, or its powerful magic may become harmful. No traditional Navajo would dare reproduce permanently such a painting on a resin surface, but some paintings are marketed that have many of the basic attributes of the curative creations.

Graphic arts have reached a level of quality which places several Indian artists into the "fine art" market. Original paintings and limited edition prints by R. C. Gorman, Fritz Shoulder and Amado Peña are sold by art galleries nationwide. These artists cater to urban clients from America's major cities, featuring highly stylized works which carry a distinctive Southwestern Indian imprint.

A small group of Indian artists have begun to produce Southwestern landscapes in both realistic and abstract styles, portraying the mountains and canyons of the Southwest, but without any distinctive Indian motif, and thus now compete with non-Indian artists.

The Indian way of life, as most Americans romanticize it to have been, is the subject for a group of non-Indian artists living in the Southwest. Both originals and limited edition prints are sought after by collectors nationwide. Depictions of Sioux, Blackfoot, Apache, and Comanche warriors have become a very popular art form, with original works by artists such as Frank McCarthy, Howard Terpning, and Olaf Wieghorst often selling for over US$100,000. A young Southern California artist, Bev Doolittle, has developed a style that portrays the spiritualism of the Indian's totemic beliefs with a combination of stark realism and impressionist images. Her limited edition prints sell for as much as US$4500 and are purchased by collectors worldwide. Although these artists are non-Indian, the impact of their work upon the native arts and crafts of the Southwest is profound. By calling attention to the romantic image of the Indian, they help to stimulate greater interest in the crafts of the contemporary Indian.

Statuary and carved pottery pieces are appearing on the Southwestern arts and crafts market. Most statuary is of a highly contemporary style but carries the Indian flavor through its native subjects. Carved pottery has become an art form of intricate detail, expanding upon the traditional polychrome designs which have for centuries been painted. Small, ornately carved pieces can sell for several thousand dollars, representing still another area where Indian art is appealing to a sophisticated buyer.

Prospect

At present the outlook for Southwestern Indian art is good, as quality remains high and public interest appears to be steadily gaining. Tribal shops and trading posts on the reservations do an active business. Urban stores have expanded beyond the areal cities and now include Indian specialty shops in many towns throughout the nation.

The 1970s and 1980s have seen a national trend toward investment in collectibles and fine art objects. Neophyte buyers can begin to learn about Southwest Indian arts through many publications which range from shopper's guides to rugs, pottery, and *kachinas* to serious historic and pictorial volumes on specific Indian art forms.

During the early 1970s, it appeared that the popularity of Southwestern Indian art had started to decline because of the overproduction of lower quality, less expensive rugs and jewelry that flooded the market, including even so-called discount stores. Many collectors began to lose interest as there was nothing "new" to purchase. Indian artists and dealers recognized the need for innovation. In addition, they realized that the mass-produced "junk" that was finding its way to the marketplace was creating a negative image among true collectors. Changes in design, use of new materials—such as gold—and introduction of more contemporary color schemes in Navajo rugs, together with the development of the graphic arts all point to a new vitality which now also attracts a young, affluent market. Interior designers now advocate the use of so-called primitive arts as strong accents, combining these works with more contemporary furnishings in offices and public rooms as well as in private homes.

This assessment of the Indian crafts of the Southwest suggests that massive in-migration and mass tourism have not been disruptive. Rather, the contact with Anglo society offered extended markets that served to heighten artistic productivity and to revive old traditions. It might be argued that in contrast to the "trinketization" crafts in other milieus—e.g., plastic totem poles or printed textiles that simulate hand block prints—the very nature of the materials with which Indians work, and the designs that are integral to their culture, are not easily transferred to the "fake art" that clutters touristic markets elsewhere. Cheap pot metal adorned with fake stones abounds but is patently not Indian, and the difference is clearly evident even to a novice.

Further, the revival of Southwestern handwork has served to strengthen Indian identity, pride in heritage, and perhaps most importantly, local income as an alternative to out-migration to jobs or joblessness in an urban setting.

Main Edition Art Gallery
Scottsdale, Arizona

12

Creating Antiques for Fun and Profit: Encounters Between Iranian Jewish Merchants and Touring Coreligionists

Antiques collecting as a form of ethnic art is a tangential tourist activity, usually confined to knowledgeable and well-to-do travelers and to geographically restricted areas with ancient traditions, such as Iran. Increased tourism heightens demand for a limited, dwindling product and may lead to the creation of spurious antiques. In Iran, tourism is an important industry for Persian Jews who own many of the upper-category hotels and at least one of the active and highly regarded travel agencies, specializing in handling foreign visitors. This involvement as well as the antique trade, including the "fake art" made and marketed to tourists, has positive values supportive of an ethnic minority struggling to survive as a distinct entity in an unfavorable clime.

Of Iran's total population of 26,676,000 (1968), the Jewish population approximated 80,000, of whom 50,000 lived in the capital city, Teheran, with lesser numbers in the tourist centers of Shiraz (8500) and Isfahan (3500), and the remainder scattered in provincial cities. Nowhere do the Jews represent more than 3 percent of the total resident population. In 1968, fewer than 250,000 tourists visited Iran. Jewish tourists were most certainly less than 5 percent of the total and possibly as little as 2 percent. Nevertheless, their presence has had an effect disproportionate to their relative numbers on both native Jews in the tourist industry and, indirectly, on Iranian Jewry in general. Evaluated here are the effects of interaction between a limited segment of the Iranian tourist trade and a likewise restricted portion of the Iranian population having contact with them.

Isolation of Persian Jewry

During the 8th century B.C.E., Jews were forcibly settled in the mountains of Kurdistan by conquering Assyrians. By the sixth century B.C.E., there is good evidence of Jewish settlement in western Iran where they have lived for more than twenty-five hundred years. The social conditions of this Diaspora have varied considerably over time. Long periods of persecution, forced conversion, harassment, exploitation, and segregation from non-Jewish neighbors have alternated with short periods of comparative tranquility. The general insecurity of this milieu was capped by nearly three hundred years of severe repression ending only in 1925. Jews were often denied the right to participate in the primary subsistence activities of the region, agriculture and pastoralism, and thus gravitated to urban settlement and marginal subsistence means including shopkeeping (Loeb 1970). The past fifty years, which have been quiet by contrast, have afforded Jews an opportunity for social, economic, and intellectual development unparalleled in this millennium.

For nearly a thousand years, the Jews of Iran were largely isolated from their coreligionists, with catastrophic consequences for their cultural development. Literacy declined, familiarity with the Jewish Great Tradition was reduced, and major creative innovations were minimal. Beginning in the 1870s, contact was reestablished with Jews in Palestine and Europe, and after World War II interaction between these communities intensified considerably.

The first outside contacts were primarily missionary visits by Jews from Baghdad and Jerusalem for the purpose of collecting charitable contributions and propagating Jewish learning. These missionaries described in vivid detail the misery, poverty, and ignorance of Iranian Jewry. After 1900 representatives of Jewish social agencies including Alliance Israélite Universelle, the Jewish Agency, the American Joint Distribution Committee, and Otsar Hatorah (an orthodox religious education foundation) had considerable impact on the lives of Iranian Jews in Teheran and in the provincial cities. While the social concern and relief efforts of these institutions were most welcome by indigenous Jews, the arrogance and assumed superiority of these Western Jews were highly resented, though such sentiments were rarely verbalized. Until the early 1960s most Iranian Jews had minimal contact with foreign Jews outside the confines of these agencies.

Except for emigrants to Israel, who rarely returned home, few Iranian Jews went abroad before the 1960s. At that time, wealthy and middle-income Jews began to visit Israel, and numbers of college students were sent abroad, especially to England and the United States.

Tourism in Iran

In the 1960s, Iran became an important tourist site, attracting an increasing number of Jewish tourists from Europe, the United States, and, on occasion, Israel. Many American and European Jewish tourists were willing to spend considerable sums for the exceptionally fine art and artifacts crafted in Iran. Stories circulated about illuminated Hebrew manuscripts, rare Megillah scrolls, and prized amulets. Tourists actively sought authentic "Jewish" art and ritual objects; the more quaint, the better!

For generations, one of the most common occupations among Jews (almost exclusively identified with them) was itinerant peddling. Many Jews extensively peddled "second-hand" goods and were expert in evaluating carpets, silver, copper, mosaics, painted objects, manuscripts, and trinkets. Gold and silversmithing were also plied by many Jews because Islamic law prohibits the sale of gold or silver by Muslims at a greater value than their metal is worth. Because there could be no profit to a Muslim in working or dealing in gold or silver, these professions were largely taken over by Jews and Christians. These various, traditional Jewish occupations have given rise to skilled, shrewd managers of the best located gift/antique shops in the major tourist centers, Teheran and Isfahan.

Jewish entrepreneurship in the tourist trade is pervasive and supports the worldwide observation that ethnic minorities are frequently associated with this industry. In Iran, tourism has had considerable impact on the economic well-being of those participating directly in the trade of tourist goods, and has created a new "home" industry with a spin-off of petty, secondary entrepreneurship. Tourism has also been a source of acculturative ideas from the West, a wellspring of socioeconomic contacts all over the world, and an opportunity for personal interaction with far-flung coreligionists for the first time in centuries.

Persian Ethnic Art

Jewish tourists coming to Iran are bedazzled, as are all tourists, by the variety and superior quality of Iranian artisanship. They are equally impressed by the monuments to Persia's past glory and bewildered by the strange customs of the local populace. Most touring Jews crave something familiar within this environment and thus actively seek contact with local coreligionists and their institutions, especially the synagogue.

It is a noteworthy pattern of Western Jewish tourist culture that Jews, who are totally disinterested in Jewish life at home, become avid anthropologists abroad. Their overseas observations become anecdotal "back home," and they strive (in the "show-and-tell" manner) to take back items of material culture having historical, social, and religious import. If the goods are aesthetically pleasing, so much the better.

Since the turn of the century, traveling Jewish scholars have obtained prized manuscripts and artifacts on their infrequent sojourns through Iran. The more astute Jewish merchants catering to foreign tourists had already noted this predilection amongst their touring coreligionists. By the early 1960s, Jewish merchants had delved into communal resources, finding quantities of talismans and amulets, some handwritten manuscripts (including a few poorly illuminated ones), printed cloth, and silver and copper objects of dubious ritual significance. To further enhance their status with touring coreligionists and to attract them away from non-Jewish competitors in the antique trade, merchants put up easily understood symbols of commonality. Most popular of these is a sign reading: *barukh habba*, Hebrew for "welcome." Although active wooing of Jewish clientele might have the potential of discouraging non-Jewish tourists, the latter are unmoved by such symbols, and probably do not understand them.

In fact, the "aware" non-Jew sometimes picked up the wrong set of signals. On one occasion, my wife and I observed a fascinating exchange that took place early one evening in a non-Jewish tourist shop in Isfahan. A group of Iraqi tourists were considering the purchase of mosaic boxes, when one of the more perceptive members of the group noted the hexagonal pattern of stars adorning the many boxes. Well-indoctrinated Muslims, they stormed out of the store protesting that the proprietors must be Jewish since the mosaic was full of Zionist symbols!

By 1967, the once inexpensive, authentic Jewish artifacts had become scarce and the price correspondingly high. More and more Jewish tourists were coming to Iran, and ever fewer authentic Jewish culture items were available for marketing. Further, demand for these items was increasing abroad as kinsmen of the original Iranian Jewish shopkeepers opened stores in Jerusalem, Paris, London, and New York.

Spurious Antiques

In the 1960s, traders in Iranian Jewish artifacts began to commission the manufacture of appropriate items for the Jewish tourist trade. My "scientific" interest in this industry and tourism generally began with a request from the cultural attaché at the American consulate in Isfahan. A reputable art museum in New York had purchased, for several hundred dollars, a Hebrew-character astrolabe (for fortune telling) of considerable antiquity. Since it appeared to be the first one of its kind purchased by an American museum, they required some verification as to its age, source, and authenticity.

Shirazi Jewish informants, who had been dealing in astrolabes for over fifty years, denied ever having seen or even heard of this device with Hebrew characters, which aroused both my suspicion and curiosity. The signature in Hebrew identifying the craftsman as *'Eli,* according to the museum, was in fact that of *'Ali* (a common Muslim name). A variety of evidence indicated that Isfahan was the source of the "antique," and a quick trip there confirmed my doubts. Already acquainted with the antique dealers of Isfahan, my primary suspect readily confessed to having commissioned the manufacture of these "antiques," approximately one hundred of which were then available for distribution. I purchased a smaller version of the museum astrolabe for us$10, as the workmanship proved to be quite good and the aging excellent.

The manufacture of fake "Jewish art" for the tourist market exploits a wide variety of crafts. "Authentic" antiques include: (1) ceramic tiles and plaques styled in a crude imitation of Western-styled paintings of Moses and Aaron; (2) round metal plates (mostly tin-washed copper) with Hebrew-text borders and appropriate images; (3) Kashan carpets—mostly stylized portraits of Moses and Aaron, with a few more sophisticated forms combining a variety of Jewish symbols; (4) crudely carved wooden arks and altars in sharply contrasting pastels; (5) illuminated manuscripts; (6) painted miniatures and portraits; (7) astrolabes with zodiac signs and Hebrew lettering; and (8) simple amulets and silver containers for *mzuzas* (ritual scrolls). In general, the craftsmanship of these articles is universally crude, the painting sloppy, and the Hebrew calligraphy often inaccurate and erroneous.

Authentic antique Jewish craft was, by contrast, well constructed, carefully crafted, and Hebraically accurate, although the artisanship was somewhat below the level attained by master craftsmen designing secular items. Insofar as I can determine, most of the items mentioned above, with the exception of the illuminated manuscripts and amulets, did not exist in the traditional past. In fact, very few artifacts used by Persian Jews were decorated in a specifically and uniquely Jewish manner, with the exception of some *glims* (woven carpets) and paisley cloths with Hebrew-lettered borders, used in synagogues and homes for ritual purposes, and *tora* casings of wood, velvet, and silver. Some vases, perfume or rosewater flasks, silver cups, and oil lamps used for ritual purposes may have been specially decorated, but informants could not recall having seen them. Despite these obvious shortcomings, most Jewish tourists can easily obtain ostensibly authentic items of Persian Jewish culture. The Iranian Jewish "antique" shops in Israel, New York, and Europe are filled with such artifacts. The really crude artifacts are easily identified as fakes, but good work has fooled the experts. The artisans are without peer when it comes to antiquing.

An extensive feature article in an English-language Iranian newspaper in 1968 reported the experience of a young Persian Jewish merchant who set up shop in downtown New York. He reputedly sold an ostensibly antique "portrait" of a nineteenth-century Persian Jew to an apparently gullible New Yorker for several hundred dollars. The customer returned several days later with the painting under his arm and informed the merchant—after having the painting appraised—that the painting was not as old as had been represented. The sheepish merchant reached into his pocket, intending to refund the buyer's money. But the buyer hurriedly continued that the painting was well over two hundred years old and valued at many times the purchase price. As the happy customer left clutching his "bargain" the proprietor chuckled to himself over the duping of the experts. He had had the work commissioned only several years earlier.

Iranian Jewish antique sellers are as wily and shrewd as their counterparts elsewhere, and they have undoubtedly "cleaned-up" financially from touring coreligionists, but duplicity is a two-way street. In one case, a glib French Jew, posing as a major importer of art objects and antiques, used a falsified testimonial from an important French Jewish leader as an introduction to the Isfahani antique trade. Having convinced them of his integrity, his reputation spread by word of mouth or letter of introduction throughout the country. He departed Iran, taking with him merchandise worth thousands of dollars, all on credit, and was never heard from again.

In this respect, the most astute Jewish merchants are quite vulnerable. They are constantly taken in by apparently pious foreign Jews who are able to convince them of their sincerity and authenticity. Coreligionists cannot be viewed as apt to swindle or exploit. On the contrary! Foreign Jews, having established some relationship with Persian shopkeepers, are often persuaded, with the help of a small gift, to smuggle artifacts to relatives abroad for resale. Some may be entrusted with samples as bait for large overseas orders. Usually such faith is rewarded, but sometimes the consequences are disastrous, as alluded to previously. This apparent naïvete is understandable, because major swindles of Iranian Jews by indigenous coreligionists were immediately publicized widely with harmful social and business consequences for the offender. The fact that this long arm of justice is not effective outside the country is totally foreign to the Iranian Jewish experience.

Typically, Jewish tourists are attracted to an antique shop by its location, display of goods (both quality and variety), and Hebrew ethnic symbols. The tourists are often as interested in finding an access to the local community and their way of life as they are in making a purchase. Interaction often begins as the entrepreneur expresses a guess (usually wild) as to the tourist's origin. He then attempts through questioning (usually in English or French) to evaluate the tourist's interests in merchandise, the seriousness of his intention to purchase something, and how much he might be able to convince him to spend. Frequently, as the conversation progresses about objects, their artistic merit, authenticity, and antiquity, the shopkeeper offers his customer tea and suggests he sit and make himself comfortable. If it appears that there is a good chance of the sale coming to fruition, the initial meeting and conversation may last half an hour or more. Later contacts may be even more extensive. Eventually, the shopkeeper may even host the tourist at his home—a minor triumph for the tourist, as such invitations are rare in cosmopolitan Teheran. If the tourist expresses an interest, the entrepreneur sometimes offers to guide his guest through the Jewish quarter and aid him in finding the local synagogues, especially for Sabbath worship.

An initial interest shown by the tourist in Jewish artifacts is often used by the shopkeeper to create interest in other items as well. Ritual items may thus induce tourists to buy more. With the seller having the added advantage of an appeal to piety, and common identity, the tourist may feel guilt because his purchases fall almost within the category of *zdaga* (pious charity), or a subtle, financial device to keep Iranian Jewry alive (cf. Khury 1968). Having been exposed to apparent poverty, piety, friendship, and sincerity in the proprietor, the tourist is ripe to be plucked.

While the tourist is obtaining many insights and "representative" artifacts from Iranian Jewry, to be brought home and shared with friends and acquaintances, the Iranian Jews also benefit in a number of ways from this contact. In many cases, the proprietor's best advertising is by word of mouth, and he is not loathe to sell some items at marginal profit if he suspects this will cement a long-term relationship with the tourist, a few of whom return or maintain contact by mail with the entrepreneurs.

Social Effects of Tourism

The antique dealer serves as an agent of social contact between Iranian and non-Iranian Jews. He often introduces foreign Jews to the community, or alternatively, serves in a buffer capacity to ferret out those who should be kept apart from the community. The activities of foreign Jewish teachers may have had an intense impact on Iranian Jewish acculturation to Great Tradition Judaism, but foreign Jewish tourists have also been an important source of knowledge of foreign Jewish secular life and customs.

The antique dealer benefits economically from tourism by acquisition of wealth, and socially from increased prestige through contact with foreigners. For many, successful entrepreneurship provides the means to move up from low to middle or high-middle rank within Iranian Jewish society.

The creating of "authentic Jewish antiques" for foreign Jewish tourists has forged close links between Iranian Jewry and their coreligionists from abroad. Both parties benefit from their encounters despite the underlying fraud in their business dealings. These outside contacts have been of considerable value to Iranian Jews as a means of preserving their identity in a modernizing Islamic state.

Tourism has radically altered the assessment of the values and culture of foreign Jews by at least part of Iranian Jewry. Culture shock, induced by tourists in the form of counterfraud and secularist rather than basically religious attitudes and behavior, as well as curiosity, charity, and concern shown humanistically (rather than arrogance and social administration), has forced some Iranian Jews to reevaluate their own behavior and world-view with respect to education, religion, philanthropy, and even business ethics. Tourism is thus a powerful force in the ongoing process of secular westernization and in the acculturation of the Jewish Great Tradition that Persian Jewry is presently experiencing.

Epilogue

Over ten years have passed since the initial publication of this chapter. For Iranian Jewry, the changes have been wrenching and painful. During the winter of 1978–79 the Shah was deposed and a new Islamic republic established in Iran. Jews emigrated by the tens of thousands in the first two years and hundreds have continued to leave each year since. Tourism came to a standstill and most of those antique shopkeepers and their suppliers have long abandoned this occupation or have left Iran altogether.

Are the practices described earlier and motivations behind them therefore no longer relevant in discussing Iranian Jewry? With respect to those still living in Iran, one can only guess that for the present at least, this supposition is probably accurate. But for many Diaspora Iranian Jews, whether living in Tel Aviv or New York, London or Los Angeles, Jewish artifacts, particularly "antiques," remain important to their livelihood. Their shops often proclaim a city of origin, such as Isfahan, Shiraz, or Teheran; their Persian art items are not always of the earlier high quality, but Jewish wares still appear in abundance and are often of equal or finer workmanship than that of a decade earlier. Certainly the Hebrew on some artifacts appears to be more accurate. Collectors and museums in America, at least, are still puzzled about "authentic," "antique" Persian Judaica items offered to them for sale. Old merchandizing and credit networks have been revived in the present setting and new ones have been established, sometimes extending across continents and around the world.

On Pico Boulevard and along Fairfax Avenue in "Jewish" Los Angeles, few of the shopkeepers in Judaica stores are Iranian. One is more apt to find Iranian Jews as shopkeepers in the many specialty food markets catering to the needs of their fellow countrymen with specialty imports from Iran or Iranian foods processed locally. But in Judaica shops and, more often, in the "art" and specialty shops scattered about, Iranian Jewish "antiques" can be readily purchased.

It is in Israel where the largest variety and perhaps the best quality of these goods are found. The shops of Tel Aviv and Jerusalem are strongly reminiscent of their Iranian counterpart of the previous decade. Involvement in tourism has become a way of life for many Iranian-Israelis, but much of the social content and symbolism of a decade ago has changed.

It is unlikely that the manufacture or sale of these items is still functioning in any significant way to aid in the acceptance or integration of Iranian Jewish immigrants into their new social environs; rather, the items may serve as a link to their past and to a culture now more prized because it is no longer accessible.

University of Utah, Salt Lake City

13

The Polynesian Cultural Center: A Multi-Ethnic Model of Seven Pacific Cultures

MAX E. STANTON

The Polynesian Cultural Center (PCC) is located in the community of Laie on the Northshore-Windward coast of the island of Oahu, forty miles (an hour's drive) from the prime Hawaiian tourist target of Waikiki. In the past ten years the PCC has emerged as the second most popular visitor attraction in the state (surpassed only by the U.S.S. *Arizona* Memorial at Pearl Harbor) with a paid gate attendance in excess of one million guests per year.

The "typical" visitor to the Center generally spends the better part of a vacation day at the facility, beginning with a chartered bus trip from Waikiki arriving at mid-day. Upon arrival, there are guides waiting to lead the tourist on a choice of a walking tour, or (at extra cost) a canoe or tram tour (Plate 1). Once the formal conducted tour is completed, the visitor is free to return to the various exhibits alone. At dusk, a buffet-type dinner is served, followed by a one and one-half hour music and dance review. After the evening show, the visitor then boards the bus and returns to Waikiki. There is one over-all charge for admission that all visitors must pay: us$30 for adults, us$15 for juniors, us$10 for children aged five to eleven, and children four years of age and under are admitted free. This includes admission

Plate 1.   Visitors on the popular canoe tour that passes by all of the "villages" of the center.

and participation in all PCC activities for the day (dinner, canoe pageant, walking tour of the villages, Laie tour, canoe tour, and evening "This is Polynesia" stage show). The tour companies charge an additional US$10–15 per passenger for transportation. Individuals can also rent automobiles or ride the city bus from Waikiki, reducing the transportation costs.

The PCC is privately owned and operated by the Church of Jesus Christ of Latter-day Saints (LDS), commonly known as the Mormons. The Center was established in 1963 with a three-fold purpose: (1) to preserve the culture of the Polynesians; (2) to provide employment and work-scholarship support for the students attending the Brigham Young University–Hawaii Campus (the immediate neighbor of the PCC and founded as the Church College of Hawaii in 1955; the name changed in 1974); and (3) to provide direct financial aid to BYU-Hawaii.

For most PCC visitors, the state of Hawaii is their only contact with distant Polynesia, a vast Pacific triangle that encompasses many islands within its apexes of Hawaii, Easter Island, and New Zealand. The opportunity to take a vicarious trip through time and space to "Old Hawaii" and the rest of Polynesia has obvious appeal (Plate 2). A satisfactory fiction emerges wherein a guest can imagine for a brief time that the idyllic life

Plate 2. Visitors are led through the Hawaiian "village" by their tour bus driver/guide.

of Polynesia and the "Noble Savage," described by Robert Louis Stevenson and James Michener, is a "reality." On numerous occasions, visitors have exhibited loud outbursts of exuberance because they have "seen real natives at work in their own grass huts." Most workers at the Center are accustomed to such rather naïve behavior and recognize that this type of reaction is intended to be complimentary. This image of ethnic reality is also projected in PCC promotional efforts. The student-workers also recognize that a full, less-superficial glimpse of their culture is impossible in the few hours guests spend at the facility. Thus any portrayal of their cultural heritage that might be appreciated by the visitors is better than none at all. In this case study, the concept of a model culture is examined in terms of the expectations of the guests and the economic and social requisites imposed on hosts to create and sustain the model.

The Evolution of a Dream

Laie provides a social setting well suited for the establishment of an institution such as the Polynesian Cultural Center. For well over half a century, Latter-day Saints from Hawaii, Samoa, and the other Polynesian Islands have been gathering in the area because of the presence of the Mormon Temple in the community. In 1955, construction was begun on the Church of Hawaii (CCH). The work was facilitated by over 450 volunteer workers (called Labor Missionaries by the LDS Church), many of whom hailed from Samoa, Tonga, and New Zealand. After the completion of the construction, many of these Pacific Islanders remained in Laie as students of the college.

Because of the rather isolated location of Laie and also because of the socioeconomic background of the large majority of CCH students, various income-generating possibilities were explored for possible development into student-related employment. The most promising idea was a Polynesian dance troupe that traveled twice weekly into Honolulu to perform. The first performance was staged in 1959 and proved to be an immediate success.

Although the Polynesian group in its Honolulu location was successful, many problems emerged. It was a formidable logistical task to transport a full company of seventy-five performers, plus "back-stage" personnel, on a semiweekly round trip from Laie to Honolulu. Also, the time involved in such a venture was a serious drain on the productive study time of the students involved. It soon became apparent that the only logical solution to these problems would be the establishment of an adequate performing site in Laie. Following the usual deliberations and planning associated with any large-scale project, construction of the Polynesian Culture Center was initiated early in 1962, and the facility was opened to the public on 12 October 1963.

There was a great deal of apprehension concerning the ability of a tourist facility so far from the main tourist destination center in Waikiki to attract a large enough volume of visitors to be successful. It soon became evident, however, that the car-rental and tour bus companies saw the PCC as a perfect "lure" to get the visitors out of Waikiki and into their vehicles. From its first days of operation, the Center witnessed an upward trend in its clientele, and passed the million annual visitor mark in 1976, a figure that has since been consistently maintained. The average daily attendance ranges from about fifteen hundred in the fall and winter months to nearly twenty-five hundred during the summer. During Christmas and Easter vacations, and such holidays as Memorial Day, the Fourth of July, and Labor Day, the Center entertains over five thousand visitors daily. With such a large number of persons at one time, it has become increasingly difficult to maintain the casual, relaxed atmosphere that the tourists expect.

The Functioning of a Model Culture

The Polynesian Cultural Center is a model culture that selectively attempts to portray the best of those tangible, believable aspects of Polynesian culture with which the tourist can identify. Because of the interplay of time imperatives, cultural preferences, and personal inclinations, all facets of Polynesian culture are not portrayed. Tourists are on a vacation—they are seeking a change from the routine or ordinary and want to experience the "unusual." However, they generally lack the time and the depth of experience to understand the more complex and intricate aspects of Polynesian culture. The visitor can briefly participate in a simple dance in the Tahitian village (Plate 3), look over the shoulder of a person making *tapa* (bark cloth) in the Tonga area, and is encouraged to take pictures of Polynesians in Polynesian settings. There simply is not enough time in a one-day visit to discuss the nature of the Polynesian extended family (*ramage*) with its complex variations in political, economic, and kinship elements; or to explain the economic aspects of the conscription of manual labor as a form of capital; or to explore many of the other deeper, more complex aspects of Polynesian culture. Nor

Plate 3. Teaching visitors the Tahitian *tamure*.

does the Center see its mission as a forum for addressing the long-standing social and economic injustices found throughout the Pacific.

As a model and not the reality, the process of selecting the cultural elements to be shown admittedly creates a "fake culture," one which would not be found today anywhere in the various Polynesian Islands. The alert visitor needs only to recall the trip from Waikiki to Laie to realize that the Hawaiian Village represented at the Center is unlike anything seen from the bus window. In fact, one central theme pervading most of the presentations at the PCC is that this is *not* what typically exists today in the various Polynesian Island groups. The Center is basically an attempt to reconstruct lifestyles that are vanishing or have disappeared in the wake of the vast flood of technological gadgetry of the twentieth century. The model caters to ethnic tourism, providing to the tourist an opportunity to see in one afternoon what many of the indigenous residents of the various Polynesian societies themselves rarely, if ever, see. The visitor is, through the model-culture experience, able to gain a brief insight into a selective array of Polynesian cultures without the necessity of traveling throughout the Polynesian Triangle. Another PCC purpose is to keep alive (even revive) traditional art forms and practices, giving the guest a chance to view some limited historical aspects of a life-style as it once was (Plate 4).

It is a sobering assignment to coordinate the efforts of five hundred student-workers and three hundred full-time employees so that the end product will, at 10:00 A.M. each morning, greet the first visitor as "just another happy day in Polynesia." Behind the scenes, there are electricians, payroll clerks, mechanics, florists, public relations experts, anthropologists, and a host of other persons all working to make the operation run smoothly. If one were to visit the PCC two or three hours before opening time, the at times frantic tempo of activity would be blatantly evident: "Paradise is two hours away so let's get working." It is exciting to be a part of the PCC and to realize the manifold tasks that precede the opening, so that those persons who are directly involved in face-to-face contact with the visitors are able to be at ease and sustain the illusion of spontaneity and relaxed casualness.

Technical problems frequently arise, presenting challenges (or nightmares) to the anthropological specialists who are charged with the duty of "preserving Polynesian culture" at the PCC. Health and safety regulations, building codes, budgetary concerns, bureaucracy, and sometimes misguided actions of well-intending persons often prevent a fully authentic representation of culturally correct details. For some, it is still painful to recall the episode in which an old Samoan double canoe of exquisite construction

Plate 4. Student worker in the Fijian Village making a hibiscus bark lei (*salusalu*).

showing the beautiful markings of native-grain wood was trimmed down fore and aft and painted in a bright combination of light-blue and lemon yellow "so that it would better catch the tourists' eye." Or, there was a "near disaster" when at the last moment it was discovered that a priceless piece of Hawaiian *tapa* was about to be used as a tablecloth at a staff party where punch and Chinese food (with its many delicious but viscid sauces) were to be served.

To upgrade the overall authenticity of the PCC, the Center employs one full-time cultural specialist and has recently acquired the half-time services of a BYU–Hawaii faculty member on indefinite loan to augment the cultural operation. Scholars and highly respected representatives from Polynesian cultures are also called upon for their insights. The individuals selected to supervise each of the seven cultural demonstrations, or "villages," are, whenever possible, proven experts in their own ethnic cultural background and are given a wide latitude of options concerning the presentations in their areas.

In spite of the conscious effort now being made to improve the PCC, continuing problems exist, some of which arise from naïve or uninformed tourists' expectations. Many visitors have preconceived ideas of what Polynesia "should be" and are sometimes disappointed when their expectations are not met. Some visitors are critical because no one lives in the houses at the Center. One visitor, who claimed to be a trained social scientist, observed that the women were "over-dressed," that there was not one bare-breasted woman at the Center! This person should have known that in all but the most remote parts of Polynesia, such attire (or lack of it) is not to be found today, and it would now be offensive and personally embarrassing for the women to dress (or undress) in such a manner.

Another legitimate criticism that is very difficult to resolve is the time or period theme. What date or era should the exhibits portray? In the past two to three hundred years, all of the Polynesian Islands have undergone rapid, sometimes drastic, cultural change. It is virtually impossible to place all of the buildings, costumes, material items, and live demonstrations (dances, songs, and games) within the same specific time-frame. The PCC tried to tie all portions of "village" exhibits into a functionally integrated whole, with full realization that an artifact might be removed two hundred years in authenticity from the house where it is located. Suggestions have been made to expand the Center and provide three or four clusters of buildings in each "village" to represent change through time. This task would be monumental and far transcend the original intent of the PCC. The best solution to date is to have the tour guides alert the visitors that such discrepancies do exist and point them out.

The large number of visitors per day makes it impossible to give a detailed representation of all aspects of the various Polynesian cultures. The basic emphasis is on the material culture (houses, canoes, and artifacts) and the performing arts (singing and dancing). The ideology, social organization, and world-view of each culture—so important to their personal lifestyle—are painfully absent. Only some general allusions to the nonmaterial aspects of Polynesian life are made. This is not a fault of the PCC, but merely a fact of life. As mentioned above, a detailed description of this component of Polynesian culture would require more time than the workers can give or the average visitor is willing to expend. However, individuals with deeper interests are welcome to remain in a "village" and chat with staff on duty in the exhibit. Some specialized presentations are now available to interested groups and a broader offering is planned for the future. Thus, members of a study group may spend more time at the Center as serious students of culture rather than merely interested spectators.

As a cultural model or "living museum," the Center uses a thematic approach which concentrates on certain dynamic and tangible aspects of culture. In an effort to make the visit more meaningful, each of the "villages" has developed some specific activity such as husking a coconut, learning to use a certain percussion instrument, involvement in a game of skill, or performing a dance that encourages tourist participation—all popular with visitors. The PCC is learning from its past mistakes and is now, more than ever, attempting to allay as many criticisms and deficiencies as possible. Special training sessions are held for workers who are involved with tourists on a face-to-face basis. (Not all Polynesians have an in-depth knowledge of the traditions and culture of their own specific ethnic group, and few workers have more than a superficial understanding of the culture of the other groups represented at the Center.) These training programs are designed to give guides, "villagers," and other personnel a basic understanding of the material culture, historical development, and contemporary situation of the societies represented at the facility. The sessions also help to develop personal confidence and self-assurance in greeting and instructing the daily crowds.

Over the years, the PCC has developed a number of strategies to attract not only the first-time visitors, but the return visitors as well. The local visitor is given the *kama'aina* discount of one-third of the listed price. (A kama'aina, by this definition, is a resident of Hawaii.) An aggressive local television campaign, reminding the local residents that there *is* a different place to go for that special day off, has recently proven quite successful. The evening stage show is changed on an annual basis and recent print media advertisements found locally, in selected U.S. mainland locations, and in the airline flight magazines stress the "New" Polynesian Cultural Center. In February 1987 a public announcement was made that the PCC was soon going to start a sister facility located adjacent to the existing center (named, tentatively, the "Gateway to Asia") that will feature selected Japanese, Chinese, Korean, Thai, and Filipino exhibits. Completion of this facility is targeted for the early 1990s.

The Economic Impact of the Model Culture

The Polynesian Cultural Center and its sister institution Brigham Young University–Hawaii Campus (BYU–HC) operate closely together as the two major sources of employment in Laie. Both institutions receive tax-exempt status: the BYU–HC because it is a private college, and the PCC because of its deep involvement in supporting BYU–HC through student employment and direct financial subsidies to the college. The PCC in 1987 donated more than two million dollars annually in unrestricted funds, some of which are used to upgrade the research and instructional capabilities of the faculty. Also, funds from the Center support more than 400 students who are employed at BYU–HC and who, except for this financial support, have no relationship whatever with the PCC. Further, nearly seven hundred BYU–HC students are directly employed by the Center. In total, the PCC in 1986 generated us$3.5 million in benefits to the BYU–HC and its students. In addition, the Laie community now enjoys more than us$8 million annually from the PCC in wages paid to full-time non-students.

One might look at the workload and relatively low pay of the student workers at the PCC and question whether such a successful operation as this might be exploiting the students. In the twenty-five years the Polynesian Cultural Center has been in operation an estimated 15,000 students have been employed by the institution. Of course, not all of these individuals have worked at the Center during their entire academic career and not all students who have worked there have gone on to graduate. However, the social and economic impact of the PCC has justified its symbiotic relationship with BYU–Hawaii Campus. I have worked as a member of the BYU–HC faculty since 1971 (and was myself a student at the Church College of Hawaii—now BYU–HC) and was employed at the PCC. I know personally of dozens of individuals—many of whom would have been unable to afford a college education without the presence of the PCC—who have gone on to satisfactory and rewarding careers too varied to enumerate, and who have become good citizens of their communities. In a recent trip to Fiji, I met a number of former BYU–HC students, nearly all of whom had worked at the PCC and are now school principals, government bureau chiefs, private entrepreneurs, middle management workers in international corporations, school teachers, officials in the police force, and so forth.

The economic impact of the PCC extends far beyond Laie and the surrounding communities. A large number of employees (especially married couples in which both parties are from the same cultural background, and single students) regularly send a sizeable portion of their income home to assist their families or to invest in private bank accounts. Also, as when a relative or close friend gets married or dies, those workers who, under normal circumstances, would not be expected to contribute are expected to help out financially. Events such as church dedications or drives to assist in the cost of tuition for others are, as well, times when one is expected to willingly donate cash (even at the expense of defaulting on regular payments such as utilities or regular groceries). In the past five years the LDS Church has constructed temples in Tonga, Tahiti, and Western Samoa, and in each case local members of the Church (most of whom were employed either by the PCC or BYU–HC) were praised for their generous contributions.

When one of the older workers at the PCC was asked why so much money is sent abroad, especially in light of the high cost of living in Hawaii, this fine Tongan gentleman replied, *"Autō e manu ki tokū,"* or *"*At sunset the birds return to Toku [an island in Tonga],*"* paraphrased to mean, "In his heart and in the heart of all good Tongans, there is only one home, Tonga," and his relatives there need the money more than he does in Hawaii.

The skills learned at the Center also benefit the students regardless of their success at the college. The PCC may sometimes appear to be a "tropical state fair" with dozens of light-hearted, smiling persons "doing their own thing," but to be genuine and enthusiastic, eager to please, and quick to smile day after day, regardless of one's inner pressures, are highly prized skills. The poise and confidence gained by the workers, especially the college students, will probably stand them in good stead wherever they go. Also, the knowledge gained in becoming familiar with rapidly vanishing aspects of their culture will undoubtedly prove valuable, making these persons "cultural repositories" of an otherwise scarce and dying cultural tradition.

It would be erroneous to suggest that the Polynesian Cultural Center benefits only individuals who want to become more appreciative of their traditional heritage, or that the Center provides secure economic positions only for those who could not otherwise cope with the more demanding way of life of the mid-twentieth century. For better or worse, the economic and social realities of our era have become a fact of life throughout all the islands of Polynesia. The question is not "if" Polynesia will change, but "how" it will resolve the changes that are occurring. The PCC is a large-scale operation requiring a wide variety of professions and skills, and through cooperation with BYU–HC, the Center turns out top-quality entertainers and others skilled in the material crafts of Polynesia. Behind the scenes, students are involved with diverse, work-related experience, such as personnel management, accounting, commercial art, carpentry, foods and nutrition, secretarial skills, public relations, printing, electronics, police and security, travel ticketing, purchasing and supply, and auto mechanics.

The Center employs a large number of persons in varied occupations including highly-trained professional administrators and knowledgeable experts of specific cultures supervising the work in the respective "villages," and Laie housewives looking for a supplemental family income. Through rational planning and cooperation, the PCC can satisfy the needs of the curious tourist as well as provide for the enrichment and improvement of its employees, and thus fulfill the three-fold purpose for which it was created.

The overall effect of visitor contact at the PCC is not as great as some might imagine. The tourists are no more an imposition to the worker in one of the "villages" at the Center than a guest at a hotel is to the desk clerk or a diner is to a restaurant worker. Hospitality is good business, and it does not hurt to smile. When the working day is over, the Center employees return to their dorms and homework, or to their homes and families, and are undisturbed by outsiders until the next day's group arrives.

The workers at the PCC are not unfamiliar with tourists. For employees who originate from such places as Fiji, Tahiti, and especially Hawaii, the tourist has been a familiar fact of life for as long as they can remember. Even those from Samoa, Tonga, and Rotorua in New Zealand learned to accept and tolerate tourists long before they began their work at the Center. For most employees, this contact with and acceptance of foreigners commenced in their home areas by the presence of missionaries, educators, and administrative officials. Because of life-long contacts with persons not of their culture, together with the experience gained at the PCC, most workers are much more at ease and familiar with the visitor than is the converse. Many employees have been to Mainland U.S.A. as visitors, as Mormon missionaries, or in the military service. And, as the result of the LDS missionary program, some workers have been to Asia, Latin America, or even Europe and have gained a high degree of fluency in the languages of these respective areas. It is always a source of amusement to see the look on visitors' faces when a worker, dressed in traditional attire, approaches a group of Japanese tourists and begins to freely converse with them in Japanese. The workers at the PCC take obvious pride in their cultural heritage, and most of them appreciate the fact that through the medium of the model village they can present that which they deeply treasure and value to visitors in a positive context unfettered by the lights of Waikiki or the Hollywood makeup artist.

One interesting side effect of the multi-ethnic nature of the PCC is the opportunity it affords for persons from other Polynesian areas to live in Hawaii or for local Hawaiians to have Fijians, Tongans, and New Zealanders as neighbors. The average employee has little opportunity to interact meaningfully with a tourist at the Center, but he may live next door to people whose original home is thousands of miles distant. A genuine intercultural exchange takes place in this context, and those who benefit most from this experience are not the transient tourists, but the PCC workers themselves.

Laie was initially a "company town" with the Mormon Church (rather than a factory) as the center of power. Before the establishment of the PCC, relatively few visitors came to Laie except for kinship and religious purposes. Now all that has changed. Hawaii is receiving in excess of two million visitors annually, and half of them visit the PCC. However, the facility is equipped to handle large numbers of guests during the full course of the day, so that there is very little tourist "spill-over" into the community at large. In fact, the frequent outpouring of anti-tourist sentiment found in so many other communities of Hawaii is conspicuously absent among the permanent, long-term residents of Laie. However, during my seventeen years' residence in the community I have observed, as the result of the location of the Center in Laie, a marked increase in income and the material welfare of its inhabitants; and tourism *per se* has not significantly or directly disrupted local life-styles. (A job at the Center is substantively little different than is any other occupational task. A job as a mechanic, secretary, or commercial artist at the PCC varies little from the same job anywhere else.)

The Polynesian Cultural Center is successful as a "model culture" in Laie's social context in two principal ways. First, as outlined extensively above, it is the reconstruction of the exotic, more popular elements of Polynesia and puts "on stage" for the visitors selected aspects of Polynesian life, especially in the realm of material culture and aesthetics, which are not now the normal way of life in Laie, Hawaii, or anywhere else in Polynesia. (No one in Hawaii still lives in a thatched hut; the outboard motor and Bruce Lee-type Kung Fu films are making their imprint in the Marquesas Islands; and commercial television is beamed daily to the Manu'a Group in Samoa.)

The second principal justification for considering the PCC to be an adequate "model culture" is that the presence of visitors does not interfere with the daily lives of the people of Laie. Students attend grade school, a college functions effectively, the bank opens and closes; in general, people work *away* from the prying eyes of the tourist. Basic local values are not disrupted, and neither does the "model culture" disrupt the strong religious orientation of the community. Because it is a church-sponsored institution, the PCC actually serves to enhance Mormon norms and values by not operating on Sunday and by giving release-time consideration for persons having special church-related assignments. In fact, the location of the PCC at the edge of Laie, rather than in the middle of the community, ensures much less interference with local habits than in similar "model cultures" such as Leavenworth, Washington; Cherokee, North Carolina; or, Rothenburg-ob-der-Tauber in Germany. The relationship between Laie, the PCC and BYU–HC is somewhat analogous to Oberammergau—a town that, for religious purposes, becomes host to short-term guests once every decade for the world-renowned Passion Play. The people of this small community in the German Alps are thoroughly modern and live similar to the life-style in other villages in the region. Their involvement with mass tourism reinforces rather than disintegrates their sense of community and cohesion.

The overall impact of the "model culture" of the PCC in the lives of the workers, especially the students, has the following consequences that may be both positive and negative in nature. First, their involvement at the Center affords them the opportunity for an education that, in many cases, could not otherwise be financed. However, because of the often vast distances from home and the necessity for reduced course loads because of working and church-related assignments, it is not uncommon for a student to undergo a long-term separation from home and family, but a sense of total isolation seldom occurs because the extended family is still quite effective in most Polynesian societies. A student often has a fellow member of his family at school, or an older sibling or other close relative may have immigrated to Laie or a nearby community. A second, and important, feature of the "model culture" is that many students who previously had little direct contact with their cultural heritage now have their ethnic identity reinforced through their association with the Center. This has been especially true for students from New Zealand, French Polynesia, and Hawaii, as well as for migrant families from such areas as Samoa and Tonga whose children have little opportunity for enculturation within their original ethnic group. Exposure to Polynesian culture other than one's own is a third aspect of the model culture nature of the PCC. By close association with persons from a common cultural heritage, a great wealth of information is exchanged and absorbed on an informal, unstructured, one-to-one basis. As a result, students often request the opportunity to become involved with another group. Similarly, students who are ethnic minorities in their homelands (e.g., East Indians from Fiji, Filipinos from Hawaii, and Chinese from French Polynesia) have an opportunity, often for the first time in their lives, to cross the cultural line and gain insight and even participate in the dominant culture. At home, these doors to intercultural communication are frequently closed, if not barred. The fourth result of this "model culture" is the fact that students from the less-developed realms of Polynesia who come to BYU–HC and the PCC live in the urban cosmopolitan cultural milieu of modern Hawaii, with wide exposure to Western values and technology. But, the very fact of residing in Hawaii may well lead to a fifth feature: many students receive a distorted, atypical view of the modern world. Hawaii is one of the premier tourist resort areas of the world, and Oahu also has one of the highest concentrations of military personnel-per-population-size in America. As a result, the students from elsewhere in Polynesia see many people with a lot of time and money on their hands. Their view of reality is not corrected by looking inwardly at Laie either, because the Mormon Church plays such an overwhelming, dominant role in shaping community affairs and local norms. Few students get a fair chance to see the broad spectrum of "mainstream" America. A sixth feature is the fact that students gain skills in tourism, the performing arts, and other work experience, which can at a later time prove to be of worth in their homeland or in their private lives. Seventh, their involvement at the PCC enables them to do what few college students can elsewhere—earn extra funds to send home to their families, thereby enhancing their image among their families and as members of their community. This involvement in the financial and social structure also serves to validate their church membership by showing that an LDS student in Hawaii can still be an asset to the home community. Also, the student's comparative affluence, derived from mass tourism, may reinforce the financial potential of tourism at home.

As a last feature, after years of student catering to the superficial "smile all the time" expected at the PCC, there is a real danger that some of the more pressing problems of one's homeland might be overlooked, or that the partial image of the culture that is daily portrayed will, in fact, become the cultural reality of the hosts. Either eventuality would greatly diminish the overall potential of the Center to be more than a "tropical amusement park" and should be carefully considered in evaluating its impact.

A Model Culture in a Real World

The Polynesian Cultural Center is a highly successful social and economic operation that is effectively meeting the multiple needs for which it was, rather daringly, conceived. However, the problems encountered in any large establishment are to be found at the PCC, including labor disputes, differences of opinion, problems in communications, personality clashes, and other difficulties that occur when large numbers of persons work together. Despite their existence, I believe that the task of presenting diverse Polynesian cultures on a mass scale has been highly successful, and that the problems are only minimally apparent to the paying guest.

Anyone contemplating the establishment of a facility such as the Polynesian Cultural Center must fully consider the range and multitude of problems. Because of the large number of employees (over eight hundred), the cultural differences, and the high volume of visitors each day, the management of a model culture must be acutely aware of the problems as they arise and must act quickly to meet and solve problems, real or imagined, as they emerge. Pressures from within the institution, as well as from those outside the direct sphere of operation, can make management a difficult task. By dealing with "in house" problems as they arise and trying to create a feeling of rapport with the working staff, administrators can be free to deal with outside concerns such as transportation companies, labor unions, sales and promotion groups, tour agencies, and other parties exerting their special pressures to gain preferential treatment from the Center.

Possibly a prerequisite in maintaining a sense of cooperation and cohesion is a spirit of dedication and cooperation. The PCC has a definite advantage in the common Latter-day Saint affiliation of most of the personnel at the Center, which tends to minimize conflict and reinforce understanding. This is not to say that service problems do not arise, but when problems do arise, cultural and personnel differences that might otherwise prove to be irreconcilable can be dealt with beginning from a basic philosophical orientation as Mormons, which often transcends cultural differences.

The Polynesian Cultural Center is fortunately located on an island that is one of the busiest tourist centers of the world. Its popularity is well established, but it is doubtful if it could be as successful if it were located elsewhere, other than on Oahu in the state of Hawaii. It is not unique as a cultural center. Other centers such as Rotorua in New Zealand, Orchid Island in Fiji, or the cultural center in Ponape exist and prove to be popular local attractions. But, as is the case of the Polynesian Cultural Center, these "model culture" centers generally draw visitors *after the fact*. The centers are visited because the guest has been drawn to the area by one of the various types of tourism: recreational, ethnic, or cultural. The Polynesian Islands are too remote to hope for model culture exhibits to pull in clientele on their own merits. Even the PCC in its active promotional efforts in the United States, Canada, and Japan, plays heavily on the theme ". . . when in Hawaii, visit us." Places such as French Polynesia, Micronesia, Samoa, and Tonga, which are contemplating a rapid thrust into tourism and resort development, may well be advised to explore the potential of a "model culture" site, but such endeavors should also be realistically planned within the rational bounds of potential, and probably operational costs. A serious miscalculation in either of these two areas could seriously jeopardize the successful longevity of such an undertaking.

Brigham Young University—Hawaii

V

TOWARDS A
THEORY OF
TOURISM

Tourism is a complex phenomenon, as illustrated by the preceding case studies, and thus becomes an intriguing subject for analysis. Contemporary social scientists believe that knowledge of the theoretical components of a discipline, such as tourism, provides the tools for its better expansion or development, and for its wise application. Applied anthropologists in particular have become deeply involved in and committed to directing culture change in the diverse fields of medical anthropology, health delivery systems, family planning, mitigation of archaeologic sites, criminal justice—and tourism. The appended bibliography now contains many examples of "applied tourism": the use of theory to study and implement tourist development, and to mitigate sociocultural problems which arise from its existence.

Nuñez (chapter 14) provides an initial theoretical statement which may well become classic, touching as it does on so many facets of anthropological inquiry. By contrast, Lett has succinctly and effectively examined the literature of the past decade to illustrate that, indeed, anthropologists could and should become the paramount culture brokers as tourism changes the world and is itself changed in response to human needs and values.

14

Touristic Studies in Anthropological Perspective

THERON NUÑEZ
WITH EPILOGUE BY JAMES LETT

Since its beginning little more than a decade ago, the study of tourism by anthropologists has been characterized largely by serendipity. This, however, is not an irony, for many of the now traditional and established interests of anthropologists derive from fortuitous observations or accidental "discoveries" while researching other or unrelated topics or problems. For the last ten years, anthropologists have gone to study other things or other people and almost everywhere have discovered tourists.

Why then have anthropologists only recently found tourism of scholarly interest? The answer, I think, lies in the observation that the study of tourism finally has become respectable. That is to say, anthropologists have been aware for many years of the impact of tourism on indigenous societies but may have refrained from publishing their observations in systematic form because the study of tourism was somehow not considered "proper" or within the traditional purview of the discipline. This volume clearly demonstrates the demise of that view and the acceptance of tourism as a legitimate field of inquiry under a variety of traditional anthropological rubrics. What follows, then, is an examination of those approaches that have been used or might be used in modified form to further the study of tourism.

The acculturation model is the most obvious. Anthropologists have known for more than a half century many of the things likely to eventuate when different cultures come into contact, and this knowledge can readily apply to contact between tourists and indigenous, or "host," societies. Acculturation theory explains that when two cultures come into contact of any duration, each becomes somewhat like the other through a process of borrowing. However, the nature of the contact situation, the distinctive profiles of the contact personnel, different levels of sociocultural integration, numerical differences in the populations, and other variables typically result in asymmetrical borrowing. Furthermore, acceptance or rejection of alien traits or artifacts conditioned by the foregoing considerations may have far-reaching indirect consequences because the functional model of societies explains that a perturbation of one aspect of a social system is likely to disturb or change other aspects.

Tourists are less likely to borrow from their hosts than their hosts are from them, thus precipitating a chain of change in the host community. The notion that people in more or less continuous, first-hand, face-to-face contact become more like each other should not be ignored just because tourists come and go. A tourist clientele tends to replicate itself. As a host community adapts to tourism, in its facilitation to tourists' needs, attitudes, and values, the host community must become more like the tourists' culture. That is what tourists in search of the exotic and "natural" vacation setting mean when they say that a place has been "spoiled" by tourism, i.e., those who got there before them and required the amenities of home. Anthropologists are often in the forefront of those who deplore the dilution and adulteration of traditional cultures, what Mexican intellectuals have called the *Cocacolaización* of the native way of life. However, the alteration of one culture by another has always been a fact of existence. Some societies have remained in relative isolation from others for long periods of time, but in this century virtually no community is immune from outside contact, and the tourist is more ubiquitous than any other kind of representative of other cultures. Although anthropologists decry, as they should, the exploitation of any people by another, they should realize better than most that communities dedicated to tourism from an economic point of view must maximize the exploitation of the tourist clientele to the fullest. The ethical question is who or how many profit from the exploitation, which I will address later.

Perhaps the most striking example of the asymmetry in host-guest relationships is to be found in linguistic acculturation in which the usually less literate host population produces numbers of bilingual individuals, while the tourist population generally refrains from learning the host's language. The cadre of bilingual individuals in a tourist-oriented community or country is usually rewarded. The acquisition of a second language for purposes of catering to tourists often results in economic mobility for people in service positions. Interpreters, tour guides, bilingual waiters, clerks, and police often are more highly compensated than the monolinguals of their communities. In the history of acculturation phenomena, rarely has a community, a country, or a culture been a willing host but rather has had another people and aspects of another way of life foisted or forced upon them.

Today, however, tourists are literally being invited, encouraged, and enticed to bring themselves and their alien ways even to places and countries where their countrymen have but recently been ejected by revolution or rejected by successful independence movements. In the modern world, the underdeveloped or developing nations are those most often encouraging and promoting tourism. Within the last few decades, many newly independent countries and some emerging from relative feudal isolation into a wider world have realized that their competitive status in a world money economy is precarious at best. Tourism is seen as an avenue, along with others, depending on the country's resources, toward development and modernization. This situation indicates an interesting irony: in order to survive and perpetuate their cultural identity and integrity, emerging new nations or quite traditional cultures caught up in a competitive world economy encourage and invite the most successful agents of change (short of political or military agents) active in the contemporary world. This kind of initiative on the part of a host culture introduces a novel variable into the traditional equation of acculturation.

Finally, the anthropological study of tourism, with some exceptions contained in this volume, has followed the same ontogeny as the study of acculturation. Historically, anthropologists were interested in the effects or results of contact between what were usually called dominant and subordinate cultures, but this generally meant that they focused almost exclusively upon changes in the subordinate culture or with sifting, after the fact, which culture traits were of indigenous origin and which were alien. Only as acculturation theory became more sophisticated did the functional nature of acculturation become more apparent, and then anthropologists understood that they must examine both parties within the situational nature of contact if more complete understanding of the phenomenon were to be approached. This is the sequence that has been generally followed in the more specific studies of tourism, and we are just now beginning to realize that the tourists themselves, the donor personnel as representatives or agents of an alien culture (although never fully representative of it) must also be studied.

The varieties of cultural and social change that are likely to occur with the advent of tourism are obviously going to affect the lives of individuals in the host cultures more radically than those of the transient cultures. I would suggest that the traditional approaches of innovation theory and personality theory within anthropology are applicable here.

Many anthropologists agree that two classes of individuals are likely to be innovators within their own communities and/or the first to accept and possibly promulgate an alien trait or behavior. These classes of people have been described as those who hold traditional positions of prestige within their communities and those who are somehow culturally marginal. There is also some scholarly agreement among those who study culture change that traditionally prestigious individuals may be successful innovators when a community is undergoing gradual, orderly change, whereas culturally marginal individuals are more likely to be innovators during periods of rapid, stressful change. This thesis involves a number of assumptions: that prestige is often related to leadership, that traditional leadership at the community level is usually conservative and respected, that an innovation advocated by a prestigious traditionalist may be emulated with little risk so long as such changes involved occur in a more or less gradual and orderly fashion; conversely, marginal individuals are less often prestigious in traditional societies, less often are associated with leadership, less likely to be emulated, etc. However, a further assumption is that the above holds true so long as successful leadership provides solutions to the mundane problems of existence, so long as the status quo or gradual change is existentially satisfying to the community. It is assumed that during periods of rapid, stressful culture change traditional leadership may fail to innovate in the solution of problems or be unwilling to integrate novelty within community norms, whereas culturally marginal individuals, being less conservative, perhaps more imaginative, may assume positions of leadership and may become successful innovators during periods of accelerated, disquieting change.

The foregoing may be an oversimplification of a body of anthropological thought, but I submit that for the study of tourism this outline does have heuristic merit. The advent of tourism, either at the community or national level, occurs almost invariably during periods of rapid change or precipitates rapid change. Elements within national governments may make policy commitments to the promotion and development of tourism as a quick expedient to shore up a quaking economy, and a local community may be "discovered" overnight as one of the "last" unspoiled tourist meccas. This is the arena for the marginal individual to appear in as a leading performer.

Now, the term "marginal man" has meant many things to many social scientists. It has meant psychologically marginal, biologically marginal, economically marginal, and biographically marginal—in other words, an individual who differs from some cultural norm or norms and who behaves and is treated accordingly. I would submit that some forms of marginality are likely to allow some individuals to adapt more readily than others to the stresses and changes brought on by tourism and that they may therefore become the more successful innovators with a potential for economic and social mobility and possible leadership. The kind of marginal individual I have in mind is what has come to be called the culture broker. It is a matter of being able to turn to advantage his or her marginality, demonstrating that entrepreneurship, for example, may be more adaptive than traditional economic subsistence pursuits. The marginal individual is one who may be psychologically inclined or motivated to cope with anxieties creatively, perhaps becoming bilingual. Or, he or she may have had more previous exposure than others to education, travel, bi-cultural or bi-racial experience. This does not mean to say that all marginal individuals within a culture or a community will emerge as successful innovators or will better adapt to change than nonmarginals. I think it is a matter of probabilities to be computed in terms of local or cultural variables in equation with the touristic situation and its personnel. But it is clear that in most situations a handful of people, no more economically or intellectually advantaged than their peers, appear to emerge as culture brokers. They learn the necessary second or third language; they change occupations from subsistence or salaried to entrepreneurial; they migrate to potential or developing resort areas, etc.; and, if they are successful, they are emulated by the previously less daring.

One is tempted at this juncture to speculate that if we had a full operational picture of the development of tourism from its incipient phase to full-blown established resort status that we might often find "revitalization" theories metaphorically apt, with previously marginal individuals becoming prophets or proselytizing disciples and becoming, with the advent of a new "steady state," the prestigious community leadership, attempting to revive or pressure that which attracted tourists in the first place and acting conservatively in the face of further development.

When the anthropologist is involved in empirical field research, however, he is usually concerned with the daily round of life and the annual cycles of events that engage the whole community or the largest segments of it. His approach, traditionally, is participant observation, obtaining information from a representative range of individuals and specialized data from "key" informants. The ethnographic routine need not be varied when studying tourism at the community level, except that the tourists, be they infrequent or regular visitors or part-time residents of the community, must be taken into account. This further involves an understanding of patterns of interaction between local residents, the hosts, and individual tourists or groups of tourists. In long-established tourist centers, where tourism may properly be called an industry (i.e., Bermuda and Monaco), tourists and hosts are likely to understand each other rather fully, and patterns of interaction have become routinized and may be easily understood and interpreted by the ethnographer. However, when tourism is new or recent to a traditional community, a more difficult series of chores confronts the participant-observer.

An ethnographer new to a field site is always faced with a problem of role definition: what image does he project to the people he is there to study? If he is the sole alien present, as is often the case, he and his hosts usually work out his role definition and status within the community through a somewhat mutual trial-and-error learning experience. Both the hosts and the ethnographer try to find a place where he will "fit" certain established categories of age, sex, and demeanor. However, in a community where tourists are a factor and the subject of study as well, the ethnographer is likely to be identified with the tourist population, stereotyped and classified as a member of a group or category of outsiders. The ethnographer is, of course, almost always an outsider, but most, given a reasonable degree of training, sensitivity, and persistence, establish sufficient rapport with their informants to allow them to gain a limited insider's perspective on the community. Any attempt to study an indigenous population and a tourist population in interaction will probably require talents similar to that of the Roman rider, with a foot on each horse. To make complete, accurate, and empathetic observations of both populations will necessitate a delicate balancing act. Indeed, as some of the chapters of this volume indicate, the anthropologist is likely to be most empathetic toward the host population and even hostile to the very notion of tourism, much less wishing to be identified as a tourist. To be able to achieve a degree of mutual rapport and identity with both populations requires a kind of objectivity and tough-mindedness that is often lacking in social science. It seems, then, that the investigator must, in fairness to his discipline and to his informants, be a participant-observer in both camps. Having personally done this, I have found myself playing what might be considered a boundary role, attempting to interpret each culture to representatives of the other. And since most anthropologists are educators as well as researchers, the boundary role is not only objectively sound but satisfying from a philosophical and humanistic point of view.

But what is the nature of the interaction between hosts and tourists? Their relationship is almost always an instrumental one, rarely colored by affective ties, and almost always marked by degrees of social distance and stereotyping that would not exist amongst neighbors, peers, or fellow countrymen. One has a much easier task when one studies and interprets social interaction within a "natural" community where values and attitudes are more mutually shared and understood. The greater the ethnic and cultural distance between the host and tourist personnel, the greater the confusion and misunderstanding the two groups are likely to encounter and the less natural they are likely to act. However, this is not a novelty to the anthropologist familiar with other kinds of acculturational situations.

How is the anthropologist to present his understanding and interpretation of host-tourist interaction; what models are available to him that go beyond the traditional hypotheses of acculturation? The "dramaturgical" studies of Erving Goffman come immediately to mind. Tourists and more often their hosts are almost always *on stage* when they meet in face-to-face encounters. They have prepared for their performances backstage: the tourist has read his travel brochures, consulted previous visitors, planned his wardrobe, and thumbs through his dictionary and phrase book before going on stage; his host may count the house, assess the mood of the audience, arrange the lighting and props, consult with fellow performers, and rehearse a friendly smile. These metaphors are often not far from reality. Tourists often alter their demeanor when away from home, and their hosts are likely to engage in roles designed to accommodate tourists that they would never play before their peers. A taxi driver might become an instant expert on the archaeological ruins of his region. Or a tourist might assume the airs of an aristocrat in a country where his money goes twice as far as at home. I am aware that we all wear many masks, but our performances are usually more exaggerated before an audience of strangers for whom we must perform, often to the point of obfuscation. Thus the anthropologist must attempt to find his way backstage as well as view the performance from the audience.

An overview of tourism as a subject of anthropological inquiry must contend with the range and diversity of phenomena involved. Traditionally, science has approached this kind of problem by establishing taxonomies and typologies. It is too early in the development of touristic studies to attempt an exhaustive or definitive statement. This volume represents most of what anthropologists now know about the subject. However, we have some guidelines.

Ethnic and environmental tourism have been distinguished, the latter referring to the tourists' interest primarily in the aesthetic or recreational resources of features of the environment. It should be noted that it is unlikely that great numbers of tourists may be drawn to truly inhospitable environments, regardless of how exotic or interesting the host people may be. However, such situations do exist (as in Eskimo country) and tend to result in closer than usual guest-to-host population ratio. As a consequence, tourist impact might be more severe than otherwise. Other typological categories suggest themselves: internal, domestic tourism vs. international tourism; "packaged and programmed" tourism vs. individual tourism; resort tourism vs. "off-the-beaten-track" tourism; religious vs. secular tourism; recreational vs. educational or "cultural" tourism; and mass vs. elite tourism. This is not intended to exhaust the list of possible alternatives and indeed suggests that various permutations of the above categories are probable. A tourist often wants to enrich his leisure and travel to the fullest. A tourist's motives will undoubtedly be reflected in his expectations and behavior within the context of the host's environment.

The chapters in this volume leave many questions unanswered, as they should, but suggest others, as they must. For example, little is known aside from rather obvious generalizations regarding communication facilities, accessibility, accommodations, and publicity as to why tourists make the kinds of choices they make between one vacation and another. Or, why do Italian, Japanese, or American tourists find different tourist areas of interest? Studies of different tourist nationalities and their predilections for locale, entertainment, recreation, souvenirs, or other ethnic groups might fall within the tradition of national character studies as well as prove interesting to students of personality and culture.

I think we yet have no clear idea of how tourists form stereotypes of their hosts, and only limited evidence of how their hosts form stereotypes of them. Nor are we certain how intergroup status relationships are shaped or shared. An understanding of these processes might shed significant light on the symbolic content of each culture, especially where a host community has the opportunity to stereotype and evaluate representatives of more than one nationality.

Not to be overlooked is the fact that some host communities are themselves multi-ethnic and present a culturally pluralistic profile to the tourist. Such populations may be logically expected to react differentially to tourism, positively or negatively, or one or more segments of a multi-ethnic community might profit or suffer at the expense of others. For example, as tourism invades Surinam on the verge of independence from the Netherlands, which peoples—the Bush Negroes, East Indians, urban blacks, Creoles, or the Dutch—will profit or lose, and who will make the policy decisions regarding the direction and development of tourism?

And what about those countries even now committed to tourism as their principal economic activity; those governments whose budgets are tied to continued income from tourists; those communities that have abandoned traditional subsistence schemes to compete for tourist monies?

Some of the foregoing questions lead us to consider, jointly, questions of applied anthropology and anthropological ethics.

Those familiar with the Fox "action anthropology" project and the Cornell-Vicos cooperative applied program of development know that some things can be done by anthropologists to help people consolidate their goals and find means to certain ends. Those anthropologists who wish or feel that they must intervene on behalf of the welfare of the people they study should remember that changes in a local community are more often accepted or opposed in a larger context. Tourism is more often *caused* than it occurs by happenstance, and is more often welcome at the outset than rejected by potential hosts, even enough promoted for economic reasons at governmental levels little concerned with long-range results at the community level. I hope that anthropologists can isolate major economic, social, and political inequities that may be brought about by the development and promotion of tourism and attack resultant inequities through their professional associations and as individuals. And, they might well be solicited to give professional guidance to communities and governments as to the most positive means for establishing mutually agreed-upon ends. Certainly, it is ethical and probably desirable that anthropologists, given the opportunity, should suggest logical alternatives to tourism as a means of economic development.

Prudence should require, however, that the anthropological community resist the temptation to condemn tourism as unnecessarily intrusive, as exploitive, as deculturative. Who are we to say that improved roads, water purification projects, and rural electrification, as spinoffs from tourist development, are not as beneficial to, let us say, rural peasants and craftsmen as they are to their governments and to tourists? At the present state of our knowledge it is difficult to demonstrate that tourism *per se* is uniquely destructive or evil. It may be in some instances the best alternative available to a community or a country; it might also prove to be destructive of natural and human resources.

As anthropologists we would not be acting ethically, however, if we did not expose the cultural fakes and the human zoos for what they are. We must equally resist the temptation to view indigenous peoples as unable to adapt and to assimilate to a changing world. We cannot keep them as pristine pets on anthropological reservations.

It remains true that most tourists represent the "haves" of the world and that many host communities and countries are relative "have-nots." It has also been observed by a number of politically astute anthropologists that modernization and industrialization programs in developing countries, more often than not those receiving aid from Western nations, often exacerbate the status quo, with the rich getting richer and the poor becoming poorer. These are ultimately international problems not immediately soluble in purely anthropological terms. I raise this dilemma merely to suggest that in economic exchanges between tourists and others—although the carriers, travel agencies, and governments may profit enormously—the monies expended by tourists for goods and services at the local, community level, in the markets and bazaars, in taxies and in taverns, for meals and gratuities, may bring greater prosperity and well-being to members of the host community than they might have found possible by any other means in their lifetimes. At the risk of oversimplification, what I am suggesting is that a form of what anthropologists have called a redistributive economic system is operative here. That is, monies spent by tourists are surplus monies, redistributed by an international elite amongst those who have little opportunity for producing such surpluses. One may not ideologically approve of such a system, but one may describe it within the context of economic anthropology.

In summary, as a subject of scholarly study, tourism may be new, but it may be treated within traditional methods and theories of anthropological research for the present and will benefit from the application of more recent, more sophisticated models as data and understanding accumulate. By the time a discipline begins to attempt definitions and prepare taxonomies, as this book does, the subject has achieved legitimacy.

Although the articles in this volume and those cited in the bibliography represent the bulk of the literature concerning tourism, it is certain that many other anthropologists and other scholars have considerable unpublished data in their possession. It is hoped that this effort will encourage them to bring forth their findings and to extend their research in this area. As sufficiently more substantive data accumulate, more elegant and precise theoretical postulates may replace these preliminary observations.

University of Florida, Gainesville

Epilogue, by James Lett

I spent the autumn of 1979 studying hosts and guests on the island of Virgin Gorda, but my field research on tourism was *not* occasioned by serendipity. It was my express intention to study the impacts of touristic development, and I had been awarded research grants to do so from the Inter-American Foundation in Washington, D.C., and the Division of Sponsored Research at the University of Florida. That research, which was designed with the assistance of Theron Nuñez (who was then chairperson of my supervisory committee), resulted in my master's thesis ("Tourism and Culture Change on Virgin Gorda") and provided the data for several subsequent articles (Lett 1982; 1983; 1985). In all of this, I think, I was very typical.

To be specific about it, my personal experience is reflective of the two major trends that have characterized the anthropological study of tourism in the decade since the original edition of this volume appeared. In the first place, the serendipitous approach to touristic studies within anthropology is a thing of the past. Today ethnographers are applying for research funds to study tourism *per se,* and their applications are being met with approval. Ten years ago, as Nuñez observed, the study of tourism had achieved legitimacy and respectability within the discipline; now it is recognized and accepted as a primary area of interest and research for a growing number of anthropologists. In the second place, there has been a veritable explosion of anthropological publications on the subject of tourism. Scores of articles have appeared, and several journals have devoted entire issues to the anthropological analysis of tourism, including *Studies in Third World Societies* ("Tourism and Behavior," 1978, No. 5, and "Tourism and Economic Change," 1978, No. 6), *Cultural Survival Quarterly* ("The Tourist Trap," 1982, Vol. 6), and *Annals of Tourism Research* ("Tourism and Development: Anthropological Perspectives," 1980, Vol. 7, and "The Anthropology of Tourism," 1983, Vol. 10). Anthropologists have responded in full cry to Nuñez's call to publish what they know about tourism.

In short, what was once accidental and unnoticed within anthropology has become deliberate and ubiquitous. Both of these developments deserve another word or two of comment.

The fact that anthropologists have, lately, purposely turned their attention to the study of tourism can only be seen as a welcome and overdue development. In the second half of this century, anthropologists have discovered tourists everywhere they have gone, as Nuñez says, for the simple reason that tourists are everywhere. Modern tourism accounts for the single largest peaceful movement of people across cultural boundaries in the history of the world. Given that, tourism is unavoidably an anthropological topic. As a discipline whose raison d'être is the exploration and explication of cultural similarities and differences, anthropology cannot ignore the phenomenon of tourism and retain its identity.

The fact that anthropologists have begun to build a sizeable body of literature on the subject of tourism has had several predictable results, including the fact that anthropologists have disagreed about the best theoretical approach to take in examining tourism. The anthropological literature on tourism can be broadly divided into two categories—a division that is reflected in the two articles that make up part I of this volume. On the one hand, there are those anthropologists, like Nelson Graburn, who are interested in exploring the culturally defined meanings that the experience of tourism holds for the tourist and those he or she encounters; on the other hand, there are those anthropologists, like Dennison Nash, who are interested in assessing the range of empirical effects that tourism has upon the sociocultural systems of host societies.

Professors Graburn and Nash, in fact, have been actively involved in a debate about the best way to study tourism since the first edition of this volume was published in 1977. In the past decade, two major theoretical overviews on the anthropology of tourism have appeared, one by Nash (1981) and the other by Graburn (1983a). Graburn has argued that tourism can best be analyzed as a near-universal manifestation of the pan-human need for play and recreation whose origin is grounded in the invariable tendency for human beings to assign meaning to their activities, while Nash has argued that tourism can best be viewed as a near-universal form of travel pursued by people at leisure whose origin cannot be determined but whose cultural variability can be assessed. Graburn (1983) suggests that tourism is preeminently a secular ritual, and that in many contemporary societies it fulfills functions once met by sacred (or, more precisely, supernatural) rituals. Nash (1984) questions Graburn's contention that the need to alternate between ordinary and non-ordinary experiences is innate or universal, and he asks why such a need, if it did exist, would necessarily express itself in touristic form. While Graburn would prefer to explore the symbolic meaning of tourism, Nash would prefer to analyze the political and economic effects of touristic development.

These two perspectives are not necessarily contradictory, however; indeed, as the articles in this volume attest, they can easily be seen as complementary. The theoretical difference between Professors Graburn and Nash is a common one in anthropology, for it reflects the distinction between those who wish to study *the maintenance of human identity* and those who wish to study *the maintenance of human life*. These phrases are ones I have used elsewhere (Lett 1987) to characterize the basic duality of the anthropological domain of inquiry. By "the maintenance of human identity," I mean those activities whose primary function is to define and demarcate human status, or those activities whose express origin lies in the human tendency to impose symbol-mediated meanings upon the world. *Cross-culturally, the maintenance of human identity is most frequently accomplished through such activities as ritual, play, and art.* By "the maintenance of human life," I mean those activities whose primary function is to satisfy the physical and metabolical requirements of survival. *Cross-culturally, the maintenance of human life is invariably accomplished, except in the most extraordinary circumstances, through learned and shared subsistence strategies.* While most cultural phenomena simultaneously involve, in some aspect, the maintenance of both human life and human identity (this is certainly true of tourism), most anthropologists tend to focus on one set of issues or the other when researching any cultural phenomenon (and this, again, has been true of the anthropological approach to tourism). Thus in analyzing tourism most anthropologists have either described the ways in which tourism is used as a symbolic means of expressing and maintaining human identity, or they have described the social, political, economic, and environmental effects that result from using touristic modes of production to maintain human life.

In the past decade, both approaches have been characterized by greater articulation and greater sophistication. With regard to the study of tourism as a means of maintaining human life, we now have a considerable literature on the impact of tourism in a variety of societies. Nash (1981), one of the principal proponents of this point of view, has helped to sharpen the focus of our analysis by reminding us that association and causality are not necessarily the same thing. (There was a tendency, in early anthropological studies of tourism, to attribute all social changes to tourism and to downplay or ignore other sources of change.) Nash and Nuñez have both challenged anthropologists to explain the causes of touristic variability—to explain, among other things, why tourists make the choices they do—and several of their colleagues have responded with particular case studies, including Smith (1979) and Moore (1985). In addition, the literature on the impacts of tourism is notably more balanced than it was ten years ago; anthropologists have heeded Nuñez's warning not to automatically condemn all forms of tourism in all cases (witness Professor Greenwood's observation, in his epilogue to Chapter 8, that tourism *does* occasionally engender creative and positive responses).

With regard to the study of tourism as a means of maintaining human identity, the literature is both richer ethnographically and more complex ethnologically. Graburn (1983) has taken the lead in analyzing tourism as a form of secular ritual, building especially upon the work of Huizinga (1950), Leach (1961), Norbeck (1974), and Turner (1969; 1974). Other anthropologists have applied the concepts of play, ritual, and liminality to the study of tourism in the past decade, including most notably Wagner (1977), Moore (1980), and Lett (1983).

Whether anthropologists have chosen to study tourism as a means of maintaining human life or human identity, they have virtually all agreed upon one thing: there is no need for a particular or specific "theory of tourism"—rather, there is a need to apply existing anthropological theories to the study of tourism, as Nuñez suggested when he said that tourism could be studied under a variety of traditional anthropological rubrics. In analyzing contemporary anthropological theory (Lett 1987), I have suggested that the paradigms of cultural materialism and symbolic anthropology are best suited for the analysis, respectively, of human life and human identity, and I would suggest that that holds true as well for the study of tourism. (Indeed, that seems to be the general theoretical track most anthropological students of tourism have followed in recent years.)

In the final analysis, what unites all anthropological approaches to tourism is the discipline's uniquely holistic and comparative perspective. This is the one thing that has characterized all anthropological analyses of tourism to date, and it is the one thing, ultimately, that separates anthropological accounts of tourism from studies conducted by psychologists, economists, political scientists, or sociologists. Valene Smith (1980, p. 16) has made this point elsewhere, but it is one that bears repeating. Anthropologists may differ as to whether they wish to study symbolic systems of meaning or behavioral systems of adaptation, but all anthropologists agree that all aspects of sociocultural systems are interrelated—and all anthropologists agree that their theories must be applicable to all peoples in all places at all times.

In sum, the anthropology of tourism is as broad as the field of anthropology itself. The major paradigmatic challenges facing contemporary anthropologists are ones that can readily be pursued in the context of touristic studies, as Professor Greenwood notes in this volume when he observes that the "broadest theoretical issues in the discipline" include "culture as representation" (the critical issue for symbolic anthropologists) and "the links between political economy and systems of meaning" (an abiding concern for cultural materialists). The anthropological study of tourism has scarcely begun. Nuñez speaks of having played a boundary role, as an ethnographer, between hosts and guests of different backgrounds, and his personal experience is likely to be prophetic. Anthropologists are uniquely well-suited to be culture brokers, and in a world where cross-cultural encounters are becoming commonplace, thanks to tourism, anthropologists will find increasing opportunities to fulfill that role.

Indian River Community College
Fort Pierce, Florida

REFERENCE LIST AND BIBLIOGRAPHY

The bibliography, although extensive, is not exhaustive. It lists additional works by the contributors to this volume, as well as important books and/or articles in related disciplines, and is intended to serve as a starting point for research. The principal tourism journals published in the U.S., the *Annals of Tourism Research* and the *Journal of Travel Research*, both have a respective index and therefore are not fully referenced here.

Appreciation is extended to Veronica Long and Carol Cameron for their able assistance in library research and programming.

Abbey, J. R. 1978. The relevance of life-style and demographic information in designing package travel tours. Ph.D. dissertation, Utah State University, Logan.

Adams, J. 1972. Why the American tourist abroad is cheated: A price theoretical analysis. *Journal of Political Economics* 80 (1): 203–7.

Adams, R. McC. 1974. Anthropological perspectives on ancient trade. *Current Anthropology* 15: 239–58.

Addison, W. 1951. *English spas.* London: Batsford.

Adebiaye, T. W. 1973. Le Tourism international et le development des Etats d'Afrique Noire Francophone. Thesis, Université des Sciences Sociales de Toulouse, Toulouse.

Aerni, M. J. 1972. Social effects of tourism. Letter to the editor in *Current Anthropology* 13 (2): 162.

Ahmed, N. 1979. Tourism and the historical and cultural heritage of Bangladesh. *World Travel* 150: 36–40.

AIEST. 1972. Tourism research methods and their application to developing countries and regions. *Proceedings* 13.

————. 1985. *Trends of tourist demands.* Vol. 26. Bern, Switzerland.

Aiken, S. R., and Moss, M. R. 1976. Man's impact on the natural environment of peninsular Malaysia. *Biological Conservation* 3: 279–82.

Airey, D. 1978. Tourism and the balance of payments. *Tourism International Research-Europe* 3: 2–16.

————. 1979. Tourism education in the United Kingdom. *The Tourist Review* 34 (3): 13–15.

'Akau'ola, L., 'Ilaiu, L., and Samate, 'A. 1980. The social and cultural impact of tourism in Tonga. In *Pacific tourism: As islanders see it,* F. Rajotte and R. Crocombe, eds., pp. 17–24. Fiji: South Pacific Social Sciences Association and The Institute of Pacific Studies, University of the South Pacific.

Akoglu, T. 1971. Tourism and the problem of environment. *Tourist Review* 26: 18–20.

Albert, B. W. 1982. Travel and rehabilitation. *Mainstream* 7 (5): 18–29.

Alexander, D. 1972. *Holiday in the Seychelles.* Cape Town/London/New York: Purnell.

Alexander, L. M. 1953. The impact of tourism on the economy of Cape Cod, Massachusetts. *Economic Geography* 29: 320–26.

Allsop, K. 1972. Across Europe and out of sight, man. *Punch* 2 August: 130–32.

Aminuddin, M. 1981. Domestic tourism: Its importance and potentialities. *Dawn* 19 May: 3.

Amory, C. 1952. *The last resorts.* New York: Harper and Bros.

Anan'yev, M. A. 1968. *Mezhdunarodnyy turizm* (International tourism). Moscow: Izdatel'stvo "Mezhdunarodnyye otnosheniya."

Andersson, A., and de Jong, H. 1986. *Recreatie in een Veranderende Maatschappij: Een literatuurstudie.* Landbouw: Hogeschool Wageningen.

Andric, N. 1980. *Turizam i regional razvoj.* Zagreb: Informator.

Andronicou, A. 1979. Tourism in Cyprus. In *Tourism: Passport to development?* E. de Kadt, ed., pp. 237–64. New York: Oxford University Press.

Angell, R. C. 1967. The growth of transnational participation. *Journal of Social Issues* 23: 108–29.

Annis, S. n.d. The museum as a staging ground for symbolic experience. Master's thesis, Dept. of Geography, University of Chicago.

Anolik, A. 1977. *The law and the travel industry.* Corte Medera, California: Alchemy Books.

Anuario El País. 1987. Madrid: Ediciones El País.

Apter, H. 1974. Counting the (social) cost of tourism, part I. *The Travel Agent* (16 December): 24–29.

————. 1975. Counting the (social) cost of tourism, part II. *The Travel Agent* (6 February): 54–58.

Archer, B. H. 1976a. *Demand forecasting in tourism.* Cardiff: University of Wales Press.

————. 1976b. Uses and abuses of multipliers. In *Planning for tourism development: Quantitative approaches,* G. E. Gearing, W. W. Swart, and T. Var, eds., pp. 115–32. New York: Praeger.

————. 1977a. Tourism in the Bahamas and Bermuda: Two case studies. Bangor Occasional Papers in Economics No. 10. Cardiff: University of Wales Press.

————. 1977b. Tourism multipliers: The state of the art. Bangor Occasional Papers in Economics No. 11. Cardiff: University of Wales Press.

Archer, B. H., Shea, S., and Vane, R. 1974. *Tourism in Gwynedd: An economic study.* Bangor: Institute of Economic Research, University College of Wales.

Archer, E. D. G. 1980. Effects of the tourist industry in Barbados, West Indies. Ph.D. dissertation, University of Texas, Austin.

Argyle, M. 1982. Intercultural communication. In *Cultures in contact*, L. B. Bochner, ed., pp. 61–80. Oxford: Pergamon Press.

Ascher, F. 1980. Tourisme et developpement: La fin des illusions. *Le Monde Diplomatique* (August).

———. 1985. *Tourism transnational corporations and cultural identities*. Paris: UNESCO.

Ascher, F., and Schecht-Jacquin, J. 1978. *La production du tourisme*. Paris: Ardu-Cordes, Université de Paris.

Ascher, J. D. 1979. A sociological approach to crowding in outdoor recreation: A study of the Yosemite National Park back country. Ph.D. dissertation, University of California, Berkeley.

Ash, J. 1974. To hell with paradise. *New Internationalist* (February).

Ashton, G. 1964. Tourism as culture contact: A bibliographic survey on the impact of tourism as planned economic development. Paper presented to the Symposium on Tourism, Central States Anthropological Society, 14–16 May 1964, Milwaukee, Wisconsin.

Ashworth, G. 1984. Recreation and tourism. In *Man and environment*, D. Burtenshaw, ed. London: Bell-Hyman.

Ashworth, G., and de Haan, T. 1985. The touristic historic city: A model and application in Norwich. *Field Studies Series* No. 6. Groningen: GIRUG.

———. 1986. Uses and users of the tourist-historic city: An evolutionary model in Norwich. *Field Studies Series* No. 10. Groningen: GIRUG.

Asian Institute of Tourism. 1982. *Annotated bibliography on Philippine tourism*. Division of Tourism Research and Publications. Quezon City: University of the Philippines.

Asian Women's Liberation, Asian Women's Association. 1980. Prostitution, tourism. No. 3, June 1980. Tokyo: Japan.

Aspelin, P. L. 1978. Indirect tourism and political economy: The case of the Mamainde of Mato Grosso, Brazil. In *Tourism and economic change*. Studies in Third World Societies No. 6. V. Smith, ed., pp. 1–18. Williamsburg, Virginia: William and Mary Press.

———. 1982. "What you don't know, won't hurt you." *Cultural Survival Quarterly* 6 (3): 20–21.

Atac-Rosch, I. 1984. Public planning for tourism: A general method for establishing economic, environmental, social and administrative criteria. Ph.D. dissertation, University of Washington, Seattle.

Auten, H. R., Jr. 1980. A short haul airline transport for the People's Republic of China. DBA dissertation, United States International University, San Diego, California.

Awekotuku, A. N. 1980. Maori culture and tourist income. In *Pacific tourism: As islanders see it*, F. Rajotte and R. Crocombe, eds., pp. 153–62. Fiji: South Pacific Social Sciences Association and The Institute of Pacific Studies, University of the South Pacific.

Axtell, R. E., ed. 1985. *Do's and taboos around the world*. Elmsford, New York: The Benjamin Company.

Badea, L. 1969. Le premier colloque national de la géographie du tourisme (Bucarest, September 1968). *Revue Roumaine de Géologie, Géophysique, et Géographie, Serie de Géographie* 13 (1): 91–93.

Bagus, G. N. 1976. *The impact of tourism upon the culture of the Balinese people.* Washington DC: UNESCO/IBRD, pp. 8–10.

Bailey, F. G. 1973. *Debate and compromise: The politics of innovation.* Oxford: Basil Blackwell.

Bainbridge, S. 1979. *Restrictions at Stonehenge: The reactions of visitors to limitations in access: Report of a survey.* London: Social Survey Division, Office of Population Censuses and Surveys, HMSO.

Baines, G. B. K. 1982. South Pacific island tourism: Environmental cost and benefits of the Fijian example. In *The impact of tourism development in the Pacific,* F. Rajotte, ed. Peterborough: Trent University.

Balandier, G. 1951. La situation coloniale: Approche théorique. *Cahiers Internationaux de Sociologie* 11: 44–79.

Ball, D. A. 1971. Permanent tourism: A new export diversification for less developed countries. *International Development Review* 13 (4): 20–23.

Balossier, R. 1967. Approche sociologique de quelques problémes touristiques. *Cahiers de Tourisme,* Series C., No. 3.

Balsdon, J. P. V. D. 1966. *Life and leisure in ancient Rome.* London: Bodley Head.

Barber, D. 1987. New Zealand's about-face on Pacific overstayers. *Far Eastern Economic Review* (19 March): 30.

Barbier, B., and Billet, J. 1980. Developpement touristique et espace natural. *Revue de l'AIEST* 21: 11–21.

Barbose, Y. 1970. Trois types d'intervention du tourisme dans l'organization de l'espace littoral. *Annals de Géographie* 79: 446–68.

Baretje, R. 1969. Bibliographie touristique. In *Collection Etudes et Memoires* 22 (11): 104. Aix-en-Provence: Centre d'Etudes du Tourisme.

Baretje, R., and Defert, P. 1972. *Aspects économiques du tourisme.* Paris: Editions Berger-Lavrault.

Barratt, P. J. H. 1972. *Grand Bahama.* Newton Abbot: David and Charles.

Barth, F., ed. 1963. *The role of the entrepreneur in social change in northern Norway.* Bergen: Scandinavia University.

———. 1967. On the study of social change. *American Anthropologist* 69: 661–69.

Barthes, R. 1973, *Mythologies.* London: Paladin.

Baud-Bovy, M., and Lawson, F. 1976. *Tourism master plan.* Toronto: Management Development Institute, Ryerson Polytechnical Institute.

———. 1977. *Tourism and recreation development.* London: Architectural Press.

Bauge, R. 1975. Le developpement du tourisme rural en France et en Afrique de l'Ouest Francophone par l'intervention du credit agricole (Senegal Case Study). Toulouse: Université des Sciences Sociales de Toulouse.

Baumgartner, F. 1978. Le tourisme dans le tiers-monde: Contribution au developpement? *Revue du Tourisme* 1: 14–17.

Beard, J., and Ragheb, M. 1983. Measuring leisure motivation. *Journal of Leisure Research* 15: 219–28.

Beck, B., and Bryan, F. 1971. This other Eden: A survey of tourism in Britain. *The Economist* 6683: 25.9, xxiv.

Beesley, M. E. 1965. The value of time spent in traveling: Some new evidence. *Economica* 32 n.s.: 174–85.

Beioley, S. 1981. *Tourism and urban regeneration: Some lessons from American cities.* London: English Tourist Board.

Belardinelli, E. 1970. *Problemi attuali degli approdi tutistici.* Milan: Giuffrè.

Belasco, W. 1979. *Americans on the road: From autocamp to motel, 1910–1945.* Cambridge, Massachusetts: The MIT Press, pp. 37–52.

Belisle, F. J. 1980. Hotel food supply and local food production in Jamaica: A study in tourism geography. Ph.D. dissertation, University of Georgia.

Bell, T. A. 1973. The metamorphosis of Tahiti: Change and tradition in a transforming landscape. *Yearbook of the Association of Pacific Coast Geographers* 35: 103–13.

Bendre, V. P. 1979. *Tourism in India.* Aurangabad, India: Parimal Prakashan.

Bennett, C. M. 1970. Tourism and its effect on the peoples of the Pacific. *Proceedings of the 19th Annual Pacific Area Travel Association (PATA) Conference,* 13–17 April 1970, Auckland, New Zealand, pp. 78–81.

Ben Salem, T. 1970. Aspects humains du developpement du tourisme dans le Cap Bon. *Revue Tunisienne du Science Sociales* 20: 31–68.

Bergerot, J., et al. 1974. *Etude du developpement touristique de l'archipel des Comores.* Paris: Ministere de l'Education Nationale et du Tourisme.

Berlyne, D. E. 1962. New directions in motivation theory. In *Anthropology and human behavior,* T. Gladwin and W. C. Sturtevant, eds., pp. 150–73. Washington DC: Anthropological Society of Washington.

Berriane, M. 1980. *L'Espace touristique Marocain.* Poitiers: CNRS–Université de Poitiers et Tours.

Berthoud, G. 1972. Introduction: Dynamics of ownership in the circum-Alpine area. *Anthropological Quarterly* 43 (3): 117–24.

Bevan, D. L., and Soskice, D. W. 1976. Appraising tourist development in a small economy. In *Using shadow prices,* Little and Scott, eds. London: Heinemann.

Bhattia, A. K. 1978. *Tourism in India.* New Delhi: Sterling Publishers.

Biddlecomb, C. 1981. *Pacific tourism.* Suva, Fiji: Lotu Pasifika Productions.

Bielckus, C. L. 1977. Second homes in Scandinavia. In *Second homes: Curse or blessing?* J. T. Coppock, ed., pp. 35–46. Oxford: Pergamon.

Birnbaum, S. 1981. 'Intruders' Cuna natives mingle in San Blas Islands. *The Denver Post Roundup* 1 February: 45.

Bishop, J. M. 1986. The marketing of Tarascan culture in Michoacan, Mexico. Paper presented at the Symposium on Rural Tourism, Annual Meeting of the Society for Applied Anthropology, 26–30 March, Reno, Nevada.

Bisilliat, J. 1979. Problèmes posés par l'expansion du tourisme dans les pays en voie de developpement. *Peuples Mediterranéens.* Paris: Institute d'etudes Mediterranéennes, No. 7.

Blake, E. W. 1974. Stranger in paradise. *Caribbean Review* 6: 9–12.

Blake, G. W., and Lawless, R. 1972. Algeria's tourist industry. *Geography* 57: 148–52.

Blanchard, R. D. 1976. Lifestyle and travel demand of the elderly: A case study of Los Angeles County. Ph.D. dissertation, University of California, Los Angeles.

Blizovsky, Y. 1973. The role of tourism in the economy. In *The second million: Israel tourist industry, past, present, future,* C. H. Klein, ed., pp. 117–28. Tel Aviv: Amir Publishing.

Blumin, S. M. 1980. *The short season of Sharon Springs: Portrait of an American village.* Ithaca, New York: Cornell University Press.

Bocca, G. 1963. *Bikini beach.* London: W. H. Allen.

Bochet, G. 1971. Souvenir-hunting—. *Tam-Tam* 5: 1–3. Abidjan: Ivory Coast Information Journal, Ministry of Tourism of the Ivory Coast.

Bochner, L. S., ed. 1982. *Cultures in contact.* Oxford: Pergamon Press.

Bodine, J. 1964. Symbiosis at Taos and the impact of tourism on the Pueblo: A case of "unplanned" economic development. Paper presented to Symposium on Tourism, Central States Anthropological Society, 14–16 May 1964, Milwaukee, Wisconsin.

Boek, W. S. 1964. Touring as planned economic development: Coordinating diverse local interests with outside capital. Paper presented to the Symposium on Tourism, Central States Anthropological Society, 14–16 May 1964, Milwaukee, Wisconsin.

Boeke, J. H. 1953. *Economics and economic policy of dual societies as exemplified by Indonesia.* New York: International Secretariet, Institute of Pacific Relations.

Boissevain, J. 1977. Tourism and development in Malta. *Development and Change* 8: 523–38.

———. 1978. Tourism and development in Malta. In *Tourism and economic change.* Studies in Third World Societies No. 6., V. Smith, ed., pp. 37–56. Williamsburg, Virginia: William and Mary Press.

Boissevain, J., and Inglott, P. S. 1979. Tourism in Malta. In *Tourism: Passport to development?* E. de Kadt, ed., pp. 265–84. New York: Oxford University Press.

Bolabola, C. A. B. 1980. The impact of tourism on Fijian woodcarving. In *Pacific tourism: As islanders see it,* F. Rajotte and R. Crocombe, eds., pp. 93–98. Fiji: South Pacific Social Sciences Association and The Institute of Pacific Studies, University of the South Pacific.

———. 1981. Does tourism cause malnutrition? They seem to be connected. *Pacific Perspectives* 10 (1): 72–77.

Bonapace, U. 1968. Il turismo nella neve in Italia e i suoi aspetti geografici. *Revisita geografica italiana* 75 (2): 157–86 and 75 (3): 322–59.

Bond, M E., and Ladman, J. R. 1971. Tourism: A regional growth phenomenon. *Rocky Mountain Social Science Journal* 8 (2): 23–32.

———. 1972. Tourism: A strategy for development. *Nebraska Journal of Economics and Business* 2 (1): 37–52.

———. 1974. The tourist industry: What impact on Arizona? *Arizona Business* 20: 20–26.

Boon, J. A. 1974. The progress of the ancestors in a Balinese temple group. *Journal of Asian Studies* 34 (1): 7–25.

Boorstin, D. 1962. *The image, or what happened to the American dream.* New York: Atheneum.

———. 1975. *The image: A guide to pseudo-events in America.* New York: Atheneum.

Bornet, B. 1974. Tourisme et environnement: Faut-il souhaiter une concentration ou une deconcentration touristique? *Les Cahiers du Tourisme,* Series C, No. 20. Aix-en-Provence: Centre d'Etudes du Tourisme.

Bornet, B., et al. 1979. La politique de la formation professionnelle touristique au service de l'emploi. *Revue du Tourisme* (July–September): 2–88.

Bornschier, V. 1980. Multinational corporations, economic policy and national development in the world system. *International Social Science Journal* 32 (1): 158–74.

Bosselman, F. P. 1978. *In the wake of the tourist: Managing special places in eight countries.* Washington DC: The Conservation Foundation.

Bossen, L. 1984. *The redivision of labor.* Albany: State University of New York Press.

Boulduc, J. 1974. *Selective bibliography: Tourist facilities and development policies in the French-speaking third world and Canada.* Ottawa: Institute of International Co-operation.

Bouman, A., and Lengkeek, J. 1986. Een vergelijking van toeristische recreatieve ontwikkelingsplannen. *Vrije Ti jden Samenleving* 4 (3): 10–15.

Bouret, R. E. 1972. *Tourism in Puerto Rico.* San German: Inter-American University Publications.

Boutillier, J. L., et al. 1978. *Le Tourisme en Afrique de l'Ouest: Panacee ou nouvelle traite?* Paris: Maspero.

Boyer, M. 1972. *Le tourisme.* Paris: Editions du Seuil.

Boynton, L. 1986. The effect of tourism on Amish quilting patterns. Paper presented at the Symposium on Rural Tourism, Annual Meeting of the Society for Applied Anthropology, 26–30 March 1986, Reno, Nevada.

Brameld, T., and Matsuyama, M. 1978. *Tourism as cultural learning: Two controversial case studies in educational anthropology.* Washington DC: University Press of America.

Brancher, D. M. 1972. The minor road in Devon—a study of visitors' attitudes. *Regional Studies* 6: 49–58.

Breslin, P., and M. Chapin. 1984. Conservation, Kuna style. *Grassroots Development* 8 (2): 26–30.

Brewer, J. D. 1978. Tourism, business, and ethnic categories in a Mexican town. In *Tourism and behavior, Studies* in Third World Societies No. 5, V. Smith, ed., pp. 83–100. Williamsburg, Virginia: William and Mary Press.

British Tourist Authority. 1975. Is there "Welcome" on the mat? London.

———. 1981. The economic significance of tourism within the European community. London.

Britton, R. 1978. International tourism and indigenous development objectives: A study with special reference to the West Indies. Ph.D. dissertation, University of Minnesota.

———. 1979. Some notes on the geography of tourism. *Canadian Geographer* 23: 276–82.

———. 1980a. Alternatives to conventional mass tourism in the third world. Paper presented to the 76th Annual Meeting, Association of American Geographers, 13–16 April 1980, Louisville, Kentucky.

———. 1980b. The dark side of the sun. *Focus* 31 (2): 10–16.

Britton, S. G. 1980a. The spatial organization of tourism in a neocolonial economy: A Fiji case study. *Pacific Viewpoint* 21 (2): 144–65.

———. 1980b. The evolution of a colonial space-economy: The case of Fiji. *Journal of Historical Geography* 6 (3): 251–74.

———. 1982a. The political economy of tourism in the third world. *Annals of Tourism Research* 9: 331–58.

———. 1982b. International tourism and multinational corporation in the Pacific. In *The Geography of Multinationals,* M. Taylor and N. Thrift, eds. London: Croom-Helm.

———. 1983. *Tourism and underdevelopment in Fiji.* Canberra: The Australian National University.

Brougham, J. E. 1978. Resident attitudes towards the impact of tourism in Sleat. Ph.D. dissertation, University of Western Ontario, London, Ontario.

Brougham, J. E, and Butler, R. W. 1977. *The social and cultural impact of tourism: A case study of Sleat, Isle of Skye.* Edinburgh: Scottish Tourist Board.

Brower, C. H. 1986. Gender roles and social change: A Mexican case study. *Ethnology* 26 (2): 89–106.

Brown, C. 1984. Tourism and ethnic competition in a ritual form—the firewalkers of Fiji. *Oceania* 54 (3): 223–44.

Brown, D., Ellet, A., and Giemza, G. 1982. *Hawaii recalls: Selling romance to*

America, nostalgic images of the Hawaiian Islands, 1910–1950. Honolulu: Editions Limited.

Brown, J. 1970. Sex division of labor among the San Blas Cuna. *Anthropological Quarterly* 43 (2): 57–63.

Brown, N. O. 1959. *Life against death*. London: Routledge and Kegan Paul.

Brown, T. L., and Connelly, N. A. 1984. Tourism in the Adirondack region of New York. Natural Resources Research and Extension Series 21. Ithaca, New York: Cornell University.

Browne, R.-J. 1986. Tribal tourism development on American Indian reservations in the western United States. Master's Thesis, Oregon State University, Corvallis.

Brownrigg, M., and Greig, M. A. 1975. Differential multipliers for tourism. *Scottish Journal of Political Economy* 21: 261–75.

———. 1976. *Tourism and regional development*. Speculative Papers No. 5. Glasgow: Fraser of Allander Institute.

Bryan, W. 1957. A geographic study of the tourist industry of Mexico. Master's thesis, Dept. of Geography, Oklahoma State University.

Bryden, J. 1973. *Tourism and development: A case study of the commonwealth Caribbean*. New York: Cambridge University Press.

Bryden, J., and Faber, M. 1971. Multiplying the tourist multiplier. *Social and Economic Studies* 20 (1): 61–82.

Buck, R. C. 1978a. Boundary maintenance revisited: Tourist experience in an old order Amish community. *Rural Sociology* 43 (2): 221–34.

———. 1978b. From work to play: Some observations on a popular nostalgic theme. *Journal of American Culture* 1 (3): 543–53.

———. 1979. Bloodless theater: Images of one old order Amish in tourism literature. *Pennsylvania Heritage* 2 (3): 2–11.

Budowski, G. 1976. Tourism and environmental conservation: Conflict, coexistence, or symbiosis. *Environmental Conservation* 3: 27–31.

Bugnicourt, J. 1977. Tourism with no return. *Development Forum* 5 (5): 2–3.

Burde, J. H., and Lenzini, J. 1980. Timber harvest and aesthetic quality: Can they coexist? In *Tourism planning and development issues*, D. E. Hawkins, E. L. Shafer, and J. M. Rovelstad, eds., pp. 121–32. Washington DC: George Washington University Press.

Burgelin, O. 1967. Le tourisme juge. *Communications* 10: 65–97. Special edition, Vacances et tourisme.

Burger, A. V. 1978. The economic impact of tourism in Nepal: An input-output analysis. Ph.D. dissertation, Cornell University, Ithaca, New York.

Burkart, A. J., and Medlik, S. 1974. *Tourism: Past, present and future*. London: Heinemann.

Burke, K. 1980. The development of a small tourist enterprise. In *Pacific tourism: As islanders see it*, F. Rajotte and R. Crocombe, eds., pp. 25–31. Fiji: South Pacific Social Sciences Association and The Institute of Pacific Studies, University of the South Pacific.

Burn, H. P. 1975. Packaging paradise—the environmental costs of international tourism. *Sierra Club Bulletin* 80 (5): 25–28.

Burnet, M. L. 1970. Pays en voie de developpement et tourisme. *Bulletin de l'Association des Géographes Francais* 377–78.

Burrough, P. 1985. Geografische informatiesystemen: Gereedschappen voor landschaps-en milieuanalyse. *Landschap* 2: 269–76.

Burton, T. L. 1971. *Experiments in recreation research*. London: Allen and Unwin.

Butler, R. W. 1974. The social implications of tourist development. *Annals of Tourism Research* 2 (2): 100–14.

———. 1975a. Tourism as an agent of social change. In *Tourism as a factor in national and regional development*, Department of Geography Occasional Paper 4, pp. 85–90. Peterborough, Ontario: Trent University.

———. 1975b. *The development of tourism in the North and implications for the Inuit*. Renewable Resources Project, Vol. 9. Ottawa: Inuit Tapirisat of Canada.

———. 1980. The concept of a tourism area cycle of evolution: Implications for management of resources. *Canadian Geographer* 24: 5–12.

Callimanopulos, D. 1982. Tourism in the Seychelles: A counterfeit paradise. *Cultural Survival Quarterly* 6 (3): 24–25.

Cals, J. 1974. *Turismo y política turística en España: Una aproximación*. Barcelona: Ariel.

Cameron, J. M., and Bordessa, R. 1981. *Wonderland through the looking glass*. Ontario: Canada Belstein Publishing.

Canadian Government Office of Tourism. 1982. *Tourism is important to all of us*. Ottawa.

Caribbean Ecumenical Consultation for Development. 1971. *The role of tourism in Caribbean development*. Study Paper No. 8. Bridgetown, Barbados.

Caro Baroja, J. 1963. The city and the country: Reflections on some ancient commonplaces. In *Mediterranean countrymen*, J. Pitt-Rivers, ed., pp. 27–40. The Hague: Mouton.

———. 1968. Mascaradas y alardes' de San Juan. In *Estudios sobre la vida tradicional española*, J. Caro Baroja, ed., pp. 167–82. Barcelona: Ediciones Peninsula.

Carone, G. 1959. *Il turismo nell'economia internazionale*. Milan: Giuffré.

Carpenter, B. R. 1962. Puerto Rico's tourist industry. *Annals of the Association of American Geographers* 52: 323–24 (abstract).

Carpenter, E. 1972, 1973. *Oh, what a blow that phantom gave me!* New York: Holt, Rinehart and Winston.

Casson, L. 1971. After 2000 years tours have changed but not tourists. *Smithsonian* 2 (6): 52–60.

Castro Farinas, J. A. 1969. Los medios de communication social y el desarrollo de turismo. *Estudiant Information* 9 (1): 55–71.

Catholic Publishing House. 1984. *Kisaeng tourism*. Seoul, Korea.

Caufield, C. 1982. Can scientific tourists save Panama's rainforests? *New Scientist* 24 June: 833.

Cazes, G. 1968. Le developpement du tourisme à la Martinique. *Cahiers d'Otre Mer* 2 (83): 225–26.

———. 1972a. Tourisme, developpement et amenagement: l'example de Puerto Rico. *Les Cahiers du Tourisme*, Series B, No. 16. Aix-en-Provence: Centre d'Etudes du Tourisme.

———. 1972b. Le role du tourisme dans la croissance economique. *Revue du Tourisme* No. 3 (July–September): 93– 98; No. 4 (October–December).

Cazes, G. Lanquar, and Raynouard, Y. 1980. *L'Amenagement touristique*. Paris: Presses Universitaires de France.

CETIM. 1977. *Tourisme dans le tiers-monde: Mythes et realités*. Geneva: Centre Europe Tiers-Monde.

Chadwick, R. A. 1981. Some notes on the geography of tourism: A comment. *Canadian Geographer* 25: 191–97.

Chalip, L., Csikszentmihalyi, M., Kleiber, W., and Larson, R. 1984. Variations of experience in formal and informal sport. *Research Quarterly for Exercise and Sport* 55: 109–16.

Chen, P. 1972. Social pollution—with special reference to Singapore, *NYLTI Journal* (Singapore) (May) 117–25.

Cheng, J. R. 1980. Tourism: How much is too much? Lessons for Canmore from Banff. *Canadian Geographer* 24: 72–80.

Chen-Young, et al. 1977. *Transnationals of tourism in the Caribbean.* London: Commonwealth Secretariat.

Chesnutwood, C. M. 1958. Computing a qualitative tourist industry index. *Annals of the Association of American Geographers* 48: 356 (abstract).

Chib, S. N. 1980. Financing tourism development: A recipient's view. *International Journal of Tourism Management* 1 (4).

Chirstaller, W. 1955. Beitrage zu einer geographie des fremdenverkehrs. *Erdkunde* 9 (1): 1–19.

———. 1964. Some considerations of tourism of Europe. The peripheral regions—underdeveloped countries—recreation areas. *Papers of the Regional Science Association* 12: 95–105.

Chiti, M. P. 1970. *Profilo pubblico del turismo.* Milan: Giuffrè.

Choi, C. 1986. Politics and commercialization of shamanic healing in Korea. Paper presented at meetings of the American Anthropological Association, 3–7 December 1986, Philadelphia, Pennsylvania.

Chow, W. T. 1978. *Tourism and regional planning: The legends of Hawaii.* Bellingham: Western Washington University.

Clark, R. N., Hendee, J. C., and Campbell, F. L. 1971. Values, behavior and conflict in a modern camping culture. *Journal of Leisure Research* 3 (3): 143–59.

Clarke, C. D. 1978. An analysis of the determinants of demand for tourism in Barbados. Ph.D. dissertation, Fordham University, New York City.

Clement, H. G. 1961. *Future of tourism in the Pacific and Far East.* U.S. Department of Commerce. Washington DC: U.S. Government Printing Office.

Cleveland, H., Mangone, C. J., and Adams, J. C. 1960. *The overseas Americans.* New York: McGraw-Hill.

Cleverdon, R. 1979. *The economic and social impact of international tourism on developing countries.* London: The Economist Intelligence Unit.

Clout, H. D. 1977. Residence secondaries in France. In *Second homes: Curse or blessing?* J. T. Coppock, ed., pp. 47–62. Oxford: Pergamon.

Cobb, C. 1986. Panama: Ever at the crossroads. *National Geographic* (April): 466–96.

Cohen, E. 1971. Arab boys and tourist girls in a mixed Jewish Arab community. *International Journal of Comparative Sociology* 12 (4): 217–33.

———. 1972. Toward a sociology of international tourism. *Social Research* 39: 164–82.

———. 1973. Nomads from affluence: Notes on the phenomenon of drifter-tourism. *International Journal of Comparative Sociology* 14 (1–2): 89–103.

———. 1974. Who is a tourist? *Sociological Review* 22 (4): 527–53.

———. 1976. *Tourism in the Pacific Islands.* Exchange Bibliography #1155. Monticello, Illinois: Council of Planning Librarians.

———. 1979a. The impact of tourism on the hill tribes of Northern Thailand. *Internationales Asienforum* 19: 5–38.

———. 1979b. A phenomenology of tourist experiences. *Sociology* 13: 179–202.

———. 1979c. Rethinking the sociology of tourism. *Annals of Tourism Research* 6: 18–35.

————. 1984. The sociology of tourism: Approaches, issues and findings. *Annual Review of Sociology* 10: 373–92.

Coker, J. A. 1950. Tourism and the peasant in the Grisens. *Scottish Geographical Magazine* 66: 107–16.

Cole, J. W. 1972. Cultural adaptation in the eastern Alps. *Anthropological Quarterly* 45 (3): 158–76.

Cole, N. 1979. Museums for the people. *Tourism in England.* London: English Tourist Board.

Cole, R. G. 1972. Sixteenth-century travel books as a source of European attitudes toward non-white and non-western culture. *Proceedings of the American Philosophical Society* 116 (1): 59–67.

Colenutt, R. J. 1969. Modelling travel patterns of day visitors to the countryside. *Area* 2: 43–47.

Colley, G. 1967. International tourism today. *Lloyds Bank Review* 85: 29–41.

Colley, G., Whearcroft, S., and Baretje, T. 1965. *Study on the impact of tourism on national economies and international trade.* Geneva: IUOTO.

Colloque d'Antrans—Grenoble. 1973. Tourisme et emploi dans les Alpes. *Revue de Géographie Alpine* 61 (4): 509–70.

Commonwealth Geographical Bureau. 1982. *Workshop on the impact of tourism on small developing countries: Preliminary report.* Suva: Fiji School of Social and Economic Development, University of the South Pacific.

Cook, K. 1982. Guidelines for socially appropriate tourism development in British Columbia. *Journal of Travel Research* 21 (1): 22–28.

Cooper, C. E. 1947. Tourism. *Journal of Geography* 41: 115–20.

Coppock, J. T. 1977. Second homes in perspective. In *Second homes: Curse or blessing?* J. T. Coppock, ed. New York: Pergamon.

————. 1982. Geographical contributions to the study of leisure. *Leisure Studies* (1): 81–91.

Coppock, J. T., and Rogers, A. W. 1975. Too many Americans out in the wilderness. *Geographical Magazine* 47 (8): 508–13.

Cosgrove, I., and Jackson, R. 1972. *The geography of recreation and leisure.* London: Hutchinson.

Costa-Pau, M. 1966. *Turistes, sirenes i gent del pais.* Barcelona: Ariel.

Cowan, G. 1975. Cultural impact of tourism with particular reference to the Cook Islands. In *A new kind of sugar: Tourism in the Pacific,* B. R. Finney and K. A. Watson, eds., pp. 79–86. Honolulu: East-West Cultural Learning Institute.

Cowan, R. A. 1987. Tourism development in a Mexican coastal community. Ph.D. dissertation, Southern Methodist University, Dallas.

Cox, J. R. 1980. The management of a heathland and sand dune landscape subject to heavy tourist and recreational pressures. In *Tourism and the environment,* M. Romeril and D. Hugher-Evans, eds., pp. 57–61. London: Institute of Environmental Sciences.

Crampson, L. J., and Tan, T. K. 1973. A model of tourism flow into the Pacific. *Revue de Tourisme* 3: 98–104.

Crandall, R. 1980. Motivations for leisure. *Journal of Leisure Research* 12 (1): 45–54.

Crandon, L., and Shepard, B. 1984. *Women, enterprise and development.* Chestnut Hill, Massachusetts: The Pathfinder Fund/AID.

Cribier, F. 1983. Retirement to tourist resorts on the French coast. In *Leisure, tourism, change,* Proceedings of IGU Commission of the Geography of Tourism and Leisure. Edinburgh: Tourism and Recreation Research Unit, Edinburgh University.

Crick, M. 1985. "Tracing" the anthropological self: Quizzical reflections on field work, tourism and the Ludic. *Social Analysis* 17: 73–94.

Crittendon, A. 1975. Tourism's terrible toll. *International Wildlife* 5 (3): 4–12.

Crocombe, R. 1972. Preserving which tradition? The future of Pacific cultures. *Pacific Perspective* 1 (1): 1–5 and 1 (2): 28–49.

———. 1973. *The new South Pacific*. Rutland, Vermont: Charles E. Tuttle.

Crowley, D. J. 1977. Tourism in Ghana. *Insight and Opinion* 6 (2): 109.

Crystal, E. 1976. Ceremonies of the ancestors. *Pacific Discovery* 29 (1): 9–18.

Cullell, R. 1987. Su querida España. *El Pais Negocios* (4 July): 1–3.

Cullinan, T. n.d. *Non-tourism in Latin America*. Menlo Park: Stanford Research Institute.

Curti, G. P. 1962. The isle of Man: Geographical factors in the evolution of a political enclave. *Annals of the Association of American Geographers* 52: 327 (abstract).

D'Amico-Samuels, D. A. 1986. You can't get me out of the race: Women and economic development in Negril, Jamaica, West Indies. Ph.D. dissertation, City University of New York.

D'Amore, L. J. 1976. The significance of tourism in Canada. *Business Quarterly* 41 (3): 27–35.

———. 1983. Guidelines to planning harmony with the host community. In *Tourism in Canada: Selected issues and options*, P. E. Murphy, ed., pp. 135–59. Victoria, British Columbia: University of Victoria, Western Geographical Series 21.

Danilova, N. A. 1973. Klimat pribaltiki i prodolzhitelnost' perioda, blagopriyatnogo dlya turizma (Climate of the Baltic area and duration of the period favorable to tourism). In *Geografiya i turizm*, S. A. Kovalov, et al., eds. Voprosy Geografii, vol. 93. Moscow: Izdatel'stvo "Mysl."

Dann, G. 1976. The holiday was simply fantastic. *Tourist Review* 31 (3): 19–23.

Darlington, J. W. 1981. Railroads and the evolution of the Catskill Mountain resort area, 1870–1920: The impact of transport technology on tourism landscapes. Paper presented at the 1981 Annual Meeting of the Association of American Geographers. 19–22 April, Los Angeles.

Dasmann, R. F., Milton, J. P., and Freeman, P. H. 1973. *Ecological principles for economic development*. London: John Wiley & Sons.

Data-Ray, S. 1984. Bombay: City at bursting point. *People* 2 (2): 8–17.

Davidoff, P. G., and Davidoff, D. S. 1983. *Sales and marketing for travel and tourism*. Rapid City, South Dakota: Black Hills Publishing.

Davies, E. T. 1969. *Tourism and the Cornish farmer*. Exeter: Exeter University Press.

Davis, C. R. 1984. The myth of autochthony: Ecology, ethnohistory and symbols of ethnicity in a French Alpine community. Ph.D. dissertation, University of Pittsburgh.

Davis, D. 1968. The future of tourism in the developing countries. *Finance and Development* 5 (4).

Deardon, P. 1983. Tourism and the resource base. In *Tourism in Canada: Selected issues and options*, P. E. Murphy ed., pp. 75–93. Victoria British Columbia: University of Victoria Western Geographical Series 21.

Deasy, G. F., and Griess, P. R. 1966. Impact of a tourist facility on its hinterland. *Annals of the Association of American Geographers* 56 (2): 290–306.

DeBurlo, C. 1980. The geography of tourism in developing countries. An annotated bibliography with special reference to sociocultural impacts. Vance Bibliographers, Monticello, Illinois. Bibliography: Public Administration Series P–546, 27 pp.

———. 1984. Indigenous response and participation in tourism in a southwest Pacific Island nation, Vanuatu. Ph.D. dissertation, Sycracuse University.

———. 1987. Anthropology and the tourist business. *Practicing Anthropology* 9 (2): 11–12.

De Kadt, E. 1976. *Tourism: Passport to development?* New York: Oxford University Press.

Department of Planning and Economic Development. 1983. The economic impact of tourism in Hawaii, 1970–1980. Research Report 1983–82. Hawaii: Research and Economic Analysis Division.

Dernoi, L. A. 1983. Farm tourism in Europe. *Tourism Management* 4: 155–66.

Desplanques, H. 1973. Une nouvelle utilization de l'espace rurale en Italie: l'agritourisme. *Annales de Géographie* 82 (450): 151–63.

Devons, E. 1961. World trade in invisibles. *Lloyds Bank Review* 60 n.s.: 37–50.

DeVries, P. J. 1972. From plantation to tourism: Social and economic change in Montserrat, West Indies. Paper read to the Canadian Sociological and Anthropological Association, May 1972.

Dewailly, J. M. 1985. *Tourisme et loisirs dans le Nord et le Pas de Calais.* Lille: Societé de Geographie.

Dewar, K. 1983. Old hotel registers as a tool in analyzing resort visitation and development. *Recreation Research Review* 10 (3): 5–10.

Diamond, J. 1977. Tourism's role in economic development: The case re-examined. *Economic Development and Cultural Change* 25: 539–53.

Dickerson, T. A. 1982. *Travel laws.* New York: Law Journal Seminars Press.

Dieng, I. M., and Bugnicourt, J. 1982. *Touristes-Rois en Afrique.* Paris: Editions Karthala; Dakar: ENDA.

Dieng, I. M., and Strobel, M. 1976. *Les Touristes vus par ceux que les servent.* Dakar: ENDA.

Dietvorst, A. 1982. Theoretische aspekten van de recreaiegeografie: een verkingning. De relatie theorie-pratijk in recreatie-onderzoek. *Nijmeegse Geografische Cahiers*, No. 19. Nijmegen: Geografisch en Planologisch Institut.

———. 1984. Veranderend vrijetijdsgedrag, *PRO voorstudie.* PRO: The Hague.

Dietvorst, A., and Jansen-Verbeke, M. 1986. Een geografische visie op de inter-relatie vrije tijd. *Recreatie en Tourisme*, vrije tijd en Samenleving. 4 (3): 241–56.

Dilsaver, L. M. 1976. Tour planning as a role for geographers in international tourism. Master's thesis, Dept. of Geography, California State University, Hayward.

———. 1979. Some notes on the negative impacts of international tourism. *Association of Pacific Coast Geographers.* 1979 Yearbook 41. Corvallis: Oregon State University Press.

Donehower, E. J. 1969. The impact of dispersed tourism in French Polynesia. Master's thesis, University of Hawaii.

Doswell, R. 1978. *Case-studies in tourism.* London: Barrie & Jenkins.

Doswell, R., et al. 1979. *Further case-studies in tourism.* London: Barrie & Jenkins.

Doumbia, Y. 1974. *Consideration sur le developpement touristique au Mali.* Talence: Ecole Internationale de Bordeaux.

Dower, M. 1965. Fourth wave: The challenge of leisure. *Architect's Journal* (20 January).

———. 1973. Recreation, tourism and the farmer. *Journal of Agricultural Economics* 24: 465–77.

———. 1975. Tourism and conservation in Europe. *Ekistics* 232: 192–95.

Doxey, G. V. 1983. Leisure, tourism and Canada's aging population. In *Tourism in Canada: Selected issues and options*, P. E. Murphy, ed., pp. 57–72. Victoria British Columbia: University of Victoria, Western Geographical Series 21.

Doxey, G. V., and Associates. 1971. *The tourist industry in Barbados: A socio-economic assessment.* Kitchener, Ontario: Dusco Graphics.

Driss, A. 1969. La planification touristique et son integration, dans les pays en voie de developpement. *Rapport sur le Seminaire Tourisme et Developpement* 16 May–6 June 1969, Berlin, Germany.

Duchet, R. 1949. *Le tourisme à travers les ages.* Paris: Vigot Frères.

Duffield, B. S. 1977. Tourism: A tool for regional development. Edinburgh: Edinburgh University.

Dumazedeir, J. 1967. *Towards a society of leisure.* New York: Free Press.

Dunkle, J. R. 1950. The tourist industry of southern California: A study in economic and cultural geography. Master's thesis, Dept. of Geography, University of California, Los Angeles.

Dunning, J. H., and McQuenn, M. 1977. *The role of transnational corporations in international tourism: A preliminary survey.* United Nations: Centre on Transnational Corporations.

Dupront, A. 1967. Tourisme et pelegrinage, reflexions de psychologie collective. *Communications* 10: 97–121.

Durand, M. G. 1966. Une ênquete sur le tourisme social et familial. *Revue de Geographie Alpine* 54 (1): 73–95.

Durkheim, E. 1912. *Elementary forms of religious life.* London: Allen and Unwin.

Durrell, L. 1969. *Spirit of place: Letters and essays on travel.* New York: Dutton.

Dutt, A. K., and Noble, A. G., eds. 1982. India cultural patterns and processes. Boulder, Colorado: Westview Press.

Easdale Holiday Village. 1981. Conflict in tourism: The case of the Easdale Holiday Village Developmental Proposal. *Tourism Review* 36 (3): 10–15.

Eckbo, G. 1969. The landscape of tourism. *Landscape* 18: 29–31.

Ecumenical Council on Third World Tourism. 1986. *Third world people and tourism: Approaches to a dialogue.* Bangkok.

Edelmann, K. M. F. 1975. Major problems of tourism growth in developing countries. *Annals of Tourism Research* 2 (1): 33–43.

Edgell, M. C. R., and Farrell, B. H., eds. 1974. *Themes on Pacific lands.* Western Geographical Series, vol. 10. Victoria, British Columbia: University of Victoria.

Edgerton, R. B. 1979. *Alone together: Social order on an urban beach.* Berkeley, California: University of California Press.

Edington, W. R. 1982. Regulatory objectives and the expansion of casino gambling. *Nevada Review of Business and Economics* 6 (3): 4–13.

Edwards, A. 1976. *International tourism development: Forecasts to 1985.* London: Economic Intelligence Unit.

Egan, M. 1967. *The visitor industry in American Samoa.* Report for the Hawaii Visitors Bureau, Honolulu.

Eidsvik, H. K. 1983. Parks Canada, conservation and tourism: Review of the seventies—a preview of the eighties. In *Tourism in Canada: Selected issues and options*, P. E. Murphy, ed., pp. 241–69. Victoria, British Columbia: University of Victoria, Western Geographical Series 21.

Eiselin, E. 1945. Tourist industry of a modern highway: U.S. 16 in South Dakota. *Economic Geography* 21: 221–30.

———. 1955. A tourist-geographer visits Iquitos, Peru. *Journal of Geography* 55: 176–82.

Elkan, W. 1973. *Employment in the East African hotel and tourist industries: A survey.* Nairobi: University for Development Studies.

———. 1975. The relation between tourism and employment in Kenya and Tanzania. *Journal of Development Studies* 11: 123–30.

Ellis, D. J. 1976. *The impact of tourism on cultural manifestations: Arts and crafts.* Washington DC: UNESCO/World Bank.

England, R. 1980. Architecture for tourists. *International Social Science Journal* 32 (1): 44–55.

English, E. P. 1986. *The great escape? An examination of North-South tourism.* Ottawa: The North–South Institute.

English Tourist Board. 1977. A 5 £ billion industry. *Tourism in England* 23: 4–5.

———. 1978a. *Planning for tourism in England.* London: ETB.

———. 1978b. *Bude to Wadebridge: A new growth point for tourism.* London: ETB.

———. 1978c. *Scarborough: A new growth point for tourism.* London: ETB.

———. 1979. *English cathedrals and tourism: Problems and opportunities.* London: ETB.

———. 1981a. *Planning for tourism in England.* London: ETB.

———. 1981b. *Tourism and the inner city.* London: ETB.

English Tourist Board and Trades Union Congress. 1976. *Holidays: The social need.* London: ETB.

Enzenberger, H. 1962. *Einzelheiten.* Frankfurt am Main: Suhrkamp Verlag.

Erbes, R. 1973. *International tourism and the economy of developing countries.* Paris: OECD.

Ergun, C. 1979. The effects of personality on recreational travel behavior. Ph.D. dissertation, Northwestern University, Evanston, Illinois.

Erheil, H. S. 1985. Trends and patterns in international tourism in Jordan. Ph.D. dissertation, University of Cincinnati.

Esh, T., and Rosenblum, I. 1975. *Tourism in developing countries: Trick or treat? A report from Gambia.* Uppsala: SIAF.

Esman, M. 1984. Tourism as ethnic preservation: The Cajuns of Louisiana. *Annals of Tourism Research* 11: 451–67.

Evans, N. H. 1978. Tourism and cross-cultural communication. In *Tourism and behavior,* Studies in third world Societies No. 5, V. Smith, ed., pp. 41–53. Williamsburg Virginia: William and Mary Press.

———. 1979. The dynamics of tourism development in Puerto Vallarta. In *Tourism: Passport to development?* E. de Kadt, ed., pp. 305–20. New York: Oxford University Press.

———. 1986. The tourism of Indian California: A neglected legacy. Paper presented to the Symposium on Rural Tourism, Annual Meetings of the Society for Applied Anthropology, 26–30 March, Reno Nevada.

Fabiane, D. 1971. Information sources on international travel and tourism. *The Professional Geographer* 23 (3): 234–36.

Fabos, J. 1979. *Planning the total landscape: A guide to intelligent land use.* Boulder Colorado: Westview Press.

Fairburn, A. N. 1951. The grand tour. *Geographical Magazine* 24 (3): 118–27.

Fanon, F. 1968. *The wretched of the earth.* New York: Grove Press.

Farber, M. 1954. Some hypotheses on the psychology of travel. *The Psychoanalytic Review* 41: 267–71.

Farrell, B. H. 1974. The tourist ghettos of hawaii. In *Themes on Pacific lands,* M. C. R. Edgell and B. H. Farrel, eds., pp. 181–221. Victoria, British Columbia: University of Victoria, Western Geographical Series.

Farrell, B. H., ed. 1977. *The social and economic impact of tourism on Pacific communities.* Santa Cruz California: Center for South Pacific Studies.

——. 1982. *Hawaii: The legend that sells.* Honolulu: University of Hawaii Press.

Ferrario, F. 1977. The tourist landscape: A method of evaluating tourist potential and its application to South Africa. Ph.D. dissertation, University of California, Berkeley.

Fieguth, W. 1967. Historical geography and the concept of the authentic past as a regional resource. *Ontario Geography* 1: 55–60.

Field, J. A., Jr. 1971. Transnationalism and the new tribe. *International Organization* 25 (3): 353–72.

Finney, B. R. 1973. *Polynesian peasants and proletarians.* Cambridge, Massachusetts: Schenkman.

Finney, B. R., and Watson, K. A. 1975. *A new kind of sugar: Tourism in the Pacific.* Honolulu: East-West Culture Learning Institute.

Fletcher, T. R. G. 1982. *Tourism in Canada: Past, present, future.* Ottawa: Canadian Government Office of Tourism.

Flori, P. 1978. Une analyse generale de l'impact touristique. *Espaces: Tourisme, Loisirs, Environnement* No. 31, Paris.

Fong, P. 1980. Tourism and urbanization in Nausori. In *Pacific tourism: As islanders see it,* F. Rajotte and R. Crocombe, eds., pp. 87–88. Fiji: South Pacific Social Sciences Association and The Institute of Pacific Studies, University of the South Pacific.

Force, R. W. 1975. Tourism and change: Stimulation and recreation. Paper read at the Pacific Science Congress, August 1975, Vancouver, British Columbia.

Force, R. W., and Bishop, B., eds. 1975. *The impact of urban centers in the Pacific.* Honolulu: East-West Culture Learning Institute.

Forster, E. 1923. *Room with a view.* New York: Knopf.

Forster, J. 1964. The sociological consequences of tourism. *International Journal of Comparative Sociology* 5 (12): 217– 27.

Fox, M. 1975. The social impact of tourism—a challenge to researchers and planners. In *A new kind of sugar: Tourism in the Pacific,* B. R. Finney and K. A. Watson eds., pp. 27–47. Honolulu: East-West Culture Learning Institute.

Francillon, G. 1974/75. *Bali: Tourism, culture and environment.* Report No. SHC-75/WS/17. Bali, Indonesia and Paris: Universitas Udayana and UNESCO.

Francke, L. 1976. Sun spots. *Newsweek.* 5 January, pp. 44–50.

Fraser, R. 1973. *Tajos: The story of a village on the Costa del Sol.* New York: Pantheon.

Frater, J. M. 1983. Farm tourism in England: Planning funding, promotion and some lessons from Europe. *Tourism Management* 4: 167–79.

Frey, V. H. 1976. The impact of mass tourism on a rural community in the Swiss Alps. Ph.D. dissertation, University of Michigan, Ann Arbor.

Friedheim, E. 1976a. Turista: The medical battle begins. *The Travel Agent* 143 (8) 82–83.

——. 1976b. Turista war: A win is possible. *The Travel Agent* 143 (9): 74–75.

Friedman, J. A. 1983. From plantation to resort: Tourism and dependency in a West Indian island. Camden: Rutgers University.

Friends of Micronesia. 1973. Tourism: A special report. *Newsletter* 3: 4 Berkeley, California.

Fukunaga, L. 1975. A new sun in North Kohala. In *A new kind of sugar: Tourism in the Pacific,* B. R. Finney and K. A. Watson, eds., pp. 199–228. Honolulu: East-West Culture Learning Institute.

Fussell, P. 1979. The stationary tourist. *Harper's* (April): 31–38.
———. 1980. *Abroad.* New York: Oxford University Press.
Galt, G. 1974. *Investing in the past: A report on the profitability of heritage conservation.* Ottawa: Heritage Canada.
Gamper, J. 1982. The impact of tourism on two Alpine communities in Austria. Ph.D. dissertation, University of California, Berkeley.
———. 1985. Reconstructed ethnicity: Comments on MacCannell. *Annals of Tourism Research* 12: 250–53.
Gasparovic, F. 1984. The development of tourism and the environment on the Adriatic coast of Yugoslavia. *Industry and Environment* 14 (11/2).
Gaulis, L., and Creux, R. 1975. *Pionniers Suisses de l'hotellerie.* Paudex (Suisses): Editions de Fontainemore.
Gavira, M. 1976. *The mass tourism industry in Spain.* Washington, DC: UNESCO/IBRD.
Gearing, C. E., Swart, W. W., and Var, T., eds. 1976. *Planning for tourism development.* New York: Praeger.
Gebhardt, R. 1976. Blacktop bid for the tourist: How the road came to Baja. In Travel and Resort Section, *New York Times,* 18 January 1976.
Geddes, L. 1966. The tourist industry today. *Journal of the Royal Society of Arts* 114: 448–59.
Gee, C. Y., Choy, D. J. L., and Makens, J. C. 1984. *The travel industry.* Westport Connecticut: AVI Publishing.
Geertz, C. 1957. Ethos, world view, and the analysis of sacred symbols. *Antioch Review* 17:4.
———. 1959. Form and variation in Balinese village structure. *American Anthropologist* 61: 911–1001.
———. 1963a. *Agricultural involution.* Berkeley: University of California Press.
———. 1963b. *Peddlers and princes.* Chicago: University of Chicago Press.
———. 1966. Religion as a cultural system. In *Anthropological approaches to the study of religion,* M. Banton, ed., pp. 1–46. London: Tavistock.
———. 1972. Deep play: Notes on the Balinese cock fight. *Daedalus* 101: 1–37.
Geographical Review 25 (1936): 507–9. Some geographical aspects of tourism.
Gerakis, A. S. 1966. Economic man: The tourist. *Finance and Development* 111 (1): 41–48.
Gerassi, J. 1963. *The great fear: The reconquest of Latin America by Latin Americans.* London: Macmillan.
Geshekter, C. L. 1978. International tourism and African underdevelopment: Some reflections on Kenya. In *Tourism and economic change,* Studies in Third World Societies No. 6, V. Smith, ed., pp. 57–88. Williamsburg, Virginia: William and Mary Press.
Getz, D. 1977. The impact of tourism on host populations: A research approach. In *Tourism: A tool for regional development,* B. S. Duffield, ed. pp. 9.1–9.13. Edinburgh: University of Edinburgh.
———. 1986. Models in tourism planning: Towards integrating theory and practice. *Tourism Management* 7 (1): 21–32.
Ghali, M. A. 1976. Tourism and economic growth: An empirical study. *Economic Development and Cultural Change* 24: 526–35.
———. 1977. *Tourism and regional growth.* Leiden: Martinus Nijhoff.
———. 1978. Tourism and economic growth: An empirical study. *Economic Development and Cultural Change* No. 3.
Gillmor, D. C. 1973. Irish holidays abroad: The growth and destinations of chartered inclusive tours. *Irish Geography* 6 (5): 618–25.

Gimigliano, M. N. 1979. Experiences along the Cherry Valley turnpike: The education of a traveler. Ph.D. dissertation, University of Michigan, Ann Arbor.

Ginier, J. 1964. Quelques aspects du tourisme americain en France. *Annales de Geographie* 73 (397): 297–318.

———. 1965. *Geographie touristique de la France.* Paris: Societe d'Edition d'Enseignement Superieur.

———. 1969. *Les touristes etrangers en France pendant l'été.* Paris: Genin.

Gluckman, M. 1947. Malinwoski's "functional" analysis of social change. *Africa* 17: 106–21.

Goethe, J. W. 1962. *Italian journey (1786–88).* New York: Pantheon.

Goffman, E. 1959. *The presentation of self in everyday life.* New York: Doubleday.

———. 1967. *Interaction ritual.* New York: Doubleday.

Gold, S. M. 1980. *Recreation planning and design.* New York: McGraw-Hill.

Goldberg, A. B. 1981. Commercial folklore and voodoo in Haiti: International tourism and the sale of culture. Ph.D. dissertation, University of Indiana, Bloomington.

Goldsmith, E. 1974. Pollution by tourism. *The Ecologist* 48 (1): 47–48.

Goldstein, V. 1975. Planning for tourism on the island of Hawaii: The effects of tourism on historical sites and culture. In *A new kind of sugar: Tourism in the Pacific,* B. R. Finney and K. A. Watson, eds., pp. 161–64. Honolulu: East-West Culture Learning Institute.

Gonen, A. 1981. Tourism and coastal settlement processes in the Mediterranean region. *Ekistics* 290: 378–81.

Goodfriend, D. E. 1982. Shahjahanabad-Old Delhi: Tradition and planned change. *Ekistics* 49 (297): 472–75.

Gooding, E. G. B. 1971. Food production in Barbados, with particular reference to tourism. In *The tourist industry in Barbados.* Report for G. V. Doxey and Associates. Kitchener, Ontario: Dusco Graphics.

Goonatilate, S. 1978. *Tourism in Sri Lanka: The mapping of international inequalities and their internal structural effects.* Montreal: Centre for Developing Area Studies, Working Paper 19.

Graburn, N. H. 1980. Teaching the anthropology of tourism. *International Social Science Journal* 32 (1): 56–68.

———. 1983a. The anthropology of tourism. *Annals of Tourism Research* 10 (1): 9–33.

———. 1983b. *To pray, pay and play: The cultural structure of Japanese domestic tourism.* Aix-en-Provence: Université du droit, d'economie et des sciences, Centre des hautes études touristiques.

———. 1984. The evolution of tourist arts. *Annals of Tourism Research* 11: 393–419.

Graburn, N. H. H., ed. 1976. *Ethnic and tourist arts: Cultural expressions from the fourth world.* Berkeley and Los Angeles: University of California Press.

Graef, R., Csikszentmihalyi, M., and McManama, G. S. 1983. Measuring intrinsic motivation in everyday life. *Leisure Studies* 2: 155–68.

Gravel, J. P. 1979. Tourism and recreational planning: A methodological approach to the valuation and calibration of tourism activities. In *Urban and regional planning in a federal state: The Canadian experience,* W. T. Perks and I. M. Robinson, eds., pp. 122–34. Stroudsburg, Pennsylvania: Dowden, Hutchinson & Ross.

Graves, C. 1957. *Royal riviera.* London: Heinemann.

Graves, R., and Hodges, A. 1973. *The long weekend.* London: Penguin.

Gray, H. P. 1970. *International travel-international trade.* Lexington, Massachusetts: D. C. Heath.

———. 1974. Towards an economic analysis of tourism policy. *Social and Economic Studies* 23 (3): 386–97.

Gray, R. D. 1967. *Goethe: A critical introduction.* London: Cambridge University Press.

Green, R. H. 1979. Toward planning tourism in African countries. In *Tourism: Passport to development?* E. de Kadt, ed., pp. 79–100. New York: Oxford University Press.

Greenwood, D. J. 1970. *Agriculture, industrialization and tourism: The economics of modern Basque farming.* Ann Arbor: University of Microfilms.

———. 1972. Tourism as an agent of change: A Spanish Basque case. *Ethnology* 11: 80–91.

———. 1976. Tourism as an agent of change. *Annals of Tourism Research* 3 (3): 128–42.

———. 1982. Cultural authenticity. *Cultural Survival Quarterly* 6 (3): 27–28.

Groupe Huit. 1979. The sociocultural effects of tourism in Tunisia: A case study of Sousse. In *Tourism: Passport to development?* E. de Kadt, ed., pp. 285–304. New York: Oxford University Press.

Gubler, W. H. 1967. Las Vegas: An international recreation center. Master's thesis, University of Utah, Salt Lake City.

Gultart, C. 1982. U. K. charter flight package holidays to the Mediterranean, 1970–78. *Tourism Management* 3: 16–39.

Gunn, C. A. 1977. Industry pragmatism vs. tourism planning. *Leisure Sciences* 1: 85–94.

———. 1979. *Tourism planning.* New York: Crane, Russak & Company.

Gunter, B. G. 1979. Properties of the leisure experience. In *Leisure: A psychological approach,* H. Ibrahim and R. Crandall, eds. Los Alamitos, California: Hwong.

Gvishiani, D. M. 1980. Development problems, contemporary science and technology. *International Social Science Journal* 32 (1): 151–57.

Haahti, A. J., and Yavas, U. 1983. Tourists' perceptions of Finland and selected European countries as travel destinations. *European Journal Of Marketing* 17 (2): 34–43.

Haden-Guest, A. 1972. *Down the programmed rabbit hole.* London: Hart-Davis, Macgibbon.

Haines, G. H. 1976. The problem of the tourist. *Housing and Planning Review* 32: 7–11.

Hall, G. D. 1982. *Slocan Valley planning program: Tourism analysis.* Victoria, British Columbia: Ministry of Municipal Affairs, Province of British Columbia.

Hall, S. 1969. Hippies: An American moment. In *Student power,* J. Nagel, ed. London: Merlin.

Hallowell, A. J. 1957. The backwash of the frontier. In *The frontier in perspective.* W. D. Wyman and C. B. Kroeber, eds. Madison: University of Wisconsin Press.

Hanna, M., and Harris, T. 1979. *English cathedrals and tourism.* London: English Tourist Board.

Hannah, W. 1972. Bali in the seventies. Part I: Cultural tourism. *American Universities Field Staff Reports,* Southeast Asia Series 20: 2.

Harper, W. 1981. The experience of leisure. *Leisure Sciences* 4: 113–26.

———. 1986. Freedom in the experience of leisure. *Leisure Sciences* 8: 115–30.

Hart, E. J. 1983. *The selling of Canada: The CPR and the beginnings of Canadian tourism.* Banff: Altitude Press.

Hartzog, G. B. 1984. A national parks ministry: A model for ministry in the context of leisure tourism. Ph.D. dissertation, Theology, Claremont, California.

Hassan, R. 1975. International tourism and intercultural communication. *Southeast Asian Journal of Social Sciences* 3 (2): 25–37.

Haug, C. J. 1976. Urban development and tourism: Nice, a case study, 1750–1914. Ph.D. dissertation, University of Kansas.

Haulot, A. 1981. Social tourism: Current dimensions and future developments. *Tourism Management* 2: 207–12.

Hawkins, D., Shafer, E., and Rovelstad, J. 1980a. *Summary and recommendations.* International symposium on tourism and the next decade. Washington DC: George Washington University.

———. 1980b. *Tourism marketing and management issues.* Washington DC: George Washington University.

———. 1980c. *Tourism planning and development issues.* Washington DC: George Washington University.

Healy, K., and Zorn, E. 1983. Taquile's homespun tourism. *Natural History* 92: 80–91.

Heely, J. 1980. The definition of tourism in Great Britain: Does terminological confusion have to rule? *The Tourist Review* 35 (2): 11–14.

Heiberg, T. 1980. Centre-periphery tourism and self-reliance. *International Social Science Journal* 32 (1): 69–98.

Hekker, A. 1983. Recreatie en toerisme: Begrip en beleid. *Recreatie en Tourisme* 15 (2): 19–24.

Helleiner, F. 1981. The regionalization of waterway: A study of recreational boat traffic. *Canadian Geographer* 25 (1): 60–74.

Helms, M. 1970. Matrilocality, social solidarity and culture contact: Three case histories. *Southwest Journal of Anthropology* 26: 197–212.

Hendee, J. C. 1975. Sociology and applied leisure research. *Annals of Tourism Research* 2 (3): 155–63.

Hennessey, J. 1975. Increasing competition in tourism. *Eastern Economist* 61 (3): 12–33.

Henry, I., and Bramham, P. 1986. Leisure, the local state and social order. *Leisure Studies* 4 (5): 189–209.

Henry, W. R., Jr. 1980. Relationships between visitor use and tourist capacity for Kenya's Amboseli National Park. Ph.D. dissertation, Colorado State University, Fort Collins.

Henshall, B. D. 1981. *Background information on the New Zealand tourism industry and factors affecting industry prospects for the 1980s.* Working Paper NTA/81/1, June.

———. 1982. *Tourism and New Zealand—A strategic analysis: Final report.* Working Paper NTA/81/8, August.

Henshall, B. D., and Marsh, N. R. 1981. *A social values marketing model of tourism and New Zealand.* Working Paper NTA/81/3, September.

Hermans, D. 1981. The encounter of agriculture and tourism: A Catalan case. *Annals of Tourism Research* 8 (3): 462–79.

Herrera, F. 1972. Aspectos del desarollo economico y social de los Indies Cunas de San Blas, Panama. *American Indigena* 32 (2): 187–95.

Hetherington, A. 1987. *Rural tourism marketing.* Sacramento, California: California State Office of Tourism.

Heutz de Lemp, C. 1964. Le tourisme dans l'archipel des Hawaii. *Cahiers d'Outre Mer* 17 (65): 9–57.

Hibbert, C. 1969. *The grand tour.* London: Weidenfeld and Nicolson.

Hicks, B. 1976. Perceptual conflict as the snake in a tourist's paradise. Paper read at the Symposium on Tourism and Culture Change, American Anthropological Association, 18 November 1976, Washington DC.

Hill, A. 1971. Tourism in Africa: Africa's tourist growth confounds the experts. *African Development* 5: 75.

Hillendahl, W. H. 1971. Economic rate of return of tourism. Paper read to the third travel research seminar, Pacific Area Travel Association, 10 November 1971, Singapore.

———. 1973. Political and economic variations in the world and their effect on travel. Paper read to the fifth travel research seminar, Pacific Area Travel Association, 16 October 1973, Suva, Fiji.

Hiller, H. L. 1974a. Where is tourism traveling? *Journal of Interamerican Studies and World Affairs* 16 (4): 508–15.

———. 1974b. Caribbean tourism and the university. *Caribbean Educational Bulletin* 1 (1): 15–22.

———. 1974c. Commentary on things tourismic. *Caribbean Review* 6 (4): 8 and 50–52.

———. 1975. The organization and marketing of tourism. In *A new kind of sugar: Tourism in the Pacific*, B. R. Finney and K. A. Watson, eds., pp. 237–46. Honolulu: East-West Culture Learning Institute.

Hills, T. L., and Lundgren, J. 1974. The impact of tourism. Paper read at the International Geographical Union Regional Meeting, December 1974, Palmerston North, New Zealand.

———. 1977. *The impact of tourism in the Caribbean—a methodological study.* Montreal: Department of Geography, McGill University.

Himan, H. R. 1970. *Tourism and economic development: the British Honduras case.* Winston-Salem, North Carolina: Overseas Research Center, Wake Forest University.

Hiranyakit, S. 1984. Tourism planning and the environment. *Industry and Environment* 14: 11–12.

Hoffman, N. 1979. *A survey of tourism in West Malaysia and some socioeconomic implications.* Singapore: Institute of Southeast Asian Studies.

Hogan, T. D., and McPheters, L. R. 1981. *Tourism and travel in Arizona.* Tempe: Bureau of Business and Economic Research, Arizona State University.

Holden, P., Horlemann, J., and Pfafflim, G. F., eds. 1983. *Tourism prostitution development.* Bangkok: Ecumenical Coalition on Tourism.

Holloman, R. 1969. Developmental change in San Blas. Ph.D. dissertation, Northwestern University, Evanston, Illinois.

———. 1975. Ethnic boundary maintenance, readaption, and societal evolution in the San Blas Islands of Panama. In *Ethnicity and resource competition in plural societies*, Leo Despres, ed. Chicago: Aldine.

Hong, E. 1978. Tourism: Its environmental impacts in Malaysia. Paper presented at the Symposium on the Malaysian Environment, 16–20 September 1978, RECSAM Complex, Penang.

Horoi, S. R. 1980. Tourism and Solomon handicrafts. In *Pacific tourism: As islanders see it*, F. Rajotte and R. Crocombe, eds., pp. 111–14. Fiji: South Pacific Social Sciences Association and The Institute of Pacific Studies, University of the South Pacific.

Houseal, B. 1986. Indigenous cultures and protected areas in Central America. *Cultural Survival Quarterly* 10 (2): 10–20.

Houts, D. van. 1978. *International tourism in Africa: ALA Bibliography No. 1.* Antwerp: Institute for Developing Countries.

Hovinen, G. 1981. A tourist cycle in Lancaster County, Pennsylvania. *Canadian Geographer* 25 (3): 283–85.

Howe, J. 1982. Kindling self-determination among the Kuna. *Cultural Survival Quarterly* 6 (3): 15–17.

————. 1986. *The Kuna gathering: Contemporary village politics in Panama*. Latin American Monographs No. 67. Institute of Latin American Studies. Austin: University of Texas Press.

Howell, C. D. B. 1978. Tourism in Tortola, British Virgin Islands: Perceptions toward land carrying capacity. Ph.D. dissertation, University of Florida, Gainesville.

Huber, R., Jr. 1986. Kuna Indians move to preserve rainforest. *Naturalist* 6 (7): 12–17.

Hudman, L. E. 1980. *Tourism: A shrinking world*. Columbus, Ohio: Grid.

Hudson, E. 1973. *Vertical integration in the travel and leisure industry*. Paris: Institute de Transport Aerien.

Hughes, C. C. 1960. *An Eskimo village in the modern world*. Ithaca: Cornell University Press.

Huizinga, J. 1950. *Homo Ludens: A study of the play element in culture*. Boston: Beacon.

Hunt, J. D. 1986. Tourism comes of age in the 1980s. *Parks and Recreation* 21 (10): 31–36, 66–67.

Husbands, W. 1981. Centres, peripheries, tourism and sociospatial development. *Ontario Geography* 17: 49.

Hutson, J. 1971. A politician in Valloire. In *Gifts and poison*, F. G. Bailey, ed., 68–96. New York: Shocken Books.

IBO. 1979. *Arab travel in the 80's*. International Business Opportunities. Report on statements made at the first Arab Conference on Tourism, February 1979, London.

Idacipta, P. T. 1976. Master plan for South Sulawesi tourist development. *Rencana Induk Pengembangan Pariwisata Sulawesi Selastan*, vol. 2 Djakarta: Government Printing Office.

Ietswaart, H. F. P. 1980. A successful development project in Ecuador: The Institute of Economic Research. *International Social Science Journal* 32 (1): 175–78.

Inkeles, A. 1969. Making men modern: On the causes and consequences of individual change in six developing countries. *American Journal of Sociology* 78: 208–25.

Inskeep, E. L. 1975. Physical planning for tourist development. In *A new kind of sugar: Tourism in the Pacific*, B. R. Finney and K. A. Watson, eds., pp. 247–52. Honolulu: East-West Culture Learning Institute.

International Journal of Environmental Studies. 1985. Tourism and the environment. Special issue, 25: 215–64.

ISIS: International Bulletin. International Feminist Network. 1979 Tourism and Prostitution. Rome, No. 13, 40 pp.

Iso-Ahola, S. E. 1979a. Basic dimensions of definitions of leisure. *Journal of Leisure Research* 11: 28–39.

————. 1979b. Some social psychological determinants of perceptions of leisure: Preliminary evidence. *Leisure Sciences* 2: 305–413.

————. 1980. *The social psychology of leisure and recreation*. Dubuque, Iowa: William C. Brown.

Jackson, E. L., and Schinkel, D. R. 1981. Recreational activity preferences of resident and tourist campers in the Yellowknife region. *Canadian Geographer* 25: 350–64.

Jackson, E. L., and Wong, R. A. G. 1982. Perceived conflict between urban cross-country skiers and snowmobilers in Alberta. *Journal of Leisure Research* 14 (1): 47–62.

Jackson, J. B. 1963. Rise and fall of tourism in the southwest. *Annals of the Association of American Geographers* 53: 599 (abstract).

Jackson, R. T. 1969. Uganda's place in world tourism. *Seminar Papers*. Nairobi: Makerere University College, Dept. of Geography.

———. 1973. Problems of tourist industry development on the Kenyan coast. *Geography* 58 (1): 62–65.

Jafari, J. 1973. Role of tourism on socio-economic transformation of developing countries. Master's thesis, Cornell University.

———. 1974a. The components and nature of tourism: The tourist market basket of goods and services. *Annals of Tourism Research* 1 (3): 73–90.

———. 1974b. Socio-economic costs of tourism to developing countries. *Annals of Tourism Research* 1 (7): 227–63.

———. 1975. Creation of the inter-departmental World Tourism Organization. *Annals of Tourism Research* 2 (5): 237–46.

———. 1978. Study of tourism within the context of the social sciences. In *The 1978 Proceedings of the Association Internationale d'Exports Scientifiques du Tourisme* 19: 339–45.

———. 1979. The tourism market basket of goods and services: The components and nature of tourism. *Tourism Recreation Research* 4 (2): 11–18.

———. 1980. Expatriates and tourism development: Application of some anthropological perspectives. *Revue de l'AIEST* 21: 76–107.

———. 1983. Understanding the structure of tourism. In *Tourism and culture: A comparative perspective*, E. C. Nebel III, ed., pp. 65–84. New Orleans: University of New Orleans Press.

———. 1984. Unbounded ethnicity—the tourist network and its satellites. *Revue de tourisme* No. 3

———. 1985. The tourist system: A theoretical approach to the study of tourism. Ph.D. dissertation, University of Minnesota, Minneapolis.

Jakle, J. 1985. *The tourist: Travel in twentieth-century North America*. Lincoln/London: University of Nebraska Press.

Jansen-Verbeke, M. 1985a. The inner city as a leisure product. *World Leisure and Recreation* 20 (2): 6–17.

———. 1985b. Inner city leisure resources. *Leisure Studies* 4: 142–57.

———. 1986. Recreational behavior and attitude of inner city dwellers: Some issues of a case-study. *Tijdschrift van de Belische Vereniging voor Aardrijkskundige Studies* 2: 239–59.

Jenkins, C. L. 1980. Education in tourism policy-makers in developing countries. *International Journal of Tourism Management* 1 (4): 238–42.

Jeune Afrique. 1979. Quel tourisme pour l'Afrique? No. 956: 31–66.

Johnson, R. B. 1978. The role of tourism in Tongan culture. In *Tourism and behavior*, Studies in Third World Societies No. 5, V. Smith, ed., pp. 55–68. Williamsburg, Virginia: William and Mary Press.

Johnston, B. R. 1987. *The political ecology of development: Changing resource relations and the impacts of tourism in St. Thomas, United States Virgin Islands*. Amherst: University of Massachusetts Press.

Jones, P. M., Dix, M. C., Clarke, M. I., and Heggie, I. G. 1983. *Understanding travel behavior*. Brookfield, Vermont: Gower Publishing.

Jones, S. B. 1933. Mining and tourist towns in the Canadian Rockies. *Economic Geography* 19: 368–78.

Jopling, C. 1974. Women's work: A Mexican case study of low status as a tactical advantage. *Ethnology* 13 (2): 187–95.

Jordan, J. W. 1980. The summer people and the natives: Some effects of tourism in a Vermont vacation village. *Annals of Tourism Research* 7 (1): 34–55.

Jud, G. D. 1975. Tourism and crime in Mexico. *Social Science Quarterly* 56: 324–30.

Jules-Rosette, B. 1984. *The messages of touristic art: An African semiotic system in comparative perspective.* New York: Plenum Press.

Jursa, P. E., and Winkates, J. F. 1974. Tourism in Ethiopia: A case study. *Issue* 4(1): 45–49.

Kaiser, C., and Hebler, L. E. 1978. *Tourism: Planning and development.* Boston, Massachusetts: CBI Publishing.

Kamaruzaman, Y. 1981. *Recreation demand: A case study of Desaru Resort.* Serdang: University of Malaysia.

Kaminske, V. 1981. Zur systematische stellung einer geographie des freizeitverhaltens. *Geographische Zeitschrift* H3: 217–33.

Kanywanyi, J. L. 1973. Tourism benefits the capitalists. In *Tourism and socialist development,* I. G. Shivji, ed., pp. 52–65. Tanzanian Studies No. 3. Dar es Salaam: Tanzania Publishing House.

Kaplan, M. 1960. Leisure in America: A social inquiry. New York: John Wiley.

Kaspar, C. 1977. Social needs and their realization in tourism. *Proceedings of AIEST* 18: 19–20. Berne, Switzerland.

Kaviolis, V. 1970. Post-modern man: Psychological responses to social trends. *Social Problems* 17 (4): 435–48.

Kayser, B. 1962. La geographie appliquée au tourisme. *Colloque national de geographie appliquée,* Strasbourg 1961. Paris: Edition du Centre National de la Recherche Scientifique.

Keller, A. 1970. He said: "Tourists never take the mail boat"—that clinched it. *New York Times,* section 10, 24 May 1970.

Keller, C. P. 1985. Centre-periphery tourism development and control. In *Leisure tourism and social change,* J. Long and R. Hecock, eds., pp. 77–84. Edinburgh: Centre for Leisure Research.

Kelley, J. 1977. Tourism, land alienation and foreign control in Hawaii. In *The Melanesian environment,* J. H. Winslow, ed. Canberra: Australian National University Press.

Kelly, E. M., ed. 1986. *Perspectives: Leisure and tourism.* Wellesley, Massachusetts: Institute of Certified Travel Agents.

Kelly, J. 1981. Leisure interaction and the social dialectic. *Social Forces* 60: 304–22.

———. 1983. *Leisure identities and interactions.* London: Allen and Unwin.

Kemper, R. V. 1978. Tourism and regional development in Taos, New Mexico. In *Tourism and economic change,* Studies in Third World Societies No. 6, V. Smith, ed., pp. 89–103. Williamsburg, Virginia: William and Mary Press.

Kendall, K. W., and Var, T. 1984. *The perceived impacts of tourism: The state-of-the-art.* Tourism Research Publications. Social Science Research Institute and School of Travel Industry Management. Honolulu: University of Hawaii.

Kent, J. 1972. *Solomon Islands.* Newton Abbott, England: David and Charles.

Kent, N. 1971. Escape mecca of the world. *Hawaii Pono Journal* 1 (4): 32–58.

———. 1975. A new kind of sugar. In *A new kind of sugar: Tourism in the Pacific,* B. R. Finney and K. A. Watson, eds., pp. 169–98. Honolulu: East-West Culture Learning Institute.

Keogh, B. M. 1969. The role of travel in the recreational day-trip. Master's thesis, University of Western Ontario, London, Ontario.

Kerins, E. 1983. Panama's primitive San Blas Islands: Indians manage to hold on to the Pre-Colombian lifestyle amid cruise ships. *The Hartford Courant,* 13 November, p. F1.

Khury, F. 1968. The etiquette of bargaining in the Middle East. *American Anthropologist* 70: 698–706.

Kii, L. 1980. Laulasi Island welcomes tourists. In *Pacific tourism: As islanders see it,* F. Rajotte and R. Crocombe, eds., pp. 115–20. Fiji: South Pacific Social Sciences Association and The Institute of Pacific Studies, University of the South Pacific.

Kim, J.-M. 1986. An analysis of Korean residents' attitudes toward the impact of tourism. Ed.D. dissertation, George Washington University.

Kim, S. N. 1986. Farewell dancing of spirits in a Korean healing ritual. Paper presented at the meetings of the American Anthropological Association, 3–7 December 1986, Philadelphia, Pennsylvania.

Kirch, D. C. 1984. Tourism as conflict in Polynesia: Status degradation among Tongan handicraft sellers. Ph.D. dissertation, University of Hawaii, Honolulu.

Kirkby, A. 1985. Leisure as commodity: The role of the state in leisure provision. *Progress in Human Geography* 1: 64–84.

Kloke, C. 1975. South Pacific economies and tourism. In *A new kind of sugar: Tourism in the Pacific,* B. R. Finney and K. A. Watson, eds., pp. 3–26. Honolulu: East-West Culture Learning Institute.

Knebel, H. J. 1960. *Soziologische strukturwanderlungen im modernen tourismus.* Stuttgart: F. Enke Verlag.

Knox, J. M. 1978. *Classification of Hawaii residents' attitudes toward tourists and tourism.* Tourism Research Project: Occasional Paper no. 1, Mimeographed. Honolulu: University of Hawaii.

———. 1979. *Research priorities in Hawaii and the Pacific: An overview.* Tourism Research Project: Occasional Paper no. 3. Mimeographed. Honolulu: University of Hawaii.

Koea, A. 1977. Polynesian migration to New Zealand. In *A new kind of sugar: Tourism in the Pacific,* B. R. Finney and K. A. Watson, eds., pp. 68–69. Honolulu: East-West Culture Learning Institute.

Koning, H. 1974. Travel is destroying a major reason for travelling. *New York Times,* 17 November 1974.

Korzay, M., and Var, T. 1985. *Resident perception of tourist and tourism: Istanbul, Turkey.* Burnaby, British Columbia: Simon Fraser University, Faculty of Business Administration.

Kosters, M. I. 1981. *Focus on tourism: An introduction in the field.* Den Haag, Holland: VUGA Publishers.

Koth, B. A., Field, D. R., and Clarke, R. N. 1984. Cruise ship travelers to Alaska. In *On interpretation: Sociology for interpreters of natural and cultural history,* G. E. Machlis and D. R. Field, eds., pp. 95–107. Corvallis: Oregon State University Press.

Kousis, M. 1984. Tourism as an agent of social change in a rural Cretan community. Ph.D. dissertation, University of Michigan, Ann Arbor.

Krause, W., and Jud, G. D. 1973. *International tourism and Latin American development.* Studies in Latin American Business No. 15. Austin: University of Texas, Graduate School of Business.

Kreutzwiser, R. D. 1973. A methodology for estimating tourist spending in Ontario counties. Unpublished Master's thesis, University of Waterloo, Ontario.

———. 1978. Socio-economic impact of Walt Disney World, Central Florida. Unpublished paper, Dept. of Geography, University of Guelph, Ontario.

Krippendorf, J. 1987. *The holiday-makers: Understanding the impact of leisure and travel.* Vera Andrassy, trans. London: Heinemann.

Krizan, B. 1971. The economic impact of tourism on the American Virgin Islands. Master's thesis, Southern Illinois University.

La temporada turistica 1985 a Catalunya. 1986. Barcelona: Generalitat de Catalungy, Departament de Comerc, Consum i Turisme.

Labor, G. 1969. Determinants of international travel between Canada and the U.S. *Geographical Analysis* 1 (4): 329–36.

Lagelee, G. 1976. Le developpement du tourisme au Senegal. Thesis, Université de Paris.

Laine, P. 1980. *Liberons le tourisme.* Paris: Fayolle.

Lamborn, B. N. A. 1974. Energy economics of tourist travel. *Florida Environmental and Urban Issues* 1: 4–5.

Lancaster, J. R., and Nichols, L. L. 1971. *A selected bibliography of geographical references and related research in outdoor recreation and tourism, 1930–71.* Exchange Bibliography #190. Monticello, Illinois: Council of Planning Librarians.

Lane, L. W., Jr. 1975. Tourism: A sound economic partner and a good environmental influence. Paper read to the New Zealand National Travel Association Seminar, 9 April 1975, Wellington, New Zealand.

Lanfant, M. F., 1980. Introduction: Tourism in the process of internationalization. *International Social Science Journal* 32 (1): 14–43.

Lanquar, R. 1977. *Le tourisme international.* Paris: Presses Universitaires de France.

Lansing, J. 1968. The effects of migration and personal effectiveness on long distance travel. *Transportation Research* 2: 329–38.

Lansing, J. S. 1973. *Evil in the morning of the world: Phenomenological approaches to a Balinese community.* Ann Arbor: University of Michigan Center for South and Southeast Asian Languages.

Larrabee, E., and Meyersohn, R., eds. 1952. *Mass leisure.* Glencoe: Free Press.

Latouche, R. 1963. Un colloque scientifique sur le tourisme á Nice. *Revue de Geographie Alpine* 51 (2): 369–70.

Lavery, P. Resorts and recreation. In *Recreational geography,* P. Lavery , ed., pp. 167–96. New York: Wiley and Sons.

Lawler-Brook, D. J. 1986. An inquiry into tourism and education in San Cristobal de las Casas (Mexico). Boulder: University of Colorado.

Lawrence, H. W. 1983. Southern spas: Source of the American resort tradition. *Landscape* 27 (2): 1–12.

Lawson, F., and Baud-Bovy, M. 1977. *Tourism and recreational development.* London: Architectural Press.

Lea, D. A. M. 1980. Tourism in Papua New Guinea: The last resort. In *Of Time and place: Essays in honour of O. H. K. Spate,* J. N. Jennings and G. J. R. Linge, eds. Canberra: Australian Natural University Press.

Leach, E. 1961. *Rethinking anthropology.* London: Athlone Press, University of London.

Lederhans, M. A. 1979. An investigation of intra-family vacation-travel purchasing decisions among husbands and wives over 65 years of age. Ph.D. dissertation, Virginia Polytechnic Institute and State University, Blacksburg.

Lee, J. 1978. *Tourism and the development of the mid-Pacific Islands.* Hawaii: University of Hawaii.

Lee, R. L. 1978. Who owns boardwalk: The structure of control in the tourist industry of Yucatan. In *Tourism and economic change,* Studies in Third World Societies No. 6, V. Smith, ed., pp. 19–35. Williamsburg, Virginia: William and Mary Press.

Lefeuvre, A. 1980. *Religious tourism and pilgrimage: On the move.* 10 (30): 80–81. Vatican City: Pontifical Commission on Migration and Tourism.

Le Fevre, T. 1975a. Who gets what from tourists? In *A new kind of sugar: Tourism in the Pacific,* B. R. Finney and K. A. Watson, eds., pp. 101–10. Honolulu: East-West Culture Learning Institute.

———. 1975b. Making do with leftovers from Pacific tourism. In *The Pacific way,* S. Tupouniua, R. Crocombe, and C. Slatter, eds., pp. 215–21. Suva, Fiji.

———. 1975c. Rarotonga airport: A preliminary view of the possible balance sheet. In *A new kind of sugar: Tourism in the Pacific,* B. R. Finney and K. A. Watson, eds., pp. 87–100. Honolulu: East-West Culture Learning Institute.

Lehmann, A. C. 1980. Tourists, black markets and regional development in West Africa. *Annals of Tourism Research* 7: 102–19.

Leiper, N. 1980. An inter-disciplinary study of Australian tourism. Master's thesis, University of New South Wales, Sydney, Australia.

Lengyel, P., ed. 1980. The anatomy of tourism. *International Social Science Journal* 32 (1): 1–13.

Lent, J. A. 1978. Advertising and national development: The case of Malaysia. In *Tourism and behavior,* Studies in Third World Societies No. 5, V. Smith, ed., pp. 69–81. Williamsburg, Virginia: William and Mary Press.

Lerner, S. C. 1977. Social impact assessment: Some hard questions and basic techniques. Unpublished workshop paper, University of Waterloo, Ontario.

Lester, D., ed. 1979. *Gambling today.* Springfield, Illinois: Charles C. Thomas.

Lett, J. 1982. The British Virgin Islands tourism industry: Problems and prospects for the 1980's. Paper presented at the seventh annual meeting of the Caribbean Studies Association, 26–30 May 1982, Kingston, Jamaica.

———. 1983. Ludic and liminoid aspects of charter yacht tourism in the Caribbean. *Annals of Tourism Research* 10 (1): 35–56.

———. 1985. Playground in the sun. *Chartering* 2 (4): 22–23.

———. 1987. *The human enterprise: A critical introduction to anthropological theory.* Boulder, Colorado: Westview Press.

Leugger, J. 1958. Weitere soziologische aspekte des fremdenverkehrs. *Revue de Tourisme* 13 (1): 9–16.

Lévi-Strauss, C. 1970. *Tristes tropiques.* J. Russell, trans. New York: Atheneum.

Levitt, K., and Gulati, I. 1970. Income effect of tourist spending: Mystification multiplied; a critical comment on the Zinder Report. *Social and Economic Studies* 19 (3): 325–43.

Lewis, G. 1972. *The Virgin Islands.* Evanston: Northwestern University Press.

Lewsey, C. D. 1978. Assessing the environmental effects of tourism development on the carrying capacity of small island systems: "The case of Barbados." Ph.D. dissertation. Cornell University, Ithaca, New York.

Leys, C. 1975. *Underdevelopment in Kenya: The political economy of neocolonialism, 1964–1971.* Berkeley: University of California Press.

Liegeois, F., and Magis, J. 1967a. Le tourism: Fait sociologique. *Ethnie Française* (March–April): 13–18.

———. 1967b. Tourisme: Nouvelle demension social (le). *Documents CEPESS* 6 (5): 3–125.

Light, I. 1974. From Vice District to tourist attraction: The moral career of American Chinatowns. *Pacific History Review* 43 (8): 367–94.

Lin, V. L., and Loeb, P. D. 1977. Tourism and crime in Mexico: Some comments. *Social Science Quarterly* 58: 164–67.

Linnekin, J. 1982. Selling Hawaiian culture. *Cultural Survival Quarterly* 6 (3): 29.

Liu, J. 1979. The economic impact of tourism on an island economy: A case study of Victoria BC. Ph.D. dissertation, Simon Fraser University, Burnaby, British Columbia.

———. 1980a. Differential multipliers for the accommodation sector. Working paper no. 80–07. Honolulu: University of Hawaii, School of Travel Industry Management.

———. 1980b. Tourist income multipliers at the establishment level. Working paper no. 80–08. Honolulu: University of Hawaii, School of Travel Industry Management.

———. 1980c. The Japanese tourist in Hawaii. Paper presented at the Fifth Annual Pacific Islands Studies Conference, University of Hawaii.

Lloyd, S. 1975. *Sociology of tourism and travel motivations.* Turin: UIOOT, CIEST.

Lockefeer, H. 1974. Derde wereld ziet nadelen van toerisme. *Volkskrant* 29.

Loeb, L. D. 1970. *The Jews of southwest Iran: A study of culture persistence.* Ann Arbor: University Microfilms.

Loki, M. 1975. How Fijians can benefit from tourism and how to milk the tourists. In *The Pacific way,* S. Tupouniua, R. Crocombe, C. Slatter, eds., pp. 222–26.

Lonati, C. 1985. Impact of tourism on the enlightenment of the Mediterranean basin: Communication by the Secretary-General of the WTO. *World Travel* 184: 25–26.

London, M., Crandall, R., and Fitzgibbons, N. 1977. The psychological structure of leisure: Activities, needs, people. *Journal of Leisure Research* 9: 252–63.

Loukissas, P. J. 1977. *The impact of tourism on regional development: A comparative analysis of the Greek Islands.* Ithaca: Cornell University Press.

———. 1978. Tourism and environment in conflict: The case of the Greek island of Myconos. In *Tourism and economic change,* Studies in Third World Societies No. 6, V. Smith, ed., pp. 105–32. Williamsburg, Virginia: William and Mary Press.

Lowenthal, D. 1962. Tourists and thermalists. *Geographical Review* 52 (1): 124–27.

———. 1962–63. Not every landscape pleases. *Landscape* 13 (2): 19–23.

Lua, H. 1980. A heavy hearted Hawaiian. In *Pacific tourism: As Islanders see it,* F. Rajotte and R. Crocombe, eds., pp. 135–38. Fiji: South Pacific Social Sciences Association and The Institute of Pacific Studies, University of the South Pacific.

Lundberg, D. E. 1971. Why tourists travel. *Cornell Hotel and Restaurant Administration Quarterly* 11 (4): 75–81. Ithaca: Cornell University, School of Hotel Administration.

———. 1972. A new look in social tourism. *The Cornell Hotel and Restaurant Administration Quarterly* 13 (3): 62–71.

———. 1980. *The tourist business.* Fourth ed. Boston: CBI Publishing.

Lundgren, J. 1982. *The development of tourist accommodation in the Montreal Laurentians recreational land use: Perspectives on its evolution in Canada.* Carleton Library Series No. 126. G. Wall and J. Marsh, eds., pp. 175–89. Ottawa: Carleton University.

Lundgren, L. O. J. 1973. The development of the tourist travel systems. *Revue de Tourisme* 28 (1): 2–14.

Macaulay, R. 1949. *Fabled shore.* London: Hamish Hamilton.

MacCannell, D. 1973. Staged authenticity: Arrangements of social space in tourist settings. *American Journal of Sociology* 79 (3): 589–603.

———. 1976. *The tourist: A new theory of the leisure class.* New York: Schocken Books.

————. 1984. Reconstructed ethnicity: Tourism and cultural identity in third world communities. *Annals of Tourism Research* 11: 375–91.

Machlis, G. E., and Field, D. R. 1984. *On interpretation: Sociology for interpreters of natural and cultural history.* Corvallis: Oregon State University Press.

Machlis, G. E., Field, D. R., and Van Every, M. 1984. A sociological look at the Japanese tourist. In *On interpretation: Sociology for interpreters of natural and cultural history,* G. E. Machlis and D. R. Field, eds., pp. 77–93. Corvallis: Oregon State University Press.

MacKenzie, M. 1977. The deviant art of tourism: Airport art. In *Social and economic impact of tourism of Pacific communities,* B. H. Farrell, ed., pp. 83–85. Santa Cruz: Center for South Pacific Studies, University of California.

Madden, M. S., and Cohn, S. L. 1966. The legal status and problems of the American abroad. *Annals of the American Academy of Political and Social Science* 368: 119–31.

Magubane, B. 1973. The Xhosa in town, revisited urban anthropology: A failure of method and theory. *American Anthropologist* 75: 1701–15.

Mann, T. 1930. *Death in Venice.* New York: Knopf.

Mannell, R. C. 1979. A conceptual and experimental basis for research in the psychology of leisure. *Society and Leisure* 2: 179–96.

Manning, F. 1973. *Black clubs in Bermuda: Ethnography of a play world.* Ithaca: Cornell University Press.

————. 1974. Cup match and carnival: Secular rites of revitalization in decolonizing tourist-oriented societies. Paper presented to Burg Wartenstein Symposium 64. New York: Wenner-Gren Foundation for Anthropological Research.

————. 1979. Tourism and Bermuda's black clubs: A case of cultural revitalization. In *Tourism: Passport to development?* E. de Kadt, ed., pp. 157–76. New York: Oxford University Press.

————. 1982. The Caribbean experience. *Cultural Survival Quarterly* 6 (3): 13–14.

Marcano, E., Aquilar, M., and Castro, N. 1982. Ingreso de pasajeros hacia la Isla de Margarita via maritima. Universidad do Oriente, Nuclew do Nueva Esparta, Escuela de Hoteleria y Turismo. Unpublished manuscript.

March, K., and Taque, R. 1986. *Women's informal associations in developing countries.* Boulder, Colorado: Westview Press.

Mark, S. M. 1975. Tourism and quality growth in the Pacific area. In *A new kind of sugar: Tourism in the Pacific,* B. R. Finney and K. A. Watson, eds., pp. 147–52. Honolulu: East-West Culture Learning Institute.

Marnham, P. 1971. *The road to Katmandu.* London: Macmillan.

Marsh, J. S. 1975a. Hawaiian tourism: Costs, benefits, alternatives. *Alternatives* 4 (3): 34–39.

————. 1975b. Tourism and development: The East African case. *Alternatives* 5 (1): 15–22.

Martinez, T. M. 1983. *The gambling scene.* Springfield, Illinois: Charles C. Thomas.

Mathieson, A., and Wall, G. 1982. *Tourism: Economic, physical, and social impacts.* London: Longman Group.

Mathieu, S. 1982. Authenticity of Haitian folk dances as opposed to voodoo ceremonial dances. Unpublished Honors thesis, Dept. of Anthropology, Cornell University.

Matley, I. M. 1976. *The geography of international tourism. Association of American Geographers Resource Paper* 76–1.

Matthews, H. G. 1975. International tourism and political science. *Annals of Tourism Research* 2 (4): 195–204.

————. 1978. *International tourism: A political and social analysis.* Cambridge, Massachusetts: Schenkman.

Matznetter, J., ed. 1974a. *Studies in the geography of tourism.* Frankfurt am Main: J. W. Goethe-Universitat.

————. 1974b. Reports of working groups. Geography of tourism and recreation. *I.G.U. Bulletin* 25 (1): 7.

————. 1976. Die differenzin in der auffassung einer geographie des tourimus und der naherholong. *Deutscher Geographentage,* Innsbruck, 1975, pp. 661–72. Tagungsbericht und Wissenschaftliche Handlungen. Wiesbaden: Franz Steiner Verlag.

Maurer, J. L. Tourism and development in a socio-cultural perspective: Indonesia as a case-study. *Itineraires* No. 24. Geneva: Institut Universitaire d'Etudes du developpement.

Maxtone-Graham, J. 1985. *Liners to the sun.* New York: Macmillan.

May, R. J. 1975. Tourism and the artifact industry in Papua New Guinea. In *A new kind of sugar: Tourism in the Pacific,* B. R. Finney and K. A. Watson, eds., pp. 125–34. Honolulu: East-West Culture Learning Institute.

Mayer, P. J. 1978. No land too remote: Women travelers in the Georgian age— 1750–1830. Ph.D. dissertation. University of Massachusetts, Amherst.

Mayo, E. J., and Jarvis, L. P. 1981. *The psychology of leisure travel.* Boston: CBI Publishing.

McClaskie, S. L. Napier, T. L., and Christensen, J. E. 1986. Factors influencing outdoor recreation participation: A state study. *Journal of Leisure Research* 18: 190–205.

McDonald, J. R. 1980. The tourist business. *Focus* 31 (2): 1–9.

McDowell, D. E. 1979. *Tourism in Alaska native villages.* Juneau, Alaska: Bureau of Indian Affairs.

McEachern, J., and Towle, W. L. n.d. *Ecological guidelines for island development.* Morges, Switzerland: International Union for Conservation of Nature and National Resources.

McGeary, J. 1986. Gone but not forgotten: In Panama and ex-Peace Corps volunteer finds a surprising legacy. *Time* 127 (April 14): 28, 31.

McGrevy, N. L. 1975. The polynesian cultural center: A model for cultural conservation. Paper read at the Symposium on Tourism and Culture Change, American Anthropological Association, 6 December 1975, San Francisco, California.

McGuire, F. A. 1984. A factor analytic study of leisure constraints in advanced adulthood. *Leisure Sciences* 6: 313–26.

McGuire, J. W. 1963. *The future growth of Hawaiian tourism and its impact on the state and on the neighbor islands.* Honolulu: University of Hawaii, Economic Research Center.

McIntosh, R. W. 1972. *Tourism principles, practices and philosophies.* Columbus: Grid.

McKay, J. 1986. Leisure and social equality in Australia. *Australian and New Zealand Journal of Sociology* 22 (3): 343–67.

McKean, P. F. 1972. Tourist-native interaction in paradise: Locating some partial equivalence structures in Bali. Paper read at the 71st Annual meeting, American Anthropological Association. In *Masyarakat Indonesia* (Indonesian Society), Jakarta.

————. 1976a. Tourism, culture change and culture conservation. In *World anthropology: Ethnic identity in modern Southeast Asia,* D. Banks, ed. The Hague: Mouton.

————. 1976b. An anthropological analysis of the culture-brokers of Bali: Guides, tourists, and Balinese. Background paper for the UNESCO/World Bank seminar on the socio-cultural impacts of tourism, 7–11 December 1976, Washington DC.

———. 1977. From purity to pollution? A symbolic form in transition: The Balinese *ketjak*. In *The imagination of reality: Symbol systems in Southeast Asia*, A. Becker and A. Yengoyan, eds. Tucson: University of Arizona Press.

———. 1982. Tourists and Balinese. *Cultural Survival Quarterly* 6 (3): 32–33.

McLaughlin, W. J., and Harris, C. C. 1985. The first Governor's Conference on tourism looking to the future of undiscovered America. Moscow, Idaho: The University of Idaho Press.

McLeod, E. M. 1974. Bibliography of studies and documents on Caribbean tourism. Appendix VII, vol. 6: *Tourism, Caribbean regional study*. Washington DC: International Bank for Reconstruction and Development.

McTaggart, W. D. 1980. Tourism and tradition in Bali. *World Development* 8 (5–6): 457–66.

Mead, W. E. 1914. *The grand tour in the eighteenth century*. New York: Benjamin Blom.

Medlik, S. 1966. *Higher education and research in tourism in western Europe*. London: University of Surrey.

Medlik, S., and Middleton, V. T. C. 1973. The tourist product and its marketing implications. *International Tourism Quarterly* 3: 28–35.

Meeker, J. W. 1984. Red, white and black in National Parks. In *On interpretation: Sociology for interpreters of natural and cultural history*, G. E. Machlis and D. R. Field, eds., pp. 127–38. Corvallis: Oregon State University Press.

Meinke, H. 1968. *Turismus and wirtschaftlichen entwicklung*. Göttingen: Van den Hoek and Ruprecht.

Meleisea, M., and Meleisea, P. 1980. "The best kept secret": Tourism in Western Samoa. In *Pacific tourism: As islanders see it*, F. Rajotte and R. Crocombe, eds., pp. 35–46. Fiji: South Pacific Social Sciences Association and The Institute of Pacific Studies, University of the South Pacific.

Mercer, D. C. 1970a. The geography of leisure: A contemporary growth point. *Geography* 55: 261–73.

———. 1970b. Discretionary travel behavior and the urban mental map. *Australian Geographical Studies* 9 (2): 133–43.

———. 1970c. The role of perception in the recreation experience: A review and discussion. *Journal of Leisure Research* 3: 261–76.

Mercer, K. C. R. 1976a. Why do people take holidays. *New Society* 37 (724): 438–40.

———. 1976b. The application of motivational research to tourism. *Tourist Review* 31 (4): 10–11.

———. 1977. Needs, motives, recreation and tourism. *Rural Recreation and Tourism Abstracts* 2: 1–5.

Merlini, G. 1968. Problemi geografici del turismo in Italia. *Bollettino della Società Geografica Italiana*, series IX, 9 (1–3): 1–30.

Metelka, C. J. 1977. Tourism and development: With friends like these, who needs enemies? Paper presented at the Fifth Pacific Regional Science Conference, August 1977, Vancouver, British Columbia.

———. 1986. *Dictionary of tourism*. Second edition. Wheaton, Illinois: Merton House Publishing.

Micssec, J. M. 1972. La croissance du tourisme en Tunisie. *L'Information Geographique* 36 (4): 169–78.

Middleton, V. T. C. 1974. *Tourism policy in Britain: A case for a radical reappraisal*. London: The Economist Intelligence Unit.

Mieczkowski, Z. T. 1981. Some notes on the geography of tourism: A comment. *Canadian Geographer* 25: 186–91.

Mihovilovic, M. A. 1980. Leisure and tourism in Europe. *International Social Science Journal* 32 (1): 99–113.

Mill, R. C., and Morrison, A. M. 1985. *The tourism system.* Englewood Cliffs, New Jersey: Prentice-Hall.

Miller, J. J. B. 1974. The tourist as the counter-agent in cultural diffusion. In *Cultural discord in the modern world,* L. J. Evenden and F. F. Cunningham, eds., pp. 75–81. British Columbia Geography Series No. 20. Vancouver British Columbia: Simon Fraser University.

Milner, G. B. 1972. Samoan lesson. *New Society* 27 (July 26).

Mings, R. C. 1966. *The role of the commonwealth government in the growth and development of the Puerto Rico tourist industry.* Ann Arbor: University Microfilms.

————. 1969. Tourism's potential for contributing to the economic development in the Caribbean. *Journal of Geography* 68: 173–77.

————. 1970. Research on the tourist industry in Latin America: Its present status and future needs. In *Geographic Research in Latin America,* B. Lentnek. R. L. Carmin, and T. L. Martinson, eds., pp. 315–23. Proceedings of the Conference of Latin American Geographers, vol. 1.

————. 1974. *The tourist industry in Latin America: A bibliography for planning and research.* Exchange Bibliography #614. Monticello, Illinois: Council of Planning Librarians.

————. 1978. Tourist industry development: At the crossroads. *Tourist Review* 33 (3): 2–9.

————. 1980. A review of public support for international tourism in New Zealand. *New Zealand Geographer* 36: 20–29.

Mishan, E. J. 1971. *Cost-benefit analysis: An introduction.* New York Praeger.

Missouri, University of. 1986. *Tourism USA: Guidelines for tourism development.* Columbia Missouri: Department of Recreation and Park Administration, University Extension.

Mitchell, B. 1979. *Geography and resource analysis.* New York: Longman.

Mitchell, F. H. 1968a. *The costs and benefits of tourism in Kenya.* Report to the Kenya Tourist Development Corp. Nairobi, Kenya: University College, Institute for Development Studies.

————. 1968b. *The impact of tourism on national income.* Nairobi, Kenya: University College, Institute for Development Studies, Staff Paper No. 30.

————. 1970a. The value of tourism in East Africa. *East African Economic Review* 1 (2): 1–21.

————. 1970b. Evaluating the role of tourism in Tanzanian development. In *Tourism and Socialist development,* I. G. Shivji, ed., pp. 23–24. Dar es Salaam: Tanzania Publishing House.

Mitchell, L. S. 1969. Recreational geography: Evolution and research needs. *The Professional Geographer* 21 (2): 117–19.

————. 1980. Geographic analysis: Implications for tourism. *Business and Economic Review* 26 (5): 38–42.

————. 1984. A geographical analysis of leisure activities: A life style case study. In *Leisure, tourism and social change,* J. Long and R. Hecock, eds., pp. 35–44. Edinburgh: Centre for Leisure Research.

Mitchelson, R. L. 1979. An examination of the psycho-physical functions in travel mode-choice behavior. Ph.D. dissertation, Ohio State University, Columbus.

Mitford, N. 1959. The tourist. *Encounter* 13 (3): 3–7.

Moimoi, T., and Samate, A. 1980. Tongans in Fiji tourism. In *Pacific tourism: As islanders see it*, F. Rajotte and R. Crocombe, eds., pp. 31–32. Fiji: South Pacific Social Sciences Association and The Institute of Pacific Studies, University of the South Pacific.

Moir, E. 1964. *Discovery of Britain: The English tourists, 1540–1840*. Fernhill House Ltd. Distributed by Humanities Press, Highland, New Jersey.

Mone, S. E. 1980. Tourism in reverse: The reaction of islanders abroad. In *Pacific tourism: As islanders see it*, F. Rajotte and R. Crocombe, eds., pp. 164–67. Fiji: South Pacific Social Sciences Association and The Institute of Pacific Studies, University of the South Pacific.

Montgomery, G. 1981. *An evaluation of the tourism potential of the cruise ship industry of BC*. Victoria, British Columbia: Ministry of Industry and Small Business Development.

Moore, A. 1980a. Walt Disney World: Bounded ritual space and the playful pilgrimage center. *Anthropological Quarterly* 53: 207–18.

———. 1980b. Planners, tourists and Indians: National policy, regional development and the San Blas Cuna. *Practicing Anthropology* 2 (5/6): 19–20.

———. 1984. From council to legislature: Democracy, parliamentarianism, and the San Blas Cuna. *American Anthropologist* 86: 28–42.

———. 1985. Rosanzerusu is Los Angeles: An anthropological inquiry of Japanese tourists. *Annals of Tourism Research* 12 (4): 619–43.

Moore, K. 1970. Modernization in a Canary Island village: An indicator of social change in Spain. *Journal of the Steward Anthropological Society* 2: 19–34.

Moreno, O. 1974. Las limitaciones en el desarrolle turistico. *Comercio Exterior* 25 (3): 308–14.

Moret, Rmo. R. Joseph. 1763. *Empeños del valor, y bizarros, desempeños, o sitio de Fuenterrabia*. Manuel Silvestre de Arlequi, trans. Joseph Miquel de Esquerro, Impressor de los Reales Tribunales de Navarra, originally written 1654, facsimile edition published by the Ministerio de Información y Turismo de España, Industrias Gráficas Valverde, San Sebastián, 1968.

Morrison, H. B. 1972. *The golden age of travel*. Reprint of 1951 edition. New York: American Museum of Science Books.

Morss, E., and Gow, D. 1985. Sustaining project benefits. In *Implementing rural development projects*, E. Morss and D. Gow, eds., pp. 217–43. Boulder, Colorado: Westview Press.

Moulin, C. 1980. Existe-t-il des limites socio-psychologiques au developpement touristique? *Revue de l'AIEST* 21: 121–29.

Mozoomdar, A. 1974. Tourism and the BOP in a developing country. International Union of Official Travel Organizations (IOUTO) seminar paper.

Murdie, R. A. 1965. Cultural differences in consumer travel. *Economic Geography* 41 (3): 211–33.

Murphy, P. E. 1975. The role of attitude in the choice decisions of recreational boaters. *Journal of Leisure Research* 7 (3): 216–24.

———. 1979. Development and potential of tourism. In *Vancouver island: Land of contrasts*, C. N. Forward, ed., pp. 289–307. Victoria, British Columbia: University of Victoria, Western Geographical Series.

———. 1980. Tourism management using land-use planning and landscape design: The Victoria experience. *Canadian Geographer* 24: 60–71.

———. 1981. Community attitudes to tourism: A comparative analysis. *International Journal of Tourism Management* 2 (3): 189–95.

———. 1982. Tourism planning in London: An exercise in spatial and seasonal management. *Tourist Review* 37 (1): 19–23.

——. 1985. *Tourism: A community approach*. New York: Methuen.

Murphy, P. E., and Rosenblood, L. 1974. Tourism: An exercise in spatial search. *Canadian Geographer* 18 (3): 201–10.

Myers, N. 1975. The tourist as an agent for development and wildlife conservation: The case of Kenya. *International Journal of Social Economics* 2 (1): 26–42.

Nagenda, J. 1969. Parading the primitive to woo tourists. *African Development* 3 (8): 15.

Naibavu, T., and Schutz, B. 1974. Prostitution: Problem or profitable industry. *Pacific Perspective* 3 (1): 59–68.

Narduzzi, N. 1973. Prevision de la demande et formation du capital dans le domaine du tourisme. *Revue de Tourisme* 2: 74–76.

Nash, D. 1970. *A community in limbo: An anthropological study of an American community abroad*. Bloomington: Indiana University Press.

——. 1978. An anthropological approach to tourism. In *Tourism and economic change*, Studies in Third World Societies No. 6, V. Smith, ed., pp. 133–52. Williamsburg, Virginia: William and Mary Press.

——. 1979. Tourism in pre-industrial societies. *Les Cahiers du Tourisme* series C, n. 51, 31 pp.

——. 1981. Tourism as an anthropological subject. *Current Anthropology* 22 (5): 461–81.

——. 1984. The ritualization of tourism: Comment on Graburn's 'The Anthropology of Tourism.' *Annals of Tourism Research* 11 (3): 503–7.

Native Brotherhood of British Columbia. 1980. *The development of native tourism in British Columbia*. Victoria, British Columbia: Ministry of Tourism.

Nayacakalou, R. 1972. The leasing of native land for tourist plant development in Fiji. In *Change and development in rural Melanesia*. pp. 151–58. Canberra: A.N.U. Research School for Pacific Studies.

Naylor, J. 1967. Tourism—Spain's most important industry. *Geography* 5 (1:234): 23–40.

Nelson, L. P. 1986. Experiences of black tourists in Africa. Ed.D. dissertation, Columbia University Teacher's College.

Nelson, R. 1985. *The evolution of tourism and tourist landscapes: Nelson, British Columbia 1890–1984*. Master's Thesis, University of Waterloo, Ontario.

Nettekoven, L. 1979. Mechanisms of intercultural interaction. In *Tourism: Passport to development?* E. de Kadt, ed., pp. 135–145. New York: Oxford University Press.

Newby, P. T. 1981. Literature and the fashioning of tourist taste. In *Humanistic geography and literature: Essays on the experience of place*, D. C. Peacock, ed., pp. 130–41. London: Helm.

Ngabonzina, A. 1974. *Reflections sur le developpement du tourisme au Rwanda*. Talence: Ecole Internationale de Bordeaux.

Ngitol, T. 1975. *L'Intervention de l'etat dans le secteur touristique au Cameroun*. Yaounde: Universite de Yaounde.

Nicholls, L. L. 1978. Regional tourism development in "Third World America": A proposed model for Appalachia. Paper presented at the symposium on Tourism and Regional Development, 38th annual meeting, the Society for Applied Anthropology, 4 April 1978, Merida, Mexico.

Nieto, J. A. 1976. Tourism: Its penetration and development on a Spanish island. Ph.D. dissertation, New School for Social Research, New York.

Niukula, P. 1980. The impact of tourism on Suvavou Village. In *Pacific tourism: As islanders see it*, F. Rajotte and R. Crocombe, eds., pp. 83–86. Fiji: South Pacific Social Sciences Association and The Institute of Pacific Studies, University of the South Pacific.

Nolan, M. L. 1986. Pilgrimage as rural tourism: The European example. Paper presented at the Symposium on Rural Tourism, annual meetings of the Society for Applied Anthropology, 26–30 March, Reno, Nevada.

Nolan, S. D., Jr., and Nolan, M. L. 1978. Variations in travel behavior and the cultural impact of tourism. In *Tourism and behavior*, Studies in Third World Societies No. 5, V. Smith, ed., pp. 1–17. Williamsburg, Virginia: William and Mary Press.

Norbeck, E. 1971. Man at play. *Natural History* (special supplement): 48–53.

———. 1974. The anthropological study of human play. *Rice University Studies* 60: 1–8.

Nordyke, E. C. 1979. Relationship between tourism and population growth. Paper presented at a workshop of the Commission on Population and the Hawaiian Future, Honolulu. Mimeographed.

Noronha, R. 1979. Paradise reviewed: Tourism in Bali. In *Tourism: Passport to development?* E. de Kadt, ed., pp. 177–204. New York: Oxford University Press.

Norris, F. 1985. *Gawking at the Midnight Sun: The tourist in early Alaska*. Studies in History No. 170. Juneau, Alaska: Alaska Historical Commission.

———. 1987. Showing off Alaska: The northern tourist trade, 1878–1941. *Alaska History* 2 (2): 1–18.

Northwest Territories. 1983. *Community based tourism: A strategy for the Northwest Territories tourism industry*. Yellowknife: Department of Economic Development and Tourism.

Nuñez, T. A. 1963. Tourism, tradition and acculturation: Weekendismo in a Mexican village. *Ethnology* 2 (3): 347–52.

———. 1964. Authority versus anarchy: The impact of urban tourism on a rural milieu in Mexico. Paper read at the Symposium on Tourism, Central States Anthropological Society, 14–17 May 1964, Milwaukee, Wisconsin.

Nur, M. N. 1983. Tourism prospects in Pakistan. *Dawn* 1 November: I–II.

Ogilvie, F. W. 1933. *The tourist movement*. Staples Press.

———. 1934. Tourist traffic. *Encyclopedia of Social Sciences* 13: 661–64. New York: Macmillan.

Oglesby, M. K. 1982. Tourism in Malta. *Leisure Studies* 3 (2): 147–61.

O'Grady, R. 1982. *Tourism in the third world: Christian reflections*. Maryknoll, New York: Orbis Books.

Okotai, T. 1980. Tourism in the Cook Islands. In *Pacific tourism: As islanders see it*, F. Rajotte and R. Crocombe, eds., pp. 49–56. Fiji: South Pacific Social Sciences Association and The Institute of Pacific Studies, University of the South Pacific.

O'Loughlin, C. 1967. *Economic and political change in the Leeward and Windward Islands*. New Haven: Yale University Press.

———. 1970. Tourism in the tropics: Lessons from the West Indies. *Insight and Opinion* 5 (2): 105–10.

Olwig, K. F. 1980. National parks, tourism and local development: A West Indian case. *Human Organization* 39 (1): 22–30.

Ontario Ministry of Industry and Tourism. 1976. *Tourism development in Ontario: A framework for opportunity*. Toronto.

Organization for Economic Cooperation and Development. 1974. *Tourism policy and international tourism in OECD member countries*. Paris: OECD.

———. 1977. *Tourism policy and international tourism in OECD member countries*. Paris: OECD.

———. 1980. *The impact of tourism on the environment*. Paris: OECD.

Ossipow, P. W. 1963. Le role de l'automobile dans le tourisme. *Tourist Review* 18: 17–24, 61–73.

Oswalt, W. H. 1979. *Eskimos and explorers.* Novato, California: Chandler & Sharp.

Ouma, J. P. B. 1970. *Evolution of tourism in East Africa.* Nairobi: East African Literature Bureau.

Overton, J. 1980. Tourism development conservation and conflict: Game laws for caribou protection in Newfoundland. *Canadian Geographer* 24: 40–49.

Pacione, M. 1977. Tourism: Its effects on the traditional landscape in Ibiza and Formentera. *Geography* 62: 43–47.

Packer, L. V. 1974. *Tourism in the small community: A cross-cultural analysis of developmental change.* Ann Arbor: University Microfilms.

Papson, S. 1979. Tourism: World's biggest industry in the twenty-first century? *The Futurist* 12: 249–57.

Parker, A., and Neal, A. 1977. *Molas: Folk art of the Cuna Indians.* New York: Crown.

Parker, S. 1986. A review of leisure research around the world. *World Leisure and Recreation* 1: 7–10.

Parkes, J. 1925. *Travel in England in the seventeenth century.* London: Oxford University Press.

Parsons, J. J. 1973. Southward to the sun: The impact of mass tourism on the coast of Spain. *Yearbook of the Association of Pacific Coast Geographers* 35: 129–46.

Passariello, P. 1986. Novelty's pilgrims: Change and tourism in a Mexican beach community. Ph.D. dissertation, University of California, Berkeley.

de Pater, B. C. 1983/84. *Sociaal geografische aspekten van de vrije tijdsbeseding.* Breda en Amsterdam: Centrum voor Vrije Landeskunde/Geografische en Planologisch Instituut.

———. 1984. Ruimtelijke en sociale begrippen in de sociale geografie. *Bijdragen tot de sociale geographie en Planologie.* No. 11. Amsterdam: Vrije Universiteit.

Patera, C. 1984. *Mola making.* Piscataway, New Jersey: New Century Publisher.

Patterson, W. D. 1976. Can culture survive tourism? PATA, Twenty-fifth Anniversary Conference.

Pearce, D. 1981. *Tourist development.* London: Longman.

———. 1987. *Tourism today: A geographical analysis.* London: Longman.

Pearce, P. L. 1981. Environmental shock: A study of tourists' reactions to two tropical islands. *Journal of Applied Social Psychology* 11: 268–80.

———. 1982a. Tourists and their hosts: Some social and psychological efforts of intercultural contact. In *Cultures in contact,* L. S. Bochner, ed. Oxford: Pergamon Press.

———. 1982b. *The social psychology of tourist behavior.* Oxford: Pergamon.

Pearce, P. L., and Moscardo, G. M. 1985a. The relationship between travellers' career levels and the concept of authenticity. *Australian Journal of Psychology* 37 (2): 157–74.

———. 1985b. Tourist theme parks: Research practices and possibilities. *Australian Psychologist* 20 (3): 303–12.

Pearce-Sales, J. 1959. *Travel and tourism encyclopaedia.* London: Blandford.

Pearson, R. 1957. The geography of recreation on a tropical island: Jamaica. *Journal of Geography* 56: 12–22.

Pere, B. 1980. Commercializing culture or culturizing commerce? In *Pacific tourism: As Islanders see it,* F. Rajotte and R. Crocombe, eds., pp. 139–45. Fiji: South Pacific Social Sciences Association and The Institute of Pacific Studies, University of the South Pacific.

Perea, L. 1978. *Case study: Hikkaduwa. The role of tourism in the social and economic development of Sri Lanka*. Colombo, Sri Lanka: Social Science Research Centre.

Perez, L., Jr. 1973–74. Aspects of underdevelopment: Tourism in the West Indies. *Science and Society* 37: 473–80.

Perpillou, A. 1966. Quelques études recèntes sur les problèmes géographiques du tourisme. *Annales de Geographie* 75 (409): 341–45.

Persaud, B. 1970. Impact of tourism. *West Indies Chronicle* (July): 329–31.

Persaud, L. 1973. European tourism "not the answer." *West Indies Chronicle* (December): 485–96.

Peters, M. 1969. *International tourism: The economics of the international tourist trade*. London: Hutchinson.

Petit-Skinner, S. 1977. Tourism and acculturation in Tahiti. In *Social and economic impact of tourism on Pacific communities*, B. H. Farrell, ed., pp. 85–87. Santa Cruz: Center for South Pacific Studies, University of California.

Phillips, M. 1982. Tourism in the Amazon. *Cultural Survival Quarterly* 6 (3): 19.

Phongpaicht, P. 1982. Bangkok masseuses. *Cultural Survival Quarterly* 6 (3): 34–5.

Piesse, R. D. 1970. Tourism, aboriginal antiquities, and public education. In *Aboriginal antiquities in Australia: Their nature and preservation*, F. D. McCarthy, ed. Australian Aboriginal Studies, No. 22. Canberra: Australian Institute of Aboriginal Studies.

Pi-Sunyer, O. 1973. Tourism and its discontents: The impact of a new industry on a Catalan community. *Studies in European Society* 1: 1–20.

———. 1979. The politics of tourism in Catalonia. *Mediterranean Studies* 1 (2): 47–69.

———. 1982. The cultural costs of tourism. *Cultural Survival Quarterly* 6 (3): 7–10.

Pittock, A. B. 1967. Aborigines and the tourist industry. *Australian Quarterly* 39 (3): 87–95.

Pitt-Rivers, J. 1964. Pilgrims and tourists: Conflict and change in a village of southwestern France. Paper read at the symposium on Tourism, Central States Anthropological Society, 14–16 May 1964, Milwaukee, Wisconsin.

Pizam, A., and Pokela, J. 1983. The 1979 U.S. gasoline shortage and its impact on the tourism industry. *Tourism Management* 4: 94–101.

Planina, J. 1962. Turizem kot druzbena en ekonomska kategarija. *Economisk Revy* 13 (1): 29–37.

Plog, S. C. 1974. Why destination areas rise and fall in popularity. *Cornell Hotel and Restaurant Administration Quarterly* (February).

Pollard, H. J. 1976. Geographical variation within the tourist trade of the Caribbean. *Journal of Tropical Geography* 43: 49–62.

Pool, I., Keller, S., and Bauer, R. A. 1956. The influence of foreign travel on political attitudes of American businessmen. *Public Opinion Quarterly* 20 (1): 161–75.

Pope, R. H. 1964. Touristry: A type of occupational mobility. *Social Problems* 2: 336–66.

Poser, H. 1939. Geographische studien uber den fremdenverkehr im riesengebirge: Ein beitrag zur geographischen betrachtung des fremdenverkehrs. *Abhandlungen der Gesellschaft der Wissenschaften zu Gottingen, Mathematisch-Physikalishe Klasse*, Dritte Folge, Heft 20, pp. 1–173.

Pospisil, L. 1975. Tyrolean peasants of Obernberg. Paper read at the conference of the Wenner-Gren Foundation, August–September 1975, Burg Wartenstein, Austria.

Pouris, D., and Beerli, C. 1963. *Culture and tourism*. Paris: Organization for Economic Cooperation and Development.

Preister, K. 1987. Issue-centered social impact assessment. In *Anthropological praxis: Translating knowledge into action*, R. M. Wulff and S. J. Fiske, eds., pp. 39–55. Boulder and London: Westview Press.

Press, C. M., Jr. 1978. *Hustling* in a touristic setting. Paper presented at the symposium on Tourism and Regional Development, 38th annual meeting, The Society for Applied Anthropology, 4 April 1978, Merida, Mexico.

Press, I. 1969. Ambiguity and innovation: Implications for the genesis of the culture broker. *American Anthropologist* 71: 206–17.

Price, R. L. 1980. A geography of tourism: Settlement and landscape on the Sardinian littoral. Ph.D. dissertation, University of Oregon, Eugene.

Problèmes Economiques. 1979. Le tourisme international dans les pays de L'Est. *Problemes Economiques* No. 1626: 9–14.

Przeclawski, K. 1985. The role of tourism in contemporary culture. *The Tourist Review* 40: 2–6.

Pye, E. A., and Lin, T. 1983. *Tourism in Asia: The economic impacts*. Ottawa: International Development Research Centre (available through Singapore University Press).

Quandt, R. E., ed. 1970. *Demand for travel: Theory and evaluation*. Lexington, Massachusetts: Lexington Books.

Quintana, B. B., and Floyd, L. G. 1972. *Que Gitano! Gypsies of southern Spain*. New York: Holt, Rinehart and Winston.

Quirt, J. H. 1962. Airlines: Profitless progress. *The Exchange* 23: 4.

Radke, D., and Donner, H. J. 1975. *Contribution of international tourism to the economic and social development of Sri Lanka*. Berlin: German Development Institute.

Rae, J. B. 1971. *The road and the car in American life*. Cambridge: Massachusetts Institute of Technology.

Rae, W. F. 1891. *The business of travel*. London: Thos. Cook & Son.

Rajotte, F. 1977. Evaluating the cultural and environmental impact of Pacific tourism. *Pacific Perspective* 6: 41–48.

———. 1978. *A method for evaluation of tourism impact in the Pacific*. University of California, Data Paper No. 9. Santa Cruz: Center for South Pacific Studies.

———. 1980. Tourism impact in the Pacific. In *Pacific tourism: As islanders see it*, F. Rajotte and R. Crocombe, eds., pp. 1–14. Fiji: South Pacific Social Sciences Association and The Institute of Pacific Studies, University of the South Pacific.

Rajotte, F., and Crocombe, R. 1980. *Pacific tourism: As islanders see it*. Fiji: South Pacific Social Sciences Association and The Institute of Pacific Studies, University of the South Pacific.

Ramaker, J. G. 1966. *Toeristen en toerisme: Sociaal-economische beschouwingere over het moderne toerisme*. Assen: Van Gorcum.

Rambaud, P. 1967. Tourisme et urbanisation de Campagne. *Sociologica Ruralis* 7: 311–55.

———. 1980. Tourisme et village: Un debat de societé. *Sociologica Ruralis* 4: 232–49.

Rapoport, A. 1982. *The meaning of the built environment: A non-verbal communication approach*. Beverly Hills, California: Sage Press.

Ray, D. J. 1975. *The Eskimos of Bering Straits, 1650–1898.* Seattle: University of Washington Press.

Ray, N. 1983. Mountains and monasteries. *Geographical Magazine* 55 (12): 645–50.

Reason, J. 1964. *Man in motion: The psychology of travel.* New York: Walker and Co.

Redcliff, M. 1973. The effects of socio-economic change in a Spanish pueblo on community cohesion. *Sociologia Ruralis* 13 (1): 1–14.

Redfield, R., Linton, R., and Herskovits, M. 1936. Memorandum in the study of acculturation. *American Anthropologist* 38 (1): 129–52.

Redfoote, D. L. 1984. Touristic authenticity, tourist angst, and modern reality. *Qualitative Sociology* 7: 291–309.

Reed, R. R. 1979. The colonial genesis of hill stations: The genting exception. *Geographical Review* 69: 463–68.

Reilly, R. T. 1980. *Travel and tourism marketing techniques.* Wheaton, Illinois: Merton House Publishing.

Reiter, R. R. 1977. The politics of tourism in a French alpine community. In *Hosts and guests: The anthropology of tourism,* V. Smith, ed. pp. 139–48. Philadelphia: University of Pennsylvania Press.

Renaud, B. 1972. The influence of tourism growth on the production structure of island economies. *Review of Regional Studies* 2 (3): 41–56.

Renschler, R. 1982. Die Anthropologische dimension: Bedrohung and erweiterung der identitat von gast und gastgeber. In *Tourismus-das phanomen des reisens,* H. Ringeling and M. Svilar, eds., pp. 75–90. Bern: Paul Haupt.

Reynoso y Valle, A., and de Regt, J. P., 1979. Growing pains: Planned tourism development in Ixtapa-Zihuatanejo. In *Tourism: Passport to development?* E. de Kadt, ed., pp. 111–34. New York: Oxford University Press.

Richards, G. 1972. *Tourism and the economy.* Guildford: University of Surrey.

Richter, L. K. 1980. The political uses of tourism: A Philippine case study. *Journal of Developing Areas* 14 (1): 237–57.

———. 1982. *Land reform and tourism development: Policy-making in the Philippines.* Cambridge, Massachusetts: Schenkman.

Rickson, I. 1973. Planning and tourism. *Journal of Royal Town Planning Institute* 59: 269–70.

Rifkind, C. 1981. Tourism and communities: Process, problems, and solutions. *Livability Digest* 1 (1): 4–45.

Ritchie, J. E. 1975. The honest broker in the cultural marketplace. In *A new kind of sugar: Tourism in the Pacific.* B. R. Finney and K. A. Watson, eds., pp. 49–60. Honolulu: East-West Culture Learning Institute.

Ritter, W. 1966. *Fremdenverkehr in Europa.* Leiden: A. W. Sijthoff.

———. 1974. Tourism and recreation in the Islamic countries. In *Studies in the geography of tourism,* J. Matznetter, ed., pp. 273–81. Frankfurt-am-Main: J. W. Goethe-Universitat.

Rivers, P. 1972. *The restless generation: A crisis in mobility.* London: Davis-Poynter.

Robben, C. G. M. 1982. Tourism and change in a Brazilian fishing village. *Cultural Survival Quarterly* 6 (3): 18.

Roberts, R. 1981. *Trans-Tasman tourism prospects to 1985.* Working Paper NTA/ 81/2, Department of Management Studies, University of Auckland, New Zealand.

Robertson, A. 1965. The sunshine revolution. *The Geographical Magazine* 37 (12): 926–39.

Robineau, C. 1975. The Tahitian economy and tourism. In *A new kind of sugar: Tourism in the Pacific*, B. R. Finney and K. A. Watson, eds., pp. 61–78. Honolulu: East-West Culture Learning Institute.

Robinson, G. W. S. 1957. Tourism in Corsica. *Economic Geography* 23: 337–48.

———. 1972. The recreation geography of south Asia. *Geographical Review* 62: 561–72.

Robinson, H. 1979. *A geography of tourism*. Plymouth: MacDonald & Evans.

Rodriguez, S. 1986. Constructed and reconstructed ethnicity in Taos. Paper presented at the meetings of the American Anthropological Association, 3–7 December 1986, Philadelphia, Pennsylvania.

Roebuck, J., and McNamara, P. 1973. Ficheras and freelancers: Prostitution in a Mexican border city. *Archives of Sexual Behavior* 2 (3): 231–44.

Rogalewski, O. 1980. International tourism originating from Poland. *International Social Science Journal* 32 (1): 114–27.

Rogozinski, J. 1980. The impact of tourism in the economy: The Mexican case. Ph.D. dissertation, The University of Texas at Austin.

Romeril, M. 1985. Tourism and conservation in the Channel Islands. *Tourism Management* 6 (1): 43–49.

Romeril, M., and Hughes-Evans, D., eds. 1980. *Tourism and the environment*. London: Institute for Environmental Sciences.

Ropponen, P. J. 1976. Tourism and the local population. In *Planning and development of the tourist industry in the E. C. E. Region*, Economic Commission for Europe, pp. 104–9. New York: United Nations.

Rosenow, J. E., and Pulsipher, G. L. 1979. *Tourism: The good, bad, and the ugly*. Lincoln, Nebraska: Century Three Press.

Ross, D. R., and Farrell, B. H., eds. 1975. *Source materials for Pacific tourism*. Santa Cruz: University of California, Center for South Pacific Studies.

Roy, L. 1975. Planning for tourism on the island of Hawaii: The effects of tourism on natural resources, natural beauty and recreation. In *A new kind of sugar: Tourism in the Pacific*, B. R. Finney and K. A. Watson, eds., pp. 165–68. Honolulu: East-West Culture Learning Institute.

Ruberstein, C. 1980. Survey report on how Americans view vacations. *Psychology Today* (May): 62–67.

Rudelius, W., Pennington, A. L., and Ross, I. 1971. Analyzing state tourism: A case study of the Midwest. *Journal of Leisure Research* 3 (4): 250–60.

Rudney, R. S. 1979. From luxury to popular tourism: The transformation of the resort city of Nice. Ph.D. dissertation, University of Michigan, Ann Arbor.

Rutazibwa, G. 1973. L'étude des problèmes de l'industries touristique. *Revue de Tourisme* 1: 30–33.

———. 1974. Le transports et le tourism international. *Revue de Tourisme* 3: 93–99.

Ryan, B. 1965. The dynamics of recreational development on the south coast of New South Wales. *Australian Geographer* 9 (6): 331–48.

Ryan, J. B. 1969. Tourism in the U.S. Virgin Islands: Its growth and economic impact in the post-War period. Master's thesis, University of Kansas.

Sadler, P. 1983. Ski area development in the Canadian Rockies: Past lessons, future prospects. In *Tourism in Canada: Selected issues and options*, P. E. Murphy, ed. Victoria, British Columbia: University of Victoria, Western Geographical Series 21.

Sadler, P., and Archer, B. H. 1974. The economic impact of tourism in developing countries. Tourist Research Paper No. 4. Institute of Economic Research. Bangor: University College of North Wales.

Saglio, C. 1976. *Case-study and cultural integration of tourism in four villages of Lower-Casamance (Senegal)*. World Bank, Agency for Cultural and Technical Coordination.

Salato, R., and Ilaiu, M. 1980. Tamavua Village: For tourists only. In *Pacific tourism: As islanders see it*, F. Rajotte and R. Crocombe, eds., pp. 89–92. Fiji: South Pacific Social Sciences Association and The Institute of Pacific Studies, University of the South Pacific.

Salter, M. A. 1977–78. *Play: Anthropological perspectives. Proceedings of the Association for the Anthropological Study of Play*. West Point, New York: Leisure Press.

Samarasuriya, S. 1982. *Who needs tourism? Employment for women in the holiday industry of Sudugama, Sri Lanka*. Colombo-Leiden: Research Project Women and Development.

Samy, J. 1973. Who does what to whom in Pacific tourism? Paper read at the Seminar on Social Issues in Development Planning in the South Pacific, 29 November–3 December 1973, Suva, Fiji.

———. 1975. Crumbs from the table? In *The Pacific way*, S. Tupouniua, R. Crocombe, and C. Slatter, eds., pp. 205–14. Suva: South Pacific Social Science Association. Also in *A new kind of sugar: Tourism in the Pacific*, B. R. Finney and K. A. Watson, eds., pp. 11–24. Honolulu: East-West Culture Learning Institute.

———. 1980. Crumbs from the table? The workers' share in tourism. In *Pacific tourism: As islanders see it*, F. Rajotte and R. Crocombe, eds., pp. 67–82. Fiji: South Pacific Social Sciences Association and The Institute of Pacific Studies, University of the South Pacific.

Sanday, P. 1973. Toward a theory of the status of women. *American Anthropologist* 75: 1682–99.

Sandor, T. L. 1971. Economic analysis of resort development. *Cornell Hotel and Restaurant Administration Quarterly* 11 (4): 43–49.

Sandru, I. 1970. Considerations sur la géographie du tourisme, avec spécial regard sur la Roumanie. *Revue Roumaine de Géologie, Géophysique, et Géographie, Serie de Géographie* 14 (1): 175–80.

Sargent, J. R., et al. 1967. The limits of tourism as a growth generator. *Development Digest* 5 (2): 82–86.

Saskatchewan Tourism and Small Business. 1983. *A tourism development strategy for the province of Saskatchewan*. Regina: Tourism and Small Business.

Schadler, K. 1979. African arts and crafts in a world of changing values. In *Tourism: Passport to development?* E. de Kadt, ed., pp. 146–56. New York: Oxford University Press.

Schaer, U. 1978. Traffic problems in holiday resorts. *Tourist Review* 33 (2): 9–15.

Schild, G. V. H. 1978. Development of a model for marketing of international tourism: The case of South Korea. DBA dissertation, George Washington University, Washington DC.

Schmidt, C. J. 1979. The guided tour: Insulated adventure. *Urban Life* 7 (4): 441–67.

———. 1980. *Tourism: Sacred sites, secular seer*. Stoney Brook: State University of New York Press.

Schmitt, R. C. 1968. Travel, tourism and migration. *Demography* 5 (1): 306–10.

Schmoll, G. A. 1977. *Tourism promotion*. London: Tourism International Press.

Schneider, H. 1976. Tourism development in Africa: Scope and critical issues. *Afrika Spectrum* 1: 5–15.

Schouten, R., and Osgood, D., eds. 1975. *The impact of tourism on regional devel-*

opment: A case study of Taos, New Mexico. Dallas: Southern Methodist University, Dept. of Anthropology.

Schudson, M. S. 1979. Review essay: Tourism and modern culture. *American Journal of Sociology* 84: 1249–59.

Scottish Tourist Board. 1975. *The economic impact of tourism: A case study in Greater Tayside.* Edinburgh: Tourism and Recreation Research Unit, University of Edinburgh.

Sealy, N. D. 1982. *Tourism in the Caribbean.* London: Hodder and Stoughton.

Sebeok, T. A. 1980. The domain of the sacred. *Journal of Social Biological Structure* 3: 227–29.

Sedeuilh, M. 1974. Public health aspects of tourism. *WHO Chronicle* 28 (6): 293.

Sessa, A. 1983. *Elements of tourism economics.* Rome: CATAL.

Sethom, N. 1974. *L'influence du tourisme sur l'economie et la vie regionales dans la zone de Nabeul-Hammamet.* Master's thesis, Institut de Géographie, Université de Paris I.

Seveck, C. A. 1973. *Longest reindeer herder.* Fairbanks: Arctic Circle Enterprises.

Seward, S. B., and Spinrad, B. K. 1982. *Tourism in the Caribbean: The economic impact.* Canada: International Development Research Center.

Shanklin, E. 1980. The Irish go-between. *Anthropological Quarterly* 53 (3): 162–72.

Shaw, S. M. 1985. The meaning of leisure in everyday life. *Leisure Sciences* 7 (1): 1–24.

Sheldon, P. J., and Mak, J. 1985. The demand for package tours: A mode choice model. Honolulu: University of Hawaii, unpublished manuscript.

Sheldon, P. J., and Var. T. 1984. Resident attitudes to tourism in North Wales. *Tourism Management* 5 (1): 40–47.

———. 1985. Tourism forecasting: State-of-the-art. *Journal of Forecasting* 4: 183–95.

Shepard, P. 1955. The nature of tourism. *Landscape* 5 (1): 29–33.

Sherzer, J. 1983. *Kuna ways of speaking: An ethnographic perspective.* Austin: University of Texas Press.

Sherzer, J., and Sherzer, D. 1976. Mormaknamaloe: The Cuna mola. In *Ritual and symbol in native America,* P. Young and J. Howe, eds. University of Oregon Anthropological Papers, No. 9.

Shivji, I. G. 1973. Tourism and socialist development. *Tanzanian Studies No. 3.* Dar es Salaam: Tanzania Publishing House.

Sigaux, G. 1966. *History of tourism.* J. White, trans. London: Leisure Arts.

Signorelli, M. J., Jr. 1978. A study of selected hotel officials and managers with respect to assessment of job attitudes. Ed.D. dissertation, University of Nevada, Las Vegas.

Sikivou, J. 1980. A conversation with two swordsellers. In *Pacific tourism: As islanders see it,* F. Rajotte and R. Crocombe, eds., pp. 99–100. Fiji: South Pacific Social Sciences Association and The Institute of Pacific Studies, University of the South Pacific.

Sikorski, K. A. 1968. Modern Hopi pottery. *Utah State University Monograph Series* 15 (2): 9–10.

Simmel, G. 1950. *The sociology of George Simmel.* Glencoe: The Free Press.

Simms, D. M. 1981. Tourism, entrepreneurs, and change in southwest Ireland. Ph.D. dissertation, State University of New York, Albany.

Simpson, A. 1968. *The new Europeans.* London: Hodder and Stoughton.

Simpson, J. 1975. Research for tourism in the Hawaii Visitors Bureau. In *A new kind of sugar: Tourism in the Pacific,* B. R. Finney and K. A. Watson, eds., pp. 153–56. Honolulu: East-West Culture Learning Institute.

Sinclair, J. T. 1960. Current development of the tourist industry and its future in the economy of El Salvador. *Annals of the Association of American Geographers* 50: 346 (abstract).

Skinner, R. J. 1980. The impact of tourism on Niue. In *Pacific tourism: As islanders see it,* F. Rajotte and R. Crocombe, eds., pp. 61–64. Fiji: South Pacific Social Sciences Association and The Institute of Pacific Studies, University of the South Pacific.

Sládek, G. 1966. *Zahraničný Cestovný Ruch* (Foreign tourism). Bratislava: Vydavateľstvo Politickej Literatúry.

Sloane, L. 1987. Crossroads in Panama. *New York Times,* Travel Section 15 February: 23, 32.

Smaoui, A. Tourism and employment in Tunisia. In *Tourism: Passport to development?* E. de Kadt, ed., pp. 101–10. New York: Oxford University Press.

Smith, D. C. 1972. Issues in the economic development of Micronesia: Tourism as an example. In *Micronesian realities: Political and economic,* F. M. Smith, ed., pp. 218–34. Santa Cruz: University of California, Center for South Pacific Studies.

Smith, M. E. 1982a. The process of sociocultural continuity. *Current Anthropology* 23: 127–42.

———. 1982b. Tourism and Native Americans. *Cultural Survival Quarterly* 6 (3): 10–12.

Smith, V. L. 1953. Travel geography courses for a new field. *Journal of Geography* 52 (2): 68–72.

———. 1961. Needed: Geographically-trained guides. *The Professional Geographer* 13: 6.

———. 1976. Tourism and culture change. *Annals of Tourism Research* 3 (3): 122–26.

———. 1978. The editor's perspective. In feature book review, "Hosts and guests: The anthropology of tourism." *Annals of Tourism Research* 5 (2): 274–77.

———. 1979. Women: The taste-makers in tourism. *Annals of Tourism Research* 6: 49–60.

———. 1980. Anthropology and tourism: A science-industry evaluation. *Annals of Tourism Research* 7: 13–33.

———. 1981. Controlled vs. uncontrolled tourism: Bhutan and Nepal. *RAIN* 40 (October): 4–6.

Smith, V. L., ed. 1978a. *Tourism and behavior.* Studies in Third World Societies No. 5. Williamsburg, Virginia: William and Mary Press.

———. 1978b. *Tourism and economic change.* Studies in Third World Societies No. 6. Williamsburg, Virginia: William and Mary Press.

Spencer, J. E., and Thomas, W. L. 1948. Hill stations and summer resorts of the Orient. *Geographical Review* 38: 637–71.

Stanfield, C. A., Jr. 1971. The geography of resorts: Problems and potentials. *The Professional Geographer* 23 (2): 164–66.

State of Hawaii. 1975. *What Hawaii's people think of the visitor industry.* Honolulu: Department of Planning and Economic Development.

———. 1983. *The economic impact of tourism in Hawaii: 1970 to 1980.* Research Report 1983–2. Honolulu: Department of Planning and Economic Development.

Steffen, B. D. 1986. Tourism and culture change in West Africa Bakau Old Town: A case study. Ed.D. dissertation, George Washington University.

Sternlieb, G., and Hughes, J. W. 1983. *The Atlantic City gamble.* Cambridge: Harvard University Press.

Stitcher, J. H. 1964. The United States Indian Service responds to a felt need in planned tourism development. Paper presented to the Symposium on Tourism, Central States Anthropological Society, 14–16 May, Milwaukee, Wisconsin.

Stoffle, R. W., Last, C. A., and Evans, M. J. 1978. Reservation-based tourism: Implications of tourist attitudes for native American economic development. Paper presented at the symposium on Tourism and Regional Development, 38th annual meeting, The Society for Applied Anthropology, 4 April 1978, Merida, Mexico.

Stoffle, R. W., and Rascl, D. L. 1979. *Alone together: Social order on an urban beach.* Berkeley: University of California Press.

Stott, M. 1980. Tourism in Mykonos: some social and cultural responses. *Mediterranean Studies* 1 (2).

Stuckart, J. M. 1982. Barniz de Pasto: The impact of tourism on a traditional craft. Ph.D. dissertation, University of Pittsburgh.

Stuyt, G. A. M. 1979. Ethnic festivals: Cultural preservation and tourism: A comparative study. Ph.D. dissertation, Texas A & M University, College Station, Texas.

Sutton, H. 1980. *Travelers: The American tourist from stagecoach to space shuttle.* New York: Morrow.

Sutton, W. A., Jr. 1967. Travel and understanding: Notes on the social structure of touring. *International Journal of Comparative Sociology* 8 (2): 218–23.

Svendsen, A. S. 1969. Det moderne reiseliv og det private massekonsum av reiser og rekreasjon. *Ad Novas* 8: 124–28.

Swain, M. B. 1977. Cuna women and ethnic tourism: A way to persist and an avenue to change. In *Hosts and guests: The anthropology of tourism.* V. Smith, ed., pp. 71–82. Philadelphia: University of Pennsylvania Press.

———. 1978. Ailigandi women: Continuity and change in Cuna female identity. Ph.D. dissertation, University of Washington, Seattle.

———. 1982. Being Cuna and female: Ethnicity mediating change in sex roles. In *Sex roles and social change in native lower Central American societies,* C. Loveland and F. Loveland, eds. Urbana: University of Illinois Press.

Sweet, J. D. 1981. Tewa ceremonial performances: The effects of tourism on an ancient Pueblo indian dance and music tradition. Ph.D. dissertation, University of New Mexico, Albuquerque.

Swinglehurst, E. 1982. *Cook's tours: The story of popular travel.* Poole: Blandford Press.

Syme, F. 1980. Thoughts on the consequences of tourism. In *Pacific tourism: As islanders see it,* F. Rajotte and R. Crocombe, eds., pp. 57–58. Fiji: South Pacific Social Sciences Association and The Institute of Pacific Studies, University of the South Pacific.

Talbot, N. 1974. A note on tourism in the West Indies. *Science and Society* 38: 347–49.

Tangil, M. 1977. Tourism and the environment. *AMBIO* 6 (6): 336–41.

Tanirono, E. 1980. The impact of tourism on Solomon culture. In *Pacific tourism: As islanders see it,* F. Rajotte, and R. Crocombe, eds., pp. 109–10. Fiji: South Pacific Social Sciences Association and The Institute of Pacific Studies, University of the South Pacific.

Taumoepeau, S. P. 1986. *Visitor statistics 1986.* Nuku'alofa, Kingdom of Tonga: The Tonga Visitor's Bureau.

Taylor, J. L. 1953. Waikiki: A study in the development of a tourist community. Ph.D. dissertation, Clark University.

Teas, J. 1976. I'm studying monkeys: What do you do? Youth and travelers in Nepal. Unpublished manuscript.

Teuscher, H. 1983. Social tourism for all: The Swiss travel savings fund. *Tourism Management* 4: 216–19.

Teye, V. E. B. 1982. Examination of some factors influencing the development of international tourism in Africa: A comparative study of Zambia and Ghana. Winnipeg: The University of Manitoba Press.

Thomas, J. S. M. 1977. Blacks on the South Carolina sea islands: Planning for tourist and land development. Ann Arbor: University of Michigan Press.

Thomas, W. L. 1978. Progressive rather than centralized tourism: A recommendation for improving international tourism in the Philippines. *Philippine Geographical Journal* 22 (2): 55–82.

Thompson, P. T. 1970. *The use of mountain recreational resources: A comparison of recreation and tourism in the Colorado Rockies and the Swiss Alps.* Ann Arbor: University Microfilms.

Thurot, J. M. 1973. Le tourisme tropical balneaire: Le modèle Caraibe et ses extensions. Doctoral dissertation, Centre d'Etudes du Tourisme, Université d'Aix-Marseille, France.

———. 1979. *The impact of tourism on socio-cultural values.* New York: International Bank of Reconstruction and Development.

Tice, K. 1986. Grassroots development and the distribution of resources by gender. Paper presented at the meetings of the American Anthropological Association, 3–7 December 1986, Philadelphia, Pennsylvania.

Tideman, M. C. 1982. Cost-benefit analysis of congress tourism. *Tourist Review* 37 (4): 22–25.

Tobin, G. A. 1974. The bicycle boom of the 1890s: The development of private transportation and the birth of the modern tourist. *Journal of Popular Culture* 8: 838–49.

Todt, H. 1965. *Uber die räumliche ordnung von reisezielen.* Berlin: Duncker and Humbolt.

Tokuhisa, T. 1980. Tourism within, from and to Japan. *International Social Science Journal* 32 (1): 128–50.

Tombaugh, L. 1962. Tourism and mobility. *Landscape* 11.

Tong, P., and Tanentoa, B. 1980. Urbanization, tourism and natural environment. In *Pacific tourism: As islanders see it*, F. Rajotte and R. Crocombe, eds., pp. 127–32. Fiji: South Pacific Social Sciences Association and The Institute of Pacific Studies, University of the South Pacific.

Tourism Canada. 1985. *Tourism tomorrow: Towards a Canadian tourism strategy.* Ottawa: Tourism Canada.

Tourism and Recreation Research Unit (TRRU). 1972. *The tourism caravan in Scotland: Supply-demand report.* Edinburgh: University of Edinburgh.

———. 1981. *The economy of rural communities in the national parks of England and Wales.* TRRU Research Report 47. Edinburgh: Tourism and Recreation Research Unit, University of Edinburgh.

Tourism USA. 1986. *Guidelines for tourism development.* Department of Recreation and Park Administration. Columbia, Missouri: University of Missouri.

Tourist Association of Yugoslavia. 1980. *Tourism in Yugoslavia: Statistical data, 1960–1979.* Beograd: Turisticki Savez Jugoslavije.

———. 1981. *Tourist traffic in Yugoslavia: 1979–1980.* Beograd: Turisticki Savez Jugoslavije.

Towner, J. 1984a. The grand tour: Sources and a methodology for historical study of tourism. *Tourism Management* 5 (3): 215–22.

———. 1984b. *The European grand tour, circa 1550–1840: A study of its role in the history of tourism*. Ph.D. dissertation, University of Birmingham, Alabama.

Travis, A. S. 1980. The need for policy action. In *The impact of tourism on the environment*, pp. 79–97. Paris: OECD

Trease, G. 1967. *The grand tour*. London: Heinemann.

Triantis, S. G. 1979. Economic impact of tourism and recreation in Muskoka. In *Recreational land use in Southern Ontario*, Publication Series No. 13., pp. 273–79.

Troisgros, S. 1979. *Le tourisme social face au developpement touristique et aux societés transnationales*. Brussels/Paris: BITS/UNESCO.

Tupouniua, S., Crocombe, R., and Slatter, C., eds. 1975. *The Pacific way—social issues in national development*. Suva, Fiji: South Pacific Social Sciences Association.

Turnbull, C. 1981a. A pilgrimage in India: Where tourism is economically unthinkable, the pilgrimage may serve a similar function. *Natural History* 90 (7): 14–20.

———. 1981b. Holy places and people of India. *Natural History* 90 (9): 76–81.

Turner, E. S. 1967. *Taking the cure*. London: Michael Joseph.

Turner, F. J. 1920. The frontier in American history. New York: Holt, Rinehart and Winston.

Turner, L. 1974/1973. *Multinational companies and the third world*. London/New York: Allen Lane/Hill & Wang.

———. 1974. Tourism and the social sciences, from Blackpool to Benidorm and Bali. *Annals of Tourism Research* 1 (6): 180–205.

———. 1976. The international division of leisure: Tourism and the third world. *World Development* 4: 253–60.

Turner, V. 1969. *The ritual process*. Chicago: Aldine.

———. 1974. Liminal to liminoid in play, flow, and ritual: An essay in comparative symbology. *Rice University Studies* 60: 53–92.

Turner, V., and Turner, E. 1978. *Image and pilgrimage in Christian culture*. New York: Columbia University Press.

Tyagi, A. K. 1986. Recreated identity: Tourists in India. Paper presented at the American Anthropological Association meetings, 3–7 December 1986, Philadelphia, Pennsylvania.

Tyner, G. E., and Tyner, J. A. 1978. Tourism in Canada's Northwest Territories: Aspects and trends. *California Geographer* 18: 137–49.

UGTS. 1978. Le tourisme au Senegal. In *Notre Afrique: Debats sur le Tiers-Monde*, pp. 63–82. Paris: Maspero.

UNESCO. 1966. Resolution on the preservation and presentation of the cultural heritage in connection with the promotion of tourism. General Conference, XIVth Session, November 1966, Paris.

U.S. Department of Commerce. 1972. *A study of Japanese travel habits and patterns*. Washington DC: Government Printing Office.

U.S. Department of Commerce, Office of Regional Development and Planning. 1967. *Tourism and recreation: A state of the art*. Prepared by Arthur D. Little, Inc. Washington DC: Government Printing Office.

U.S. Travel Data Center. 1980. *The economic impact of foreign spending in the United States*. Washington DC: Government Printing Office.

Urbanowicz, C. F. 1975a. Tourism in the Polynesian Kingdom of Tonga. Paper read at the Santa Cruz Pacific Seminar on the Social and Economic Impact of Tourism on Pacific Communities, 5 May 1975, Santa Cruz, California.

———. 1975b. Drinking in the Polynesian Kingdom of Tonga. *Ethnohistory* 22 (1): 33–50.

———. 1977. Integrating tourism with other industries in Tonga. In *Social and economic impact of tourism on Pacific communities*, B. H. Farrell, ed., pp. 89–93. Santa Cruz: Center for South Pacific Studies, University of California.

Van den Berghe, P. 1980. Tourism as ethnic relations: A case study of Cuzco, Peru. *Ethnic and Racial Studies* 3 (4): 375–92.

Van den Berghe, P., and Keyes, C. 1984. Introduction: Tourism and re-created ethnicity. *Annals of Tourism Research* 11: 343–52.

Van Doren, C. S. 1981. Outdoor recreation trends in the 1980s: Implications for society. *Journal of Travel Research* 19: 3–10.

———. 1983. The future of tourism. *Journal of Physical Education, Recreation, and Dance* 54: 27–29, 42.

Van Stone, J. W. 1955. Archaeological excavations at Kotzebue, Alaska. *Anthropological Papers of the University of Alaska* 3: 75–155.

Var, T. 1984. Tourism, recreation development and local economics. *Recreation Canada* 42 (2): 16–20.

Varley, R. C. G. 1978. *Tourism in Fiji: Some economic and social problems*. Occasional Papers in Economics 12. Bangor: University of Wales Press.

Vaughan, R. 1977a. *The economic impact of tourism in Edinburgh and the Lothian Region*. Edinburgh: Scottish Tourist Board.

———. 1977b. *The economic impact of the Edinburgh Festival 1976*. Edinburgh: Scottish Tourist Board.

———. 1977c. Tourism: A tool for regional development. In *Leisure studies association conference*. Edinburgh Tourism and Recreation Research Unit, University of Edinburgh.

Veal, A. 1986. Planning for leisure: Alternative approaches. *The Planner* 9–12.

Vergniol, R. G. 1977. Mythes et realités economiques du tourisme international dans les pays pauvres. *Revue de Tourisme* 1: 8–12.

Vidal-Folch, X. 1987. Mar, sexo, y sol. *El Pais* 21 July: 16–17.

Villepontoux, E. J. M. 1981. Tourism and social change in a French Alpine community. Ph.D. dissertation, University of Massachusetts, Amherst.

Vincent, J. A. 1980. The political economy of Alpine development: Tourism and agriculture in St. Maurice. *Sociologia ruralis* 4: 250–71.

Vine, P. 1973. Tourism: What priority should it get? *African Development* 7: 18.

Vogt, J. W. 1978. Wandering: Youth and travel behavior. In *Tourism and behavior, Studies in Third World Societies* No. 5, V. Smith, ed., pp. 19–40. Williamsburg, Virginia: William and Mary Press.

Voigt, P. 1981. *Tourismus und Mexico: Eine untersuchung uber die auswirkungen interkultureller kontakte in der dritten welt*. Munich: Wilhelm Fink.

Volkman, T. A. 1982. Tana Toraja: A decade of tourism. *Cultural Survival Quarterly* 6 (3): 30–31.

———. 1986. Reinventing ritual: Tourism and its objects in Tana Toraja, Indonesia. Paper presented at the annual meeting of the American Anthropological Association, 3–7 December, Philadelphia, Pennsylvania.

Vries, P. de. 1981. The effects of tourism on marginalized agrarian systems: West Indian perspectives. *Canadian Journal of Anthropology* 2 (1): 77–84.

Vroon . J. A. 1981. Socio-cultural aspects of tourism: Trends in tourism planning for the 1980s. *Revue de l'AIEST* 19.

Vusoniwailala, L. 1980. Tourism and Fijian hospitality. In *Pacific tourism: As islanders see it*, F. Rajotte and R. Crocombe, eds., pp. 101–6. Fiji: South Pacific Social Sciences Association and The Institute of Pacific Studies, University of the South Pacific.

Wagner, U. 1977. Out of time and out of place—mass tourism and charter trips. *Ethnos* 42: 38–52.

Wahab, S. 1975. *Tourism management*. London: Tourism International Press.

Wahlers, R. G., and Etzel, M. J. 1985. Vacation preference as a manifestation of optimal stimulation and lifestyle experience. *Journal of Leisure Research* 17: 283–95.

Wales Tourist Board. 1974. *Farm tourism in Wales: A practical guide for Welsh farmers*. Cardiff: Wales Tourist Board.

———. 1981. *Survey of community attitudes in Wales*. Cardiff: Strategic Planning and Research Unit.

Wall, G., and Sinnott, J. 1980. Urban recreational and cultural facilities as tourist attractions. *Canadian Geographer* 24 (1): 50–59.

Wall, G., and Wright, C. 1977. *The environmental impact of outdoor recreation*. Waterloo, Ontario: University of Waterloo, Department of Geography Publication Series, 11.

Walter, J. A. 1982. Social limits of tourism. *Leisure Studies* 1: 295–304.

Walton, J. K. 1983. *The English seaside resort: A social history 1750–1914*. Leicester: Leicester University Press.

Ward, M. 1971. *The role of investment in the development of Fiji*. Department of Applied Economics Occasional Paper 26. Cambridge, England: Cambridge University Press.

Waroka, J. 1980. Planning for tourism in Solomon Islands. In *Pacific tourism: As islanders see it*, F. Rajotte and R. Crocombe, eds., pp. 121–24. Fiji: South Pacific Social Sciences Association and The Institute of Pacific Studies, University of the South Pacific.

Waters, S. R. 1966. The American tourist. *Annals, American Academy of Political and Social Sciences* 46: 109–18.

Waters, S. R., and Patterson, W. D. 1987. *Travel industry world yearbook: The big picture—1987*. New York: Child and Waters.

Weaver, D. Z. B. 1986. The evolution of a heliotropic tourism landscape: The case of Antigua. Ph.D. dissertation, University of Western Ontario, London, Ontario.

West, C. B. 1985. *The Chuck West story: Forty years of Alaska tourism 1945–1985*. Seattle: Weslee Publishing.

White, J. 1967. *History of tourism*. London: Leisure Art.

White, P. E. 1974. *The social impact of tourism on host communities: A study of language change in Switzerland*. Oxford: Oxford University Press.

Williams, A. J., and Zelinsky, W. 1970. On some patterns in international tourist flows. *Economic Geography* 46 (4): 549–67.

Williams, R. 1972. *The country and the city*. London: Chatto and Windus.

Williams, T. A. 1979. Impact of domestic tourism on a host population: The evaluation of a model. *Tourism Recreation Research* 4 (2): 15–21.

Willis, F. R. 1977. Tourism as an instrument of regional economic growth. *Growth and Change* 8 (2): 43–47.

Wilson, D. 1979. The early effects of tourism in the Seychelles. In *Tourism: Passport to development?* E. de Kadt, ed., pp. 205–36. New York: Oxford University Press.

Winsburg, M. F. 1966. Overseas travel by American civilians since World War II. *Journal of Geography* 65 (2): 73–79.

Withington, W. A. 1961. Upland resorts and tourism in Indonesia: Some recent trends. *Geographical Review* 51: 418–23.

Wolbrink and Associates. 1973. *Physical standards for tourist development.* Honolulu: Pacific Islands Development Commission.

Wolf, E. 1973. Aspects of group relations in a complex society. In *Contemporary cultures and societies in Latin America,* D. B. Heath and R. N. Adams, eds., pp. 85–101. New York: Random House.

Wolf, K., and Jurczek, P. 1986. *Geographie der freizeit und des tourismus.* Stuttgart: Ulmer.

Wolfe, R. I. 1962. The summer resorts of Ontario in the 19th century. *Ontario History* 54: 149–61.

———. 1966. Recreational travel—the new migration. *Canadian Geographer* 10 (1): 1–14.

———. 1982. Recreational travel—the new migration revisited. *Ontario Geography* 19: 103–24.

Wood, R. E. 1979. Tourism and underdevelopment in Southeast Asia. *Journal of Contemporary Asia* 9 (3): 274.

———. 1980. International tourism and cultural change in Southeast Asia. *Economic Development and Cultural Change* 28 (3): 561–81.

World Council of Churches. 1970. *Leisure-tourism: Threat and promise.* Geneva: World Council of Churches.

World Tourism Organization (WTO). 1985a. Identification and evaluation of existing and new factors and holiday and travel motivations influencing the pattern of present and potential domestic and international tourist demand. PG (V) B.2.1—1985, 25 pp.

———. 1985b. Methodology for the establishment and implementation of tourism master plans, at both domestic and regional level, to ensure that the approach to tourism's social, cultural and educational functions advocated by the Manila Declaration is progressively reflected in the short and medium term objectives of tourism plans. PG (V) B.3.1.—1985.

———. 1985c. The security and legal protection of the tourist. PG (V) B.2.3—1985, 37 pp.

———. 1985d. The state's role in protecting and promoting culture as a factor of tourism development and the proper use and exploitation of the national cultural heritage of sites and monuments for tourism. PG (V) B.4.2—1985.

Yablonsky, L. 1968. *The hippie trip.* New York: Pegasus.

Yeates, M., and Garner, B. 1980. *The North American city.* New York: Harper and Row.

Yefremov, Y. K. 1973. Geografiya i Turizm (Geography and tourism). In *Geografiya i Turizm,* S. A. Kovalev, et al., eds. Voprost Geografii, vol. 93. Moscow: Izdatel'stvo "Mysl."

Young, G. 1973. *Tourism: Blessing or blight?* Harmondsworth: Penguin Books.

Young, J. 1973. The hippie solution: An essay in the politics of leisure. In *Politics and deviance,* I. and L. Taylor, eds. London: Penguin Books.

Young, R. C. 1977. The structural context of the Caribbean tourist industry: A comparative study. *Economic Development and Cultural Change* 25: 657–72.

Zehnder, L. E. 1975. *Florida's Disneyworld: Promises and problems.* Tallahassee: Peninsular Books.

Zelinsky, W. 1971. The hypothesis of the mobility transition. *Geographical Review* 61: 219–49.

Zimmerman, R. C. 1980. European tourism. *Landscape* 24: 31–32.

Zinder, H., et al. 1968. *Essential elements of a tourist development programme: A critical commentary.* Published by the author, Washington DC.

———. 1969. *The future of tourism in the eastern Caribbean.* Published by the author, Washington DC.

Zito, L. 1982. Settling down: Bedouin in the Sinai. *Cultural Survival Quarterly* 6 (3): 22–23.

INDEX